Our Life With

Teacher's Manual

Our Life With Jesus

Teacher's Manual

Faith and Life Series
Revised Edition
BOOK THREE

Ignatius Press, San Francisco
Catholics United for the Faith, Steubenville, Ohio

Director of First Edition: The late Rev. Msgr. Eugene Kevane, Ph.D.
Assistant Director and General Editor of First Edition: Patricia Puccetti Donahoe, M.A.
First Edition Writer: Sister Theresa Wynne, I.H.M.

Revision Writers: Colette Ellis, M.A. and Marilyn Hogan
Director and General Editor of Revision: Caroline Avakoff, M.A.
Editors of Revision: Christopher Bess and Matthew Ramsay

Catholics United for the Faith, Inc. and Ignatius Press gratefully acknowledge the guidance and assistance of the late Reverend Monsignor Eugene Kevane, former Director of the Pontifical Catechetical Institute, Diocese of Arlington, Virginia, in the production of the First Edition of this series. The First Edition intended to implement the authentic approach in Catholic catechesis given to the Church through documents of the Holy See and in particular the conference of Joseph Cardinal Ratzinger on "Sources and Transmission of Faith." The Revised Edition continues this commitment by drawing upon the *Catechism of the Catholic Church* (Libreria Editrice Vaticana, 1994, 1997).

Scripture quotations are from the Holy Bible, Revised Standard Version, Catholic Edition. Old Testament © 1952; Apocrypha © 1957; Catholic Edition, incorporating the Apocrypha © 1966; New Testament © 1946; Catholic Edition © 1965, by the Division of Christian Education of the National Council of the Churches of Christ in the United States of America. All rights reserved.

© 1987, 2003 Catholics United for the Faith, Inc.
All rights reserved
ISBN 0-89870-709-9
Printed in Hong Kong

Contents

Introduction to the Revised Edition vi
For Teachers and Catechists viii
1. God Loves Us 1
2. God Created the World 11
3. Learning about God 21
4. The Promise of a Savior 31
5. Abraham: The Father of God's People 41
6. The Prophet Moses 51
7. God's Laws of Love 61
8. King David 71
9. Loving God Most of All 81
10. The Lord's Day 91
11. Obedience and Love 101
12. Purity and Truth 111
13. God's Tender Mercy 121
14. Meeting Jesus in Confession 131
15. The Christ Child Is Born 141
16. Jesus Grows in Age and Wisdom 151
17. Signs and Wonders 161
18. The Last Supper, Our First Mass 171
19. Jesus Gives His Life for Us 181
20. Offering Gifts of Love 191
21. The Holy Mass 201
22. Offering Jesus to the Father 211
23. The Bread of Life 221
24. Jesus Comes to Us in the Holy Eucharist 231
25. Jesus Rises in Splendor 241
26. The Coming of the Holy Spirit 251
27. God's Family on Earth 261
28. Our Life in the Church 271
29. Mary, Our Mother and Queen 281
30. The Communion of Saints 291
    Appendix A A-1
    Appendix B B-1

Introduction to the *Faith and Life* Revised Edition

The *Faith and Life* series, which includes a student text, Teacher's Manual, and *Activity Book* for grades 1–8, has been used in schools and parishes across the country since its original publication in 1987. This revision of the original series continues our commitment to the faithful transmission of the teachings of the Roman Catholic Church by emphasizing the importance of Scripture and the *Catechism of the Catholic Church*.

The Student Textbook:

The *Faith and Life* student texts have undergone minimal revision. The beautiful and inspiring religious artwork has been maintained, for faith has inspired art for centuries, and religious art has, in turn, inspired our faith. Art is a valuable educational tool, especially in the teaching of religious truths to children, for it offers a visual image in addition to the oral and written word. Art can also be a source of meditation for students and teachers as they investigate the paintings, discuss the religious imagery, and come to understand the beautiful symbols and the artistic expressions they communicate.

In the primary grades, the *Faith and Life* student texts are written at an advanced reading level. In these early years a child's oral comprehension far surpasses his reading ability (e.g., children can understand a religious video though they would have a difficult time reading the script). Doctrine is presented in a way that both challenges the student's intellect and avoids the boredom that is often fatal in catechetical efforts.

New vocabulary in all the grades is now indicated by bold type. New words have been added to enhance each lesson in the revised text, and each definition can now be found both within the chapter and in the glossary.

The questions provided for memorization in each chapter have been expanded and carefully revised for age-appropriateness; relevant references to the *Catechism of the Catholic Church* are indicated next to every question. Each chapter in the revised text opens with an appropriate Scripture passage, with relevant Bible verses quoted throughout. These changes demonstrate Biblical backing for the faith as well as the significance of the new *Catechism* to the Church as a fruit of Vatican II. Additional common Catholic prayers have been inserted in the revised text, with an expansive list of prayers at the back of the student text.

The Teacher's Manual:

The *Faith and Life* Teacher's Manuals are the most heavily updated and expanded aspects of this extensive revision process. Useful information previously provided in the supplemental Resource Binders of the original series has been incorporated into the new Teacher's Manuals, thus eliminating the need for individual binders.

Each chapter of the Teacher's Manuals begins with a list of important references to the *Catechism of the Catholic Church* and Scripture passages that support the chapter lessons. This is followed by a clear and succinct summary of the doctrine discussed in the preceding four lessons; this summary may be used as a guide for once-a-week catechism or CCD classes.

The revised Teacher's Manual provides a full week of detailed lesson plans for each chapter with four days of teaching and one day of review and assessment. Each color-coded lesson clearly indicates the teaching aims and materials necessary for that day. Optional craft materials, songs, appendix pages, and additional video and book resources are also included. The lesson plans themselves are designed to be guides in teaching even the most complex truths of the faith with age-appropriate examples.

Comprehensive chapter quizzes and optional unit tests can be found in Appendix A. In the primary grades, these quizzes may be completed together in class. Appendix B contains additional activities such as stories, games, crafts, and skits.

One entirely new addition to the revision is the "Catholic Culture and Tradition" box found on the second page of each lesson. These boxes include supplemental materials for the teacher, lives of the saints, explanations of terms, descriptions of Church traditions and rituals, relevant citations, suggestions for activities, additional resources, and prayers.

To assist Parish and CCD Programs, "once-a-week lesson plans" can be formulated by using the summary boxes for doctrinal content from the chapter introductory page and the italicized sections throughout the four lessons. A recommended format would be: read the entire chapter, use a lesson plan consisting of the italicized sections, which cover the necessary material and doctrines with sufficient development, then spend time reinforcing the material with the memorization of questions, vocabulary, and prayers. The quizzes can then be sent home for family reinforcement and review. The unit quizzes can still be administered in class once a month to assist the teacher in monitoring the students' progress.

The Activity Book:

The *Faith and Life* Activity Books have been significantly expanded to include one activity for each lesson, that is, four activities per chapter. The goal was to offer the teacher a wide variety of reinforcement tools in a separate text without losing the interest of the students. In the primary grades the activities focus on drawing, coloring, and simple puzzles and exercises, while in the later years reading comprehension and memorization are emphasized.

The *Faith and Life* series, revised edition, aspires to aid teachers and parents (the primary educators) in transmitting the truths, doctrines, wealth of traditions, and richness of culture found in the Roman Catholic Church.

For Teachers and Catechists

Text and Grade Level
The third grade text, *Our Life With Jesus*, is a simple introduction to Bible stories and teachings of the faith. The third grader has an active imagination and is easily convinced by his emotions as well as his reason. The teacher should, therefore, make use of creative presentations reinforced through repetition, such as those included in this manual, in addition to the catechist's personal good example.

Catechesis: Nature and Purpose
Catechesis is the systematic instruction of children, young people, and adults into the Catholic faith and the teachings of the Church with the goal of making them into Christ's disciples (cf. CCC 5). It is the handing-on of Christ's message to His people. The *General Catechetical Directory* describes catechesis as a form of ministry of God's Word, "which is intended to make men's faith living, conscious, and active, through the light of instruction" (GCD 17; 1971).

The Catechist: God's Instrument
To be a catechist is to be God's instrument. Every catechist has a responsibility to teach the fullness of the truth faithfully, while witnessing to those entrusted to his care. A fervent sacramental life and regular prayer life are the catechist's best personal preparation. Any instructor can use textbooks and teaching tools, learn various methods for effective classroom participation, and develop lesson plans to facilitate an academic environment. But nothing is as important as witnessing through your words and deeds and petitioning God for the on-going formation and spiritual growth of the students. No matter how much knowledge you impart to your students, you should recognize that you merely plant the seeds of faith that God Himself must cultivate in their souls.

John Paul II states in *Catechesi Tradendae*: "at the heart of catechesis we find . . . the Person of Jesus of Nazareth . . . in catechesis it is Christ . . . who is taught . . . and it is Christ alone who teaches . . ." (CT 5,6). Religious education must always be centered on the Triune God and on Christ Himself. God chose to reveal Himself throughout salvation history, through His creation, the prophets, the Scriptures, and most perfectly in the Person of Jesus Christ. This revelation, preserved faithfully through Sacred Scripture and Tradition, has been entrusted to the Church that every catechist is called to serve.

Catechesis in today's ministry is often coupled with evangelization—a first hearing of the Good News of Salvation. Through catechesis, you should guide your students to seek, accept, and investigate profoundly the Gospel so that they in turn may become witnesses of Christ. The new *Catechism of the Catholic Church*, together with Sacred Scripture, provides catechists with the tools necessary to achieve this.

The Role of Parents: The First Catechists
The family provides the first and most important introduction to Christian faith and practice for any child, since parents are the primary educators of their children. Instruction in the faith, which begins at an early age, should include not only the parents' good Christian example, but also a formation in prayer and an explanation and review of what students have learned from religious instruction and attending liturgical events.

Parental cooperation is very important to a teacher's success as a catechist. You should try to involve parents in their children's instruction. Discuss with them the program and methods you are using, consult them about better ways to teach their children, and ask for assistance if problems arise. Let parents know that you are there to help them fulfill their duties in forming and educating their children in Christ (cf. GCD 78, 79).

Methodologies
The *General Catechetical Directory* provides an overview of various successful methodologies you may find useful. Knowledge can be transmitted through prayer and liturgy, through words and deeds, or through texts and activities, but the students learn it primarily from you, the catechist.

Induction and Deduction:	Inductive methods serve well in the presentation of facts and in considering and examining those facts in order to recognize their Christian meaning. Induction is the process of reasoning from a part to a whole, from particular to general principles. It is not independent of deductive methods, which reason from the general to the particular and include interpretation and determining cause and effect. These two methods, taken together, aid in the students' understanding of the unity of the faith, the inter-relation of topics, and most importantly their practical applications.
Formulas:	Expressing thoughts or ideas succinctly and accurately in a memorable form allows for ease of memorization and better understanding of a topic. In the early stages of education, memorization should be utilized more frequently since children first need language to communicate meaning. In theology, semantics are very important, for Christians have died for their faith and schisms have occurred because of word use (e.g., the *Filioque* in the Nicene Creed). Such formulas also provide a uniform method of speaking among the faithful.
Experience:	Personal experience is reflective and practical, and it transforms abstract theories into applicable and memorable concepts. Catechists should use concrete examples in class and encourage their students to judge personal experience with Christian values.
Creativity:	Creative activities enable students to meditate upon and express, in their own words, the messages they have learned.
Groups:	In catechesis the importance of group instruction is becoming more apparent. Groups aid the social and ecclesial formation of students, and they foster a sense of Christian co-responsibility and solidarity.

The Catechism of the Catholic Church: An Important Tool

Today's classrooms are filled with children who have various needs and backgrounds. Complicated by an atmosphere of religious indifference, religious hostility, and an apparent absence of Catholic culture, knowledge, and meaningful practice, your catechetical work becomes especially valuable. One important tool that belongs to all the faithful is the *Catechism of the Catholic Church*, which is divided into four sections: the Creed, the Sacraments, the Moral Life, and Prayer.

The Creed:	The Creed is a summary of the faith and the Church's baptismal promises. As a public profession of faith, Catholics find in it their identity as members of Christ's Mystical Body. This is the faith handed down from Christ to the Apostles and to the entire Church.
Sacraments:	The seven sacraments are outward signs instituted by Christ to confer grace. Active participation in the sacramental life of the Church, such as attending Mass prayerfully and faithfully, should be encouraged from a young age.
The Moral Life:	The moral life does not limit; instead it provides the boundaries that define the Catholic identity and allow for proper love of God and neighbor. A right moral life is man's gift to God, a response to His unconditional love. Every Catholic should be an example to others.
Prayer:	Prayer unites a person with God (through words, actions, silence, and presence), and it should be encouraged and put into practice from early childhood. There are many forms of prayer, but each brings the soul closer to God.

The *Faith and Life* Teacher's Manual provides much of what you will need to be an effective catechist, but it will only be fruitful depending on how you utilize it and how you teach and minister the Word of God to your students. Take very seriously your responsibilities as a catechist. Frequently call upon Christ as His witness and disciple to help you hand on His message. Persevere and draw near to God, bringing your students with you.

Additional material may be found at www.CatecheticalResources.com and www.Domestic-Church.com

CHAPTER ONE
GOD LOVES US

Catechism of the Catholic Church References

Dignity of the Human Person: 1700–1712
Equality and Differences among Men: 1934–46
God as Creator of Heaven and Earth: 279–81, 325–27
God Continues to Care for His Creation: 302–14, 321–24
God Creates out of Wisdom and Love, 295, 315
God is Love: 218–21, 231
God Transcends Creation and Is Present to It: 300–301, 320
God's Omnipotence: 268–78
Heaven: 1023–29, 1053
Holy Trinity: 249–56, 266
Jesus as Teacher and Model: 468–69, 516–21, 561
Jesus at Prayer: 2598–2606, 2620
Jesus Teaches Us How to Pray: 2607–15, 2621
The Lord's Prayer: 2777–854

Lord's Prayer as Summary of Gospel: 2761–76
Man as Body and Soul: 362–68, 382
Man Created in Image of God: 355–57, 380–81
Perfections of God Known through Creation: 293–95, 315, 341
Prayer: Blessing and Adoration 2626–28; Intercession 2634–36; Petition 2629–33; Praise 2639–43; Thanksgiving 2637–38
Revelation of God as Trinity: 238–48, 261–64
Seven Petitions of Lord's Prayer: 2803–6, 2857
Ways of Knowing God: 31–38, 46–48, 286
What Is Prayer: 2559–65, 2590, 2644
World as Created for the Glory of God: 293–94, 319

Scripture References

Creation on the Sixth Day: Gen 1:24–31

The Lord's Prayer: Mt 6:9–13; Lk 11:1–4

Background Reading: *The Fundamentals of Catholicism* by Fr. Kenneth Baker, S.J.

Volume 2:
Creation, pp. 121–145
"Body and Soul," pp.146–48

"The Most Holy Trinity," pp.77–79
"Jesus Is the Perfect Image of the Father," pp.93–95

Summary of Lesson Content

Lesson 1

God is eternal.

God is almighty, all holy, all wise, all perfect, all loving, and all merciful. These attributes of God are called His perfections.

God made each person unique, out of love, and gave him free will.

Lesson 2

Man is made in the image of God.

Man is made of body and soul.

God remains with His creation and He continues to love and care for it.

God is pure spirit.

Lesson 3

There is only One God in three Divine Persons. This mystery is called the Holy or Blessed Trinity.

God the Son became Man in the Divine Person of Jesus.

Jesus taught us much about God.

Lesson 4

Jesus chose and taught the Twelve Apostles.

Jesus taught His followers about prayer.

He taught the Apostles to pray the Our Father.

Prayer is talking with and listening to God.

LESSON ONE: WHO IS GOD?

Aims

The children will learn the following perfections of God: eternal, almighty, all holy, all wise, all perfect, all beautiful, all loving, and all merciful.

The students will learn that God made each person unique.

Materials

- Name tags
- Pictures of creation that show God's perfections
- Cue cards with examples of God's perfections; e.g., God sent a powerful flood in the time of Noah.
- *Activity Book*, p. 1
- Pencils, paper, and crayons

Optional:
- "All people that on earth do dwell," *Adoremus Hymnal*, #622

Begin

Have the students introduce themselves to each other. You may give or have them make name tags. Also give the children their student texts and *Activity Books*. Have them look through their student texts and take turns telling you what they already know about God or what their student texts tell them about God. They may even use a picture from their student text as a reference. Have each student take a turn; e.g., "My name is Jill. The picture on page 6 helps me to know that God is the Creator."

---

1 God Loves Us

O give thanks to the LORD, for he is good,
    for his steadfast love endures for ever.
O give thanks to the God of gods,
    for his steadfast love endures for ever.
O give thanks to the Lord of lords,
    for his steadfast love endures for ever. . . .

Psalms 136:1–3

Did you know that God has lived for ever? Close your eyes and imagine billions and billions of years ago. God was alive. He existed before time began. Now imagine billions of years stretching into the future. God will still be alive. God is eternal, which means He had *no* beginning and He will *never* die. He is all powerful, all holy, all wise, and **all perfect**. His love and mercy are **infinite**. That means they are far too great to be measured.

God was thinking of you, loving you, and wanting you from all eternity. Long before He put one star in the sky, He knew you. He knew your name. He knew your face. He knew the color of your eyes and the sound of your voice. You are very precious to Him. He could have made some other person, but He wanted you. So He made you just the way you are.

God loves you so much that He made you in His image. He made a part of you that, like Him, will never die. This part of you is called your soul. It is a spirit. You cannot see it. Your soul gives you the power to think and the power to love. With your soul, you can learn things, enjoy music and stories, talk, and laugh. Without your soul, you would be no more intelligent than a rock. Without your soul, you could never love anyone. When God made us in His image, He opened up many treasures for us.

Develop

1. Read paragraphs 1–3 with the students. They may take turns reading sentences aloud.

2. Using pictures, illustrate the perfections of God. Some examples might include: a picture of the earth (God is eternal. He existed long before the earth was made); a picture of a pretty flower (God is all beautiful); and a picture of Jesus on the Cross (God is all merciful—even from the Cross He forgave our sins).

3. Write the perfections of God on the board in different columns. Have the children draw from pre-written cue cards and decide under which attribute they should be placed. Have them each take a turn placing a card under an attribute. This can also be done by having the children go outside to find something in nature that reflects the perfections of God. Students can then place their findings in the proper category.

4. Reread paragraph 3 with the children. Ask the children what makes them different from other people. Stress that God made them special and with gifts, because He loves them and wants them to have these gifts. If possible, have the children put on a little talent show or show-and-tell in order to share these gifts with the class.

5. Have the children talk about how they reflect God's perfections. For example, Suzy reminds us of God's eternal life because her soul will live forever. Bobby reminds us that God is all powerful because he is so strong. John reminds us that God is all wise because of his knowledge of animals and dinosaurs and how they live with other creatures. Mary reminds us of God's love because of her love for her family, friends, and even her dog.

6. Lead the children in a prayer of thanksgiving for all our gifts, which remind us of God.

Name:_____

Who is God?

1. How long has God lived?

   God has lived forever.

2. How long will God live?

   God will live forever.

3. How do we know God is almighty?

   Answers will vary.

4. How do we know God is all holy?

   Answers will vary.

5. How do we know God is all wise?

   Answers will vary.

6. How do we know God is all merciful?

   Answers will vary.

7. How do we know God loves us?

   God made us in His image.

Faith and Life Series • Grade 3 • Chapter 1 • Lesson 1

Reinforce

1. Have the students work on *Activity Book*, p. 1.

2. If time permits, you may have them write prayers praising God for His perfections or thanking Him for the gifts He has given to each of them.

3. Teach the children to sing "All people that on earth do dwell," *Adoremus Hymnal*, #622.

Conclude

Lead the students in prayer, thanking God for His perfections and gifts and, in particular, for each student's unique gifts.

Preview

In the next lesson, the children will learn more about being made in God's image and likeness. They should bring pictures of themselves to the next class.

GOD'S PERFECTIONS

- Eternal—God was, is, and always will be

- All powerful—God made everything out of nothing

- All holy—God is all good; all creation worships God

- All wise—all creation works together according to God's plan

- All merciful—God can forgive us when we sin

- All loving—God gave us free will

NOTES

_____
_____
_____
_____
_____
_____
_____
_____
_____

LESSON TWO: GOD MADE MAN

Aims

The students will learn that they are made in the image and likeness of God.

They will understand that they are in God's image both in body and soul even though God is pure spirit.

Materials

- Pictures of the children or a polaroid camera and film.
- *Activity Book*, p. 2
- Children's Bible (Gen 1:24–31)
- Coloring pencils
- Treasure hunt (holy medals or prayer cards)

Optional:
- "All people that on earth do dwell," *Adoremus Hymnal*, #622

Begin

Before class begins, hide the treasure.

Begin the class by reviewing the perfections of God that the students learned in the previous lesson. Have the students think of concrete examples that show God's perfections in the world around them. Discuss how God used those perfections in creating each of the students. He was wise in making Johnny funny, Sally gifted in music, Joseph artistic, etc. He is all powerful in giving us life and all holy in giving us the capacity to love Him.

Our greatest treasure is God Himself. He is always with us. He knows everything about us: who we are, what we do, and even our thoughts. He loves us far more than anyone else loves us. He gave each of us a soul so we could love Him in return. Sometimes this seems hard to do because we cannot see or hear God, since God is pure spirit.

There is only one God, but in God there are three Divine Persons: God the Father, God the Son, and God the Holy Spirit. Jesus is God the Son. He is the Second Person of the Blessed Trinity. He came to earth as a sign of God's love for us. Because Jesus, Who is God, became a man like us, it is easier for us to know and love Him. We know that He is gentle, kind, and good. He taught us to put God first. He taught us to obey God, even when we do not feel like it. He taught us that by loving each other, we give glory to God and show our love to Him.

Jesus taught His Apostles—and us—how to pray to our Heavenly Father. Sometimes Jesus went out into the desert to pray. This showed us that it is good to take special times to be alone with God. Other times, Jesus prayed with a gathering of friends or a great multitude. We follow His example when we pray with our family or classmates or others in our parish.

Once the Apostles asked Jesus how to pray. He taught them a prayer that is still used in our Church. We hear it every time we go to Mass. It is called the Our Father or the Lord's Prayer:

> Our Father who art in Heaven, hallowed be thy name. Thy Kingdom come. Thy will be done on earth, as it is in Heaven. Give us this day our daily bread, and forgive us our trespasses, as we forgive those who trespass against us, and lead us not into temptation, but deliver us from evil. *Amen.*

Develop

1. Have the students take turns reading sentences aloud from paragraphs 4 and 5.

2. Read Genesis 1:24–31 from the children's Bible with the students.

3. Ask the children what an image is. It is something that is similar in appearance or that reminds us of something else. A mirror gives us a good image of what we look like. Another good image is a photograph. Did the children bring in photographs? If not, take individual pictures of the children and let them watch the pictures develop. An image is not the same as the person, for a picture of Sally is not Sally. It cannot talk, laugh, sing, play, etc. The picture reminds us of Sally and what she looks like.

4. Ask the children how they are images of God? Do they look like Him? No, because God does not have a body. He is pure spirit. They are in God's image though. You may need to ask some leading questions as follows:
- Can we show some of God's perfections by our examples? (for example, if Anne is wise, does she remind us of God's wisdom?)
- What about God's eternal life? Will we live forever?
- What about our intellect?
- What about the way we can care for God's creation?
- What about loving one another? Are we in God's image when we love one another?

5. Ask the children to name some of the great treasures God has given to us. You may use examples from the created world. Have the children look for the hidden treasure. Ask the children why God is their greatest treasure. Ask the children how they should seek out a treasure and how they should treat it once they have found it. Ask them how they should love God.

Name:_____

Made in God's Image

1. God made me in His image because

   Answers will vary.

2. My soul is like God because

   It will never die.

3. My body reminds me of God's goodness because

   Answers will vary.

4. God is my greatest treasure because

   God is always with us. He knows everything about us. He loves us more than anyone else. He gave us a soul so we can love Him.

5. Even though I cannot see God, I know He exists because

   Answers will vary.

Faith and Life Series • Grade 3 • Chapter 1 • Lesson 2

GREAT TREASURES GOD HAS MADE FOR US

In Nature:
- Mountains
- Rivers
- Forests
- Stars
- Clouds
- Oceans

In Our Families:
- Our parents
- Our brothers and sisters
- Our pets

In Our Neighborhood:
- Our friends
- Our neighbors

In Ourselves:
- Our imaginations
- Our bodies
- Our sense of humor

Reinforce

1. Have the students work on *Activity Book*, p. 2

2. Have the students help the teacher make a display for a bulletin board in the classroom or in the hallway. Be sure to put only the students' first names on display in public.

Conclude

1. Have the students sing "All people that on earth do dwell," *Adoremus Hymnal*, #622.

2. Have the students pray the Glory Be. This prayer should be a review for them. You may want to write it on the board so they can read it.

Preview

In the next lesson, the students will learn the doctrines of the Trinity and the Incarnation.

NOTES

LESSON THREE: KNOWING GOD

Aims

The students will learn that there is only one God in three Divine Persons. This mystery is called the Holy or Blessed Trinity.

They will also learn that God the Son became Man in the Divine Person of Jesus.

The students will learn how Jesus taught us about God.

Materials

- Cut-out of a three-leaf clover, three candles, and a match
- *Activity Book*, p. 3

Optional:
- "Patrick: Brave Shepherd of the Emerald Isle," video; CCC of America, available through Ignatius Press
- "All people that on earth do dwell," *Adoremus Hymnal*, #622

Begin

Begin the class by reviewing the perfections of God and remind the students that we are made in His image.

Ask the children the ways we can come to know God. We can know that God exists from the world around us. He gave us the Bible. He came in the Divine Person of Jesus Christ (God made Man). Today we will learn more about God and how Jesus taught us about Him.

In this prayer we praise God, we say we are sorry for our sins, we ask for His love and forgiveness, and we ask Him to watch over us. **Prayer** is talking with God. It is important to pray every day because it keeps us close to Him.

Words to Know:

all perfect   infinite   prayer

Q. 1 *Who created us?*
God created us, body and soul, in His image (CCC 704–5).

Q. 2 *What purpose did God have in mind when He created us?*
God created us to know Him, to love Him and to serve Him in this life, and then to be happy with Him forever in the next life, in Heaven (CCC 358).

Q. 3 *Who is God?*
God is the all-perfect pure spirit. God is three Divine Persons: God the Father, God the Son, and God the Holy Spirit (CCC 202, 307).

Q. 4 *What does "all-perfect" mean?*
"All-perfect" means that every good is found in God, without defect and without limit. In other words, it means that He has endless power, wisdom, goodness, and love (CCC 41, 213).

Develop

1. Read paragraph 6 with the children.

2. Review the doctrine of the Trinity with the students. You may use the shamrock to explain that there is one God (one shamrock) and three Divine Persons (three leaves). You may also use three candles (which each share the same flame) as an example. You may diagram this on the board using three circles linked together. Ask the children for other examples that remind them of the Trinity.

3. Diagram on the board the three Persons of the Trinity, reviewing them in order: the First Person is the Father, the Second Person is the Son, and the Third Person is the Holy Spirit. This may be illustrated by a diagram of three circles that form a triangle with a center circle that reads "God." You may attach each circle to "God" with a line that says "is" and connect them to each other with lines that read "is not." The Father is God, the Son is God, and the Holy Spirit is God, but the Father is not the Son, and the Father is not the Holy Spirit. Likewise, the Holy Spirit is not the Son. Each Person of the Trinity is fully God, yet distinct from the others. This is the mystery we call the Blessed Trinity: there is one God in three Divine Persons.

4. Add to this diagram a line coming from the Son. Write "The Son became Man in the Divine Person of Jesus Christ." Explain to the students that Jesus is God the Son made Man. Therefore, Jesus is God. This mystery of God made Man is called the Incarnation.

5. Explain to the children that Jesus taught us much about God because He is God. He taught us about God by what He said and did. He also taught us about God because of Who He is. Because Jesus loves us, we know God loves us, etc. Ask the children what Jesus taught us about God.

Name:_____

Word Search!

Use your textbook to fill in the blanks.

God loved you from all <u>eternity</u>. Long before He put one star in the sky, He <u>knew</u> you. He knew your <u>name</u>. He knew your <u>face</u>. He knew the sound of your <u>voice</u>. God <u>loves</u> you so much that He made you in His <u>image</u>. He made a part of you that, like Him, will never die. This part of you is called your <u>soul</u>. You cannot see it. But your soul gives you the <u>power</u> to think and the power to <u>love</u>. With your soul, you can <u>learn</u> things. Without your soul, you would be no more <u>intelligent</u> than a rock. Our best treasure is <u>God</u> Himself. He is <u>always</u> with us. He loves us more than anyone else loves us. He gave us our soul so we could love <u>Him</u> in return.

Then find the words in the puzzle below.

H	I	M	G	D	E	V	I	Y	T	S	P	I	R	I	T	H
O	M	S	I	L	S	O	L	D	P	D	I	E	H	V	A	E
T	A	P	R	E	X	I	Z	U	S	L	S	T	U	P	R	V
H	G	T	F	A	G	C	V	P	P	P	T	E	Y	E	S	E
S	E	R	N	R	K	E	I	L	O	V	E	R	A	N	O	R
A	Y	E	I	N	T	Y	N	T	W	E	K	N	E	W	U	Y
L	W	D	N	T	I	N	G	S	E	G	Y	I	K	O	N	T
W	L	S	L	I	G	A	V	O	R	I	A	T	G	W	E	H
A	K	T	L	T	H	M	O	U	M	G	E	Y	O	U	N	Z
Y	E	R	F	A	C	E	L	L	O	V	E	S	D	J	N	
S	R	E	T	Z	O	U	X	H	T	S	R	N	E	L	M	X
A	U	S	I	N	T	E	L	L	I	G	E	N	T	A	Y	S

ST. PATRICK OF IRELAND

Saint Patrick was born in Scotland around the year 385 to Roman parents living in Britain in charge of the Roman colonies there. Around the age of fourteen he was captured and taken to Ireland as a slave and shepherd, at a time when Ireland was a land of Druids and pagans. He learned their language and customs, then at age twenty, escaped to the coast where sailors returned him to Gaul. He became a priest and then a bishop, and returned to Ireland in 433. Patrick preached the Gospel, converted thousands, and built churches all over Ireland. He used the shamrock to teach the Trinity. He is the patron saint of Ireland; his feast day is March 17.

Reinforce

1. List on the board the many examples of things Jesus taught us about God. (These are the answers the children will give to Question 5 in Develop.)

2. Have the students work *Activity Book*, p. 3.

3. Have the children review the Sign of the Cross and the Glory Be, and explain how these prayers remind us of the Trinity. Review the Incarnation by making the Sign of the Cross and reminding the children that Jesus died on the Cross for us.

4. If you have a video on Saint Patrick, such as "Patrick: Brave Shepherd of the Emerald Isle," from CCC of America (available through Ignatius Press; 30 minutes) show it to the class.

Conclude

1. Sing with the children "All people that on earth do dwell," *Adoremus Hymnal*, #622.

2. Pray the Sign of the Cross and the Glory Be.

Preview

In the next lesson, the students will learn about prayer, specifically the Our Father.

NOTES

LESSON FOUR: TEACH US TO PRAY

Aims

The students will learn that Jesus chose and taught twelve Apostles.

They will learn that Jesus taught His followers about prayer, and He taught the Apostles to pray the Our Father.

They will also learn that prayer is talking with and listening to God.

Materials

- Children's Bible (Mt 6:9–13, Lk 11:1–4)
- *Activity Book*, p. 4

Optional:
- "All people that on earth do dwell," *Adoremus Hymnal*, #622

Begin

Review with the students that Jesus taught us about God by Who He is, what He said, and what He did. We know Jesus is God by His words and deeds as well as the miracles he performed. We are children of God and, like Jesus, we can call Him "Father." Ask the children how a Father loves His children. Also, Jesus taught us that prayer was important because He prayed often, and He taught His disciples how to pray. Today we will learn more about the prayer that Jesus taught us. It is called the Our Father or the Lord's Prayer.

Q. 5 *Does God have a body as we have?*
No, God does not have a body, for He is a perfectly pure spirit (CCC 370).

Q. 6 *Where is God?*
God is in Heaven, on earth, and in every place: He is the unlimited Being (CCC 300, 326).

Q. 7 *Has God always existed?*
Yes, God always has been and always will be: He is eternal (CCC 212).

Q. 8 *Does God know all things?*
Yes, God knows all things, even our thoughts: He is all knowing (CCC 216, 2500).

Q. 9 *What is prayer?*
Prayer is talking with and listening to God (CCC 2559–61).

Q. 10 *What is the Our Father?*
The Our Father is the prayer Jesus taught His Apostles to pray. We still say this prayer today (CCC 2759).

Develop

1. Using the children's Bible, read the account of Jesus teaching His Apostles to pray the Our Father in Mt 6:9-13 and Lk 11:1-4.

2. Ask the children if they know the Our Father. When do they pray it? At Mass. This prayer has been passed on to all Jesus' disciples. When we are baptized, we become children of God and we can, therefore, call God our Father.

3. Have the students take turns reading sentences from the student text aloud.

4. Review with the children the definition of prayer: it is the lifting of our hearts and minds to God. When we pray we talk with and listen to God. Just as we need to speak with our mothers and our fathers to have a good relationship and understand one another, this is also true of our relationship with God. We need to pray every day!

5. Go through the Our Father line by line and explain it.
- *Our Father Who art in Heaven:* If God is the Father of us all, we must love one another. God is in Heaven, and He is everywhere. Heaven is our final home.
- *Hallowed be Thy Name:* May God's name and presence be honored as holy.
- *Thy Kingdom Come:* May Jesus reign first on earth in the Church and forever in Heaven.
- *Thy will be done on earth as it is in Heaven:* May we seek to know and do God's will.
- *Give us this day our daily bread:* We ask God to care for all our needs, especially by giving us the Eucharist.
- *And forgive us our trespasses as we forgive those who trespass against us:* May God forgive our sins as we forgive others.
- *And lead us not into temptation, but deliver us from evil:* May God protect us and help us always to do good.

Name:_____

Our Father

God's	needs	good	greater
children	hears	grace	joy
Heaven	merciful	strength	holy

By praying this...	*We can know this...*
Our Father	We are **children** of God.
Who art in Heaven	To be with God means to be in **Heaven**.
Hallowed be Thy Name	God is **holy**.
Thy Kingdom come	We want **God's** Kingdom of goodness, peace, and joy to spread to all people.
Thy will be done on earth as it is in Heaven	God wills only what is **good**.
Give us this day our daily bread	God provides for our **needs**.
And forgive us our trespasses	God is **merciful**.
As we forgive those who trespass against us	With God's **grace**, we can and must show love and mercy to others.
And lead us not into temptation	God gives us free will, but He **hears** us when we ask for help to avoid sin, and He gives us **strength**.
But deliver us from evil. Amen.	God is **greater** than the devil.

4 Faith and Life Series • Grade 3 • Chapter 1 • Lesson 4

PRAYER CHART (SAMPLE DIAGRAM)

List each of the students and check off or give stickers to reward them for all the prayers they have memorized. You may put this on display. The prayers they should already know are:

- Sign of the Cross
- Glory Be
- Our Father

Throughout the year, you may add more prayers. As the children memorize them, they may add a sticker to the chart. At the end of the year, reward the students who have memorized all of their prayers.

Reinforce

1. Have the students think of examples to fulfill each of the petitions of the Our Father.

2. Have the students complete *Activity Book*, p. 4.

3. Have the students break into pairs and quiz each other over the questions found on pp. 11 and 12 of the student text.

4. Do a general review of the content the students learned this week to prepare them for their quiz in the next lesson.

Conclude

1. Sing "All people that on earth do dwell," *Adoremus Hymnal*, #622.

2. End by praying the Sign of the Cross, the Our Father, and the Glory Be.

3. Remind the students to study for their quiz in the next lesson.

Preview

In the next lesson, the students' knowledge of the material covered this week will be reviewed and assessed.

NOTES

CHAPTER ONE
REVIEW AND ASSESSMENT

Aims

The students' knowledge and understanding of the material covered this week will be reviewed and assessed.

Materials

- Quiz 1, Appendix, p. A-1

Optional:
- "All people that on earth do dwell," *Adoremus Hymnal*, #622

Review

1. Quiz the students to ensure that they understand the definitions of the perfections of God. For example, to say that God has always existed and will always exist means that God is _____ (eternal). Do this for all the perfections learned in this chapter: eternal, almighty, all holy, all wise, all loving and all merciful.

2. Review with the children that they are made in God's image. Ask them ways they can use their bodies and souls to reflect God to others. Sample answers:
- Body: we care for creation, we bring love to others through acts of charity, we are persons, etc.
- Soul: our souls will live forever, God is pure spirit, our souls are pure spirits, and our souls are intelligent.

3. Review the doctrines of the Trinity and the Incarnation.

4. Review the definition of prayer: lifting our hearts and minds to God to talk with and listen to Him.

5. Review the prayers the children have learned this week, including the petitions of the Our Father.

6. Review the Memorization Questions for this chapter as a group.

Name: _____

God Loves Us   **Quiz 1**

Word Bank

never	love	star	see	end	talking
lived	all wise	voice	fault	everything	three

Fill in the blanks with the correct words from the Word Bank.

1. God has **lived** forever. Billions of years ago God was alive. Billions of years from now He will be just as powerful and alive.

2. God is eternal, which means He had no beginning and He will **never** die.

3. God is all perfect, which means that all good is found in God. He is without any **fault**.

4. God is almighty, all holy, and **all wise**.

5. His power and beauty are infinite, which means without **end**.

6. There is only one God, but in God there are **three** Persons: God the Father, God the Son, and God the Holy Spirit.

7. God was thinking of you, loving you from all eternity. Long before He put one **star** in the sky, He knew you.

8. He knew your name. He knew your face. He knew the color of your eyes and the sound of your **voice**. You are precious to Him.

9. God knows **everything** about us, even our thoughts.

10. God gave each of us a soul that will never die. He gave us souls so that we could **love** Him.

11. God is pure spirit. We cannot **see** or hear Him, but we know He is always with us.

12. Prayer is **talking** with God. We need to do it everyday because it keeps us close to Him.

Faith and Life • Grade 3 • Appendix A   A - 1

Assess

1. Distribute the quizzes and read through them with the students to be sure they understand the questions.

2. Administer the quiz. As they hand in their work, you may orally quiz them on the Memorization Questions for this chapter.

3. After all the quizzes have been handed in, you may wish to review the correct answers with the class.

Conclude

End by singing "All people that on earth do dwell," *Adoremus Hymnal*, #622.

CHAPTER TWO
GOD CREATED THE WORLD

Catechism of the Catholic Church References

Perfections of God Known through Creation: 293–95, 315, 341
Catechesis on Creation: 282–89
Definition of Sin: 1849–51, 1871
God Continues to Care for What He has Made: 302–14, 321–24
God Creates an Ordered and Good World: 299
God Creates out of Nothing: 296–98, 317–18

God Creates out of Wisdom and Love: 295, 315
Heaven: 1023–29
"Lord": 466
Man in Paradise: 374–79, 384
Man's Vocation to Beatitude: 1718–24, 1726–29
Mystery of Creation: 295–301, 315–318, 320
Ways of Knowing God: 31–38, 46–48, 286

Scripture References

Creation of Man: Gen 1—2

Background Reading: *The Fundamentals of Catholicism* by Fr. Kenneth Baker, S.J.

Volume 2:
"Where Does the Human Soul Come from?" pp. 149–51

Original Justice and Original Sin, pp. 155–170

Summary of Lesson Content

Lesson 1

God is Creator of Heaven and earth.

The story of Creation teaches us about God.

Lesson 2

Creation is good.

God cares for creation.

God is Lord and Master of all creation.

Lesson 3

God has a plan for every person.

God gave man free will.

Sin is the rejection of God's plan for man, whereby man offends God and neighbor.

Lesson 4

Heaven is man's greatest hope.

Heaven is a state of union with God forever. Every person is called to eternal life in Heaven.

LESSON ONE: CREATION

Aims

The students will learn the story of Creation.

They will also learn that God is the Creator of Heaven and earth.

Materials

- Appendix, pp. B-1–B-6
- Colored chalk/dry erase markers for board
- *Activity Book*, p. 5
- Children's Bible (Gen 1—2).

Optional:
- "All creatures of our God and King," *Adoremus Hymnal*, #600

Begin

Have the children distinguish between "to make" and "to create." Teach them that to make something requires materials, such as noodles, water, and tomato sauce to make spaghetti, or bread, tomato sauce, and cheese to make pizza. (As a class, you may want to make some food—sandwiches or tacos). Only God can create something from nothing. The Apostles' Creed teaches us that God is the Creator of Heaven and earth. The Nicene Creed adds "of all that is seen and unseen."

---

2 God Created the World

> In the beginning God created the heavens and the earth. The earth was without form and void, and darkness was upon the face of the deep; and the Spirit of God was moving over the face of the waters.
>
> Genesis 1:1–2

In the beginning, there was only a great darkness. There was no earth, no light, no people, or animals, or trees.

God was perfectly happy, so He did not need to create these things. But in His infinite goodness and love, He wanted to share His life. So He created all of Heaven and earth.

Creating something means making it out of nothing. When a carpenter makes a chair, he cannot do it without his hammer, nails, and wood. When a baker makes a cake, he cannot do it without eggs and sugar and milk. But God **created** the world, which means He made it out of nothing. Only God is so powerful that He can make something just by thinking of it and willing it to be.

First God said, "Let there be light!" and the sun and moon and millions of stars brightened the sky. Then He created the sparkling sea and the land. He put birds in the air and animals of all shapes and sizes on the earth. Finally, God made a man and a woman in His own image and likeness. They were Adam and Eve, our first parents. God made them to know, love, and serve Him by loving and helping each other, ruling the earth, and enjoying its beauty together.

Everything that God created is good. We believe in God's wisdom and love because everything in nature has a purpose. For

13

Develop

1. Have the students work on *Activity Book*, p. 5.

2. *Using the children's Bible, read Genesis 1—2 (the story of Creation) with the children. List on the board what was made on each day:*
   - *Day 1: light (day and night)*
   - *Day 2: waters and sky*
   - *Day 3: land, water, and vegetation*
   - *Day 4: sun, moon, and stars*
   - *Day 5: water creatures and air creatures*
   - *Day 6: land creatures, man, and woman*
   Notice how God first made space and then filled it with life.

3. Reread the Creation story and have the students take turns drawing the different stages of Creation on the board. Have them say what they are drawing and describe how each stage shows God's goodness.

4. Using the Creation Play found in the Appendix, pp. B-1–B-6, have the students dramatize the story of God's Creation. Ask how each creature gives glory to God, e.g., the sun shines brightly and gives off heat and light.

5. Have the students take turns reading sentences from the first three paragraphs from the student text aloud.

6. *Ask the students about the special role of man and woman. They were to take care of God's creation. They were "stewards." Ask the students how they can be stewards in the world today. Ideas may include picking up litter, planting trees and plants, recycling, not polluting, adopting an abandoned pet, etc.*

7. Make up a Litany of Creation, in which the children thank God for all His gifts, for example:
For the sun and moon, we thank you Lord...

Name:_____

God Creates. Man Makes.

Only God can create. Name some things He has created.

Man can make things. Name some things man can make.

Faith and Life Series • Grade 3 • Chapter 2 • Lesson 1   5

Reinforce

1. Have the students work on *Activity Book*, p. 5.

2. Draw and dramatize the story of Creation.

3. Reinforce the difference between making and creating—only God can create.

4. Have the students do a "stewardship project." Have the class collect litter on the playground, plant flowers (or bulbs) in a garden, or adopt a pet (such as a bunny).

Conclude

1. Teach the students to sing "All creatures of our God and King," *Adoremus Hymnal*, #600.

2. Lead the children in praying their Litany of Creation.

Preview

In the next lesson, the students will learn of the goodness of creation, God's wisdom in creation, and God's care for creation.

ST. FRANCIS OF ASSISI

Saint Francis was born into a wealthy family in Assisi, Umbria (present-day Italy), around the year 1181. According to a legend that dates from the fifteenth century, he was born in a stable like Our Lord. As a young man he enjoyed music, fine clothes, and a showy display. He was called by God to reject the things of this world and instead embraced poverty. Francis founded the Franciscan Order in 1209 by permission of Pope Innocent III. He died October 3, 1226; he was canonized by Gregory IX on July 16, 1228. The feast day of St. Francis of Assisi is October 4.

NOTES

_____
_____
_____
_____
_____
_____
_____
_____
_____

LESSON TWO: GOD IS LORD

Aims

The students will learn that creation is good.

The students will learn about God's wisdom in His creation and His care for creation.

They will learn that God is Lord and Master of all creation.

Materials

- *Activity Book*, p. 6
- Materials to test the senses, e.g., sandpaper, colorful balloons, perfume, music, candy, etc.

Optional:
- "Adam and Eve," video; In the Beginning: Stories from the Bible series, available through Ignatius Press
- "All creatures of our God and King," *Adoremus Hymnal*, #600

Begin

Begin the class by singing "All creatures of our God and King," *Adoremus Hymnal*, #600. What creatures are named? How are they good? Are all of God's creatures good? What about frogs and snakes? What about germs—yes, they, too, can help people! What about rain and snow? Note that all of creation is good—God made it that way. You may review the creation account from the children's Bible, pointing out that, at the end of each stage of creation, God said that it was good.

Develop

1. Ask the children how things work together. For example, how does a plant know to get its nutrients from water, soil, and the sun? The plant does not know in the same way that a human being knows because it does not have an intellect.

2. Review the types of creation:
   - *Non-living things/objects, such as rocks, land, and water. These do not have life, but they are good for they give life and shelter to living things.*
   - *Plant life, such as grass, flowers, vegetables, and trees. These have the lowest level of life. They grow and can turn towards the sun. They are not mobile and provide food for other creatures.*
   - *Animals, such as cats, dogs, and frogs. These have a higher level of life. They can move around and some can even be trained. They may be food for another creature (e.g., birds eat worms), but they do not have intellects—for example, your pet dog cannot do math nor can it choose to do a good thing or a bad thing.*
   - *Man. Men are higher than plants and animals. We can eat them and take care of them. We have immortal souls. We have intellects and can choose to do good and avoid evil. We can also share in God's life of grace! We can live forever with God in Heaven.*
   - *Angels. Angels do not have bodies, but they are still God's creatures. They have free will and are intelligent. They, too, will live forever because they are spiritual beings.*

3. Explain to the children that God's creation works together for the good. He cares for all His creation—he holds it in existence! All of this shows God's wisdom and love. God is the Lord and Master of all creation—he made it and directs it toward its end. For example, a plant provides food for man. God gives the plant all it needs to grow and produce food. Have the children think of other examples.

Name:_____

God Created the World

1. How did everything come to be? Was it always there?

God created everything out of nothing.

2. What special gifts were given to man and woman? What were they to do?

Adam and Eve were to know, love, and serve God by loving and helping each other, ruling the earth, and enjoying its beauty together.

3. Why do we believe in God's wisdom?

We believe in God's wisdom because everything in nature has a purpose.

4. What is God's purpose for you?

God's purpose for me is to be happy with Him in Heaven.

5. What are you to do in this world?

God wants us to enjoy our gifts.

6. What ruins God's plans for us?

Sin ruins God's plans for us.

7. Does God take care of us?

Yes, God takes care of us!

Reinforce

1. Have the students work on *Activity Book*, p. 6.

2. Have the students do a group project to show how they can work together to do something they could not do individually. An example might be to create a poster/display of creation, or students can help a parishioner with yard work, etc.

3. Test the children's senses and help them to appreciate and enjoy creation's goodness. For example, have them listen for wind in the leaves, smell a flower, or taste sweet honey, etc.

4. Have the students begin working on their Memorization Questions.

5. If you have time remaining, show the first part of the video "Adam and Eve," from the In the Beginning: Stories from the Bible series (available through Ignatius Press; 30 minutes). Stop the tape before the Fall.

Conclude

1. Have the children pray their Litany of Creation.

2. End with the Glory Be.

3. Lead the children in singing "All creatures of our God and King," *Adoremus Hymnal*, #600.

Preview

In the next lesson, the students will learn that God has a plan for each of us and that we can choose whether to do it or not.

NOTES

LESSON THREE: FREE WILL

Aims

The students will learn that God has a plan for every person.

They will learn about free will—that we can choose to follow God's plan or not.

They will learn that sin is the rejection of God's plan for man, whereby man offends God and neighbor.

Materials

- *Activity Book*, p. 7
- Children's Bible

Optional:
- "Adam and Eve," video; In the Beginning: Stories from the Bible series, available through Ignatius Press
- "All creatures of our God and King," *Adoremus Hymnal*, #600

Begin

Review the five senses and the types of things God has created, which we enjoy through each of our senses. List these on the board in vertical columns:
SIGHT—*sunset, rainbow, forest*
SOUND—*music, speech, birds*
TASTE—*honey, candy, fruit*
SMELL—*flowers, pizza, perfume*
TOUCH—*cotton, grass, rain*
Ask the children to name some of their favorite things in the world. Then, ask them to explain how these favorite things come from God.

---

example, a porcupine's funny needles are not for decoration. God planned them so that a porcupine could protect himself from danger. A mother kangaroo's pouch is not an accident. God planned that soft, warm place to keep her babies safe.

The things in nature work together. When a bee takes food from a flower, his legs get full of pollen which is needed for little flower seeds. As he flies away, the pollen scatters so lots of new flowers will grow. God made the mountains tall so they can catch snow. Then the snow high above the ground melts slowly and trickles down to water the earth all year.

We believe that God is the **Lord**, or master of all things. It takes a brilliant plan to make all of nature work this way. That is why we believe it comes from God.

God has a purpose for you, too. He created you to one day be happy with Him in Heaven. He also created you first to be a part of this world. At Baptism He gave His life, called grace, to your soul. He gave you talents to serve His Kingdom. He gave you five senses, so you can see, hear, taste, touch, and smell the beautiful things on this earth. Naturally, God wants you to enjoy these gifts and be happy.

Only one thing ruins His plan for our happiness: **sin**. When we sin, we do not use God's gifts in the way He wants us to use them. When we sin we do not feel right inside. We feel wrong and upset. We turn our backs on our loving God.

God gave us our mind and will so we can choose to live His plan for us. We can choose to do what is right and good. When we obey our parents, study well, are kind to our neighbors and friends, and respect animals and nature, we please God. We feel right inside.

To be happy forever, we must get to Heaven. **Heaven** is our greatest hope. God promises He will take us there if we love and serve Him in this world. We will be completely happy forever in

Develop

1. Read from "God has a purpose for you too" to the end of the paragraph that begins with "God gave us our mind."

2. Explain to the children that everything was made for a reason. For example, mountains collect snow, which becomes water for crops. Trees give us fruit, protection from the sun, and serve as homes for animals. Dogs make good pets and protect our homes. They are helpful for hunting, too. People were created to know, love, and serve God in this life and to be happy forever with God in Heaven. This is God's plan for us! (What a wonderful plan!)

3. To know, love, and serve God means that we must use our minds, hearts, and bodies well. We must be faithful to God, body and soul! This is not always easy. As humans, we have what is called free will. This means we can choose to do good and avoid evil. Why would we ever want to do bad things? Sometimes that which is evil appears to be good. For exam-

ple, eating lots of our favorite candy seems good, but it can make us sick. Because of our free will we can choose to eat too much candy and make ourselves sick.

4. When we choose to do something that is bad or against God, we sin. By sinning, we turn away from God by choosing not to obey His plan for us. When we sin, we feel badly inside. In order to sin, we must freely choose to do something we know is wrong. Ask the children what examples of sin might be and how they are against God's plan.

5. To do something good we must choose to do something good with good circumstances. An example might include giving food to the poor if we have food to share, but we cannot steal the food for this purpose. A good act requires that the object, intention, and means be good. Give the children many examples and have them think of some. Remind the children that in choosing to do good, we feel good, too!

Name: _____

God Created You!

Find the words for each blank and then complete the puzzle.

God gave you talents to serve His __(1)__. God __(2)__ He will take us to Heaven if we love and serve Him. You are made up of __(3)__ __(3)__ __(3)__. God wants us to use our minds to __(4)__ what is right and good. Everything in nature (including you) has a __(5)__. This shows God's wisdom. In __(6)__ we will see God face to face and be happy forever. God gave you five senses to enjoy the __(7)__ things on earth. God created man and woman in His image. Adam and Eve are our __(8)__ __(8)__. God made man and woman to __(9)__ __(9)__ __(9)__ each other. By sinning, we turn our backs on __(10)__, Who loves us. Before God created, He was perfectly __(11)__, and He wants to share this with you, so you can be __(11)__ forever with Him in Heaven. Only God is so __(12)__ that He can make something just by thinking about it and willing it to be. Adam and Eve were to __(13)__ the earth and enjoy its beauty together.

1. KINGDOM
2. PROMISED
3. BODY AND SOUL
4. CHOOSE
5. PURPOSE
6. HEAVEN
7. BEAUTIFUL
8. FIRST PARENTS
9. LOVE AND HELP
10. GOD
11. HAPPY
12. POWERFUL
13. RULE

Faith and Life Series • Grade 3 • Chapter 2 • Lesson 3

Reinforce

1. *Activity Book*, p. 7

2. Work on the Memorization Questions for this chapter.

3. Give the students examples of amoral situations and have them build on them to make them either morally good or morally bad actions:
e.g., feed the dog
• Good: feed the dog everyday
• Bad: feed the dog poison or feed him only once a month
e.g., read a book
• Good: read books that teach us about our faith
• Bad: read a book with unholy things in it

Optional: read the story of the fall of Adam and Eve from the children's Bible or finish watching the video, "Adam and Eve," from the In the Beginning: Stories from the Bible series (available through Ignatius Press; 30 minutes). Ask the students how Adam and Eve sinned. Did they choose to go against God by their actions? Did evil seem like good? How did they feel after they sinned? How can the students learn from the mistakes made by Adam and Eve?

Conclude

Lead the children in singing "All creatures of our God and King," *Adoremus Hymnal*, #600.

Preview

In the next lesson, the students will learn more about Heaven.

CHALK TALK: WHICH ROAD WILL YOU TAKE?

NOTES

LESSON FOUR: HEAVEN

Aims

The students will learn that God wants all of us to go to Heaven. Heaven is man's greatest hope.

The students will learn that Heaven is a state of union with God forever.

Materials

- *Activity Book*, p. 8
- Two small cakes (Each must be large enough to share with the whole class)
- Sentence strips

Optional:
- "All creatures of our God and King," *Adoremus Hymnal*, #600

Begin

Let the children see only one of the cakes. Hold up the cake and ask how this cake can be used in a good way or in a sinful way. (good: to eat and share; bad: to waste). Take the cake and say "I choose not to use this cake for God's plan of eating. Instead I choose to waste it." Then, throw the cake into the garbage pail. Ask the children if, now that the cake is destroyed, it can be used for its proper end. No. Pull out the other cake and say you will share it with all the children. Explain that this is the proper use for the cake. Throughout our lives, we can either choose to do good or choose to do that which is sinful in God's eyes. All of our actions have consequences.

Heaven because we will see God face to face. We are not sure what Heaven looks like, but we know it will be even more beautiful than we can imagine. God gave us His word: "What no eye has seen, nor ear heard, nor the heart of man conceived, what God has prepared for those who love him" (1 Corinthians 2:9).

Words to Know:

create   Lord   sin   Heaven

Q. 11 *Does God take care of His creation?*
Yes, God takes care of His creation. He keeps all things in existence and directs all of them toward their own purpose with infinite wisdom, goodness, and justice (CCC 301–2).

Q. 12 *Can God do all things?*
God can do all that He wills to do: He is the all-powerful one (CCC 268).

Q. 13 *What does "Creator" mean?*
"Creator" means that God made all things out of nothing (CCC 296).

Q. 14 *What does "Lord" mean?*
"Lord" means that God is the absolute master of all things (CCC 450).

Q. 15 *What ruins God's plan for our happiness?*
Sin ruins God's plan for our happiness (CCC 1847).

Develop

1. Explain to the children that during this life, we can choose to do good (follow God's plan, e.g., share the cake) or do bad things (choose not to follow God's plan, e.g., waste the cake). Like the cake example, once it is done it cannot be reversed. Once you threw out the cake, it could not be eaten and shared. Once it was eaten and shared, it could not be thrown out. Throughout our lives, we will be held accountable for all our actions, and when we die we will not be able to change them.

2. Consequences may not be serious, as in the cake example, or they can be very serious. If we live a bad life by rejecting God and His plan for us, we will be sent to hell for all eternity. Hell is a state of eternal suffering and separation from God. Hell is so horrible that we would never wish for even our worst enemy to go there.

3. However, if we live good lives by choosing to love God and follow His plan for us, when we die, God will bring us to live with Him forever in Heaven. Heaven is our greatest hope. It is the most wonderful state in which to be. In Heaven we will be perfectly happy, forever beholding God's face.

4. We must remember that we have free will and that God allows us to choose either Heaven or hell. We must pray to know God's plan and to choose the good, asking God to help us to know the truth. (You may teach the children: WWJD— What would Jesus do?)

5. Read the rest of the chapter from the student text.

6. Stress the importance of choosing to do good and the great reward God has promised His faithful disciples.

Name:_____

What is Heaven?

The story of how much God did for all of us is found in the Bible, beginning with the creation of the world, and how much He continues to do together with us. The Bible also tells how the story will finish, when "God will be all in all," and the world will be renewed, and we will all be forever and ever with God singing to His glory!

Connect the dots and complete the picture with your own idea of Heaven.

8   *Faith and Life Series • Grade 3 • Chapter 2 • Lesson 4*

Reinforce

1. Hand out different sentence strips to the students, and have them complete the sentences.

2. Have the students work on *Activity Book*, p. 8.

3. Have the students work on the Memorization Questions in pairs.

4. Do an overall review of the content of this chapter to help the students prepare for the quiz in the next lesson.

Conclude

1. Have the students sing "All creatures of our God and King," *Adoremus Hymnal*, #600.

2. Lead the students in praying for a happy death. End with the Our Father and the Glory Be.

Preview

In the next lesson, the students' knowledge of the material covered this week will be reviewed and assessed.

SAMPLE SENTENCE STRIPS

- Heaven is more beautiful than . . .
- Heaven is better than . . .
- Heaven is bigger than . . .
- Heaven lasts longer than . . .
- Heaven is happier than . . .
- Heaven is more fun than . . .
- Heaven sounds better than . . .
- Heaven is more comfortable than . . .

NOTES

CHAPTER TWO
REVIEW AND ASSESSMENT

Aims

The students' knowledge and understanding of the material covered this week will be reviewed and assessed.

Materials

- Quiz 2, Appendix, p. A-2

Optional:
- "All creatures of our God and King," *Adoremus Hymnal*, #600

Review

1. Have the students recount the story of Creation, covering the six days in their proper sequence.

2. Have the students explain what free will is (the ability to choose good and avoid evil).

3. Have the students define sin: to choose not to follow God's plan, and thus offend Him and our neighbors.

4. Ask the children how we can know that God has a plan for us. What can we see in the world around us that shows us God's providential care for His creation? Have them give concrete examples.

5. What is God's plan for man? To know, love, and serve God in this world, and to be with Him forever in Heaven.

6. Does man have to go to Heaven? No, man can also choose by his actions to go to hell when he dies.

7. How can man go to Heaven? By loving and serving God faithfully throughout his life.

8. Have the students describe Heaven. It is an eternal state of perfect happiness, where we are united in God's eternal embrace of love.

Name: _____

God Created the World — Quiz 2

"I have loved you with an everlasting love" (Jeremiah 31:3).

Word Bank

love	created	Heaven	darkness
earth	God	good	Sin
image	everlasting	Lord	life

Fill in the blanks with the correct word from the Word Bank.

1. In the beginning, there was *darkness*, and then God created light.

2. God was happy, but He wanted to share His *life* with us.

3. God *created* the world, which means He made it out of nothing.

4. God created Heaven and *earth*.

5. God made a man and a woman in His own *image* and likeness.

6. We believe that God is the *Lord*, or Master of all things.

7. Everything that God created is *good*.

8. We will be completely happy forever in *Heaven* for we will see God.

9. God promised that He will take us to Heaven if we *love* and serve Him.

10. *Sin* is any wrong we do on purpose, which turns us away from God.

11. Our Bible verse for today is: "I have loved you with an *everlasting* love."

12. Who loves us with an everlasting love? *God*.

Assess

1. Distribute the quizzes and read through them with the children to ensure they understand the questions.

2. Administer the quiz. As the students hand in their work, orally quiz them on the Memorization Questions for this chapter.

3. After all the quizzes have been handed in, you may wish to review the correct answers with the class.

Conclude

End with a prayer and sing "All creatures of our God and King," *Adoremus Hymnal*, #600.

CHAPTER THREE
LEARNING ABOUT GOD

Catechism of the Catholic Church References

Apostolic Tradition: 75–76, 96
Christian Holiness: 2012–16, 2028–29
Church as Protector and Teacher of Revelation: 84–95, 98–100
Church's Origin, Foundation, and Mission: 758–69, 778
God Forms His People, Israel: 62–64, 72, 218, 2077
Inspiration and Truth of Scripture: 105–108, 136

New Testament: 124–27, 139, 515
Old Testament: 121–23
Parables and the Proclamation of God's Kingdom: 543–46
Perfections of God Known through Creation: 293–95, 315, 341
Role of Pope and Bishops: 880–96, 935–39
Ways of Knowing God: 31–38, 46–48, 286

Scripture References

Wise and Foolish Bridesmaids: Mt 25:1–13
Rich Man and Lazarus: Lk 16:19–31

The Good Samaritan: Lk 10:25–37

Background Reading: *The Fundamentals of Catholicism* by Fr. Kenneth Baker, S.J.

Volume 2:
"God's Absolute Perfection," pp. 38–40

Volume 3:
"Why Did Christ Establish His Church?" pp. 95–97
"Bishops Are Successors of the Apostles," pp. 104–106
"The Everlasting Church," pp. 131–33

Summary of Lesson Content

Lesson 1

From the world around him and by the use of his reason, man can know that God exists.

Man can also, by reason, know some of God's perfections.

Lesson 2

God chose to reveal Himself to man through the prophets.

Prophets speak God's truth to their fellow human beings, in order to bring them closer to God.

Moses was the greatest of the Old Testament prophets.

Lesson 3

God also chose to reveal Himself (more directly) through His Son, Jesus Christ.

Jesus revealed God to man through all He said and did and by Who He was.

Jesus taught man about God and His kingdom through parables.

Lesson 4

The Bible is made up of the Old Testament and the New Testament.

Jesus founded the Church. The Pope is the Vicar of Christ. The bishops of the world, in union with the Pope, help govern and teach the Church.

The Church safeguards God's revelation in Scripture and Tradition.

LESSON ONE: KNOWING GOD

Aims

The students will learn that from the world around him and by the use of his reason man can know that God exists.

They will learn that by the use of his reason, man can also know some of God's perfections.

Materials

- *Activity Book*, p. 9
- Pictures of nature (or if weather is good, go outside and have bags available to collect items)
- Pictures of art of various artistic styles

Optional:
- "Of the Father's love begotten," *Adoremus Hymnal*, #331

Begin

Take the time to explain to the children that all of them are Catholic. This is a great gift from God. Ask them why they are Catholic. They are Catholic most likely because their parents are Catholic and they were born into Catholic families. Explain to the children that not all people are Catholic. Some of the children may have friends who are of different religions. Explain that although not all people recognize the truth about God as taught through the Catholic Church, God is still the one true God, and He loves them. He wants all people to know and love Him. Even people who have no religion can come to know that God exists because all creation reflects the Creator.

---

3   Learning About God

"This is eternal life, that they know thee the only true God, and Jesus Christ whom thou hast sent."

John 17:3

We believe God is with us because He gives us many signs of His presence. One of the best signs is the world all around us. Everything in nature acts for a purpose. It has order, and it has great beauty. Even a person who has never heard about God can figure out that Someone very wise and powerful must have put nature together. The different parts of creation give us many clues about God, our **Creator**.

Mountains and vast forests reveal that our Creator is majestic and great. Oceans and rushing waterfalls tell us of His power. Fresh roses and sunsets reflect God's beauty. The growth and seasons of living things show us that God is wise. And the company of good, loving people teaches us more about God's own goodness and love.

God made sure we had many ways to discover Him, since He created us to know and love Him. Long ago, before the coming of Jesus, God sent messages to His people through holy men called prophets. **Prophets** were men who prepared the people for the coming of the Savior. Moses, for example, was a great prophet. Through Moses, and other Old Testament prophets, God taught mankind to be good, to stop sinning, and to trust in Him.

God later revealed Himself to us more directly through Jesus Christ, His Son, Our Savior. Remember, Jesus is God the Son, the Second Person of the Trinity. His way of life on earth showed us what God is really like. We learn through Jesus that God is gentle as well as just, slow to anger, rich in mercy, and full of love. We learn

17

Develop

1. Show the children various pieces of art and discuss how they differ from each other. An impressionist uses bold strokes and colors to give the image the desired effect. A piece from the Renaissance period may look "romantic" or idealized. As you hold up each work of art, ask the children what it tells us about God and man. For example, a religious work of art may inspire us to a deeper love of God.

2. Explain to the children that creation works the same way. By looking at creation, we can use our reason to know something of the Creator. First, we can know that because all of creation works together, it could not have been just accidentally thrown together and left abandoned. Someone very intelligent must have made the world and still cares for it. We can look at the power of waterfalls and storms and know that the Creator must be more powerful than these. We can look at the beauty of mountains and sunsets and know that the Creator is more beautiful. Read the first two paragraphs of the chapter.

3. Either look at pictures or take the children outside to show them God's perfections in nature, such as wisdom, goodness, power, beauty, infinity, holiness, love, justice, and truth. Have the children present what they find and then describe how their findings reflect God's perfections.

4. Lead the children in giving thanks to God for the beauty of His creation, which is also a way in which we can come to know Him.

5. Next, ask the children if they can know through creation that God is a Triune God. No. Can they know that Jesus Christ is the Son of God through creation? No. Can they know that God wants us to receive the sacraments through creation? No. Explain that through creation, we can know that God exists, and we can know some of His perfections. We needed God to reveal Himself to us in the Person of His Son, Jesus Christ, in order to know more about God and His plan for us.

Name:_____

Who is God?

Take time to notice God all around you!

1. There are things all around you that are powerful. Can you name some of them? An example might be a thunderstorm.

   Answers will vary.

2. There are things all around you that are beautiful. Can you name some of them? An example might be a flower.

   Answers will vary.

3. There are things all around you that work together. Can you think of some examples? An example might be bees bringing pollen for flowers.

   Answers will vary.

4. There are things all around you that are good. Can you think of some of them? An example might be an ice cream cone.

   Answers will vary.

5. There are things all around you that make you feel God is close. Can you think of some of them? An example might be how you feel when the sun hits your face.

   Answers will vary.

Faith and Life Series • Grade 3 • Chapter 3 • Lesson 1

EXAMPLES OF HOW WE SEE THE PERFECTIONS OF GOD IN NATURE

- **Wisdom:** the changing seasons and tides; a spider's web
- **Goodness:** a bird caring for its young; the rising sun
- **Power:** the roaring ocean; a thunderstorm; an earthquake
- **Perfection:** the stars in the sky; mathematics
- **Beauty:** the great forests; waterfalls; rainbows
- **Infinity:** the night sky
- **Holiness:** the gentle wind; sun shining through trees
- **Love:** flowers blooming; birds singing
- **Justice:** natural wonders throughout the world
- **Truth:** clear water that reflects your face

Reinforce

1. Lead the children in a nature hunt.

2. Have the children work on *Activity Book*, p. 9.

3. Have the students work on the first two Memorization Questions for this chapter.

4. Make a display with the students' findings showing God's perfections as reflected in nature.

Conclude

1. Teach the children to sing "Of the Father's love begotten," *Adoremus Hymnal*, #331.

2. End class by praying a Litany of Creation and the Glory Be.

Preview

In the next lesson, the students will learn more about revelation and how God revealed Himself through the prophets.

NOTES

_____
_____
_____
_____
_____
_____
_____
_____
_____
_____

LESSON TWO: PROPHETS

Aims

The students will learn that God chose to reveal Himself to man.

They will learn that God chose the prophets to speak God's truth to man in order to bring man closer to God.

Moses was the greatest of the Old Testament prophets.

Materials

- *Activity Book*, p. 10
- Children's Bible (Ex 19:5–6, 20)

Optional:
- "The Exodus," video: In the Beginning: Stories from the Bible, available through Ignatius Press
- "Of the Father's love begotten," *Adoremus Hymnal*, #331

Begin

Ask the children if they have any close friends or family members. Do they like to speak with them? What about? Do they find joy in talking about themselves, their likes and dislikes, as well as their desires? God, too, wants us to know Him. He wants to share with us Who He is and what His plan is for us. God invites us into a deeper relationship with Him, which requires that we know Him better. Because God loves us so much and wants us to love Him in return, God chose to reveal Himself to us so that we can have this relationship with Him.

---

that He forgives the greatest sins if we are sorry for them. We learn that He is always ready to heal us, help us, and be our friend.

Jesus often taught these things through parables. **Parables** are stories about ordinary people that teach us something about the Kingdom of God. Each parable is different, but they all teach one clear message from God: "Love God with all your heart and soul and might, and love your neighbor as yourself."

We find Jesus' parables and other things He said and did in a big book called the Bible. The **Bible** is the holy book God gave us. It has two parts, the Old Testament and the New Testament. The **Old Testament** is the first part of the Bible. It teaches us about creation, our first parents, and the long wait and preparation of God's people for a Savior. The **New Testament** is the second part of the Bible. It tells the story of Jesus and how the Church began. It teaches us that the Church is our ladder to Heaven.

God inspired holy men from earliest times to write down His Law and teachings. These are recorded in the Bible. That is why we call it the word of God. We also call it Scripture. God's teaching was also passed on through words and deeds that weren't written in the Bible. That teaching is called Tradition. Scripture and Tradition teach us everything we need to know to live a good and happy life that is pleasing to God.

Jesus, our Teacher, once called Himself the Good Shepherd because He watches over us and leads us to the Father. After Jesus left the earth, He gave us another shepherd to take His place. We call this shepherd the Vicar of Christ or the **Pope**. The Pope teaches and guides the Church for Christ. He encourages us to become saints. He is the head of the **bishops** all over the world. He helps them in their mission to help us keep learning and growing in our faith.

19

Develop

1. Ask the children some of ways in which we can come to know people. We can know them by what they do (e.g., if Johnny is always mean to others, we might say that Johnny is a mean boy). We can know them by what others say about them (e.g., if your mother says that Suzy is a nice girl and that you may spend more time with her, than you may think Suzy is a nice girl). We can know them by what they say (e.g., if I say that lying hurts my feelings, then you can know that I like the truth).

2. *Explain to the children that God chose to reveal Himself to man. This means that God wants us to know Him better. We can know God by what He does (e.g., He created the world so we can say God is the Creator). We can know God by what others say about Him (e.g., Jesus told us to call God our Father). We can know God by what He says about Himself (e.g., what He revealed to the prophets).*

3. *Read paragraph 3 to the class.*

4. The prophets are holy people chosen by God to speak to others on God's behalf. They are not soothsayers (although they may at times predict the future). They speak God's truth and call people to a deeper relationship with Him. For example, let's look at Moses who was God's greatest prophet (Ex 19:5–6, 20). Moses gave us the Ten Commandments, God's Laws, so that we may live in a good relationship with God and neighbor. If you have the video on "The Exodus," from the In the Beginning: Stories from the Bible series (available through Ignatius Press; 30 minutes), you may watch it. Point out that God communicates Himself to man by words and deeds.

5. *Stress how God uses natural and supernatural means to communicate with us. Speaking through the prophets and working miraculous events are supernatural. This revelation helps us come to know God.*

24

Name:_____

The Prophets!

If you were a prophet, what would you write?

<u>Answers will vary.</u>

10 Faith and Life Series • Grade 3 • Chapter 3 • Lesson 2

MOSES

Moses was the greatest prophet of the Old Testament. Born to a poor Israelite girl, Moses was placed among the rushes on the Nile River in a basket. Discovered by Pharaoh's own daughter, Moses was raised as a son within the royal house of Egypt. When he defended an Israelite slave and killed an Egyptian, Moses fled his royal position. God called to Moses from a burning bush and gave him an important job. God told Moses to lead His people out of Egypt. Moses was not a good speaker and was afraid to do what God wanted, but Moses obeyed God and led the Israelites out of Egypt.

Reinforce

1. Have the students work on *Activity Book*, p. 10. You may read examples of prophecies from the Bible to assist the students with this activity page. You may also want to stress phrases such as, "Thus says the Lord." Often blessings were given for obedience to God and curses for disobedience. There were also invitations from God to man asking man to turn away from sin and turn back to Him. The students may want to use these ideas in their "prophecies."

2. The students may work in pairs on their Memorization Questions.

Conclude

1. The students may present their "prophecies" to one another.

2. Sing "Of the Father's love begotten," *Adoremus Hymnal*, #331.

3. End with the Sign of the Cross, the Our Father, and the Glory Be.

Preview

In the next lesson, the students will learn how God revealed Himself to man through His Son, Jesus Christ.

NOTES

LESSON THREE: JESUS

Aims

The students will learn that God chose to reveal Himself more directly through His Son, Jesus Christ.

They will learn that Jesus revealed God to man through all He said and did and by Who He was. Jesus taught about God and His Kingdom through parables.

Materials

- Children's Bible: Mt 25:1–13, Lk 16:19–31, Lk 10: 25–37
- *Activity Book*, p. 11
- Appendix, pp. B-7–B-10

Optional:
- "The Story of the Good Samaritan," video: The Beginner's Bible series, available through Ignatius Press
- "Of the Father's love begotten," *Adoremus Hymnal*, #331

Begin

Ask the children how they could send an important message to a loved one. They could e-mail or fax a message. They could make a telephone call or send it through the postal system or a delivery service. In the olden days, messengers would deliver messages. The prophets are messengers of God's word. Have you ever sent someone a message that was misunderstood? What if you sent a message that read "meet me at the park?" The person who got this message might not know who he is meeting or the correct park. In order for a message to be properly understood, it is best to send it in person.

Words to Know:

Creator   prophet   parable   Bible
Old Testament   New Testament   Pope   bishop

Q. 16 *Can we know about God from the world around us?*
Yes, we can know about God from the world around us. God's goodness, wisdom, power, and beauty can be seen in His creation (CCC 34).

Q. 17 *Does creation reveal all we need to know about God?*
No, creation cannot reveal all we need to know about God, so God chose to reveal himself through prophets and, later, through His own Son, Jesus Christ (CCC 35, 50, 65).

Q. 18 *How could Jesus reveal God to us?*
Jesus could reveal God to us because Jesus is God the Son. He taught us about God through His life, actions, and words (CCC 65, 2763).

Q. 19 *Does the Bible contain all we need to know about God and His plan for men?*
No, the Bible does not contain all we need to know of God's word, but Scripture and Tradition as taught by the Church show us everything we need to know about God (CCC 67, 78, 80).

Develop

1. As a class, read paragraphs 4 and 5 of the student text. The students may take turns reading sentences aloud.

2. Explain to the children that God wanted to communicate with His people in the best possible way, so God sent His Son to earth in the Divine Person of Jesus Christ. God became man so that man could better understand God. We can know more about God by the life of Jesus—what He did and said. What does the student text say Jesus taught us about God? (God is gentle and just, slow to anger, rich in mercy, full of love, forgiving, healing, etc.)

3. Jesus taught us about God and His Kingdom through the use of parables. Who knows what a parable is? It is a little story that teaches us something. Let's read some parables from the children's Bible:

- Wise and foolish virgins Mt 25:1–13
- Rich man and Lazarus Lk 16:19–31
- Good Samaritan Lk 19:25–37

Explain the parables and what we should learn from them.

4. Break the children into groups and dramatize the parables. Have each group put on a play for the others. Let the children ask the different characters questions. For example, "Virgin number 6, what should you have done differently? Bridegroom, what are we to learn from this parable?"

5. If you have the video "The Story of the Good Samaritan," from The Beginner's Bible series (available through Ignatius Press; 30 minutes), you may show it to the class. If not, you may select other parables from the children's Bible and read them to the students.

Name:_____

Learning about God

1. How can someone come to know God?
   Answers will vary.

2. Did God send messages to His people? If so, why?
   God sent messages to prepare His people for the coming of the Savior.

3. What do we learn from the Parable of the Wise and Foolish Bridesmaids?
   Answers will vary.

4. What do we learn from the Parable of the Rich Man and Lazarus?
   Answers will vary.

5. What do we learn from the Parable of the Good Samaritan?
   Answers will vary.

6. Of whom is the Pope head?
   The Pope is head of the bishops and the Church.

7. Who safeguards the truths of Scripture and Tradition?
   The Church safeguards Scripture and Tradition.

Faith and Life Series • Grade 3 • Chapter 3 • Lesson 3   11

PARABLES FOUND IN THE GOSPELS

- The Sower and the Seeds (Mk 4:3–9; Mt 13:3–9; Lk 8:5–8)
- The Mustard Seed (Mt 13:31; Mk 4:30–32; Lk 13:18)
- The Dishonest Steward (Lk 16:1–12)
- The Two Debtors (Lk 7:41–43)
- The Hidden Treasure (Mt 13:44)
- The Pearl of Great Price (Mt 13:45)
- The Ten Virgins (Mt 25:1–13)
- The Wedding Feast (Mt 22:1–10; Lk 14:16–24)
- The Wedding Garment (Mt 22:11–14)
- The Rich Man and Lazarus (Lk 16:19–31)
- The Good Samaritan (Lk 10:25–37)
- The Prodigal Son (Lk 15:11–32)

Reinforce

1. Have the children present their parables to each other.

2. Have the students complete *Activity Book*, p. 11.

3. Have the students work on their Memorization Questions.

4. If you have not done so, show the video "The Story of the Good Samaritan," from The Beginner's Bible series (available through Ignatius Press; 30 minutes).

Conclude

1. Sing with the children "Of the Father's love begotten," *Adoremus Hymnal*, #331.

2. End class by praying the Our Father and the Glory Be.

Preview

In the next lesson, the students will learn about Scripture, Tradition, and the Church.

NOTES

LESSON FOUR: THE BIBLE

Aims

The children will learn that the Bible is made up of the Old Testament and the New Testament. God is its primary author.

They will learn that Jesus founded the Church. The Pope is the Vicar of Christ. The bishops of the world, in union with the Pope, help govern and teach the members of the Church.

They will learn that the Church safeguards God's revelation in Scripture and Tradition.

Materials

- Class set of Bibles
- *Activity Book*, p. 12

Optional:
- "Of the Father's love begotten," *Adoremus Hymnal*, #331

Begin

Distribute a class set of Bibles to the students. Teach the children that the Bible should be treated with respect, because it is the Word of God. Show the children that the Bible is made of two parts, the Old Testament and the New Testament. Have the students first open the Bible about half of the way through. Then, taking the second half, divide it in two again. This should put them around the beginning of the New Testament. Have the students work in groups to write out the names of the books in the Old and New Testaments. They may use the index for help.

> **Q. 20** *How can we be sure that the Church teaches us the truth about God and His plan?*
> We can be sure that the Church teaches us the truth because Jesus founded the Church and established Peter as the first Pope. Since then, all Popes and bishops are helped by God to guide and teach all people the truths of God (CCC 85–86).

Develop

1. Read the rest of the chapter with the children.

2. Have the children mark the Gospels on their list of books of the Bible. Note that these are the first four books of the New Testament. Stress that the Gospels are very important because they record the words and miracles of Jesus Christ. It is also in the Gospels that we find the parables. Have the students look up some of the parables listed on p. 27 of the Teacher's Manual.

3. Explain to the students that God is the author of the Bible. Although the Bible is made up of many different books and many men wrote them using different styles, it is God Who inspired their writings. They wrote no more and no less than what God wanted. The Scriptures reveal God to us in recorded word and deed.

3. Read John 21:25. Explain to the students that not everything is written in the Bible. As Catholics, we rely on both Scripture (Bible) and Tradition (the Word of God passed on through the Church but not written in the Bible). In order for the truth to be passed on without error, Jesus established the Church with Saint Peter as the head. His Church protects the truth. You may read Matthew 16:13–20 with the students.

4. Explain that the current Pope has the role of Saint Peter, the Vicar of Christ. All the bishops united with him help protect the truth passed on through Scripture and Tradition. Their special work is to help all to learn and grow in the faith through the Church. You may identify the Pope, your diocesan bishop(s), and parish priest(s). Have the children understand the roles of their local hierarchy.

5. Reinforce that we learn about God and His teachings through Scripture and Tradition and that it is safeguarded by the Magisterium (the Pope and the bishops united with him).

Name:_____

God's Revelation

1. Where do we find Jesus' parables and other things He said and did?
   <u>The Bible</u>
2. What are the two parts of the Bible?
   <u>The Old Testament and the New Testament</u>
3. About what does the Old Testament teach?
   <u>The Old Testament teaches about Creation, our first parents, and the long wait and preparation of God's people for a Savior.</u>
4. About what does the New Testament teach?
   <u>The New Testament teaches the story of Jesus and how the Church began and that the Church is the ladder to Heaven.</u>
5. Who inspired the Bible? Who wrote down everything in the Bible?
   <u>God inspired holy men from earliest times to write down everything in the Bible.</u>
6. What are other names for the Bible?
   <u>The other names for the Bible are the Word of God and Scripture.</u>
7. Other than the Bible, what teaches us everything we need to know to live a good and happy life that is pleasing to God?
   <u>Tradition</u>

Faith and Life Series • Grade 3 • Chapter 3 • Lesson 4

Reinforce

1. To demonstrate that something can be passed on either orally or in written form, use the example of passing a note. Then play the game "telephone." In this example, have one person tell the message to another. As the teacher, you will play the part of the Holy Spirit, repeating the original message at every link in the chain (just as the Church has the help of the Holy Spirit to guard the truth). This will ensure that the message is the same at the beginning and at the end of the "telephone line."

2. Have the students complete *Activity Book*, p. 12.

3. Have the students work on their Memorization Questions.

Conclude

1. Do a general review of the content taught from the entire chapter to prepare them for their quiz in the next lesson.

2. Sing "Of the Father's love begotten," *Adoremus Hymnal*, #331.

3. End class with a prayer.

Preview

In the next lesson, the students' knowledge of the material covered this week will be reviewed and assessed.

CHALK TALK: GOD'S LETTER TO US

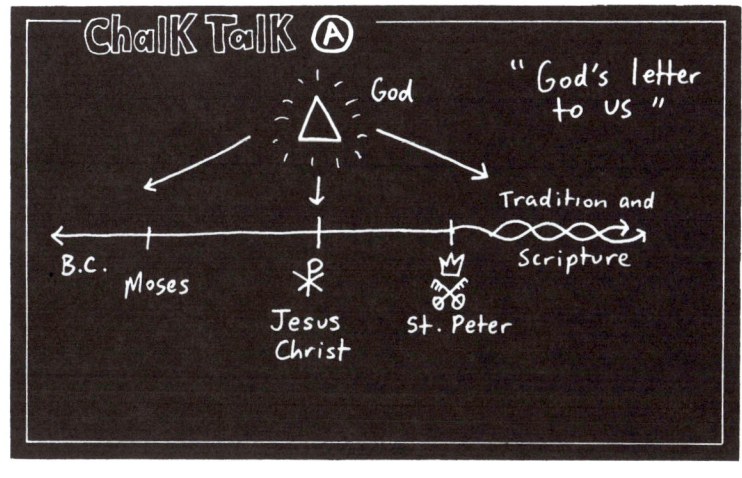

NOTES

CHAPTER THREE
REVIEW AND ASSESSMENT

Aims

The students' knowledge and understanding of the material covered this week will be reviewed and assessed.

Materials

- Quiz 3, Appendix, p. A-3

Optional:
- "Of the Father's love begotten," *Adoremus Hymnal*, #331

Review

1. Review with the children that God reveals Himself in nature, and discuss how nature reflects the perfections of God.

2. Review with the children that God reveals Himself supernaturally. He has spoken through the prophets and has revealed Himself more directly in the Divine Person of Jesus Christ, the Son of God made Man.

3. God's revelation is passed on to man in Scripture and Tradition. This revelation is kept free from error through the work of the Magisterium, which is the teaching authority of the Church (the Pope and the bishops in union with him).

4. The Bible is made up of many books. The Bible has two main parts: the Old Testament and the New Testament. The first four books of the New Testament are called the Gospels. They are Matthew, Mark, Luke, and John. The Gospels record the words and deeds of Jesus. The parables are also found in the Gospels. God is the author of the Bible. He inspired the writers to record only what God wanted recorded—no more and no less.

5. Review the Words to Know for this chapter.

Name: _____

Learning About God   **Quiz 3**

"All Scripture is inspired by God and profitable for teaching." (2 Timothy 3:16).

Word Bank

Shepherd	Jesus	Second	Savior
Bible	New Testament	Church	
Prophets	Parables	Pope	

Fill in the blanks with the correct words from the Word Bank.

1. <u>Prophets</u> were men who prepared the people for the coming of the Savior.

2. Jesus is God the Son, the <u>Second</u> Person of the Trinity.

3. The <u>Bible</u> is a holy book God gave us to tell us of His love for us.

4. The Bible is divided into two parts: the Old Testament and the <u>New Testament</u>.

5. The Old Testament tells of creation and God's people waiting for the <u>Savior</u>.

6. The New Testament tells about <u>Jesus</u>, our Savior, and the things He said and did.

7. <u>Parables</u> are stories that Jesus used to teach about the Kingdom of God.

8. Jesus, our Teacher, once called Himself the Good <u>Shepherd</u>.

9. Jesus gave us another shepherd to take his place on this earth called the <u>Pope</u>.

10. The Pope teaches and guides the <u>Church</u> for Christ.

11. Write out the Scripture verse shown at the top of this page.

_____

Faith and Life • Grade 3 • Appendix A   A - 3

Assess

1. Distribute the quizzes and read through them with the children to ensure they understand the questions.

2. Administer the quiz. As students hand in their work, orally quiz them on the Memorization Questions for this chapter.

3. After all the quizzes have been handed in, you may wish to review the correct answers with the class.

Conclude

1. Sing "Of the Father's love begotten," *Adoremus Hymnal*, #331.

2. The students may dramatize the parables for one another or continue presenting the modern-day parables they have created.

CHAPTER FOUR
THE PROMISE OF A SAVIOR

Catechism of the Catholic Church References

Angels: 328–36, 350–52
Baptism: 1213–16, 276
Baptism in the Church: 1226–28
Christian Holiness: 2012–16, 2028–29
Consequences of Original Sin: 55–58, 399–409, 416–19
Definition of Sin: 1849–51, 1871
Devils: 391–93, 414
Fall of Man: 385–90, 413
Fall of the Angels: 391–95, 414

Grace: 1996–2005, 2021–24
Grace of Baptism: 265, 1262–74, 1279–80
Heaven: 1023–29, 1053
Hell: 1033–37, 1056–57
Man's Freedom: 1730–42, 1743–48
Original Sin: 388–90, 396–401, 415
Promise of a Redeemer: 410–12, 420–21
Savior: 457, 606–7

Scripture References

The First Sin and Expulsion from the Garden: Gen 3

Background Reading: *The Fundamentals of Catholicism* by Fr. Kenneth Baker, S.J.

Volume 2:
"What Is an Angel?" pp. 177–180
"Where Did the Devil Come From?" pp. 184–86
"The Power of the Devil," pp. 190–93

Volume 3:
"Baptism into the Body of Christ," pp. 194–96
"Baptism Has Consequences," pp. 200–201
Grace: pp. 13–21

Summary of Lesson Content

Lesson 1

God created angels. An angel is a pure spirit with free will.

The battle of the angels led to the fall of the devils.

Lesson 2

Adam and Eve fell from God's grace.

The sin committed by our first parents and passed on to all people is called Original Sin.

The consequences of Original Sin include the loss of the preternatural gifts.

Lesson 3

Although Adam and Eve sinned, God did not abandon them. God promised a Savior.

Jesus is the Savior. He died on the Cross to redeem us from our sins and to bring us to eternal life in Heaven. He opened the gates of Heaven.

Through Baptism we share in the life Christ won for us by His death and Resurrection. This life is called grace.

Lesson 4

We receive grace at Baptism. We must strive to keep God's life in our souls.

Sin lessens or destroys the life of grace in our souls. Therefore we must not sin, but obey God's laws.

LESSON ONE: ANGELS

Aims

The students will learn that God created angels. They are pure spirits with free will and intelligence.

They will learn about the battle of the angels and the fall of the devils. They will know that angels are good and devils are bad.

Materials

- *Activity Book*, p. 13
- Cards with the Guardian Angel and Saint Michael Prayers
- Pictures of angels and Appendix, p. B-11
- Props for angel skit
- Paper and pencils

Optional:
- "The strife is o'er, the battle done," *Adoremus Hymnal*, #413
- "My Secret Friend: A Guardian Angel Story," video; CCC of America, available through Ignatius Press

Begin

Begin the class by teaching the students what angels are. Angels are creatures of God. They are pure spirits. Angel means "messenger." The term "angel" designates an office, rather than a species. Angels have free will and possess intelligence. Because they do not have bodies, they can move as fast as their thoughts. They are, therefore, depicted with wings. You may show the students pictures of angels. You may also teach them the names of the choirs of angels.

Develop

1. Read the first three paragraphs of the chapter with the students. They may take turns reading sentences aloud.

2. Using pictures of angels found in the student text, use Appendix, p. B-11, to present an artistic exploration of angels.

3. Explain to the students that God has given every person at least one guardian angel. These angels are there to help us reach our final goal of Heaven. They protect and guide us. You may teach them the Guardian Angel Prayer. Ask the children what they know about their guardian angels. Do they know their names? They can pray to know their guardian angels' names, and they should pray daily for the help of their angels.

4. We also know that there are seven archangels. We know the names of four: Michael, Raphael, Gabriel, and Uriel. Michael led the battle against Lucifer. Raphael helped Tobias find his wife and heal his father. Gabriel told Mary that she was chosen to be the Mother of Jesus. We can also pray to the archangels to protect us. Teach the children the Saint Michael Prayer.

5. Have the students draw pictures of the battle of the angels, their guardian angels, or a biblical story about one of the angels.

Name:_____

The Angels

1. What other creatures did God make that have the power to know and decide?
   Angels

2. What are the angels?
   The angels are pure spirits created by God.

3. What happened with the good and bad angels? Who won?
   They had fought a great battle. The good angels won.

4. With what did God reward the good angels?
   God rewarded the good angels with the joys and love of His Kingdom.

5. How did God punish the bad angels?
   God punished the bad angels by sending them to hell.

6. How did a bad angel (the devil) trick Adam and Eve?
   The devil lied by telling Eve that if she disobeyed God she would not die, but would be like God.

7. Do good and bad angels still exist? Do they try to guide us?
   Yes. Good and bad angels still exist and try to guide us.

Faith and Life Series • Grade 3 • Chapter 4 • Lesson 1   13

GUARDIAN ANGEL PRAYER

Angel of God, my guardian dear,
To whom God's love commits me here,
Ever this day be at my side,
To light and guard, to rule and guide. *Amen.*

SAINT MICHAEL PRAYER

Saint Michael the Archangel, defend us in battle, be our protection against the wickedness and snares of the devil; may God rebuke him we humbly pray; and do thou, O Prince of the Heavenly host, by the power of God, cast into hell satan and all the evil spirits who wander about the world seeking the ruin of souls. *Amen.*

Reinforce

1. Have the students work on their pictures of angels.

2. Have the students work on *Activity Book*, p. 13.

3. Have the students begin working on the Memorization Questions.

4. Teach the children to sing "The strife is o'er, the battle done," *Adoremus Hymnal*, #413.

5. Show the video "My Secret Friend: A Guardian Angel Story," CCC of America (available through Ignatius Press; 30 minutes).

Conclude

End class by praying the Guardian Angel and Saint Michael Prayers. Have them memorize these prayers.

Preview

In the next lesson, the students will learn about the fall of Adam and Eve.

NOTES

LESSON TWO: THE FALL OF MAN

Aims

The students will learn the story of the fall of Adam and Eve and the doctrine of Original Sin.

The students will discuss what life in the Garden of Eden was like before their fall from grace.

The students will discuss grace and our need for it in order to get to Heaven.

Materials

- Children's Bible: Gen 3
- *Activity Book*, p. 14
- Appendix, pp. B-12 and B-13
- Props
- Paper and markers

Optional:
- "The strife is o'er the battle done," *Adoremus Hymnal*, #413

Begin

Begin the class by telling the students what life was like in the Garden of Eden for Adam and Eve. It was so beautiful. The weather was always perfect. They got along with one another and with the animals. They knew everything they needed to know. They would never get sick or die. They even had a share in God's life of grace. These were special gifts they had from God. God loved them very much and walked with them in the garden. Truly, this was paradise.

---

4 The Promise of a Savior

The LORD God said to the serpent,
"Because you have done this,
 cursed are you above all cattle,
 and above all wild animals;
upon your belly you shall go,
 and dust you shall eat
 all the days of your life.
I will put enmity between you and the woman,
 and between your seed and her seed;
he shall bruise your head,
 and you shall bruise his heel."

Genesis 3:14–15

God made other creatures, besides man, who have the power to know and to decide. These creatures can think as we do, but they are much smarter and more powerful. They are called angels. We cannot see the angels because they are pure spirits. They have no bodies. But they are very real and alive, because God shared His life with them, too.

God created the angels out of love. He wanted them to be happy with Him in Heaven for ever. But He gave them the gift of free will so they could make a choice. Some of the angels chose to rebel against God. They refused to serve God.

The bad angels and the good angels fought a great battle. The good, obedient angels won because they had God and the truth on their side. God rewarded them with the joys and love of His Kingdom. Then God sent all the bad angels (devils) into Hell. They can

---

Develop

1. Read Genesis 3 from the children's Bible with the students. After reading the account of the fall of Adam and Eve, ask the children about the story to be sure they understand it. Suggested questions include:
   - What was God's test for Adam and Eve?
   - Who was the serpent?
   - Why was it wrong to eat of the fruit of the tree of knowledge of good and evil?
   - What happened after they ate the fruit?
   - Why did they hide from God?
   - Why did Adam blame Eve? Why did Eve blame the serpent?
   - What were the consequences of their actions?
   - Did God stop loving Adam and Eve?
   - Was God mean to take away His gifts? (No, because they were not proper to Adam and Eve)
   - What did God promise Adam and Eve? Why?

2. Using Appendix, pp. B-12 and B-13, have the students act out the fall of Adam and Eve.

3. Have the students create pictures showing before and after the fall of Adam and Eve. In order to show both before and after pictures, have the students fold a piece of paper in half, so that it divides the sheet in two. You may make a display out of the pictures.

4. *Discuss the great loss of losing the life of grace. Without grace, man cannot go to Heaven. Grace is a share in God's life. We cannot see grace. It is a supernatural gift that is very precious and important to us. God's grace is a gift that we do not deserve, and we can lose it easily. Just as Adam and Eve lost grace through Original Sin, so too, if we are not careful, can we lose through sin the grace we were given. Although Adam and Eve lost this grace for themselves and their descendants, they still had hope in God's love.*

Name:_____

God's Gift: Free Will

1. God gave us a gift called free will. What does free will allow us to do?

   <u>Free will lets us make choices.</u>

2. For what are we created? What is God's plan for us?

   <u>We were created to be God's friends forever.</u>

3. What did the angels do with their free will?

   <u>Some chose to follow God and some chose to rebel against Him.</u>

4. What did Adam and Eve do with their free will?

   <u>Adam and Eve disobeyed God.</u>

5. What is it called when you use your free will to do bad things?

   <u>Sin</u>

6. What does sin do to us?

   <u>Sin makes us sad and afraid. It hurts our friendship with God.</u>

7. How can we be freed from sin?

   <u>We can be freed from sin by Baptism.</u>

8. Who is our Savior, and what did He do?

   <u>Jesus is our Savior. He died on the Cross and rose from the dead for us.</u>

Faith and Life Series • Grade 3 • Chapter 4 • Lesson 2

Reinforce

1. Have the students work on their before/after pictures of the fall of Adam and Eve.

2. Have the students dramatize the fall of Adam and Eve.

3. Have the students work on *Activity Book*, p. 14.

Conclude

1. Sing "The strife is o'er, the battle done," *Adoremus Hymnal*, #413.

2. End class by praying the Guardian Angel and Saint Michael Prayers.

Preview

In the next lesson, the students will learn about Jesus our Savior, how He won back God's grace for us, and how He shares it with us in Baptism.

NOTES

LESSON THREE:
JESUS OUR SAVIOR

Aims

The children will learn that although Adam and Eve sinned against God, He did not abandon them; He promised them a Savior.

They will learn that Jesus is the Savior. He died on the Cross to redeem us from our sins, and He opened the gates of Heaven to all men. By Baptism, we share in the life Christ won for us by His death and Resurrection. This life is called grace.

Materials

- *Activity Book*, p. 15
- Baptism rite, doll, water, basin/font, candle, white garment
- Crucifix
- Paper, pencil, crayons
- Children's Bible

Optional:
- "The strife is o'er, the battle done," *Adoremus Hymnal*, #413
- "Jesus Dies on the Cross," video; Jesus: A Kingdom Without Frontiers series, available through Ignatius Press

Begin

Begin by reviewing with the children what life was like in the Garden of Eden before and after their fall from grace. Have them recount their preternatural gifts and the consequences of Original Sin. Stress that the gates of Heaven were closed because of Original Sin. Only with the help of God could the gates of Heaven be opened.

never see God again because they locked themselves out of Heaven when they chose to rebel against Him.

Like the angels, Adam and Eve were given free wills. They were created to be God's friends forever, but they had a choice. God tested that choice. He told Adam and Eve to enjoy all the fruits of their rich, beautiful garden, except for the fruit of one tree. He warned them that if they ate this fruit, they would die. They promised to obey God.

One day, however, the devil tricked Eve by lying to her. He told her that if she disobeyed God, she would not die, but would be like God. Eve believed the devil and broke her promise to God. Then she helped Adam to break his promise, too. This first sin was called **Original Sin**. Since Adam was the father of all people on earth, the effects of his Original Sin carry on to all generations, including our own, and to each one of us.

When Adam and Eve disobeyed God, they were worried, sad, and full of fear. They lost the gift of His life in their souls. They could no longer please Him or be His friends. Worst of all, they had to suffer and die.

God punished Adam and Eve, but He never stopped loving them. He planned a special way for them to come back to Him after their Fall. He promised a Savior, Who would make up for their sin and re-open the gates of Heaven, which were closed by Original Sin. This promise became the light and hope of the People of God.

Jesus died on the Cross to make up for our sins. He is the **Savior** of the world. He rose from the dead gaining God's eternal life for us. He wants us all to share this life, so He gave us the Sacrament of Baptism. **Baptism** pours God's life back into the soul, washing away Original Sin. When the priest poured the waters of Baptism over you, you shared in Jesus' death and Resurrection. You were born into God's family. God came to live inside of you. Because of your Baptism, you are able to go to Heaven someday.

Develop

1. Choose students to read paragraphs 8 and 9 aloud.

2. Hold up a Crucifix. Show the children what a Crucifix is and explain that Jesus died on the Cross to save us from sin and death. Christ died to win Heaven for us. He loves us so very much. You may read the Passion from the children's Bible (e.g., Mt 26—27). If you have the video, "Jesus Dies on the Cross," from the Jesus: A Kingdom Without Frontiers series (available through Ignatius Press; 30 minutes), you may show it to the class. Be sure the students understand that Jesus died on the Cross for our sins. By His sacrificial death He won back the life of grace for us.

3. Explain to the children the importance of Baptism. Baptism is a sacrament that Jesus gave us so we can have the life of grace He won for us on the Cross. We need this life of grace to go to Heaven. A sacrament is an effective outward sign of grace. Water is a sign of washing, pouring, nourishment, fun, death by drowning, life, etc. These things are happening in the soul in a very real way in the Sacrament of Baptism. Sin is washed away (including Original Sin), God's life is poured into the soul, we are nourished with God's love and life, we enter into God's family and share His love (which is fun!), we share in the death and Resurrection of Jesus, and receive the life of grace that He won for us on the Cross. This is the grace we need to get to Heaven.

4. Show the children the rite of Baptism by using a doll. Have the students act as parents and godparents.

5. Have the children make advertisements on the importance of Baptism for other third graders. Be sure they incorporate the symbols, effects, matter, and form of Baptism. You may make a display out of these.

Name:_____

God's Creation

Find these words in your textbook and use each one in a sentence.

Angel: **Answers will vary.**
_____

Free Will: _____
_____

Adam and Eve: _____
_____

Devil: _____
_____

Original Sin: _____
_____

Grace: _____
_____

Savior: _____
_____

Baptism: _____
_____

Obedience: _____
_____

Heaven: _____
_____

Hell: _____
_____

Faith and Life Series • Grade 3 • Chapter 4 • Lesson 3   15

Reinforce

1. Have the students complete *Activity Book*, p. 15.

2. Have the students talk about their Baptism advertisements.

3. The students may take turns playing godparents, parents, etc. in baptizing the doll. They may also practice performing a Baptism in case of an emergency. Be sure students memorize the formula.

4. Have the students work on the Memorization Questions for this chapter.

Conclude

1. Have the students sing "The strife is o'er, the battle done," *Adoremus Hymnal*, #413.

2. The students may make up prayers to thank God for Jesus' death on the Cross and the gift of grace they received in Baptism.

Preview

In the next lesson, the students will learn more about maintaining the life of grace in their souls.

BAPTISMAL FONTS

In the Early Church, most Baptisms, like Christ's, took place in a body of natural water. Indoor Baptism, performed for the sake of privacy and solemnity, soon became the norm. Reverence for the water, which came to receive a special blessing by the priest, developed into the construction of basins or fonts for the baptismal ceremony, and eventually, for the preservation of the water. Many fonts were built in an octagonal shape, the eight sides representing the eighth day, i.e., the day of the Resurrection. These were placed at the entrances of churches to symbolize the catechumens' entrance into the Church. Typically made of stone, metal is also an acceptable material. Upright fonts soon became more popular than full immersion basins.

NOTES

LESSON FOUR: GRACE

Aims

The students will learn that we receive grace at Baptism and that we must strive to keep God's life of grace in our souls.

They will learn that sin lessens or destroys the life of grace in our souls. Therefore, we must not sin and instead, obey God's Laws.

Materials

- Index cards with Baptism and daily "temptations" questions
- *Activity Book*, p. 16

Optional:
- "The strife is o'er, the battle done," *Adoremus Hymnal*, #413

Begin

Review with the students the definition of grace: God's life within them. Jesus won the life of grace for them by His death and Resurrection. We need grace to get to Heaven. Tell the children that grace is God's gift to us. We do not earn it, and we must work hard to keep it because we can lose it so easily. Do they know how? By sinning. Ask the children different ways that they can lose God's life in their souls. Are all sins the same, or are some more serious than others? Today we will review how to keep God's life in our souls.

You can keep your soul full of **grace** (God's life within us) by obeying and loving God. Jesus' death on the Cross teaches us that no matter how attractive a sin might appear, it is never worth the price. Sin makes us sad and afraid, and it hurts our friendship with God. Obedience and love make us happy, and they strengthen our friendship with God. If we keep our souls full of grace, we will one day rejoice with God in Heaven, our true home.

Words to Know:

Original Sin   Savior   Baptism   grace

> **Q. 21** *What is sin?*
> Sin is an offense done to God by choosing to disobey His law (CCC 1849).
>
> **Q. 22** *What is Original Sin?*
> Original sin is the sin committed by Adam and Eve. Every person receives this sin from Adam and Eve, our first parents (CCC 404).
>
> **Q. 23** *How is Original Sin taken away?*
> Original Sin is taken away by God's grace given in the Sacrament of Baptism (CCC 405).
>
> **Q. 24** *Why is man able to go to Heaven?*
> Man is able to go to Heaven because Jesus paid the price for our sins by His suffering and death (CCC 598, 601).

Develop

1. Review with the students that they first received grace at Baptism. We can continue to grow in the life of grace. We can pray, go to Mass, and receive Holy Communion. We can do good acts (good in object, intention, and circumstance—if any one of these is not good, then the act itself is not good). Have the students come up with examples.

2. Review with the children the definition of sin: choosing to offend God and neighbor by disobeying God's Laws. Sin harms our friendship with God. Ask how they would feel if you lied to them or stole from them. Would not it harm your friendship with the students? Certainly.

3. The students should know the difference between mortal sin and venial sin. Mortal sin loses the life of grace we had in our souls. To commit a mortal sin, there are three conditions:
- *It is a serious matter*
- *We know it is serious*
- *We freely choose to do it anyway*

Venial sin weakens the life of grace in our souls. It is either of a serious nature but without knowledge or free consent, or it is of a less serious nature with knowledge and/or consent.

4. Ask the students how they can receive God's grace back in their souls if they lose it by sin. Define the Sacrament of Penance for the children. Let the children know that they receive grace in this sacrament to overcome their sins, too. So, it is helpful to confess even their venial sins. If it is possible, arrange for your class to go to the Sacrament of Penance.

5. Play a review game either for points or for prizes, covering the Sacrament of Baptism, the Sacrament of Penance, and daily life tests: e.g., how can you pass/fail the test of doing homework? Pass: do it well, without being told to do it. Fail: do not do it or do it poorly.

Name:_____

Jesus, the Son of God and Our Savior

Color the picture below.

16   *Faith and Life Series • Grade 3 • Chapter 4 • Lesson 4*

SAINT THÉRÈSE AND THE LITTLE WAY

Saint Thérèse of Lisieux is a good example of someone who was very aware of the difficult journey to Heaven. Her spiritual path, called the "Little Way," has become popular in modern times. Thérèse wanted to be a saint, but she felt that she could not become a great one so she comforted herself by making small daily sacrifices. This was what she called her little way to Heaven, short and direct. By remaining childlike, she asked Jesus to carry her in His arms to the Father. She felt she was too little to attain Heaven like the saints before her, so she found her own pathway.

Reinforce

1. You may have the children go to the Sacrament of Penance or at least spend time reviewing how to receive the Sacrament of Penance. The five steps to a good confession include: making an examination of conscience (knowing your sins), having sorrow for your sins, having an amendment (decision) not to sin again, confessing your sins to a priest in the Sacrament of Penance, and receiving and doing your penance. They may role-play the five steps to prepare for the Sacrament of Penance.

2. The students may color *Activity Book*, p. 16.

3. The students may continue thinking of ways either to keep or to lose God's grace. They may work on a project doing morally good acts to grow in grace, such as making cards for seniors.

Conclude

1. You may review the Memorization Questions for this chapter.

2. Sing "The strife is o'er, the battle done," *Adoremus Hymnal*, #413.

3. End class with a prayer.

Preview

In the next lesson, the students' knowledge of the material covered this week will be reviewed and assessed.

NOTES
_____
_____
_____
_____
_____
_____
_____
_____
_____

CHAPTER FOUR
REVIEW AND ASSESSMENT

Aims

The students' knowledge and understanding of the material covered this week will be reviewed and assessed.

Materials

- Quiz 4, Appendix, p. A-4
- Unit 1 Quiz, Appendix, pp. A-5 and A-6

Optional:
- "The strife is o'er the battle done," *Adoremus Hymnal*, #413

Review

1. Review the definition of angels: pure spirits that God created. You may also review the fall of the bad angels (now called devils).

2. Review the fall of Adam and Eve. Compare life in the Garden of Eden before the fall with the consequences of Original Sin after the fall. Stress that Adam and Eve had free will. Help the children recognize what Adam and Eve's sin was.

3. Review the doctrine of Original Sin and that it is transmitted to all men. Man is born with Original Sin and without the life of grace in his soul.

4. Review that Jesus Christ won for us the life of grace by His death and Resurrection. He is the Savior of the World.

5. At Baptism, we receive this life of grace. You may review the rite, the effects, and the symbols of Baptism with the children.

6. Review the ways that we may grow in the life of grace, how we may lessen it by venial sin, and lose it by mortal sin. The students should know the difference between mortal and venial sin.

Name: _____

The Promise of a Savior　　　　　　　　　　　Quiz 4

"Therefore the child to be born will be called holy, the Son of God" (Luke 1:35).

Word Bank

Cross	chose	obey	children
Original	bodies	Adam	
promise	created	Savior	

Fill in the blanks with the correct words from the Word Bank.

1. We cannot see the angels because they are pure spirits. They have no _bodies_.

2. God _created_ the angels and gave them free will.

3. The good angels _chose_ God but the bad angels refused God.

4. Adam and Eve promised to _obey_ God when He told them not to eat the fruit of the one tree in their beautiful garden.

5. Eve broke her _promise_ to God by listening to the devil.

6. Eve helped _Adam_ break his promise to God. This first sin was called Original Sin.

7. Because Adam was the father of all people on earth, the effects of his sin are passed on to each one of us. We are all born with _Original_ Sin on our soul.

8. God promised a _Savior_ who would make up for Adam's sin and reopen the gates of Heaven.

9. Jesus is the Savior. He died on the _Cross_ to make up for our sins.

10. Baptism is the sacrament that takes away Original Sin. We receive grace, which is God's life in us, and we become _children_ of God when we are baptized.

11. Write out the Scripture verse shown at the top of this page.

_____

A - 4　　　　　　　　　　Faith and Life • Grade 3 • Appendix A

Assess

1. Distribute the quizzes and read through them with the children to ensure they understand the questions.

2. Administer the quiz. As students hand in their work, orally quiz them on the Memorization Questions for this chapter.

3. After all the quizzes have been handed in, you may wish to review the correct answers with the class.

Conclude

Lead the children in singing, "The strife is o'er, the battle done," *Adoremus Hymnal*, #413

CHAPTER FIVE
ABRAHAM: THE FATHER OF GOD'S PEOPLE

Catechism of the Catholic Church References

Abraham and the Prayer of Faith: 2570–72, 2592
Call of Abraham: 59–61, 72, 762
Characteristics of Faith:
    Faith Is a Grace: 153, 179
    Faith Is a Human Act: 154–55, 180
    Faith, the Beginning of Eternal Life: 163–65, 184
Faith and Understanding: 156–59

Faith of Abraham: 144–46, 165, 180
The Freedom of Faith: 160
God's Promise to Abraham: 705–6, 762
The Necessity of Faith: 161, 183
Perseverance in Faith: 162
Sacrifice: 2099–100

Scripture References

The Story of Abraham: Gen 12—22

Background Reading: *The Fundamentals of Catholicism* by Fr. Kenneth Baker, S.J.

Volume 1:
"Faith and the Good News," pp. 21–22
"Submission to God," pp. 23–25

Volume 3:
"The Meaning of Sacrifice," pp. 256–59

Summary of Lesson Content

Lesson 1

After the fall, man had to wait many years for the coming of the Savior.

Many people worshiped false gods.

God chose Abraham to prepare the people for the coming of the Savior.

Abraham is our father in faith.

Lesson 2

God called Abraham from the land of Ur, to go to the land God would reveal to him.

Abraham left his family, taking his wife Sarah, his nephew Lot, and their flocks to Canaan.

God promised the land of Canaan to Abraham. Canaan was the Promised Land.

Lesson 3

Abraham was blessed with flocks and riches, but not with descendants.

God blessed Abraham and Sarah in their old age with a son, Isaac.

God called Abraham to offer Isaac as a sacrifice to God. In faith and obedience, Abraham prepared his sacrifice. An angel stopped the sacrifice, saying God was pleased with Abraham.

Lesson 4

God promised Abraham descendants as numerous as the stars. From his descendants would be born the Savior.

All people face tests of obedience to God and His will. God asks that we be faithful to his laws; in doing so, we will be richly blessed.

LESSON ONE: WAITING FOR A SAVIOR

Aims

The students will learn that man had to wait many years for the coming of the Savior.

They will learn that man used to worship false gods.

They will learn that God chose Abraham to prepare his people for the coming of the Savior.

The students will learn about the virtue of faith and that Abraham had great faith.

Materials

- Treats for students
- *Activity Book*, p. 17
- False gods: pictures of sun, moon, fire, idols, etc.
- Paper and crayons

Optional:
- "Now thank we all our God," *Adoremus Hymnal*, #607

Begin

Begin the class by placing the students' treats on their desks. Tell the students that they must wait until you give them permission to eat their snacks. Remind them throughout the class that their snacks are still there and they are delicious. Let them know that waiting can be very difficult.

---

5 Abraham: The Father Of God's People

"By myself I have sworn, says the LORD, because you have done this, and have not withheld your son, your only son, I will indeed bless you, and I will multiply your descendants as the stars of heaven and as the sand which is on the seashore. And your descendants shall possess the gate of their enemies, and by your descendants shall all the nations of the earth bless themselves, because you have obeyed my voice."

Genesis 22:16–18

The people who lived after Adam and Eve waited a long time for the promised Savior. Some of them got tired of waiting and made up their own gods. They worshipped great things in nature that they could see, like fire, the moon, and the sun. They even worshipped objects they made with their hands, like animal statues made of gold.

These people forgot God, but God did not forget them. He remembered His promise to send a Savior. But first God chose certain faithful men to prepare the people for the coming of the Savior. **Abraham** was one of the first He chose. Abraham had a great gift from God, called **faith**.

God asked Abraham to leave his home and friends and go on a long journey. Abraham did not understand clearly, but because of his faith he believed in the one, true God. Also because of his faith, Abraham trusted God. **Trust** means to depend on and hope in

---

Develop

1. Have the students take turns reading sentences aloud from the first paragraph of the student text.

2. As the children list the various things people would worship, put pictures of them on the board. After reading the first paragraph, ask the children why they think people may have worshiped these things. (e.g., the sun gives light and heat and helps things to live. The moon lights up the dark night. Fire keeps us warm and can be moved by people. Gold statues are beautiful and might be considered "lucky.") Ask the students the following questions: Who made the sun? Who made the moon? Who gave us fire and gold? If God gave us all these things, is the Creator not greater than the creature?

3. Teach the children an Act of Faith so that they can affirm their faith in the One True God.

4. Read the second paragraph. Ask the children how God must have felt knowing that His people had forgotten Him. Was God faithful? Who did He choose to help prepare His people for the coming of the Savior?

5. Explain to the children that Abraham had great faith. Faith is a virtue and a habit of the will to do good. Faith is a gift from God that allows us to believe in the truths He has revealed to us, such as the Trinity and Jesus Christ as the Son of God. Can the students name some of the truths of our faith? We must exercise our virtues to become great in them. We can have weak or strong faith depending on how much we live it out. Ask the children ways they can live their faith. Examples may be: pray and go to Church, read the Bible, study their religion text books, etc. Have the students think of ways they can grow in their faith.

Name:_____

Learn Hebrew!

Hebrew is the language of God's Chosen People. This is the language God spoke to Abraham. Here are a few rules to follow:

1. Read Hebrew from right to left. So what we consider the last letter of a word of the last page of a book in English is considered the first letter of a word or the first page of a book in Hebrew.

2. Consonants are written on the line and vowels are noted above or below the line, except when a word begins with "A" (Aleph). So the word "Abraham" looks like this in Hebrew אַבְרָהָם , and is sort of read: M$_A$H$_A$ЯBA . Remember to read each line from right to left!

Study the following chart.

English	Hebrew	"English-Hebrew" Equivalent
Abraham	אַבְרָהָם	AB$_A$ЯH$_A$M
God (Aloha)	אֱלֹהֵי	$\bar{A}$L$_o$H$\bar{A}$
I am (Anochi)	אָנֹכִי	$_I$H$°$CN$_A$
Isaac (Yitzac)	יִצְחָק	X$_A$$°S_I$Y
Jacob (Yacob)	יַעֲקֹב	B$°$C$_A$Y

Use the first two columns to fill in the missing words. Then write the sentence in English. Remember to read Hebrew from right to left.

אָנֹכִי אֱלֹהֵי אַבְרָהָם אֱלֹהֵי יִצְחָק אֱלֹהֵי יַעֲקֹב

"<u>Jacob</u> of God the and, <u>Isaac</u> of God the, <u>Abraham</u> of God the am I".

Answer: <u>"I am the God of Abraham, the God of Isaac, and the God of Jacob."</u>

Faith and Life Series • Grade 3 • Chapter 5 • Lesson 1   17

ACT OF FAITH

O my God, I firmly believe that Thou art one God in three Divine Persons, Father, Son and Holy Ghost; I believe that Thy divine Son became man, and died for our sins, and that He will come to judge the living and the dead. I believe these and all the truths which the Holy Catholic Church teaches, because Thou hast revealed them, who canst neither deceive nor be deceived. *Amen*.

Reinforce

1. On the board list the ways we can grow in faith. The students may draw pictures of one of these ways to grow in this virtue.

2. Allow the students to eat their treats and praise those students who used self-control in not eating the treats until you gave them permission to do so. You may also give them an extra treat or reward for their patience.

3. Teach the students to sing "Now thank we all our God," *Adoremus Hymnal*, #607.

Conclude

End class by praying an Act of Faith.

Preview

In the next lesson, the students will learn about Abraham's journey to the Promised Land.

NOTES

_____
_____
_____
_____
_____
_____
_____
_____
_____

LESSON TWO: GOD CALLS ABRAHAM

Aims

The students will learn that Abraham was obedient to God's call.

They will trace Abraham's journey from Ur to the Promised Land.

They will understand that Abraham took his wife Sarah, his nephew Lot, and his flocks and left his family to go to Canaan. This must have been hard for him.

They will learn that God promised to give the land of Canaan to Abraham. This land is called the Promised Land.

Materials

- *Activity Book*, p. 18
- Children's Bible (Gen 12:1–7)
- Globe and Bible map, Appendix, p. B-14

Optional:
- "Now thank we all our God," *Adoremus Hymnal*, #607

Begin

Review the virtue of faith with the children and ask them how they have lived that virtue since their last class. They may have prayed or spoken to someone about God, etc. Ask them if they heard God calling to them. If not, ask them how they would feel if they had. Would they think they were crazy? Abraham didn't. He believed and obeyed!

---

someone. Abraham took his wife Sarah, his nephew Lot, and all his flocks to a faraway country called Canaan. God rewarded Abraham for his obedience. He told him, "This land I will give to you. You shall be the father of a great people. Through you all nations will be blessed." Because of this promise, this land was called "the Promised Land." Abraham did not realize it, but God's plan was that the Savior would be born from his family.

God was very good to Abraham. He gave him great riches and increased his flocks. But Abraham was worried because he had no children. When Abraham and his wife Sarah were very old, God blessed them with a child. They named the boy Isaac, which means "laughter," since he was such a surprise and delight in their lives.

One day God tested Abraham to see if he loved Him above all else. He knew Isaac was more precious to Abraham than any other treasure. One night God said to Abraham, "Take Isaac and go to a mountain that I will show you. There offer Me your son as a sacrifice." Abraham's heart was breaking, but again he put God first. He trusted and obeyed Him. He cut wood for the sacrifice, took Isaac, and walked up into the mountains. Just as Abraham was about to strike his only son, an angel sent by God stopped him. "God now knows that you truly love Him," the angel said, "for you are ready to obey Him in all things. God is pleased with you. He will bless you even more."

Abraham was very glad. He picked up a ram which was caught in the bushes and sacrificed it in thanksgiving. Then the angel told Abraham that his family would be more numerous than the stars in the sky. He told him that out of his great people, God's Chosen People, the Savior of the world would one day be born. God gave this great reward to Abraham and his children because Abraham always obeyed His voice, even when God asked him to do something very hard.

Develop

1. Read paragraph 3 from the student text to the children.

2. Next, read Genesis 12:1–7 from a children's Bible to the students.

3. Trace out Abraham's journey on the Bible map found in Appendix B, p. B-14. Using a globe, show the children where this land is and point out how small it looks on the globe. Using the globe to help, label the following bodies of water on the map: Mediterranean Sea, Jordan River, Dead Sea, Sea of Galilee, Tigris River (north), and Euphrates River (south). Pointing to the dot on the map, explain that Abraham was born in Ur, a city in the land of Mesopotamia (like Dallas, Texas, or City, State). Have the children write "Ur" where the dot is on the map. They can label the land of Canaan too. Explain that all the land between the two great rivers and the Mediterranean Sea is hot and dry. Only the land right along the Tigris, Euphrates, and Jordan rivers is green with plant life. It is called the Fertile Crescent. Have the children color the bodies of water blue, the Fertile Crescent green, and the rest of the land brown (to show the sandy desert).

4. Explain to the children that Abraham did not know where God was leading him. He simply had faith (ask a student to define faith). He packed all he could and he took his wife Sarah, his nephew Lot, and his flocks with him on his journey. He obeyed God.

5. Explain the virtue of obedience. Virtue is a habit of doing good. It must be practiced so that it will become easy and joyful to do. To obey is to do what you are asked or told to do. Ask the children how we should obey. Should we question? Should we be angry? Should we do the bare minimum, or should we try to do the best we can? How did God reward Abraham's obedience? Who should we obey? How are we rewarded? Give many examples to the children and let them think of their own examples.

Name:_____

Journey to the Promised Land!

Imagine you are Abraham, and God has called you to go on a journey to a promised land. What would you pack and why?

Write these on the suitcases below.

18   Faith and Life Series • Grade 3 • Chapter 5 • Lesson 2

SAINT BERNADETTE OF LOURDES

In 1858 Our Lady appeared to fourteen-year-old Bernadette Soubiroux in Lourdes, France. As she was crossing the River Gave, Bernadette saw a beautiful lady standing above her in the hollow of a rock. The bishop doubted the heavenly nature of her visions, so on his prompting, she asked the Lady her name and was told, I am the Immaculate Conception. This dogma had been declared only four years previously and Bernadette was a poor girl who had no knowledge of such matters, so the bishop knew it was indeed the Queen of Heaven. A miraculous spring appeared that today continues to cure the sick. The feast of Our Lady of Lourdes is February 11.

Reinforce

1. Have the children work on *Activity Book,* p. 18, and then discuss their answers. If you do not have time to work on this activity, you may play a memory game: "I'm going to the Promised Land and I'm packing..." Have each child give an answer after repeating all the previous children's answers. (e.g., "I'm going to the Promised Land and I'm packing an umbrella, a swim suit, my lunch, and some money," etc.)

2. You may display their work or their maps around the classroom.

3. Have the students work on the Memorization Questions.

Conclude

Lead the class in praying the Act of Faith and in singing, "Now thank we all our God," *Adoremus Hymnal,* #607.

Preview

In the next lesson, the students will learn how God tested Abraham.

NOTES

_____
_____
_____
_____
_____
_____
_____
_____
_____
_____

LESSON THREE: GOD TESTS ABRAHAM

Aims

The students will learn how God blessed Abraham with flocks and riches, but no descendants.

Finally, in their old age, God blessed Abraham and Sarah with a son, whom they named Isaac.

They will learn how God asked Abraham to offer Isaac as a sacrifice to God. In faith and obedience, Abraham prepared to sacrifice his son. An angel stopped the sacrifice, saying God was pleased with Abraham for his obedience.

Materials

- *Activity Book,* p. 19
- Children's Bible
- Bag of candies, materials for crafts
- Name book

Optional:
- "Now thank we all our God," *Adoremus Hymnal,* #607
- "Abraham, the Forefather," video; In the Beginning: Stories from the Bible, available through Ignatius Press

Begin

Ask the children the review questions. As they get them right, give them some candy but tell them not to eat it. After you are finished with the review, ask for all the candy back. Ask the children why they were first given the candy. Tell them the candy was a reward for getting the answers correct. Tell them you are happy because they were obedient in returning the candy. Redistribute the candy and let them eat it.

Develop

1. Read paragraph 4 from the student text with the students.

2. Explain that Abraham and Sarah had waited a long time and desired very much to have a child. In fact, they were very, very old when they had a child, and he was such a joy to them that they named him Isaac, which means "laughter." You may look up some of the students' names to see what they mean.

3. Read paragraphs 5 and 6 with the children. You may also read the same account from the children's Bible (Gen 22:1–18).

4. Discuss Abraham's test with the children. Emphasize how hard it must have been for Abraham to be obedient to God when asked to offer up his own son! How do you think Abraham was able to do this? He had great faith in God. How would they have felt if they were Abraham? or Isaac? What would they have done? How do you think Abraham felt when the angel stopped him from sacrificing his son?

5. The children may dramatize the story of Abraham's test. Choose children to be Abraham, Isaac, the angel, and the ram. They may tell the story in their own words and make costumes and masks. They may also dramatize this story in the form of a puppet show with paper-bag puppets, which they can make themselves.

Some day God may test us as He tested Abraham. He may ask us to give up something we love or want in order to follow His commands. This happens in small ways every day. God asks you to obey your mother right away, even though you would rather keep playing. God asks you to be kind to everyone, even people who have hurt you. God asks you to follow His Laws, even when it would be easier to follow another way. God has happiness and blessings in store for your love and obedience, just as He did for His faithful servant Abraham.

Words to Know:

Abraham   faith   trust

Q. 25 *Did God send a Savior right away?*
No, the people who lived after Adam and Eve waited a long time for the Savior to come (CCC 65).

Q. 26 *How did God prepare the people for the coming of the Savior?*
God chose faithful men like Abraham to prepare the people for the coming of the Savior (CCC 51, 53).

Q. 27 *How did God prepare Abraham?*
God called Abraham to leave his home and friends to go to the Promised Land. God blessed him with riches, animals, and a beloved son (CCC 59).

Name:_____

Abraham's Test

One day, God tested <u>Abraham</u> to see if he loved Him above all else. He knew <u>Isaac</u> was more precious to Abraham than any other treasure. One night <u>God</u> said to Abraham, "Take Isaac and go to a mountain that I will show you. There offer Me your son as a <u>sacrifice</u>." Abraham's heart was <u>breaking</u>, but again he put God first. He <u>trusted</u> and <u>obeyed</u> Him. He cut wood for the <u>sacrifice</u>, took Isaac, and walked up the mountains. Just as Abraham was about to strike his only son, an <u>angel</u> sent by God stopped him. "God now knows that you truly love Him," the angel said, "for you are ready to <u>obey</u> him in all things. God is <u>pleased</u> with you. He will <u>bless</u> you even more.

Draw a picture of Abraham's test.

Faith and Life Series • Grade 3 • Chapter 5 • Lesson 3

GEN 22:16–18 THE FINAL BLESSING OF ABRAHAM

God blessed Abraham with three things:
"By myself I have sworn, says the LORD, because you have done this, and have not withheld your son, your only son, I will indeed bless you, and I will multiply your descendants as the stars of heaven and as the sand which is on the seashore. And your descendants shall possess the gate of their enemies, and by your descendants shall all the nations of the earth bless themselves, because you have obeyed my voice."
1. Many descendants—a great family
2. Land of their enemies—the Promised Land
3. Blessing for all people through his family—the Savior

Reinforce

1. To dramatize the play, have the students make either costumes and masks or puppets from paper bags.

2. Have the children work on *Activity Book,* p. 19. In the box, have them draw a picture of Abraham's test.

3. Show the video "Abraham, the Forefather," from the In the Beginning: Stories from the Bible series (available through Ignatius Press; 30 minutes). Have the children look for answers to the following questions, so that they will pay close attention to the content of the movie: "Did Abraham hear or see God?" "Did the angel appear to Abraham?" "How was Isaac going to be sacrificed?" "Was Isaac obedient, too?" "What reward did God give to Abraham for his obedience in this test?"

4. Discuss the video with the class.

5. Have the students work on the Memorization Questions.

Conclude

Lead the children in praying the Act of Faith and singing "Now thank we all our God," *Adoremus Hymnal,* #607.

Preview

In the next lesson, the children will learn about the tests that we sometimes face and the promises God has in store for those who pass these tests.

NOTES

LESSON FOUR: GOD'S BLESSING

Aims

The students will learn about God's promises to Abraham: descendants as numerous as the stars, the land of their enemies (the Promised Land), and the Savior who would be born from among his descendants.

The students will learn that all people face tests of obedience to God and His will. God asks that we be faithful to His laws, and in doing so, we will be richly blessed.

Materials

- Make cards with "tests" on them for the children to discuss
- *Activity Book,* p. 20

Optional:
- "Now thank we all our God," *Adoremus Hymnal,* #607

Begin

Review Abraham's test and his virtues of obedience and faith with the students. Have the students define these virtues and explain the story of God's call to sacrifice Isaac. They can reenact this story if they want to.

Q. 28 *How did God test Abraham?*
God asked Abraham to sacrifice his beloved son, Isaac, to see if Abraham loved God above all else (Genesis 22:1–12).

Q. 29 *Did Abraham pass God's test?*
Yes, God saw that Abraham was faithful and obedient. God told Abraham that his descendents would be many, and that the Savior would come from his family (CCC 59).

Develop

1. Read the last paragraph of this chapter with the students. They may take turns reading sentences aloud.

2. Using your "test" cards (see box on facing page for suggestions), ask the children how they would respond to each situation or test of faith. Have the children make up their own tests and discuss ways of both failing and passing the tests. Make a chart on the board: on one side write "pass" and on the other side, "fail." The children may write their answers for both passing and failing the tests on the board.

3. Reread the last sentence of this chapter. With what blessings did God reward Abraham's faith and obedience?
 • Descendants—a great family
 • The Land of their enemies—the Promised Land
 • Blessing for all people through his descendants—Savior
What great blessings for Abraham! What blessings does God have in store for our faith and obedience?

4. If God blessed Abraham's faith and obedience with a great family, what is God's great family here on earth? The Church is God's family. We enter the Church at Baptism, and it is at Baptism that God gives us the gift of faith so we can exercise this virtue.

5. If God blessed Abraham's faith and obedience with the Promised Land, what land will God give to his faithful children if they obey His laws? Hint: it is not of this world. It is Heaven. If we love God and live according to His Church, in faith and obedience, God promises that we can live with Him forever in Heaven.

6. If God blessed all people through the descendants of Abraham, who is that descendent and what is that blessing? The descendant is Jesus. He is of the line of Abraham. The blessing He won for us is salvation. These are incredible blessings! Let's do our best to pass our tests.

Name:_____

Draw Pictures of God's Blessings!

God promised Abraham three things:
1. A Promised Land, 2. A Great Family,
3. A Blessing for All People

A Promised Land	A Great Family	A Blessing for All People
Heaven Our Home	The Church, God's Family	Salvation through Christ

God fulfilled these promises through Jesus Christ,
His Son and a descendant of Abraham.
1. A Promised Land—Our Home in Heaven
2. A Great Family—The Church on earth, in Purgatory, and Heaven
3. A Blessing for All People—Salvation & Grace Through Christ!

20   *Faith and Life Series • Grade 3 • Chapter 5 • Lesson 4*

SAMPLE "TESTS"

- Your friend wants you to help him cheat on a test.
- Someone who is not liked very much forgets his lunch at home.
- Your little brother needs help with his homework.
- You have to practice the piano, but it's a beautiful day outside and your friends want you to play with them.
- Your mother asks you to set the table while you are reading your favorite book or watching your favorite show.
- You find a wallet on the street. It is full of money.
- It is Sunday and you don't want to go to Mass.

Reinforce

1. Have the students work on *Activity Book,* p. 20. In the boxes, they may draw pictures to show each of God's blessings.

2. Have the students work on the Memorization Questions and prepare for the quiz in the next lesson.

Conclude

1. Lead the children in asking God for help to pass our daily tests, and say the Act of Faith.

2. They may also sing "Now thank we all our God," *Adoremus Hymnal,* #607.

Preview

In the next lesson, the students' knowledge of the material covered this week will be reviewed and assessed.

NOTES

CHAPTER FIVE
REVIEW AND ASSESSMENT

Aims

The students' knowledge and understanding of the material covered this week will be reviewed and assessed.

Materials

- Quiz 5, Appendix, p. A-7

Optional:
- "Now thank we all our God," *Adoremus Hymnal*, #607

Review

1. Review with the children that man had to wait many, many years for the coming of the Savior. Was man faithful to God? Was God faithful to man?

2. Review the journey of Abraham: God called him from the land of Ur in Mesopotamia to go through the Fertile Crescent to the land of Canaan.

3. Review the virtues of faith and obedience. The students should be able to define:
- Virtue
- Faith
- Obedience

They should be able to give examples of living the virtues of faith and obedience, and how Abraham lived these two virtues.

4. The students should be able to recount the story of God testing Abraham.

5. The students should know the blessings God gave to Abraham for his obedience.

6. The students should be able to think of ways they are tested daily and know the promises God has in store to reward their faith and obedience.

7. The students should have memorized the Memorization Questions and the Act of Faith.

Name:

Abraham: The Father Of God's People　　　　Quiz 5

"*Wait for the Lord, and he will help you*" (Proverbs 20:22).

Word Bank

| Savior | faith | everyone | born | forgot |
| gods | promise | angel | country | Abraham |

Fill in the blanks with the correct words from the Word Bank.

1. The people waited a long time for the promised _Savior_.

2. Some of the people got tired of waiting and began to worship their own _gods_.

3. These people _forgot_ God, but God did not forget them.

4. He remembered his _promise_ to send a Savior.

5. _Abraham_ was one of the men God chose to prepare the people for the coming of the Savior.

6. Abraham had a great gift from God called _faith_.

7. God asked Abraham to take his family to a faraway _country_ called Canaan.

8. God asked Abraham to offer his son Isaac in sacrifice, but as Abraham was about to strike his son an _angel_ stopped him.

9. God told Abraham that, out of his family, the Savior of the world would be _born_.

10. God asks you to obey your parents right away and to be kind to _everyone_, even to people who have hurt you.

11. Write out the Scripture verse shown at the top of this page.

Faith and Life • Grade 3 • Appendix A　　　　A - 7

Assess

1. Distribute the quizzes and read through them with the students to be sure they understand the questions.

2. Administer the quiz. As they hand in their work, you may orally quiz them on the Memorization Questions for this chapter.

3. After all the quizzes have been handed in, you may wish to review the correct answers with the class.

Conclude

1. Pray the Act of Faith.

2. Sing "Now thank we all our God," *Adoremus Hymnal*, #607.

CHAPTER SIX
THE PROPHET MOSES

Catechism of the Catholic Church References

Belief in One God: 199–202, 228
Consequences of Faith in One God: 222–27, 229
Moses and the Prayer of the Mediator: 2574–77, 2593

Obligation of the Ten Commandments: 2072–74, 2081–82
Old Law: 1961–64, 1975, 1980–82

Scripture References

The Story of Moses: Ex 1—20

Background Reading: *The Fundamentals of Catholicism* by Fr. Kenneth Baker, S.J.

Volume 1:
"Dignity of the Law," pp. 129–32

Summary of Lesson Content

Lesson 1

The descendants of Abraham grew to be a nation of people, God's chosen people, also called the Israelites.

The Israelites became slaves to the Egyptians.

Lesson 2

The Israelites became slaves because Pharaoh was fearful of the numbers of the Israelites, and jealous of their worship to God.

Pharaoh caused the slaughter of the male babies of the Israelites.

God chose Moses to bring His people out of bondage.

Lesson 3

Moses spoke on behalf of God. Moses demanded that Pharaoh free God's people.

God sent ten plagues upon the Egyptians. The greatest and last plague was the death of the Egyptian's firstborn sons.

The Israelites were spared from the final plague because they participated in the Passover.

Lesson 4

Moses led God's people out of Egypt and across the Red Sea to safety. God destroyed the army of Pharaoh in the Sea

On their way to the Promised Land, God nourished His people with manna and fresh water from a rock.

Through Moses, God gave all His people the Ten Commandments and established a covenant with them.

LESSON ONE: GOD'S CHOSEN PEOPLE ARE TESTED

Aims

The students will learn that the descendants of Abraham became God's chosen people, also called the Israelites.

They will learn that the Israelites, while in Egypt, were slaves to the Egyptians.

Materials

- *Activity Book,* p. 21
- Poster-board and markers

Optional:
- "Come, ye faithful, raise the strain," *Adoremus Hymnal,* #417
- "The Prince of Egypt," video, available through Ignatius Press

Begin

Explain to the children what God's Providence is: God's loving care for us. (Use the Chalk Talk on facing page). God watches over all things at all times, takes care of his creation, and guides things according to His plan. He showed His loving care for His creation during the time of Moses and Jesus. He still takes care of us and all things today and always, even until the end of time. God is all knowing, all wise, all good, and all loving. We can trust in His Providence even in hard times because we know God wants the very best for us.

---

6 The Prophet Moses

God said to Moses, "I AM WHO I AM." And he said, "Say this to the people of Israel, 'I AM has sent me to you.'" God also said to Moses, "Say this to the people of Israel, 'The LORD, the God of your fathers, the God of Abraham, the God of Isaac, and the God of Jacob, has sent me to you:' this is my name for ever, and thus I am to be remembered throughout all generations."

Exodus 3:14–15

As God promised Abraham, the Chosen People grew and multiplied like the stars in the sky. They spread across the land as a great and powerful people. Night and day, God watched over them and blessed them, for He loved them as His own children.

Sometimes God tests the people He loves the most. This happened to the Israelites in Egypt. They were God's favorites, His chosen ones, but God allowed them to endure a long, dark period of suffering to test their faith.

It all began with a selfish **Pharaoh**, or king of Egypt. At first, one Pharaoh had welcomed the Israelites into Egypt. But later another Pharaoh grew jealous of their loyalty to the one, true God. He also grew afraid of their great numbers and strength. He decided to control God's people by making them his slaves. Then he commanded that every one of their newborn sons be thrown into the river, so the Israelites would not be a danger to the Egyptians.

God's people were confused and full of sorrow. But God never left them. He made a plan to set His people free. He chose an Israelite called **Moses** to be His special helper. Moses' mother was

31

Develop

1. Read paragraphs 1–3 of the student text with the students.

2. You may tell the students what God's blessing was for His chosen people: abundant life—they grew numerous and became powerful, too. God loved them as His own children. (Note: If life is God's blessing to us, then we should be pro-life, which means valuing human life from conception to natural death. We should do our best to provide good conditions for all people, e.g., eliminate slavery, infanticide, etc.)

3. Remind the children of Abraham's test and our daily tests, too. It is easy to be faithful to God when things are going our way—sometimes we even forget to thank God in times like that! Sometimes, though, God tests us by taking away our comfort or the many blessings we have to see if we will still love Him. This is what happened with His chosen people, the Israelites.

4. Explain to the children that when the Israelites went to Egypt, they were given the best land and were welcomed as friends of the Pharaoh. When a new Pharaoh came to power, he became jealous of the Israelites. The Israelites remained faithful to God even though they were supposed to worship the Pharaoh. Also, the Israelites had the best land, and the Pharaoh desired it for his own. As the Israelites grew in number, the Pharaoh feared that the Israelites would fight back against the Egyptians and win. Pharaoh treated the Israelites terribly, forcing them into slavery. They were beaten, paid little, and treated like animals. In addition, Pharaoh ordered the slaughter of every Hebrew baby boy in Egypt so as to prevent the Israelites from populating and to ensure that the female Israelites would marry Egyptians when they grew up. Pharaoh thought that the massacre of the innocents would alleviate his fears. What a test this must have been! Ask the students how the Israelites should have responded to this test.

Name:_____

God Tests Israel

1. How did Abraham's descendants end up in Egypt?
The Pharaoh welcomed them into Egypt.

2. Were the descendants of Abraham numerous?
Yes

3. Did God bless Abraham's descendants?
Yes

4. What were Abraham's descendants called?
The Israelites

5. Why did God allow the Israelites to be tested?
God tested the Israelites' faith because He tests the people that He loves.

6. What test did the Israelites have to endure?
God let the Israelites become slaves of the Egyptians.

7. Why did Pharaoh become jealous?
He was jealous of their loyalty to the one true God.

Faith and Life Series • Grade 3 • Chapter 6 • Lesson 1

Reinforce

1. The students may work on *Activity Book,* p. 21.

2. You may discuss other current social justice issues.

3. Have the students create Pro-Life posters.

4. The students may watch the video "The Prince of Egypt" (available through Ignatius Press; 99 minutes). Because this film is longer than others suggested in these lessons, you may wish to show it in segments, over the course of several classes.

5. Teach the children to sing "Come, ye faithful, raise the strain," *Adoremus Hymnal,* #417.

Conclude

Lead the children in praying for the social justice issues you talked about in class, as well as whatever other intentions they may have. Allow each child to take a turn offering an intention. You may lead them in general intercessions, with the response "Lord, hear our prayer."

Preview

In the next lesson, the students will learn how God chose Moses to set his people free.

CHALK TALK: GOD'S PROVIDENCE

NOTES

LESSON TWO: GOD CHOSE MOSES

Aims

The students will learn how God chose Moses to bring His people out of bondage.

They will learn the story of Moses being sent down the Nile and saved by Pharaoh's daughter.

The students will also learn the story of God speaking to Moses from the burning bush.

Materials

- *Activity Book,* p. 22
- Children's Bible
- Props and costumes
- Construction paper, scissors, and glue

Optional:
- "Come, ye faithful, raise the strain," *Adoremus Hymnal,* #417
- "The Prince of Egypt," video, available through Ignatius Press

Begin

Review the definition of God's Providence with the students. Let them see how God knew what His People needed and that he He took care of them by asking Moses to help them. But first Moses needed to be saved from Pharaoh.

Stress that God was with the Israelites as He is with all of us. He cared for them and he cares for us, too. As the students learn about Moses today, help them to recognize that God calls all of us to help set His people free and to do His will.

---

able to save him from the Pharaoh's cruel command by putting her baby in a small basket woven of papyrus and hiding him among reeds of the river. It was the Pharaoh's daughter who discovered the child and took him home to the Egyptian palace. Moses grew up with the royal family, but he always knew he was an Israelite.

One day God spoke to Moses from a burning bush. He told Moses, "I hear the cries of My people. I know that they are suffering. Come now! I will send you to Pharaoh to lead My people, the Israelites, out of Egypt." At first Moses was afraid. He made many excuses. But finally he agreed to go because God promised him, "I will be with you and I will help you. Trust in Me."

Moses went to the Pharaoh as God commanded. "Let my people go!" he said. Moses warned the Pharaoh that he came in the name of God. The Pharaoh just laughed. He ignored Moses and treated the Israelite slaves even more harshly. God punished this cruel king by sending many plagues, or disasters, to his land. All the water in Egypt turned to blood. A huge number of frogs and bugs covered the crops and houses. Hailstorms swept across the land. Terrible illnesses hurt the Egyptian people. The country was plunged into darkness. Each time Pharaoh cried, "Stop this plague! I will let your people go!" But time and time again, the Pharaoh broke his promise. He had no intention of setting his slaves free.

Finally, God sent the most terrible plague of all. He sent the Angel of Death to kill the first-born of every Egyptian home. The Israelites were spared this tragedy because they obeyed God's command that each family share a special meal after killing a lamb and sprinkling the lamb's blood on the doorposts of their houses. When the Angel of Death saw this sign, he passed over the house and it was safe. This was called the Passover. Therefore, only the Egyptians lost their first-born children. The Pharaoh was so full of grief, he finally gave in. He let the Israelite people go.

33

Develop

1. Read paragraph 4 with the children. You may also read this account from the children's Bible in Ex 2:1–10.

2. A suggested craft: make baskets woven from strips of construction paper. You may then race them like paper sailboats in water or mud-puddles outside or fill them with things reminding the children of God's care for each of them (such as notes the children make or little things from nature that the children can collect showing God's Providence for them).

3. Read paragraph 5 with the children. Read this account from the children's Bible: Ex 3:1–4:18. The children may dramatize this story.

4. Have the children create a "burning bush." Cut out flames from red, orange, and yellow construction paper. Next, have the children cut out green leaves. On the leaves, write their prayers of thanks and trust to God and glue them on the flames. It will look like a bush not being consumed by fire.

5. Discuss with the children how God specially chose Moses to help set His people free from the Egyptians. God took great care to be sure Moses was protected from Pharaoh and then called Moses to lead the Israelites out of Egypt. How would Moses have felt? What would the students have done if they were in Moses' shoes?

6. Explain that even today God calls us to help those who are less fortunate (i.e. slaves, poor, ill, etc.) He calls us to recognize the value of all life: the unborn babies, the elderly, the sick, and the disadvantaged. Discuss with the children ways they can do God's will.

Name:_____

I will send you...

God sent Moses to lead His people out of slavery in Egypt. God calls all of us to help lead His people out of different kinds of slavery and forms of injustice.

Match the people who need help with ways you can help them be truly free.

PEOPLE WHO NEED HELP	WAYS YOU CAN HELP
Someone who is poor and hungry.	Give to missions and charities for other countries.
Children in another country must work long and hard to support their families.	Write him letters and let him know that you still care even though he is far away.
A person is sick and dying and alone in a hospital.	You can collect food for the poor.
A person at school is disliked because he is different.	You can help do yard work and visit with him.
A friend from school has to move far away from all his friends.	You can share your faith with him.
An elderly neighbor has no family to visit him.	Be friends with everybody.
A friend does not know about Jesus and is sad.	Make a get well card, or visit him.

Faith and Life Series • Grade 3 • Chapter 6 • Lesson 2

Reinforce

1. You may discuss other current social justice and pro-life issues with the students. Have them work on a project, such as visiting a nursing home, making cards for the sick, collecting goods for the poor, or visiting a crisis pregnancy center.

2. Have the children work on *Activity Book,* p. 22.

3. Show part of the video, "The Prince of Egypt" (available through Ignatius Press; 99 minutes).

4. Have the students work on the Memorization Questions.

Conclude

1. As a class, perform an act of charity.

2. Pray for those who need our prayers. Allow all the children to say their intentions.

3. Lead the students in singing "Come, ye faithful, raise the strain," *Adoremus Hymnal,* #417.

Preview

In the next lesson, the students will learn of God's mighty works in leading His people out of Egypt and into freedom.

They will learn about the Passover.

NOTES

LESSON THREE: PLAGUES

Aims

The students will learn how Moses spoke on behalf of God, and demanded that the pharaoh set God's people free.

The students will learn of God's mighty works, which show He is the One True God Who set His people free.

The students will learn about the Passover. They will also learn that Christ is the Paschal Lamb.

Materials

- *Activity Book*, p. 23
- Children's Bible: Ex 5:1—13:22; Mt 26:17–39, 27:1–50
- Passover meal
- Poster-board, markers

Optional:
- "Come, ye faithful, raise the strain," *Adoremus Hymnal*, #417
- "The Prince of Egypt," video, available through Ignatius Press

Begin

Explain to the children that in order to make someone else believe something, we may have to give proofs. For example, if I were to say to a non-Christian that Jesus is the Christ, the Son of God, what proofs could I give him? I could tell him about the many miracles Jesus performed, what He said, what others said about Him, how He fulfilled the Old Testament prophecies, etc. As an example, students can prove they have a pet by showing pictures of it, telling stories, etc.

Moses led the People of God out of Egypt to safety. The escape was full of danger, for soon the Pharaoh changed his mind again and ordered his army to chase them. God protected His children by parting the Red Sea so they could cross it. Then God closed the water, and it swallowed up the Pharaoh's men.

God protected the people in many more ways during their long journey to **Canaan**, the Promised Land. He gave them bread called manna and fresh water from a rock. He encouraged them when they were tired or losing hope. He invited Moses up to a mountain-top to receive Ten Commandments that would make His people holy and happy. Over and over again God lived up to His promise, or **Covenant**: "You will be My people, and I will be your God."

The God of Abraham and Moses is our God. There is only one, true God. He still speaks in our hearts today: "You will be My people, and I will be your God."

Words to Know:

Pharaoh   Moses   Canaan   Covenant

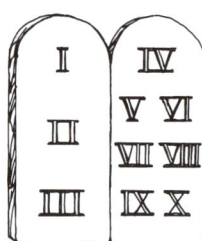

Develop

1. Read paragraphs 6 and 7 to the students as well as the account from the children's Bible: Ex 5:1—13:22.

2. Explain to the children that Moses had to prove that he was speaking on behalf of the One True God! This would have been hard because the Egyptians did not worship God. They worshiped the Nile River, the sun, even frogs and cattle! Why did God send the following plagues to the Egyptians?
- Nile turned to blood—like killing their god
- Frogs—had to get rid of frogs, which they worshiped
- Gnats and flies—only God could send these
- Cattle—they could see God is greater than the cattle they worshiped
- Boils—magic could not take these away; they were real
- Hail—destroyed crops that Egyptians offered as sacrifices
- Locusts—ate all crops, and their gods could not help them
- Darkness—to block out the sun god

- First born—This seemed very cruel, but in the ancient Egyptian world they worshiped the first born sons as gods.

God used these plagues to show His power and to teach the Egyptians that He is the One True God.

3. Explain the meaning of the Passover to the students. The lamb had to be both sacrificed and eaten. Using the children's Bible, read Mt 26:17–39, 27:1–50. Help the students to understand that Christ is the Paschal Lamb for Catholics —by His death and Resurrection we are saved from death and sin. We also eat the Paschal Lamb of Christ (Lamb of God, Who takes away the sin of the world) in the Eucharist. Just as in the Old Testament the lamb had to be sacrificed and eaten, so too, in our New Passover, Christ had to be both sacrificed and eaten (Jn 6:35–59) in order for us to share in His life. You may make a chart comparing the Old Passover and the New Passover.

Name:_____

Passover

Things to think about.

God had a plan to bring His people out of slavery in Egypt to worship Him. He commanded the Israelites to share a meal together called PASSOVER. The Israelites obeyed God and each family killed a lamb, sprinkled its blood on the doorposts of their houses, and ate the lamb for dinner. God sent His final plague upon Egypt to convince Pharaoh to set His chosen people free. God sent His angel of death to Egypt. When the angel saw the blood on the doorposts of the Israelites, he "passed over" their houses, but went to the houses of the Egyptians and killed all the first-born sons. Pharaoh was so full of grief that he set the Israelites free.

As Catholics, Jesus is our Paschal Lamb, the Lamb of God who sets us free from the slavery of sin. Jesus shed His blood on the Cross for us, and we eat His Body and drink His Blood in the Eucharist.

Faith and Life Series • Grade 3 • Chapter 6 • Lesson 3   23

Reinforce

1. Show part of the video, "The Prince of Egypt" (available through Ignatius Press; 99 minutes).

2. Celebrate a seder meal.

3. Have the students work on *Activity Book,* p. 23.

4. Have the students make posters representing each of the plagues and God's mighty works.

5. Have the students make posters comparing the Old Testament Passover and Jesus, the Paschal Lamb of God.

6. Have the students work on the Memorization Questions.

Conclude

1. Lead the children in praying for their intentions.

2. As a class, sing "Come, ye faithful, raise the strain," *Adoremus Hymnal,* #417.

Preview

In the next lesson, the students will learn about the Israelites' journey to freedom.

PASSOVER MEAL

The Passover meal, or Seder, commemorates the night that the angel of death passed over the homes of the Israelites in Egypt, sparing the firstborn sons inside houses with lambs' blood on the doorposts. The dinner is a simple meal, served just as though the family might have to flee the home at any minute. Seder, in fact, is the Hebrew word for "home."

On Holy Thursday evening many Catholic families hold a seder dinner ceremony in memory of the Jewish Passover, with roast lamb, bitter herbs, matzo, and wine. (An empty place is left for the prophet Elijah.)

NOTES

LESSON FOUR:
GOD CARES FOR HIS PEOPLE

Aims

Moses led God's people out of Egypt across the Red Sea to safety while destroying the army of Pharaoh in the sea.

God nourished His people with manna and fresh water from a rock on their way to the Promised Land.

Through Moses, God gave His people the Ten Commandments and established a covenant with them.

Materials

- *Activity Book,* p. 24
- Children's Bible

Optional:
- "Come, ye faithful, raise the strain," *Adoremus Hymnal,* #417

Begin

Discuss with the children how God led His people to freedom. Pharaoh was hard of heart and could not obey the One True God. Pharaoh would have been happy if only he could have accepted God's truth. Have the children read John 14:6 and 8:31–32 to help them understand the lesson. You may want to write these verses on the board for the children.

Q. 30 *How did God save Moses as a baby from the cruelty of Pharaoh?*
Moses was saved from Pharaoh's cruelty when his mother placed him in the river. Pharaoh's daughter found Moses and took him into her home, according to God's plan (Exodus 2:1–10).

Q. 31 *How did God speak to Moses?*
God spoke to Moses in a burning bush (Exodus 3:2–4).

Q. 32 *Why did God send the plagues to Egypt?*
God sent the plagues to Egypt to show that He is the true God, and to punish Pharaoh for not freeing God's chosen people from slavery (Exodus 10:1–2).

Q. 33 *What is Passover?*
Passover is the celebration of the night God's Angel of Death passed over the houses of the Israelites, whose doors were marked with the blood of a lamb (Exodus 12:23, 27).

Q. 34 *How did God care for His people on their way to the Promised Land?*
God gave His people the manna to eat and water from a rock to drink. He encouraged them to continue on their journey (Exodus 16:21, 17:6).

Develop

1. Read the rest of the chapter with the students. They may take turns reading aloud. You may read the same accounts from the children's Bible in Ex 14:1–31, 16:12–19, 17:1–6, 19:9—20:22.

2. How did God free His people from Pharaoh's army? Was Pharaoh defeated? Make a parallel between the crossing of the Red Sea and our Baptisms. We are freed from slavery to sin so that we, too, can enter the Promised Land of Heaven.

3. How did God take care of and nourish His people in the wilderness? You may need to explain what quail and manna are. Make a parallel between food from God and the Eucharist, which is the True Bread from Heaven that nourishes our souls on the way to our Promised Land.

4. Explain to the students that God invited Moses to receive the Ten Commandments. This would free His People from ignorance of God's laws and slavery to sin. This allowed them to live in relationship with one another and with God. We are all called to live according to God's Ten Commandments.

5. Reread John 14:6. Jesus is the way, the truth, and the life. Read John 8:31–32. The truth shall set us free! God knew that in order to be truly free, we need His love and His laws so we can live in the freedom of truth and be free from sin. Just as God led His people to Mt. Sinai to receive this truth, we receive His truth by reading the Bible, listening at Mass, receiving the Eucharist, etc.

6. Explain God's covenant with His people. It is an oath that makes us family and calls us to responsibilities (e.g., in a marriage, husbands and wives have responsibilities to each other and their children). Have the students name some of these responsibilities and tell them that this is like man's responsibility to God.

Name:_____

God's Covenant

God made a covenant with Abraham, Moses, and with all people through Jesus. In this covenant, God says to us: "You will be my people, and I will be your God." To live in this relationship, we must obey God's laws (the Ten Commandments) and the Great Law of Love. We must place God above everything (like Abraham did). By following God's laws, we will be lead to the promised land of Heaven (just like Moses and the Israelites).

Jesus made the perfect covenant with us through His sacrifice on the Cross and in sharing the Eucharist. We share God's life and are His family in His Church. We must keep God's Commandments, receive His sacraments, and pray often.

Write a prayer to God, thanking him for his covenant with you.

Dear God,
Answers will vary.

Reinforce

1. Lead a discussion with the children and ask them how they see God in their lives. Do they see him caring for them, nourishing them, and preparing them for Heaven?

2. Discuss our covenant with God. What is God's responsibility to man? What is our responsibility to God? Have the students give examples of how they can be faithful to the covenant or break the covenant.

3. Have the students work on *Activity Book,* p. 24.

4. Work on the Memorization Questions for this chapter.

Conclude

1. Lead the students in a closing prayer.

2. Sing "Come, ye faithful, raise the strain," *Adoremus Hymnal,* #417.

Preview

In the next lesson, the students' knowledge of the material covered this week will be reviewed and assessed.

SAINT MARIA GORETTI

Saint Maria Goretti is a model of Christian chastity and the love of God called to responsibility.

Threatened by a man with a knife and ordered to sin against chastity, twelve-year-old Maria Goretti was stabbed when she resisted her attacker. She chose to die rather than give up her purity.

Before dying, Saint Maria Goretti forgave her killer, demonstrating the true love of God that dwelt in her soul.

Living in a secular world that does not honor chastity, we may pray with Saint Maria Goretti to help us to remain pure and keep us from sins against chastity.

NOTES

CHAPTER SIX
REVIEW AND ASSESSMENT

Aims

The students' knowledge and understanding of the material covered this week will be reviewed and assessed.

Materials

- Quiz 6, Appendix, p. A-8

Optional:
- "Come, ye faithful, raise the strain," *Adoremus Hymnal,* #417

Review

1. The students should understand that Israel's test was slavery in Egypt.

2. The students should be able to give modern day examples of social injustice and discuss pro-life issues at an age-appropriate level.

3. The students should be able to recount the following stories:
   - Moses sent down the Nile and saved by Pharaoh's daughter
   - Moses and the burning bush
   - The plagues sent upon Egypt
   - The Passover
   - The crossing of the Red Sea and receiving the Ten Commandments.

4. The students should be able to explain that God sent the plagues to Egypt to show that He is the One True God.

5. The students should be able to explain how Jesus is the Paschal Lamb of God.

6. The students should be able to explain how crossing the Red Sea is like Baptism and why God's sending quail, manna, and water in the desert is like the Eucharist.

7. The students should be able to define a covenant and its responsibilities.

Name: _____

The Prophet Moses   **Quiz 6**

"Trust in the Lord for ever, for the Lord God is an everlasting rock"" (Isaiah 26:1-4).

Word Bank

bush	slaves	covenant	Egypt
manna	Passover	Death	
meal	plagues	Commandments	

Fill in the blanks with the correct word from the Word Bank.

1. The Pharaoh in Egypt made God's chosen people his **slaves** because he was jealous of their loyalty to the one, true God.

2. God spoke to Moses from a burning **bush** and told him to tell the Pharaoh to "Let my people go."

3. Pharaoh refused. God sent many disasters or **plagues** to the land. There were hailstorms, illnesses, frogs, and bugs.

4. Pharaoh continued to say "No," so the Angel of **Death** was sent to destroy the first-born child of every Egyptian family.

5. God commanded that each Israelite family share a special **meal** after killing a lamb and sprinkling the lamb's blood on the doorpost.

6. The homes of God's chosen people were passed over by the angel. This was called the **Passover**.

7. Pharaoh let the Israelites go. Moses led the people out of **Egypt**.

8. God protected His people on their long journey to Canaan. On their journey they received bread from Heaven, called **manna**, and fresh water from a rock.

9. Moses received the Ten **Commandments** from God on a mountain-top.

10. God lived up to His promise, or **covenant**. "You will be My people and I will be your God."

Assess

1. Distribute the quizzes and read through them with the students to be sure they understand the questions.

2. Administer the quiz. As they hand in their work, you may orally quiz them on the Memorization Questions for this chapter.

3. After all the quizzes have been handed in, you may wish to review the correct answers with the class.

Conclude

End class with a prayer and sing "Come, ye faithful, raise the strain," *Adoremus Hymnal,* #417.

CHAPTER SEVEN
GOD'S LAWS OF LOVE

Catechism of the Catholic Church References

Jesus and the Law: 574–82, 592, 2052–55, 2075
Moses and the Prayer of the Mediator: 2574–77, 2593
Obligation to the Ten Commandments: 2072–74, 2081–82
Old Law: 1961–64, 1975, 1980–82
Ten Commandments: 1084–557
Ten Commandments and the Natural Law: 2070–71, 2080

Ten Commandments as Foundation of Conscience: 1962
Ten Commandments as Path to the Kingdom of Heaven: 1724
Ten Commandments and Sacred Scripture: 2056–63, 2077
Ten Commandments in the Church's Tradition: 2064–68, 2078
Unity of the Ten Commandments: 2069, 2079

Scripture References

Moses Receives the Commandments: Ex 20:1–17

Background Reading: *The Fundamentals of Catholicism* by Fr. Kenneth Baker, S.J.

Volume 1:
"True Morality Is Based on Objective Principles," pp. 135–38

Summary of Lesson Content

Lesson 1

God protected His people on their way to the Promised Land. God gave them quail meat and manna to eat and water from a rock to drink.

Lesson 2

God nourished men's souls by giving them His Laws in the Ten Commandments.

The first three Commandments help us to love God. The last seven help us to love our neighbor.

Obeying God's Laws protects us from sin.

Lesson 3

The Ten Commandments are meant for all people and are binding, even today.

Jesus summarized the Ten Commandments with the Great Commandment of love.

Lesson 4

Keeping God's Commandments is difficult, but is good for the soul. The Commandments help us to love God and neighbor.

God has promised eternal life in Heaven to those who keep His Commandments.

LESSON ONE: ON THE WAY . . .

Aims

The students will learn that God nourished the bodies of the Israelites while they were in the desert by giving them food and drink.

They will also learn that God nourished their souls by giving them His laws, the Ten Commandments.

Materials

- Tortilla or pita bread, roasted chicken or turkey, and water for desert feast
- Children's Bible
- *Activity Book,* p. 25
- Poster Board, Markers

Optional:
- "Father, we thank thee who hast planted," *Adoremus Hymnal,* #515
- "The Ten Commandments," video; In the Beginning: Stories from the Bible, available through Ignatius Press

Begin

Prepare the desert feast in another room or at the back of the room using the ingredients listed above. Lead the children on a long walk. Say things such as, "Wow! It has been a long, long walk. We've been walking for days and days. It sure is hot out here. The desert is sandy and hot! I'm so thirsty and I'm tired of carrying all this heavy equipment. There's no food to eat! Why did Moses bring us out here? We had lots of food to eat in Egypt!" Encourage the children to grumble. After a while, stop and pray for food. After praying, enjoy the feast you prepared.

Develop

1. As the children are eating, explain to them that the Israelites grumbled against Moses and God. How foolish and ungrateful they were! They did not trust that God would take care of them. Read Exodus 16:12–19 and 17:1–6 from the children's Bible.

2. Explain that God sent miraculous food to the Israelites. Quails would fly down so the Israelites could eat them and manna (heavenly bread) would fall to them. Dew became like bread on the ground, but it was as sweet as honey. They could collect it every day, enough for each day, and then the manna would disappear. Also point out how amazing it was that water came from a rock. Surely God performed these miracles so the Israelites would know they could trust Him.

3. Lead the children in giving thanks for their desert feast.

4. *Explain that God also wanted to nourish the souls of His people. He gave them the Ten Commandments. Have the students turn to the list of the Ten Commandments in the student text. Have them take turns reading them aloud. As they read, write the first three on one "tablet" made from poster board and the last seven on a second "tablet" so they can clearly see that the Ten Commandments are divided into two sections.*

5. As the children read each commandment, have them explain it and give an example of how to keep it and how to break it. For example, the commandment, "You shall have no other gods besides me" means to worship only the One True God. You can keep this commandment by going to Mass. You can break this commandment by worshiping the Nile or the sun as did the Egyptians.

Name:_____

God Cares For You

God cared for the Israelites on their way to the promised land by giving them quail meat, manna, and fresh water. He also gave them spiritual nourishment by giving them the Ten Commandments. Think of ways God cares for you.

Write a letter to God thanking Him for caring about you.

Dear God, _____
Answers will vary.
_____
_____
_____
_____
_____
_____
_____
_____
_____
_____
_____

Faith and Life Series • Grade 3 • Chapter 7 • Lesson 1   25

COMMANDMENT MEMORY GAMES

- Assign one Commandment per child to memorize. Point to each child and have him recite his Commandment.

- Give the children examples of a Commandment and have them recite the Commandment.

- Play matching games. You give them numbers and Commandments; they match them up.

- Give the children situations and have them think of which Commandments would have been kept or broken: e.g., I told my mom I was sick when I was well, so that I wouldn't have to go to Mass: answer: 3, 4, 8.

Reinforce

1. Have the students work on *Activity Book,* p. 25.

2. The students may play memorization games to help them memorize the Ten Commandments.

3. The students may draw pictures depicting each of the Ten Commandments.

4. Teach the children to sing "Father, we thank thee who hast planted," *Adoremus Hymnal*, #515.

5. Show "The Ten Commandments," video from the In the Beginning: Stories from the Bible series (available through Ignatius Press; 30 minutes).

Conclude

Lead the children in a prayer of thanksgiving to God for the many ways He cares for us. The children may each take turns giving examples of God's loving care in this prayer.

Preview

In the next lesson, the students will learn more about the Ten Commandments.

NOTES

LESSON TWO: LAWS OF LOVE

Aims

The students will learn that the first three of the Ten Commandments help us to love God and the last seven help us to love our neighbor.

They will learn that obeying God's laws protects us from sin.

Materials

- *Activity Book,* p. 26
- Two hangers, two colors of construction paper, scissors, glue, markers, string
- Rewards for memorization of the Ten Commandments

Optional:
- "Father, we thank thee who hast planted," *Adoremus Hymnal,* #515

Begin

Play a quick review game of the Ten Commandments. Reward the children who have memorized all ten in order.

Reread the last line of paragraph 2 in the student text, "God gave them to Moses written on stone tablets, but He wants them to be written on our hearts." Explain to the children that this means God wants us to know His laws so that we can always choose to do the right thing. Knowing His laws will help us to avoid sin. Tell the students what sin is.

---

7 God's Laws of Love

"For it is not the hearers of the law who are righteous before God, but the doers of the law who will be justified."

Romans 2:13

After the children of God had safely escaped Egypt, they still had challenges to face. They had a long way to go before they reached the Promised Land. God had protected them on their way. He gave them quail meat, a bread-like food called manna, and fresh water from a rock. He gave them enough each day to satisfy their hunger and thirst.

God also wanted to nourish the souls of His children. He wanted to teach them how to love Him and be good to each other. One day, God called Moses, His prophet, to the top of **Mount Sinai** and gave him the rules of His Kingdom. We call these rules the Ten **Commandments**. God gave them to Moses written on stone tablets, but He wants them to be written on our hearts.

The first three Commandments told the people how to worship and respect God. The last seven told them how to be kind and fair to each other. The Commandments asked them to do some things and avoid others. God meant all ten of these to work together in our daily life. He also meant them to bring happiness and joy to His children's lives. He wanted to protect them from the sadness of sin.

Even though God gave the Ten Commandments to His people during the time of the Old Testament, they are meant for all God's people until the end of time.

When some people asked Jesus which of the Commandments was the greatest, He answered:

Develop

1. Read paragraph 3 of the student text with the children. Refer back to the two "tablets" you made during the previous lesson, and tell the students why they are separated into two groups. The first tablet teaches us how to love God and the second tablet teaches us how to love our neighbor.

2. You may have the children work on *Activity Book,* p. 26 at this time.

3. Hand out two colors of construction paper and scissors to each student. Have them cut out three hearts from one color and seven hearts from another color. On the three hearts have them write the first three Commandments. Have them write the number on one side and the Commandment on the other. Have them do the same thing with the last seven Commandments. Make these hearts into a mobile by crossing two hangers, tying them together, and hanging the hearts from them. Be sure to have the students write their names on their mobiles. You may hang these around the room (from the crossbars of the ceiling tiles if you have them) or on various hooks. Be sure to have the students clean up their messes.

4. Have the students break into pairs and quiz each other on the Ten Commandments. Conversely, have the students break into pairs and dramatize each of the Ten Commandments. (In the event that they choose to dramatize a Commandment, let them decide whether to act out how to keep it or how to break it). Have them explain their skit to the class.

5. Explain to the children that they must choose to keep the Ten Commandments. Even though you may tell a child that fire is hot, he may still choose to find out on his own! Encourage the students to pray to God to help them obey His Laws and to find joy in obeying them.

Name:_____

Ten Commandments

Fill in this chart below.

Commandment	What it tells us to do	What it forbids
1. See page 38 in the student text.	Answers will vary.	
2.		
3.		
4.		
5.		
6.		
7.		
8.		
9.		
10.		

26 Faith and Life Series • Grade 3 • Chapter 7 • Lesson 2

Reinforce

1. Play memory games with the students to help them memorize the Ten Commandments. Play games that also test their comprehension either by using examples or asking them for examples.

2. Have the students work on *Activity Book*, p. 26.

3. Optional: Have your class go to the Sacrament of Penance.

Conclude

1. Lead the children in a prayer asking for forgiveness for breaking the Ten Commandments and for the grace they need to keep them.

2. Sing "Father, we thank thee who hast planted," *Adoremus Hymnal*, #515.

Preview

In the next lesson the students will learn about the Great Commandment of love given to us by Jesus.

TEN COMMANDMENTS MOBILE

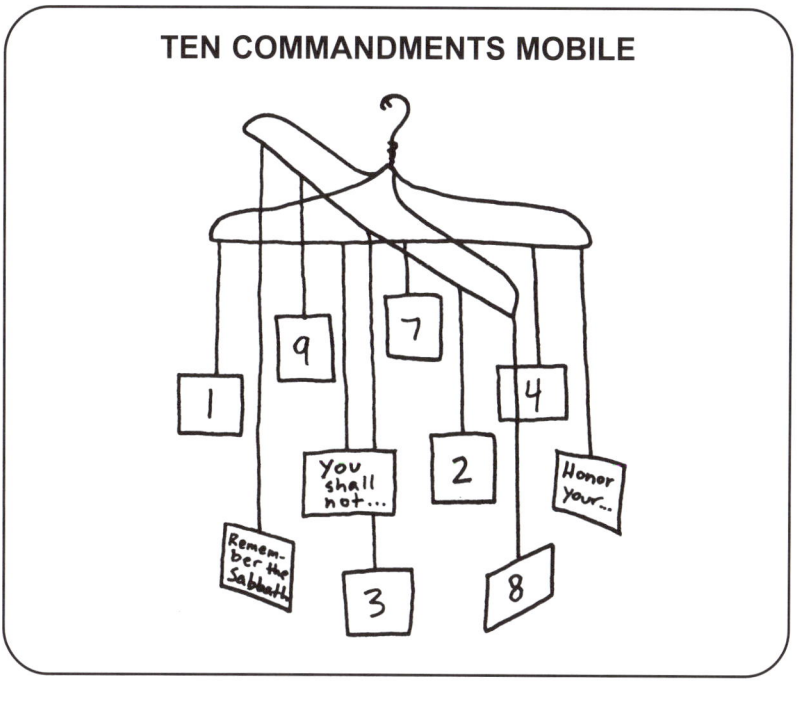

NOTES

LESSON THREE: JESUS AND THE LAW

Aims

The students will learn that the Ten Commandments are meant for all people and are binding even today.

They will learn the Great Commandment of love.

Materials

- *Activity Book*, p. 27
- Bibles
- "Father, we thank thee who hast planted," *Adoremus Hymnal*, #515

Optional:
- Appendix, p. B-15

Begin

Teach the children the Great Commandment by using hand signs: You shall love (cross your hands over your heart) the Lord (point to heaven) with all your heart (point to your heart), with all your soul (point to the sole of your shoe) with all your strength (flex your biceps muscles) and all your mind (point to your head), and your neighbor (use both hands to point to other people or simply point outward using your index fingers) as yourself (using both hands point to yourself using your thumbs).

"You shall love the Lord your God with all your heart, and with all your soul, and with all your mind. This is the great and first commandment. And a second is like it, You shall love your neighbor as yourself."

Matthew 22:37–39

Keeping God's Commandments is not always easy, but they are for our good. They help us to love God and our neighbor. Some day we will see God face to face. If we have followed His Commandments on earth, He promises to share with us the joys of Heaven that last for ever.

THE TEN COMMANDMENTS

1. I am the Lord your God; you shall not have other gods before Me.
2. You shall not take the name of the Lord your God in vain.
3. Remember to keep holy the Lord's Day.
4. Honor your father and your mother.
5. You shall not kill.
6. You shall not commit adultery.
7. You shall not steal.
8. You shall not lie.
9. You shall not covet your neighbor's wife.
10. You shall not covet your neighbor's goods.

Develop

1. Read paragraphs 4 and 5, including the quote with the children. They may take turns reading sentences aloud. As you read the Great Commandment of love, be sure the students use their hand signs.

2. Have the students search the following Biblical passages and write down their findings:
- Dt 6:5
- Mt 22:37–39
- Mk 12:30–31
- Lk 10:27

Discuss why love of God comes first. We owe God love above all things and if we love God then we will love our neighbors because He is the Father of all of us.

3. Discuss the virtue of love or charity with the students. Remind them that a virtue is a habit of the will toward doing the good. Love or charity is a theological virtue. It comes from God and directs us toward Him. There are many kinds of love: we often hear people say "I love pizza!" or "I love my pet" or "I love my mom" or "I love God." True love should help us give of ourselves to others. For example, if I love my dad, I will let him know that I love Him by giving him a hug, helping him cut the grass, making him breakfast, etc. Love often requires a sacrifice. To show your love to someone else, such as helping your brother do his homework, means that we are not focussing on ourselves (we could watch television instead of helping our brother). Who made the greatest sacrifice for us? Jesus. Jesus loves us even more than our parents do, and we know how much they love us! Charity is our way of expressing our love in action by giving to others or doing things for others because we love them.

4. Ask the following questions: Can we love strangers? Can we love our enemies? Can we love everybody?

Name:_____

God's Commandments

1. What are the Commandments of God?
The Commandments of God are the moral laws that God gave to Moses on Mount Sinai for all His people.

2. Must we keep the Commandments of God?
Yes

3. How many Commandments are there?
Ten

4. How many Commandments teach us how to love and worship God?
Three

5. How many Commandments teach us how to love our neighbor?
Seven

6. What is the Greatest Commandment? (See Lk 10:27)
"You shall love the Lord your God with all your heart, with your whole soul, and with your whole mind, and you shall love your neighbor as yourself."

7. What does the Gospel of John (Jn 14:15) teach us about the Commandments?
It teaches us that if we love God we will keep His Commandments.

8. What are the Commandments meant to do for us?
They are meant to bring us happiness and joy and to protect us from the sadness of sin.

Faith and Life Series • Grade 3 • Chapter 7 • Lesson 3

Reinforce

1. Have the students work on *Activity Book*, p. 27.

2. Have the students work on the Memorization Questions for this chapter. They may quiz each other on these questions and on the Ten Commandments.

3. Have the students think of ways they can be charitable, and if you want to, coordinate a class project of charity.

Conclude

1. Lead the students in praying the Act of Love.

2. Sing "Father, we thank thee who hast planted," *Adoremus Hymnal*, #515.

Preview

In the next lesson, the students will review daily applications of the Ten Commandments and God's promise to us for keeping them.

ACT OF LOVE

O my God, I love Thee above all things, with my whole heart and soul, because Thou art all good and worthy of all love. I love my neighbor as myself for the love of Thee. I forgive all who have injured me, and ask pardon of all whom I have injured. *Amen*.

NOTES

LESSON FOUR: KEEPING GOD'S LAWS

Aims

The students will learn daily applications of the Ten Commandments.

They will learn God's promise of eternal life in Heaven for those who keep His Commandments.

Materials

- *Activity Book*, p. 28
- Children's Bible

Optional:
- "Father, we thank thee who hast planted," *Adoremus Hymnal*, #515

Begin

Explain that rules sometimes have consequences by using an example. You may tell the children that a video game system comes with an instruction manual, which contains the rules for using the video game. The rules say to avoid putting any foreign objects into the game cartridge slot. It is possible, however, to insert a spoon of pudding into the cartridge slot. If you did this, would you break the rule? Yes. But you would also brake the video game. God's Laws work in the same way. You can break His Laws, but in doing so we hurt ourselves, our relationship with God, and our neighbor.

Words to Know:

Mount Sinai   Commandments

Q. 35 *What are the Commandments of God?*
The Commandments of God are the moral Laws that God gave to Moses on Mount Sinai for all His people (CCC 62, 2056).

Q. 36 *Must we follow the Commandments of God?*
Yes, we must follow the Commandments of God (CCC 1776, 2072–73).

"If you love me, you will keep my commandments."

John 14:15

Develop

1. Finish reading the chapter to the students.

2. Ask the children why it is important to keep the Commandments in order for us to have good relationships with God and our neighbors. Would they be friends with someone who always lied to them or stole from them? Surely not! It is important to respect people and their possessions as well as our relationships. What about God? Will He be sad if we miss Mass or worship false gods? Well, how did He treat the Egyptians? Surely God wants us to love Him just as He loves us and calls us His children.

3. You may read the story of the Prodigal Son to the students from the children's Bible (Lk 15:11–32). Use this story to demonstrate how the sins of the son hurt his relationship with his father and caused him sadness such as having to eat what the pigs ate. Also emphasize how much the father loved the son. In his sin, the son was dead to the father, but in his return and sorrow for his sin, he became alive again in the eyes of the father. How wonderful is God's love! You may also use this example to show what happens between the two sons: one was angry that the other had squandered his father's money and did not work on the farm. The father reminded him that all that he had was his. He has always been with the father and loved him. Sin can cause hard feelings even between family members, so it is important to avoid sin.

4. You may also read the story of the Rich Young Man from the children's Bible (Mt 19:16–24). Show how Jesus promises eternal life to those who keep the Commandments. Also tell the children that they must obey the Commandments out of love. Remember the parable of the rich man who did not want to sacrifice or make acts of charity to others.

5. Discuss some daily applications of the Commandments.

Name:_____

What Would Jesus Do?

Sometimes, we can't remember all of God's Commandments, or we aren't sure if we are following God's laws. The best thing we can do at times like that is to ask ourselves, "WHAT WOULD JESUS DO?" Using this rule as a guide, answer the following questions.

1. You didn't study for a big test, and you know you need to pass this test. Do you cheat by copying off your neighbor?
   Answers will vary.

2. Your best friend wants you to come over for awhile, but your brother wants you to help him with his homework. What do you do?

3. Your sister wants to borrow your toy, but you know that the last time you lent it to her, she broke it. Do you lend it to her anyway?

4. You have a letter sent home from your teacher, what do you do with it?

5. It is Sunday and you don't want to go to Mass. What do you do?

Faith and Life Series • Grade 3 • Chapter 7 • Lesson 4

DAILY APPLICATIONS OF THE COMMANDMENTS

- First: Pray to God and love Him more than anything else
- Second: Do not curse or say the Lord's name in an unprayerful way
- Third: Go to Mass cheerfully with your family on Sundays
- Fourth: Obey your parents cheerfully
- Fifth: Do not fight with or yell at others
- Sixth: Do not watch unchaste movies or shows
- Seventh: Do not use other people's things without asking
- Eighth: Do not lie
- Ninth: Be pure in your thoughts
- Tenth: Do not be jealous of other people's things

Reinforce

1. Have the students work on *Activity Book*, p. 28.

2. Play memory games with the students, reviewing their Memorization Questions, the Ten Commandments, and the Great Commandment.

3. Have the students dramatize the Prodigal Son or the Rich Young Man and discuss these parables.

Conclude

1. Lead the children in a closing prayer.

2. Sing "Father, we thank thee who hast planted," *Adoremus Hymnal*, #515.

Preview

In the next lesson, the students' knowledge of the material covered this week will be reviewed and assessed.

NOTES

CHAPTER SEVEN
REVIEW AND ASSESSMENT

Aims

The students' knowledge and understanding of the material covered this week will be reviewed and assessed.

Materials

- Quiz 7, Appendix, p. A-9

Optional:
- "Father, we thank thee who hast planted," *Adoremus Hymnal*, #515

Review

1. The students should know the Ten Commandment in order.

2. The students should know the Great Commandment.

3. The students should know that God gave us His laws:
   - To nourish our souls
   - To help us to live in a right relationship with God and neighbor
   - To protect us from sin

4. God has promised us eternal life if we keep his Commandments.

5. They should be able to recount the stories of the Prodigal Son and the Rich Young Man.

6. The students should know that WWJD stands for "What Would Jesus Do?" and that this question can help them to make good choices.

7. God asks that His Laws be written on our hearts so we can make good choices and avoid sin.

Name: _____

God's Laws of Love   Quiz 7

"The Lord is my shepherd, I shall not want" (Psalm 23:1).

Word Bank

anoint	Saul	talking	shepherd	conquered
Goliath	Psalms	David	help	near

Fill in the blanks with the correct words from the Word Bank.

1. The Israelites wanted a king. God told Samuel to **anoint** the new king by pouring oil over his head. This was a sign of God's gift of power.

2. The first king of Israel was **Saul**. He was weak and disobedient to God.

3. God chose another king named **David** to rule over His people after Saul died.

4. David was only a young **shepherd**, but he turned out to be a great and wonderful king.

5. David trusted God enough to fight the giant named **Goliath**.

6. David **conquered** Jerusalem and made it the city of his people.

7. David taught his people the importance of prayer, or **talking** with God.

8. David taught his people that, when all hope seems lost, God is **near** us.

9. God's strength and **help** are more powerful than anything in the world.

10. David wrote the **Psalms**, which are songs for God that we sing or recite after the first reading at Mass.

11. Write out the Scripture verse shown at the top of this page.

Faith and Life • Grade 3 • Appendix A   A - 9

Assess

1. Distribute the quizzes and read through them with the students to be sure they understand the questions.

2. Administer the quiz. As they hand in their work, you may orally quiz them on the Memorization Questions for this chapter.

3. After all the quizzes have been handed in, you may wish to review the correct answers with the class.

Conclude

Sing "Father, we thank thee who hast planted," *Adoremus Hymnal*, #515.

CHAPTER EIGHT
KING DAVID

Catechism of the Catholic Church References

Anointing: 695, 1293–96
David and the Prayer of a King: 2578–80, 2594
Hope: 1813, 1817–21, 1840–41, 1843
Israel as a Kingdom: 709–10
Jesus as Born into the Messianic Line of David: 437–39, 488, 559

Jesus as the Christ, the Anointed One: 436–40, 453
Psalms: 2585–89, 2596–97
Revelation of God's Plan of Salvation: 51–53, 68
Stages of Revelation: 54–55, 69–70
Typology and the Unity of the Old and New Testaments: 128–30, 140

Scripture References

The Story of David: 1 Sam 16—17

Background Reading: *The Fundamentals of Catholicism* by Fr. Kenneth Baker, S.J.

Volume 2:
"King of Kings, and Lord of Lords," pp. 282–85

Summary of Lesson Content

Lesson 1

The Israelites decided they wanted a king for their nation.

Samuel, the prophet, anointed the new king, Saul, by pouring oil over his head.

Saul was a weak king, so God chose David to be the new king.

David was a good king and loved God greatly.

Lesson 2

David taught man about God's abiding love. David knew that we should love God in return.

David slew Goliath in a battle, relying on God's help.

Lesson 3

David taught man about loving God through prayer.

David wrote many psalms praising God.

Lesson 4

God promised that the Savior would come from the descendants of David.

David foreshadowed the Savior in many ways: he was a good shepherd, he was willing to lay down his life for his people, he was a good and wise king, he listened to the Father, and he inspired people to worship God.

LESSON ONE:
A KING FOR ISRAEL

Aims

The students will learn the role of a king.

They will know that the prophet Samuel anointed the first king, Saul, by pouring oil over his head.

They will also learn that God chose David to be the new (second) king. David was a good king and loved God greatly.

Materials

- *Activity Book*, p. 29
- Oil, water, crown (can be made of construction paper)

Optional:
- "The King of love my shepherd is," *Adoremus Hymnal*, #580

Begin

Discuss what a king is with the children. A king is a leader of his people. He leads them in battle, like a general or a president. He is to lead them in worship. He represents his country when he visits other countries. He is a judge who protects the poor and neglected. He should take care of his people by giving them fair laws and making sure the people are happy. He is expected to be a good example for all and to encourage others to be good as well.

---

8   King David

"Your house and your kingdom shall be made sure for ever before me; your throne shall be established for ever."

2 Samuel 7:16

Many years after the Israelites escaped from Egypt, they decided they wanted to have an earthly **king** like the other nations. God warned them against having a king, but since the Israelites really wanted one, He said, "Yes." God told the holy prophet Samuel to **anoint** the new king by pouring oil over his head. Anointing was a sign of God's gift of power.

A man named Saul was chosen to be the king of Israel, but Saul turned out to be weak and disobedient to God. Therefore, God chose another king named David to rule over His people after Saul died. **David** was only a young shepherd boy, but he turned out to be a very great and wonderful king of Israel. He was a kind and strong leader, talented and clear-thinking in battle. He conquered Jerusalem and made it the city of his people. Best of all, King David really loved God. Sometimes he fell into sin, but he was always sorry and came back to God. He helped his people to lead good lives.

David teaches us about God's presence in our lives and His love for us. David also teaches us how we should love God in return. God was faithful to David by helping him win a victory over the cruel champion Goliath. **Goliath**, who challenged the People of God, was over nine feet tall and carried a heavy metal sword. David, who stood up for the People of God, was small and had no sword. We would think that the boy David would not have a chance. And yet, David trusted God enough to fight Goliath, and he won. David

41

Develop

1. Explain to the children that when the Israelites were in the wilderness they did not have a king. They relied on God and He protected them (e.g., from the Egyptians at the Red Sea). He provided for them (e.g., with food and drink). He was always with them and guiding them. He even spoke through the prophet Moses. Through His Laws, all were called to worship Him and to live good lives. In many ways, you could say that God was the King of Israel.

2. *Read the first two paragraphs of this chapter with the students. You may have them take turns reading sentences aloud.*

3. *Pass around oil and let the children smell it, feel it, touch it, etc. Explain that oil was used for many things:*
   - *For athletes—to escape their enemies*
   - *For beauty—it made hair healthy and skin shiny*
   - *For cooking—for eating and nourishment*
   - *For anointing prophets, priests, and kings—as a sign of*

   their sharing in God's power (priests are anointed with oil even today in the Church and lay people are anointed at Baptism and Confirmation as a sign of sharing in these ministries).

4. *Demonstrate an anointing of a king using water (not oil). Pour water over the head of a child (or let the students pour it on your head). Then crown the newly anointed!*

5. Discuss the bad king's (Saul's) qualities and the good king's (David's) qualities.

6. If a king is to be a good example to all people, what can we learn from King David?
   - To use talents well and to give glory to God
   - To love God and to be sorry if we sin
   - To help others to live good lives, etc.

Name:_____

Israel's Kings

1. Why did Israel want a king?
   Israel wanted to be like the other nations.

2. Who was the true leader and protector of Israel before they had a king?
   God

3. What did the prophets use as a sign of God's gift of power for the king?
   Anointing with oil

4. Who was Israel's first king? Was he obedient to God?
   Saul was Israel's first king and he was not obedient to God.

5. What qualities did David have that made him a good king?
   He was a kind and strong leader, talented, and clear-thinking in battle.

6. Did David love God and trust in Him? How do we know this?
   David loved God. We know this because he faced Goliath.

Faith and Life Series • Grade 3 • Chapter 8 • Lesson 1

Reinforce

1. Have the students work on *Activity Book*, p. 29.

2. Teach the students to sing "The King of love my shepherd is," *Adoremus Hymnal*, #580.

3. You may have the students look up some of King David's psalms and have them choose their favorites.

Conclude

End class by leading the children in a prayer asking God to give us the qualities of a good king. Ask God to make the children strong Christian leaders. Ask Him also to make them clear-headed in choosing good, to use their talents to give glory to God, always to be sorry for sins and turn back to God, and to help others do good, too.

Preview

In the next lesson, the students will learn about the battle of David and Goliath.

SAINT LOUIS OF FRANCE

Saint Louis was born in 1214 and was crowned King Louis IX little more than a decade later. Raised by his devout mother, Queen Blanche of Castille, Louis was taught all the necessary skills of a medieval king—Latin, fencing, and diplomacy—but he was instructed most deeply in the Catholic Faith.

In his reign as king, which lasted until his death in 1270, Saint Louis set a remarkable Christian example for his subjects, attending Mass twice daily, and saying the daily office. In 1248, he led a crusade to Egypt and was taken prisoner. After being freed and returning to France, he made peace with England. He died while leading a crusade.

NOTES

LESSON TWO: TRUST IN GOD

Aims

The students will learn how David taught man about God's abiding love and that we should love God in return.

They will learn the story of how David slew Goliath in a battle relying on God's help.

Materials

- *Activity Book*, p. 30
- Sticks from outside, elastic bands, and paper balls (discretion advised)
- Paper and markers
- Costumes and props

Optional:
- "The King of love my shepherd is," *Adoremus Hymnal*, #580
- "David and Goliath," video; In the Beginning: Stories from the Bible, available through Ignatius Press

Begin

Ask the students if they are ever afraid of anything. Are they afraid of the dark? Do they fear being unpopular? Are they ever afraid that they will not succeed at some difficult task? We all have these fears from time to time. When we are afraid or overwhelmed by something that seems too big for us to handle, we must put our trust in God and know in our hearts that with God, all things are possible. With his trust in God, a small shepherd defeated a giant and saved his homeland.

---

showed his people that even when all hope seems lost, God is near us. God's strength and help are more powerful than anything else in this world.

King David taught us the importance of prayer, or talking with God. David used his beautiful voice and musical talents to make up songs for God. These Psalms, which are messages of praise and love, are still sung in the Church today, many centuries later. We sing them or read them at Mass because the words that David sang so long ago still express the same things we believe today: God is mighty and beautiful. His mercy is everlasting. We trust and love and adore Him. We are sorry for sin. We delight in the treasures of His creation. We thank Him for sharing His life.

David was such a good king that God promised the Savior, the eternal King, would come into the world through his family. David, in fact, foreshadowed the Savior in many ways. Like Jesus, David was a good shepherd who took care of his flock. He was a wise and just king. He was willing to lay down his life for his people when he saved them from Goliath. He listened to the Father. David, the poet-king, was a hero in God's plan to save mankind.

Words to Know:

    king   anoint   David   Goliath

42

Develop

1. Read paragraph 3 of the chapter with the students. You may read the entire story of David and Goliath from a children's Bible in 1 Sam 17:1–58.

2. Let the children dramatize this story. You, being the biggest in the class, can play Goliath. The children can wear costumes and use props. Let the children retell the story in their own words.

3. Discuss the story of David and Goliath:
   - What faith did David have?
   - Did Goliath believe in God, too?
   - Why was David willing to do battle?
   - What did he take into battle? What was his protection?
   - Did King Saul expect David to win?
   - Why did no one else fight this battle?

4. You may watch the video "David and Goliath," from the In the Beginning: Stories from the Bible series (available through Ignatius Press; 30 minutes).

5. Read the last two sentences of paragraph 3 again. Explain to the students that David was very good at writing down his prayers and expressing his love and trust in God. We still have many of his prayers even today. They are called the Psalms. We hear a psalm at each Mass. His most famous psalm is Psalm 23. You may read this psalm to the class. In the next lesson, we will learn more about the Psalms.

Name:_____

King David

Here is an English translation of Psalm 23 as we pray it in the Responsorial Psalm at Mass.

Fill in the blanks using the list of words on the right.

Response: The Lord is my _shepherd_; I shall not want.

The _Lord_ is my shepherd; I shall not want.
In verdant _pastures_ He gives me repose.
Beside _restful_ waters He leads me,
He refreshes my _soul_.

The Lord is my shepherd; I shall not want.

He guides me in _right_ paths
for _His_ name's sake.
Even though I walk in the _dark_ valley
I fear no evil; for _You_ are at my side
with Your rod and Your staff that give me courage.

The Lord is my shepherd; I shall not want.

You spread the table before _me_
in the sight of my foes;
You _anoint_ my head with _oil_;
my _cup_ overflows.

The Lord is my shepherd; I shall not want.

Only _goodness_ and kindness follow me
all the days of my _life_.
And I shall _dwell_ in the _house_
of the Lord for years to come!

The Lord is my shepherd; I shall not want.

1. shepherd
2. life
3. pastures
4. house
5. oil
6. I
7. His
8. goodness
9. Lord
10. me
11. want
12. right
13. dark
14. cup
15. You
16. soul
17. my
18. restful
19. dwell
20. anoint

30   *Faith and Life Series • Grade 3 • Chapter 8 • Lesson 2*

Reinforce

1. Have the students work on *Activity Book*, p. 30.

2. They may draw pictures of David and Goliath or illustrate Psalm 23.

3. Show the video "David and Goliath," from the In the Beginning: Stories from the Bible series (available through Ignatius Press; 30 minutes).

4. Have the students work on the Memorization Questions for this chapter.

Conclude

1. Lead the children in a closing prayer.

2. End class by singing "The King of love my shepherd is," *Adoremus Hymnal*, #580.

Preview

In the next lesson, the students will learn more about prayer and the Psalms of David.

WHERE DOES THE WORD "PSALM" COME FROM?

"Psalm" is the way we write the ancient Greek word ψαλμός, which means a song that is sung to a stringed instrument. There were many authors of psalms in the ancient world, but it is the collection of 150 Psalms, composed primarily by King David that have been handed down to us through the Church. The Psalms are beautiful expressions of praise and have been used in Christian worship since the earliest days of the Church.

NOTES

_____
_____
_____
_____
_____
_____
_____
_____
_____
_____
_____

LESSON THREE: PRAYER TO GOD

Aims

The students will review prayer and its forms.

They will learn that David taught man about loving God through prayer. David wrote many psalms, praising God.

The students will review the structure of the Mass and see when we say a psalm at Mass.

Materials

- *Activity Book*, p. 31
- Missal
- Bible or children's Bible

Optional:
- "The King of love my shepherd is," *Adoremus Hymnal*, #580
- Tape/CD of psalms

Begin

Review Psalm 23 with the children. This may be your opening prayer. Explain to the students that a psalm may be set to music. In fact, it has even been said that singing is praying twice when prayerful words are set to sacred music. Surely King David knew something of this.

David taught us a great deal about prayer, and today we will learn more about prayer, the psalms, and what King David knew about prayer.

Read this Psalm from the Bible and listen carefully to the words. Why do you think King David's poems are still so important today? Can you make up a prayer of praise in words of your own?

> The Lord is my shepherd,
>   I shall not want;
>   he makes me lie down in green pastures.
> He leads me beside still waters;
>   he restores my soul.
> He leads me in paths of righteousness
>   for his name's sake.
>
> Even though I walk through the valley
>   of the shadow of death,
>   I fear no evil;
> for thou art with me;
>   thy rod and thy staff
>   they comfort me.
>
> Thou preparest a table before me
>   in the presence of my enemies;
> thou anointest my head with oil,
>   my cup overflows.
> Surely goodness and mercy shall follow me
>   all the days of my life;
> and I shall dwell in the house of the Lord
>   for ever.
>
> Psalm 23

Develop

1. Read paragraph 4 of this chapter with the students.

2. Ask the children if they remember from yesterday's readings that David taught us about God's presence, His love for us, and our love for God. Prayer is a reminder of all three of these things. We pray to God Who hears all our prayers. We pray to God because He loves us, and we love Him.

3. We can pray out loud or in our hearts. Often we pray memorized prayers, but we can also pray whatever is on our minds or in our hearts. God wants to hear about what is important to us.

4. When we pray we can fold our hands, bow our heads, kneel, sit, or even stand. You may review various gestures of prayer with the students, particularly those used at your parish.

5. Prayer expresses many things: blessing and adoration, petition, intercession, thanksgiving, and praise. Using some of the suggested psalms, find examples of each of these forms of prayer.

6. Have the students take time to read some of the Psalms. You may also read some out loud to the class. What are some things common to the Psalms?

7. When is the psalm read or sung during the Mass? Between the first and second readings on Sunday, and after the first reading but before the Gospel at weekday Masses. The psalm is usually read with a response so that all people can pray what David wrote so well. What were some of the responses listed in our text?
- God is mighty and beautiful
- God is merciful
- We trust, love, and adore God
- We are sorry for sin, etc.

Name:_____

A Poem in Praise of God

King David taught us the importance of prayer.

Write a poem in praise of God.
Answers will vary
_____
_____
_____
_____
_____
_____
_____
_____
_____
_____
_____
_____
_____
_____

Faith and Life Series • Grade 3 • Chapter 8 • Lesson 2   31

LIST OF RECOMMENDED PSALMS

- Psalm 4
- Psalm 8
- Psalm 18:1–3
- Psalm 34:1–3
- Psalm 51
- Psalm 63
- Psalm 84
- Psalm 89:1–4
- Psalm 100
- Psalm 121
- Psalm 133
- Psalm 150

Reinforce

1. Take the children to church to pray their favorite psalms before Jesus present in the tabernacle.

2. Have the students collect their favorite psalms in a booklet, which they can decorate with pictures. They can also color their pictures or underline their favorite parts.

3. Have the students work on *Activity Book*, p. 31.

Conclude

1. Let the students take turns reading the psalms they wrote.

2. End class by singing "The King of love my shepherd is," *Adoremus Hymnal*, #580.

Preview

In the next lesson the students will learn more about David and how he foreshadowed Jesus.

NOTES
_____
_____
_____
_____
_____
_____
_____
_____
_____
_____
_____

LESSON FOUR:
A SON OF DAVID

Aims

The students will learn that God promised that the Savior would come from the descendants of David.

They will learn how David foreshadowed the Savior in many ways.

Materials

- *Activity Book*, p. 32
- Children's Bible
- Posterboards and markers
- Sunday Missal
- Statue of Jesus and a crown (you may need to make one)

Optional
- "The King of love my shepherd is," *Adoremus Hymnal*, #580

Begin

Tell the children that "foreshadow" means to give a type or an example for another to follow. There are similarities between two things, but one comes before another in time. The first would "foreshadow" the other. For example, ask the students if they remember the biblical account of Joseph and the coat of many colors? He had dreams and later went to Egypt. Think of another Joseph who also had dreams sent from God and who also went to Egypt. This latter Joseph was Jesus' foster-father! We can say the first Joseph foreshadowed Jesus' foster-father, Joseph.

Q. 37 *How could David prepare God's people for Jesus?*
David could prepare God's people for Jesus because David was a shepherd who took care of his flock, like Jesus the Good Shepherd. David was a wise and just king. He was willing to lay down his life by fighting Goliath for his people (1 Samuel 16:11–17).

Q. 38 *Why was David anointed with oil?*
David was anointed with oil as a sign of his authority to be a king chosen by God (1 Samuel 16:12–14).

Develop

1. Read paragraph 5 of this chapter with the students. Have them take turns reading sentences aloud.

2. Using each of the examples below have the students look up biblical passages to show how Jesus fulfills all the types that David had set forth:

David was a shepherd; Jesus is the Good Shepherd:
- Jn 10:11–16 • Ps 23 • Mk 6:34 • Rev 7:17

David was a wise and just king; Jesus is our King:
- Mt 2:2 • Mt 25:34 • Mt 27:11
- Jn 18:37 • Rev 15:3

David was willing to lay down his life for his people; Jesus loved us to the point of death:
- Jn 10:17 • Jn 15:13 • 1 Jn 3:16 • Jn 19:26–30

David listened to God the Father; Jesus did the Father's will:
- Mt 11:27 • Mt 26:39 • Jn 15:10

David played a role in God's plan of salvation; Jesus fulfilled God's plan of salvation:
- Acts 4:12 • Mt 1:21

3. Tell the children that the feast of Christ the King is celebrated on the last day of the Liturgical year. With a Sunday Missal, read some of the passages from the feast day to show that Christ is King. What are some of your parish traditions? You may even have a crowning ceremony for Jesus.

Name:_____

Word Find

Fill in the blanks with words from your textbook.

God chose <u>David</u> to be <u>king</u>, and to rule over his people after Saul died. David was only a young <u>shepherd</u> boy, but he turned out to be a very <u>kind</u> and strong <u>leader</u>, talented and clear-thinking in <u>battle</u>. He conquered <u>Jerusalem</u> and made it the city of his people. Best of all King David really <u>loved</u> God. Sometimes he fell into <u>sin</u>, but he was always <u>sorry</u> and came back to God. He helped his people to lead <u>good</u> lives. David was such a good king that God <u>promised</u> the <u>Savior</u>, the eternal <u>King</u>, would come into the world through his <u>family</u>. David, in fact, <u>foreshadowed</u> the Savior in many ways. Like <u>Jesus</u>, David was a good <u>shepherd</u> who took care of his flock. He was a <u>wise</u> and <u>just</u> king. He was willing to lay down his <u>life</u> for his people when he saved them from <u>Goliath</u>. He listened to the <u>father</u>. David the <u>poet</u>-king, was a <u>hero</u> in God's <u>plan</u> to save mankind.

32   Faith and Life Series • Grade 3 • Chapter 8 • Lesson 4

Reinforce

1. You may have a crowning ceremony for Jesus. Have a procession and sing "The King of love my shepherd is," *Adoremus Hymnal*, #580. Allow one of your students to crown Jesus. Take some time for silent prayer. At the end of the ceremony, you may celebrate with a party.

2. Have the students work on *Activity Book*, p. 32.

3. Allow the students to work on the Memorization Questions for this chapter.

4. Have the students draw posters paralleling King David and Jesus. They may use some of the biblical quotes referenced in class.

Conclude

End class with the crowning ceremony and the song "The King of love my shepherd is," *Adoremus Hymnal*, #580.

Preview

In the next lesson, the students' knowledge of the material covered this week will be reviewed and assessed.

FEAST OF CHRIST THE KING

After World War I, Pope Pius XI sought to unify the Church in the midst of the political instability of the secular world. One of the ways he did this was to establish the Feast of Christ the King on December 11, 1925. In this beautiful feast, Catholics recognize the supremacy of Christ over all human struggles and his kingship over the Church. As Pope Pius XI wrote in His encyclical establishing the feast, The Catholic Church, which is the kingdom of Christ on earth, destined to be spread among all men and all nations, should with every token of veneration salute her Author and Founder in her annual liturgy as King and Lord, and as King of Kings.

NOTES

CHAPTER EIGHT
REVIEW AND ASSESSMENT

Aims

The students' knowledge and understanding of the material covered this week will be reviewed and assessed.

Materials

- Quiz 8, Appendix, p. A-10
- Unit 2 Quiz, Appendix, pp. A-11 and A-12

Optional:
- "The King of love my shepherd is," *Adoremus Hymnal*, #580

Review

1. The students should understand that the Old Testament kings were anointed with oil as a sign of their sharing in God's power.

2. The students should understand the role of a king as well as the qualities of a good king (as demonstrated by King David).

3. The students should be able to recount the story of David and Goliath.

4. The students should understand that David wrote many psalms, and that they are still prayed at Mass.

5. The students should understand that David foreshadowed Jesus and they should be able to list the many ways he did so.

Name: _____

King David　　　　　　　　　　　　　Quiz 8

"If you love me, you will keep my commandments" (John 14:15).

Word Bank

honor	seven	neighbor	lie	manna
heart	three	joys	Mount Sinai	holy

Fill in the blanks with the correct words from the Word Bank.

1. On the journey to the Promised Land, God fed the Israelites with _manna_.

2. On top of _Mount Sinai_, God gave Moses the tablets of the Ten Commandments.

3. The first _three_ Commandments tell us how to worship and respect God.

4. The last _seven_ Commandments tell us how to be kind and fair to each other.

5. Jesus said, "You shall love the Lord your God with your whole _heart_, with your whole soul, and with your whole mind. This is the greatest and the first commandment."

6. "And the second is like it, you shall love your _neighbor_ as yourself."

7. If we follow His Commandments, God promises to share with us the _joys_ of Heaven which last forever.

8. God wants me to follow the Ten Commandments always, which means:
    a. To _honor_ my mother and father.
    b. To keep _holy_ the Lord's Day by going to church, praying, and not doing unnecessary work.
    c. To tell the truth and not to _lie_.

9. Write out the Scripture verse shown at the top of this page.

_____

A - 10　　　　　　　　　　　　　Faith and Life • Grade 3 • Appendix A

Assess

1. Distribute the quizzes and read through them with the students to be sure they understand the questions.

2. Administer the quiz. As they hand in their work you may orally quiz them on the Memorization Questions for this chapter.

3. After all the quizzes have been handed in, you may wish to review the correct answers with the class.

4. Repeat steps 1–3 for the unit quiz.

Conclude

Lead the children in singing "The King of love my shepherd is," *Adoremus Hymnal*, #580. You may wish to direct the crowning ceremony after the quizzes.

CHAPTER NINE
LOVING GOD MOST OF ALL

Catechism of the Catholic Church References

First Commandment:
 "You shall worship the Lord your God and Him only shall you serve": 2084–86, 2133–34
 "Him only shall you serve": 2095, 2135–36
 Prayer: 2098
 Promises and Vows: 2101–3
 Sacrifice: 2099–100
 Worship: 2096–100
 "You shall have no other gods before Me": 2100
 Agnosticism: 2127–28
 Atheism: 2123–26, 2140
 Divination and magic: 2115–17, 2138
 Idolatry: 2112–14, 2138
 Irreligion: 2118–22, 2139
 Superstition: 2111, 2138
 "You shall not make for yourself a graven image": 2129–32, 2141
 Jesus Hears and Answers our Prayers: 2616, 2621
 Sacramentals: 1667–79
Second Commandment:
 The Lord's Name is Holy: 2142–49, 2160–61, 2166
 Taking the Lord's Name in Vain: 2150–55, 2162–64
 The Christian Name: 2156–9, 2165, 2167
 Sign of the Cross: 2157, 2166

Scripture References

First Two Commandments: Ex 20:2–7

Background Reading: *The Fundamentals of Catholicism* by Fr. Kenneth Baker, S.J.

Volume 1:
"Adore God, and Him Alone," pp. 138–41
"The Need for Sacrifice," pp. 141–44
"Watch and Pray," pp. 144–46
"Superstition Wears Many Faces," pp. 147–50
"Modern Idolators," pp. 150–52
"Treat Holy Things in a Holy Manner," pp. 153–55
"Blessed Be the Name of the Lord Forever," pp. 158–61
Swearing, Perjury, Vows, Blasphemy, Cursing, pp. 161–69

Summary of Lesson Content

Lesson 1

God is perfect. This lesson will review God's perfections.

Man is made to know, love, and serve God in this world so that we will be happy with him in the next. This lesson will review the virtues of faith, hope, and charity. Additionally, it will review the duties of religion: worship and prayer in its various forms.

Angels, too, are creatures who give worship to God.

Lesson 2

The First Commandment is "I am the Lord your God. You shall not have other gods before Me."

God is the One True God.

Idolatry and superstition are sins against the First Commandment.

Lesson 3

The Second Commandment is "You shall not take the name of the Lord your God in vain."

The name of God is holy and should be blessed and revered.

Blasphemy, false oaths, and any disrespectful use of God's name or the names of the saints are sins against the Second Commandment.

Lesson 4

The Second Commandment tells man to respect holy places and things.

Proper gestures and postures show our reverence in holy places.

Sacramentals are holy things that should be respected.

LESSON ONE: LOVING GOD

Aims

The students will review the perfections of God.

They will learn that man is made to know, love, and serve God in this world, in order to be happy with Him in the next.

They will review the virtues of faith, hope, and charity. In addition, they will review the duties of religion: worship and prayer.

The students will also learn that angels are creatures who worship God.

Materials

- *Activity Book*, p. 33
- Prayer cards with the Acts of Faith, Hope, and Love

Optional:
- "Holy God we praise thy name," *Adoremus Hymnal*, #461

Begin

Begin the class by asking the children why they love God. Allow each child to give an answer. Also ask them if they can ever love God too much. Use this time to review God's attributes: eternal, ever present, all loving, all good, all holy, all merciful, etc.

Develop

1. Read the first two paragraphs from the student text. Have the students take turns reading sentences aloud.

2. From the student text, review some of God's gifts. Ask the children to name some of God's gifts in their lives. Allow each child to answer.

3. In the second paragraph, the student text names some ways we can give worship to God: adoration, worship, prayer, belief, hope, love, and praise.

4. Review the reasons we were made to know, love, and serve God in this world: so we can be happy with Him forever in Heaven.

5. Explain to the children that God gave us three gifts at our Baptism that help us to love God in return: the theological virtues of faith, hope, and love.

6. Review the theological virtues with the children:
- Faith: to believe in God and to know Him
- Hope: to trust in His promises for us
- Love: to desire union with God

Have the students give examples of these virtues.

7. Teach the children the meaning of the virtue of religion: to give just worship to God because He is God. It is a way of expressing our faith, hope, and love. Which words in the student text help explain the ways in which we live our religious obedience? Worship, adoration, and praise. Ask the children how they live their religion. They go to Mass, say prayers, and love their neighbors.

8. Teach the children that even the angels adore and praise God, for they, too, are His creatures. What is the prayer of the angels in the student text? Have the children think of their own prayers of praise and adoration. You may take them to visit Jesus in the tabernacle.

---

9 Loving God Most of All

"And you shall love the LORD your God with all your heart, and with all your soul, and with all your might."

Deuteronomy 6:5

Our God is so holy and magnificent that we can never love Him too much. He is our Creator and King. He is also a loving Father Who cares for us more than anyone else in the world can. We cannot see God, but He is with us all the time. Everything we have is a gift from Him. He gave us our life, our family, our beautiful world, and many other gifts.

Because God is perfect and can do all things, we give to Him something that we do not give to anyone else. We adore and worship Him. We pray to Him, believe in Him, hope in Him, and love Him. The angels also praise and adore God. They appeared to shepherds in Bethlehem when Jesus was born, singing, "Glory to God in the highest, and on earth peace among men with whom He is pleased."

God Himself told us in the First Commandment, "I am the Lord your God. You shall not have other gods before Me." In this Commandment, He asks us to know that He is the one, true God and to love Him above all things.

The "other gods" that God told us not to worship are everyday persons, places, or things that can lead us away from Him. Some examples might be money, pleasures, toys, or nice clothes. These things are good and we can enjoy them, but we must not let them take our attention away from God. The things of this earth will pass

45

Name:_____

God's Gifts

God loves us so much! He gives us many gifts. He gives us life, our family, His Church and His word. We have so many reasons to thank God! One of the ways we can show God that we are thankful for these gifts is to give gifts back to God. Our prayer is a gift to God. Acts of charity and obedience are gifts to God. Learning about God and His Church is a gift to God. Can you think of some ways to give gifts to God?

Draw yourself giving a gift to God.

My gift to God is: _____

Faith and Life Series • Grade 3 • Chapter 9 • Lesson 1

ACT OF HOPE

O my God, relying on Thy almighty power and infinite mercy and promises, I hope to obtain pardon of my sins, the help of Thy grace, and life everlasting, through the merits of Jesus Christ, my Lord and Redeemer. *Amen.*

Reinforce

1. Have the students work on *Activity Book*, p. 33.

2. Teach the students to sing "Holy God we praise thy name," *Adoremus Hymnal*, #461. Review with them the student text and the reverent words of praise and adoration.

3. If you can, take the children to visit Jesus in the tabernacle, or arrange for a time of Eucharistic adoration.

4. Have the children work on memorizing the Acts of Faith, Hope, and Love.

Conclude

Lead the children in praying the Acts of Faith, Hope, and Love.

Preview

Ask the children to bring magazines or newspapers to the next class. You may wish to provide these for the students.

In the next lesson, the students will review the First Commandment.

NOTES

LESSON TWO: THE FIRST COMMANDMENT

Aims

The students will learn that the First Commandment is "I am the Lord your God. You shall not have other gods before Me."

They will learn that God is the One True God.

They will learn about idolatry and superstition and that they are sins against the First Commandment.

Materials

- *Activity Book*, p. 34
- Magazines, scissors, glue, paper, pencils

Optional:
- "Holy God we praise thy name," *Adoremus Hymnal*, #461

Begin

Write the First Commandment on the board. Have the children write it on the top of a piece of paper, and then break into pairs to memorize this Commandment. Discuss what this Commandment means: only God is the One True God—everything else is not. We owe God all of our love and we should worship Him because He is our God.

"O LORD, our Lord, how majestic is thy name in all the earth!"
Psalm 8:9

away, but God is for ever and He has destined us to live with Him for ever. Nothing on earth can compare with God and the treasures that He gives. That is why He comes first.

God does not want us to be superstitious. To be **superstitious** is to believe in or trust in something other than God. This would insult Our Lord instead of giving Him glory.

The Second Commandment is: "You shall not take the name of the Lord your God in vain." We are only to use the name of God to speak to Him or about Him in a **reverent** or loving way.

People in the Old Testament knew how great God is, so they were very careful when they spoke His name. When Jesus came to earth, He encouraged us to call on God's name often. He taught us a prayer that we still say together at every Mass. "Our Father, Who art in Heaven, hallowed be Thy name. . . ." Hallowed means holy. The name of God is holy and it has power. We know this because the Apostles worked many miracles in Jesus' name. Jesus promised, "Whatever you ask in My name will be done."

The name of Jesus is just as powerful today. If you are lonely or afraid, call on Jesus' name. He will come to you. If you are confused or have a problem at home or at school, call on Jesus' name. He will help you. Jesus hears us every time we call. At Benediction, we praise Him for this by joyfully saying, "Blessed be God. Blessed be His holy name."

The Second Commandment also tells us to **respect**, or think highly of, holy places and things. A church is a holy place. When we

47

Develop

1. Read paragraphs 3–5 with the students. They may take turns reading sentences aloud.

2. Ask the students to name some "other gods." Have them take out their magazines or newspaper clippings. (Encourage the students who have them to share with students who forgot them.) Have the students cut out pictures of "other gods"—everyday persons, places, and things that we can make into gods. Have each student cut out a picture and prepare an explanation to present to the class. The students' explanations should answer the question: "Why is it that the pictures you cut out can seem to be 'other gods'?" You may also ask the children what these things are meant to be used for, and how we can use such things to give glory to God. For example, television can be very good, and good programs can teach us to love God and neighbor, and even teach us about our faith! Television can become an "other god" when we choose to watch it too much, or if we watch it instead of saying our prayers or going to Mass. Have the students make their presentations.

3. Ask the students if they know any common superstitions. These may include simple superstitions such as walking under ladders, black cats, and spilt salt, etc. Ask the students why these things are wrong. If the students cannot name any, simply mention that some people place faith in things other than God. This insults God and is contrary to His Laws.

4. Review the proper ways to obey the First Commandment: faith, hope, love, and religion. Again, have the students give examples of each of these virtues.

5. This is a good opportunity to review proper church etiquette. Be sure to explain genuflecting, bowing to the altar, being silent in church, visiting Jesus in the tabernacle, paying attention at Mass, and not disturbing others.

Name:_____

Putting God First

As Catholics, we must always put God first. We do this when we worship God, when we pray, when we obey God's laws and when we love God and neighbor.

Write examples of how you can put God first.

Answers will vary.

_____
_____
_____
_____
_____

Everything God created is good, but sometimes we give things too much value. Money, power, and pleasures can all be false gods, or we we can use them to give God glory.

Write the ways we can glorify God with this gifts.

Gift	How to Use It to Give God Glory
Money	Give it to the poor
Music	**Answers will vary.**
Television	
Talents	
Toys	
Nice Clothes	
Pets	
Nice Home	

Faith and Life Series • Grade 3 • Chapter 9 • Lesson 2

SAINT THOMAS AQUINAS FACTS

Did you know that Saint Thomas Aquinas:

- Wrote many beautiful songs of love and adoration to our Lord, e.g., Tantum Ergo, O Salutaris Hostia, etc.

- Had a vision of God so beautiful that he regarded everything else on earth, even his own work, as "straw;" Saint Thomas Aquinas knew that God is more wonderful that even the greatest things on earth

Reinforce

1. Have the students work on *Activity Book*, p. 34. They may make presentations based on their work.

2. Give the students time to continue memorizing the Acts of Faith, Hope, and Love.

3. Give the students time to work on the first two Memorization Questions, which address the First Commandment. They also need to memorize the First Commandment.

Conclude

1. Lead the students in praying the Acts of Faith, Hope, and Love.

2. Sing "Holy God we praise thy name," *Adoremus Hymnal*, #461.

Preview

In the next lesson, the students will learn the Second Commandment.

NOTES

LESSON THREE: THE SECOND COMMANDMENT

Aims

The students will learn that the Second Commandment is "You shall not take the name of the Lord your God in vain."

They will learn that the name of God is holy and should be blessed and revered.

They will learn that blasphemy, false oaths, and any disrespectful use of God's name or the names of the saints are sins against the Second Commandment.

Materials

- *Activity Book*, p. 35
- Set of prayer cards (preferably of the students' patron saints)

Optional:
- "Holy God we praise thy name," *Adoremus Hymnal*, #461

Begin

Have the students work on their Memorization Questions. As they do this, set up a table and two chairs at the back of the room. Explain to the children that you will call each of them by name. When each child hears his name, he may come to you. You may give each child his prayer card when he comes to the table.

Develop

1. Stress that the children knew who you were talking about when you called their names. For example, when you called Ann's name, Elizabeth did not come. If we are trying to get someone's attention, we call him by name. Our names are very important, which is why it is mean to make fun of someone's name. Another way of demonstrating the importance of names is by reminding the children of proper forms of address. For example, they can say "Miss _____ (your name), I need help," or they could be rude and say, "hey you," or another inappropriate form of address. Which do they think would be most likely to please you?

2. *Read paragraphs 6–8 with the students. Have them take turns reading sentences aloud.*

3. Explain that calling someone's name brings his presence. For example, if they say "Mom, I need help," or "Miss ___, I need help," they will be helped. It would be wrong if they called you over and then said, "Never mind," or "I was just playing a mean game to get you to come over." It is important to say God's name only when we want to be with Him in prayer.

4. Also, ask the children how they address their parents: usually "Mom" or "Dad" or a variation of these. The students address their friends' parents as "Mr. or Mrs. _____." Their parents' adult friends address their parents by their first names. The way we address someone says something about our relationship with him. God allows us to call Him "Father." This means that God wants us to have a very close relationship with Him, for He loves us as His own children. What a special gift that is.

5. *Explain to the children that praying in Jesus' name is very powerful. When we do this, we unite ourselves to Him and His prayers, so we are never praying alone. He, too, is asking the Father that God's will be done.*

---

go into a church, we can show love for God by quietly listening to the priest and obeying our parents. We can turn to Jesus in the tabernacle or look at the image of Jesus on the crucifix, and we can pray. We should genuflect and make the Sign of the Cross when we leave. God will bless us for these acts of love.

Whether we are in a church, a park, our home, or a car, we can always praise God. We can tell Him silently or quietly that we believe in Him, hope in Him, and love Him most of all.

A Song of Praise:

HOLY GOD, WE PRAISE THY NAME

Holy God we praise Thy name!
    Lord of all, we bow before Thee!
All on earth Thy sceptre claim.
    All in Heaven above adore Thee.
Infinite Thy vast domain,
    Everlasting is Thy reign!

> **Q. 39** *What does the First Commandment, "I am the Lord your God; you shall not have other gods before Me" tell us to do?*
> The First Commandment tells us to believe in God and to love Him, to adore Him, and to serve Him alone (CCC 2084).

Name:_____

Keeping God's Commandments

1. What words are used in the text to describe God?
Holy, magnificent, Creator, King, loving Father

2. What gifts does God give us?
Everything we have is a gift from Him. He gave us our life, our family, our beautiful world, and many other gifts.

3. What do we give to God that we do not give to anyone else?
We praise and adore Him.

4. What are "other gods"?
Everyday persons, places, or things that can lead us away from Him.

5. What does the student text tell us about God's name?
God's name is holy and has power.

6. When can you call upon the name of Jesus?
When we are lonely or afraid

7. What are some holy places and things we should respect?
Churches, tabernacles, and crucifixes

Faith and Life Series • Grade 3 • Chapter 9 • Lesson 3   35

Reinforce

1. Have the students work on *Activity Book*, p. 35.

2. Have the students continue working on the Memorization Questions, the Acts of Faith, Hope, and Love, and the first two Commandments.

3. Discuss the words of "Holy God we Praise Thy Name," *Adoremus Hymnal*, #461 and how singing this song prayerfully is a way of respecting and keeping the Second Commandment.

Conclude

1. Pray the Acts of Faith, Hope, and Love.

2. Sing "Holy God we praise thy name," *Adoremus Hymnal*, #461.

Preview

In the next lesson, the students will learn how to respect holy places and things, and how to be reverent.

PATRON SAINTS

Many Catholic children are named for canonized saints. The saint for which a child is named provides both an excellent Christian example for the child and valuable intercession as the child's patron saint. According to the *Catechism of the Catholic Church*, "In Baptism, the Lord's name sanctifies man, and the Christian receives his name in the Church. This can be the name of a saint, that is, of a disciple who has lived a life of exemplary fidelity in the Lord. The patron saint provides a model of charity; we are assured of his intercession."

From the *Catechism of the Catholic Church*, #2156

NOTES

LESSON FOUR: REVERENCE

Aims

The students will learn that the Second Commandment tells man to respect holy places and things.

They will review and practice proper gestures and postures to show reverence in holy places.

The students will learn that sacramentals are holy things that should be respected.

Materials

- *Activity Book*, p. 36
- Sacramentals: e.g., prayer cards, medals, rosaries, statues, scapulars, an advent wreath, holy water, etc.
- Church tour/pictures

Optional:
- "Holy God we praise thy name," *Adoremus Hymnal*, #461
- Ceremony of the blessing of sacramentals by a priest

Begin

Have a priest come in and explain sacramentals and blessings. He can bless the children, as well as a rosary or medal for each of the children. Remind the children that sacramentals lead us closer to God; e.g., holy water reminds us of our Baptism, and recalls God's plan of salvation.

Q. 40 *What does the First Commandment tell us not to do?*
The First Commandment tells us not to put anyone or anything before God. This means we are not to be impious, superstitious, or irreligious. Also, we must not deny the truths taught to us by the Church (CCC 88, 2110).

Q. 41 *What does the Second Commandment, "You shall not take the name of the Lord your God in vain," tell us to do?*
The Second Commandment tells us to keep the name of God holy, and to honor the vows and promises we have made (CCC 2142, 2147).

Q. 42 *What does the Second Commandment tell us not to do?*
The Second Commandment tells us not to use the name of God without respect, blaspheme God or the most holy Virgin, the saints, or holy things. We also must not swear oaths that are false, unnecessary, or wrong in any way (CCC 2150, 2155).

Words to Know:

superstitious   reverent   respect

Develop

1. Finish reading the chapter with the children. They may take turns reading aloud.

2. If possible, take the children on a church tour. If it is not possible, use pictures to explain the importance of various places in the church.
   - Baptismal font—at Baptism they became God's children
   - Holy water font—blessing ourselves with holy water reminds us of our Baptism.
   - Pews—where we participate in the Mass
   - Sanctuary—this sacred area is where the Mass is celebrated
   - The altar—this is where the sacrifice of the Mass occurs, and from this table we receive Holy Communion. (We bow to the altar as a sign of reverence.)
   - The ambo—where the word of God is proclaimed. God feeds us with His word in the Liturgy of the Word. He feeds us with the Eucharist in the Liturgy of the Eucharist
   - Presider's chair—this is where the priest sits to preside over the Mass
   - Crucifix—reminds us how much God loves us and how Jesus died for our sins to give us a share in God's life
   - Choir area—the music helps us to pray the Mass. You may have the children sing "Holy God we praise thy name," *Adoremus Hymnal*, #461 in the choir area
   - Tabernacle—this is where Jesus is present. (Remind the children to genuflect.) Take a moment for silent prayer

Remind the children that church is a sacred place. They must be reverent and silent in church, so they can pray and hear God and allow others to do the same.

3. Review the various places for prayer, gestures, and types of prayer (vocal, silent, etc.). Teach them that sacramentals can help them to pray.

Name:_____

Respect and Reverence for God

The Second Commandment tells us to respect holy places and to have reverence for the name of God.

Color the picture below.

36

Faith and Life Series • Grade 3 • Chapter 9 • Lesson 4

Reinforce

1. Have the students color *Activity Book*, p. 36.

2. Have the students continue working on their Memorization Questions.

3. Lead the children in a review for the quiz to be held in the next class.

Conclude

1. Lead the children in praying the Acts of Faith, Hope, and Love.

2. Sing "Holy God we praise thy name," *Adoremus Hymnal*, #461.

Preview

In the next lesson, the students' knowledge of the material covered this week will be reviewed and assessed.

SACRAMENTALS

- What are sacramentals?

"Sacramentals are sacred signs instituted by the Church. They prepare men to receive the fruit of the sacraments and sanctify different circumstances of life.

Among the sacramentals blessings occupy an important place. They include both praise of God for his works and gifts, and the Church's intercession for men that they may be able to use God's gifts according to the spirit of the Gospel."

From the *Catechism of the Catholic Church*, #1677–78. See also #1678.

NOTES

_____
_____
_____
_____
_____
_____
_____
_____
_____
_____

CHAPTER NINE
REVIEW AND ASSESSMENT

Aims

The students' knowledge of the material covered this week will be reviewed and assessed.

Materials

- Quiz 9, Appendix, p. A-13

Optional:
- "Holy God we praise thy name," *Adoremus Hymnal*, #461

Review

1. Review the First Commandment.

2. Review the perfections of God.

3. Review the virtues of faith, hope, charity, and religion.

4. Review that even the angels give worship to God.

5. Review what some "other gods" may be.

6. Review that God is the One True God.

7. Review the Second Commandment.

8. Review the importance of God's name.
- It is to be revered
- It brings us into God's presence
- It is powerful to pray in the name of Jesus
- It must not be said in vain (needlessly or irreverently)

9. Review that holy places and things must be respected.

10. Review proper gestures and church etiquette.

11. Review sacramentals.

Name: _____

Loving God Most of All   Quiz 9

"Every day I will bless thee and praise thy name for ever" (Psalm 145:2).

Word Bank

| anything | gods | tabernacle | Name | superstitious |
| love | Lord | holy | loving | |

Fill in the blanks with the correct words from the Word Bank.

1. The First Commandment is "I am the Lord your God; you shall not have other _gods_ before Me."

2. The First Commandment tells us to adore and worship God. We pray to Him, believe in Him, hope in Him, and _love_ Him.

3. The First Commandment tells us not to put anyone or _anything_ before God.

4. God does not want us to be _superstitious_, believing that created things have powers that only God possesses.

5. The Second Commandment is "You shall not take the name of the _Lord_ your God in vain. We must never curse God's Holy Name.

6. The Second Commandment tells us to use the name of God to speak to Him or about Him in a reverent or _loving_ way.

7. Sentences such as "O God" or "O my God," when one is angry, frightened, or surprised, use God's _Name_ in the wrong way.

8. In the Our Father we say "Our Father, Who art in Heaven, hallowed by Thy Name." Hallowed means _holy_.

9. We are to show respect in holy places. In church while waiting for Mass to begin we can look at the _tabernacle_ or Jesus on the crucifix and we can pray.

10. Write out the Scripture verse shown at the top of this page.

_____

Faith and Life • Grade 3 • Appendix A   A - 13

Assess

1. Distribute the quizzes and read through them with the students to be sure they understand the questions.

2. Administer the quiz. As they hand in their work, you may orally quiz them on the Memorization Questions for this chapter.

3. After all the quizzes have been handed in, you may wish to review the correct answers with the class.

Conclude

1. Pray the Acts of Faith, Hope, and Love.

2. Sing "Holy God we praise thy name," *Adoremus Hymnal*, #461.

CHAPTER TEN
THE LORD'S DAY

Catechism of the Catholic Church References

Third Commandment:
　　Sabbath Day: 2168–73, 2189–90
　　Sunday: The Lord's Day: 1166–67
　　Day of Resurrection: The New Creation: 2174, 2191

Sunday: Fulfillment of the Sabbath: 2175–76, 2190
Sunday Mass: 2177–79
Sunday Obligation: 2180–83, 2192
Day of Grace and Rest from Work: 2184–88, 2193–95

Scripture References

The Third Commandment: Ex 20:8–11

Background Reading: *The Fundamentals of Catholicism* by Fr. Kenneth Baker, S.J.

Volume 1:
"Christ, the Rising Sun of Justice," pp. 170–72
" What about the Sunday Rest," pp. 173–75

Summary of Lesson Content

Lesson 1

In the story of Creation, God rested on the seventh day.

Man is to rest and worship God on one day of the week. In the Jewish tradition, this is Saturday, the Sabbath. In the Christian tradition, we worship and rest on Sunday, the day Our Lord rose from the dead.

Lesson 2

The Third Commandment is "Remember to keep holy the Lord's Day."

On Sunday, we celebrate the miracle of Jesus' Resurrection.

On Sunday, we go to Mass. Man is to offer himself to the Father and may receive Our Lord in Holy Communion. Man receives many blessings on Sunday.

Lesson 3

Included in the Third Commandment are the Holy Days of Obligation.

During this lesson, we will review the Sunday Mass obligation and the Holy Days of Obligation.

Lesson 4

Sunday is a day of rest and also a day to spend with family.

It is also good to perform acts of charity on Sunday.

LESSON ONE: THE LORD'S DAY

Aims

The students will learn the story of Creation, noting that God rested on the seventh day.

The students will learn that man is to rest and worship God on one day of the week. In the Jewish tradition, the Sabbath is celebrated on Saturday. In the Christian tradition, we worship and rest on Sunday, the day Our Lord rose from the dead.

Materials

- *Activity Book*, p. 37
- *Hymnal*, #610
- Children's Bible
- "The Story of Creation," video; The Beginner's Bible, available through Ignatius Press

Optional:
- "On this day, the first of days," *Adoremus*

Begin

Read the story of Creation or watch the video "The Story of Creation," from The Beginner's Bible series (available through Ignatius Press; 30 minutes). Point out that God rested on the seventh day.

The story of Creation is found in Gen 1:1—2:3.

Develop

1. Read the first paragraph from the student text.

2. Explain that the Sabbath was a holy day for the Jewish people. It was the day of rest on which man would worship God. It was a day set apart to remember our covenant with God, as well as a day on which to give God the worship that was due to Him.

3. The word "sabbath" means "set apart." One day out of each week—the seventh day, now known as Saturday—was kept holy by the Jews. The Third Commandment is "Remember to keep holy the Sabbath." It has its origin in Gen 2:2, wherein the Bible tells us that God rested on the seventh day.

4. How did the Jews keep the Sabbath? They did not do any unnecessary work. They would not cook, clean, or even walk unnecessarily. They would rest, pray, and worship God as a family.

5. In the Bible, the number 7 means "perfect." It symbolizes the perfection of all creation. Christ rose from the dead on the first day of the week, so the disciples—and now all Christians—keep the first day, Sunday, holy as the Lord's Day. Sunday is sometimes known as the eighth day (7 + 1). The number eight means "super-perfect," the super-perfection of God. Every Sunday, we celebrate Christ's victory over death in the Resurrection.

6. How do Christians keep the Lord's Day? We go to Mass, rest from unnecessary work, spend time with our families, and pray. You may ask the children what family traditions they have on the Lord's Day—some may do readings from the Bible, go to CCD, play games as a family, have a special meal, etc.

Name:_____

Sundays are Special

Sundays are special and they are holy! We are to do our best to keep them holy. We are to avoid any unnecessary work and take time for God and neighbor. We can take time for God by going to Mass, praying, reading our Bible or a holy book, or serving our neighbor. We can take time for our neighbor by spending time with family and friends, or by helping other people to come to know God through our words and actions.

Draw a picture to illustrate how you can make Sunday Special.

I can keep Sunday holy by: _____

Faith and Life Series • Grade 3 • Chapter 10 • Lesson 1   37

Reinforce

1. Have the children work on *Activity Book*, p. 37.

2. Have the students memorize the Third Commandment. Review the first three Commandments with the children.

3. Teach the children to sing "On this day, the first of days," *Adoremus Hymnal*, #610. Review the words with them. What does this song teach them about keeping the Lord's Day?

Conclude

End class by praying the Acts of Faith, Hope, and Love.

Preview

In the next lesson, the students will learn more about the Mass. You will need a class set of missals, preferably children's missals.

JEWISH TRADITIONS ON THE SABBATH

At the time of Jesus, it was customary for Jews to rest from all work on the seventh day of the week, the Sabbath. The pharisees, however, wanted a "buffer zone" around the Commandments; in particular, the Third Commandment. Not only could the Jews not work on the Sabbath, it was illegal for them to perform simple tasks, such as cooking, cleaning, picking things up. In some cases, even acts of mercy on the Sabbath were frowned upon, as we see in Lk 13:14: "...the ruler of the synagogue, indignant because Jesus had healed on the sabbath, said to the people, 'There are six days on which work ought to be done; come on those days to be healed and not on the sabbath day.'"

NOTES

LESSON TWO: THE MASS

Aims

The students will learn about the Third Commandment

The students will focus on the Mass. In the Mass, we offer ourselves to the Father and may receive Our Lord in Holy Communion. We receive many blessings on Sunday. The students will review the responses of the Mass.

Materials

- Children's missals with all the responses of the Mass.
- *Activity Book*, p. 38
- Poster boards, markers, or crayons

Optional:
- "On this day, the first of days," *Adoremus Hymnal*, #610

Begin

Read paragraphs 2 and 3 with the children. The students may take turns reading the sentences aloud.

Review the duty of attending Mass every week on Sunday or Saturday night. If there is a Mass attendance problem, ask the children to suggest ways that they can encourage their parents to take them, or find another way to Mass if their parents are not going.

---

10   The Lord's Day

> "This is the day which the LORD has made; let us rejoice and be glad in it."
>
> Psalm 118:24

When God created the world, He worked for six days and on the seventh He rested. God values the work we do, but He wants us to take one day of the week to rest, too. He also wants us to use that day to join others in worship. In the Old Testament, God's people stopped working and gathered together for worship on the Sabbath, or Saturday. However, the early Christians rested and came together to rejoice on Sunday because Jesus, Our Lord and Savior, rose from the dead on Easter Sunday morning.

We still keep Sunday as a special day to celebrate the miracle of the Resurrection. God is very pleased when we do this because His Third Commandment to us is, "Remember to keep holy the Lord's Day."

The greatest gift that we can offer to God on His day is to go to Mass faithfully. At every Mass, we give ourselves to God and join ourselves with Christ's gift of Himself to the Father. The Father in turn gives us His own Son as "the Bread of Life," Who nourishes our souls. This makes Sunday not only a day of praise but also a day of blessings and joy.

Holy Days of Obligation, like Christmas, All Saints' Day, the Feast of the Ascension, and the Feast of the Immaculate Conception are considered just as special as Sundays. They are days we mark as celebrations or feasts of special worship. God wants us to keep those days holy, too, by praying, going to Mass, and not working.

51

Develop

1. Hand out the children's missals.

2. Read through the Mass with the children. Help them to memorize the responses of the Mass.

3. Have each child make a poster to show the parts of the Mass and the appropriate responses. Sometimes there is more than one option; if this is the case, have the children include all possible responses. Using the posters, cover all the parts of the Mass. Display the posters around the classroom, and leave them up throughout the week so that they may be reviewed regularly.

Note: Very often the children know what the responses sound like, but are unsure of the words or what they mean. Be sure to go through prayers line by line and explain the meanings of harder words. Also, be sure they clearly pronounce each word. This is also a good time to review various gestures, e.g., "A reading from the Gospel according to ____." "Glory to you O Lord." (Tell them to trace little crosses on their foreheads, lips, and heart while silently praying: "May the Lord be in our thoughts, on our lips, and in our hearts.")

Regularly quiz the children on the proper responses, prayers, and gestures.

4. Ask the children which parts of the Mass are their favorites—they can point to the appropriate poster. Discuss these with the children.

5. Explain how the laity participate in the Mass: We sing the songs, pray the prayers, and say the correct responses. During the Mass, we unite ourselves with Jesus as He offers Himself to the Father in Heaven. In turn, the Father gives us His Son, Whom we receive in Holy Communion. Review the steps for receiving Communion.

Name:_____

God's Special Day

Christians keep Sundays as special days to celebrate the miracle of Jesus' Resurrection. The greatest gift we can offer to God on His day is to go to Mass faithfully. At every Mass we give ourselves to God and join ourselves with Christ's gift of Himself to the Father. The Father in turn gives us His own Son as "the Bread of Life," Who nourishes our souls. This makes Sunday not only a day of praise but also a day of blessings and joy.

1. What is the Third Commandment?

Remember the Lord's Day

2. What are we ordered to do by the Third Commandment?

Honor God on Sundays and Holy Days of Obligation by taking part in Holy Mass

3. What is forbidden by the Third Commandment?

Doing unnecessary work on Sundays and Holy Days of Obligation

38 Faith and Life Series • Grade 3 • Chapter 10 • Lesson 2

Reinforce

1. Review the steps for receiving Holy Communion:
- Be free from mortal sin (may need to the Sacrament of Penance)
- Fast for one hour (only medicine and water)
- Actively participate in the Mass
- Know Whom you are about to receive
- Receive our Lord with love and devotion
- Make a thanksgiving

2. Have the students work on *Activity Book*, p. 38.

3. Have the students work on the Memorization Questions.

Conclude

1. Lead the children in praying the Acts of Faith, Hope and Love.

2. Sing "On this day, the first of days," *Adoremus Hymnal*, #610.

Preview

In the next lesson, the students will review the liturgical calendar and the Holy Days of Obligation.

POPE SAINT PIUS X AND FIRST COMMUNION

Before 1910, many young children were not receiving Holy Communion. Except when a child's life was in question, First Communion was often deferred until well after a child had attained the age of discretion (around seven years old). Pope Saint Pius X decreed that young children should receive first Communion as soon as possible after reaching the age of discretion. In "Quam Singulari," promulgated on August 15, 1910, he called for a return to the obligations supported by the Fourth Lateran Council, the Council of Trent, and Saint Thomas Aquinas. Both of these councils and Saint Thomas determined that the Sacraments of Penance and the Eucharist should be granted as soon as a child attains the age of discretion or "some use of reason."

NOTES

LESSON THREE: THE CHURCH YEAR

Aims

The students will learn about the Church year by using the liturgical calendar.

They will learn about the Holy Days of Obligation.

They will learn that the Holy Days of Obligation are included among the obligations of the Third Commandment.

Materials

- Appendix, pp. B-16 and B-17
- Markers/crayons
- "On this day, the first of days," *Adoremus Hymnal*, #610

Begin

Review the Memorization Questions for this chapter.

What does the Third Commandment, "Remember to keep holy the Lord's Day," tell us to do?

What does the Third Commandment tell us not to do?

The Church's Calendar

Read the following to know how to color in the circular calendar on the next page. (You will need these colors: purple, green, red, and possibly a golden yellow.)

When the priest celebrates Mass, you have probably noticed that the color of his vestments changes according to the liturgical season. This liturgical calendar is basically divided into the fifty-two Sundays of the Church year.

There are two very great feasts: 1) the feast of Easter, most important for the Christian because in it we celebrate the death and Resurrection of Jesus; and 2) the feast of Christmas, December 25, which falls on a Sunday every few years, and which has three Sundays of feast after it. The priest wears white, the color of light, during these feasts; but you can use gold, too, to color in the cross and star.

Purple is a symbol of waiting and a preparing for a feast. The greater the preparation, the greater the feast! Color the four Sundays of Advent and the six Sundays of Lent in purple.

From Easter to Pentecost is "the Great Sunday": seven Sundays of feast. The priest wears white all during this Easter Season.

The eighth Sunday is Pentecost, the feast of the Holy Spirit. (Remember the meaning of the number eight!) Color Pentecost red.

The other Sundays the priest wears green. They are called Sundays in Ordinary Time.

After you have colored in your liturgical calendar, you can use it to help you and your family keep track of the liturgical seasons of the year.

B - 16   Faith and Life • Grade 3 • Appendix B

Develop

1. Read paragraph 4 with the students.

2. What are the Holy Days of Obligation in the United States? List them on the board and explain each of them:
- *Nativity of Our Lord (Christmas):* the birth of Jesus
- *Epiphany:* wise men brought gifts and worshiped Jesus
- *Ascension of Christ:* Jesus went to Heaven bodily 50 days after His Resurrection
- *Corpus Christi:* Feast of the Body and Blood of Jesus truly present in the Eucharist
- *Mary, the Mother of God:* Mary, as the mother of Jesus, is the Mother of God
- *Immaculate Conception:* Mary was conceived without Original Sin
- *Assumption of Mary:* Mary went to Heaven body and soul
- *All Saints:* celebrates everyone in Heaven

3. We are obliged to go to Mass on Sundays and Holy Days of Obligation.

4. Explain that the Church year begins on the first Sunday of Advent. Teach the children the color of each liturgical season:
- Green: Ordinary Time (life, hope, growth)
- Red: Pentecost, martyrs, Passion, and Holy Spirit (blood and fire)
- White: Easter, feasts of the Blessed Mother, saints, Jesus' life and mysteries, Baptisms, weddings, funerals, virgins, pastors (sometimes gold is worn for the mysteries of Christ)
- Purple/Violet: Advent, Lent (penance and preparation)
- Black: All Souls Day and sometimes funerals
- Rose: Halfway through advent and lent
- Blue: sometimes a priest will wear white with a blue stole for feasts of the Blessed Mother

5. Using the calendar on pp. B-16 and B-17 of the Appendix, color the weeks and add the Holy Days of Obligation.

The Church's Calendar

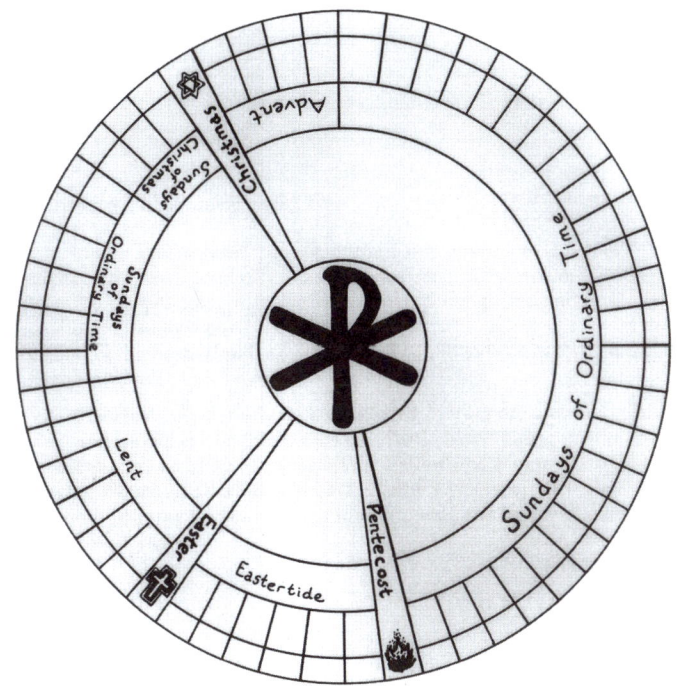

Faith and Life • Grade 3 • Appendix B B - 17

Reinforce

1. Have the children work on Appendix pp. B-16 and B-17.

2. Have the students research Holy Days of Obligation and other traditions. Have them make presentations based upon their research.

Conclude

1. Pray the Acts of Faith, Hope, and Love.

2. Sing "On this day, the first of days," *Adoremus Hymnal*, #610.

Preview

In the next lesson, the students will learn about fulfilling the law of honoring the Lord's Day.

TRADITIONS FOR HOLY DAYS OF OBLIGATION

While the Holy Days of Obligation are primarily days to refrain from servile labor and to attend Mass in remembrance of particularly important feasts in the Church, Holy Days have inspired traditions that are celebrated by many Catholics. For instance:

- **Nativity:** family creche to remember Christ's humble birth
- **Epiphany:** blessing of candles in church; families bless their homes
- **Corpus Christi:** eucharistic procession
- **Feasts of Mary:** crowning of image of Mary
- **All Saints:** pray with the saints, visit cemeteries on All Souls (November 2)

NOTES

LESSON FOUR: SUNDAY

Aims

The students will learn that Sunday is a day of worship, as well as a day of rest and family time.

They will learn that it is also good to perform acts of charity on Sunday.

Materials

- *Activity Book*, p. 39
- Lined paper and pencils

Optional:
- "On this day, the first of days," *Adoremus Hymnal*, #610

Begin

Begin the class by reviewing the obligation of going to and participating in the Holy Mass on every Sunday. Other obligations that are included in honoring the Lord's Day include going to Mass on Holy Days of Obligation. List the Holy Days and have the students explain them. Also stress that we must pay attention, respond to the Mass, pray fervently, and receive Holy Communion worthily.

Sunday is not only a day of worship but a day of joy and family closeness. It is a day when we put work aside and take time to relax. We can do that by going on a picnic, playing games, talking and laughing, or enjoying a special dinner together. It is also a good day to visit relatives or invite neighbors into our home. Just like the Risen Lord, Who spent Easter Sunday sharing peace and joy with His friends, we are meant to reach out and spread warmth and happiness to others. This is part of God's plan for our holiness.

Words to Know:

Holy Day of Obligation

> **Q. 43** *What does the Third Commandment, "Remember to keep holy the Lord's Day," tell us to do?*
> The Third Commandment tells us to honor God on Sundays and Holy Days of Obligation by taking part in the Holy Mass (CCC 2180).
>
> **Q. 44** *What does the Third Commandment tell us not to do?*
> The Third Commandment tells us not to do unnecessary work on Sundays and Holy Days of Obligation (CCC 2185).

Develop

1. Finish reading the chapter from the student text. Have the students take turns reading sentences aloud.

2. Stress that Sunday is a day for us to grow in holiness. Ask the students to think of things they can do that will help them to grow in holiness on Sunday:
- *Praying*
- *Going to Mass*
- *Spending time with family*
- *Doing works of charity, e.g., talking with a senior neighbor*
- *Resting*
- *Sharing a family meal*
- *Reading the Bible, etc.*

3. The children can reinforce this concept by playing charades. Have each child silently act out a way to grow in holiness on Sundays, and have the other children try to guess what he is acting out. Whoever guesses correctly may act out the next example. Be sure all the children who want a turn have an opportunity to participate.

4. Explain that growing in holiness is pleasing to God. It helps us to become better people and more like the angels and saints. We may ask for the help of the angels and saints especially on Sundays at Mass because they, too, are gathered around the altar. Although we cannot see them, they are there, united with us through the Communion of Saints. Ask the children what they could ask of the angels and saints, in order to grow in holiness.

Some examples of prayers to the angels and saints might be:
- Saint Michael, help me to stay away from the devils
- Saint Patrick, help me always to believe in the Holy Trinity
- Saint Francis, help me to love God in the world around me

5. Review the first three Commandments, and teach the children that they can be summarized by the Great Commandment: You shall love the Lord your God with all your heart, with all your soul, with all your strength, and with all your mind.

Name:_____

Word Search

Commandments 1, 2, and 3!

Adore	Crucifix	Holy	Resurrection
Benediction	Genuflect	Jesus	Reverent
Church	Hallowed	Lord	Tabernacle
Creator	Heaven	Prayer	Vain

```
C Y H B E N G B I C H E A V E N V R P I
H H L E E E X V M N A V F C O K A E V K
U Z T N F N D U Z U L W X Z C P I V P T
R G X E H R E S P S L J O R R J N E R H
C A K D C E D D H D O V L L H B G R A W
H B R I P S F D I V W R N D O E Q Y Q
A O R C S U R L E C E O O N L A F N E Q
L Q M T K R Y A A L D R J U Y I H T R T
E N Q I Z R R R U U E I G R S C A R Q M
P K R O X E Q R A R S L E C X L E M Y K
N C K N R C T R D A E U N N P K X H M Z
L I K A E T I F O C U R U H F O J W P H
O T P B R I Z C R U C I F I X H X C L I
R F R E X O R X E V F B L F G R X C L R
D E J X R N K T Q E H C E Z U V E V Y V
L D H N T N R J O P F H C M J S B F S D
H X J E S U S W B T J F T X W Y V D Q N
U K E C Q C A G Z G B Y Q E N U O G D T
T R V L C L A E W T A B E R N A C L E R
C R E A T O R H Z E O O S T A B S G W M
```

Faith and Life Series • Grade 3 • Chapter 10 • Lesson 4

Reinforce

1. Have the students work on *Activity Book*, p. 39. For every word in the puzzle, have them write a sentence using the word relating to the lessons they have covered in the last two chapters; e.g., "adore." I adore our Lord; "Creator." God is our Creator; this means He made us from nothing.

2. Have the students work on the Memorization Questions for this chapter.

Conclude

1. Lead the children in praying the Acts of Faith, Hope, and Love. Review how these prayers help us to live the first three Commandments.

2. Lead the children in singing "On this day, the first of days," *Adoremus Hymnal*, #610.

Preview

In the next lesson, the students' knowledge of the material covered this week will be reviewed and assessed.

HAND MOTIONS TO MEMORIZE THE GREAT COMMANDMENT

The first part of the Great Commandment: "You shall love the Lord your God with all your heart, and with all your soul, with all your strength and with all your mind" (Lk 10:27).

Teach hand-motions to memorize this:
You shall love (put your hands over your heart) the Lord your God (point to Heaven) with all your heart (point to your heart), with all your soul (point to the sole of your shoe), with all your strength (have the children make a biceps muscle by bending their arm at the elbow and point to it), and with all your mind (point to your head).

NOTES

CHAPTER TEN
REVIEW AND ASSESSMENT

Aims

The students' knowledge of the material covered this week will be reviewed and assessed.

Materials

- Quiz 10, Appendix, p. A-14

Optional:
- "On this day, the first of days," *Adoremus Hymnal*, #610

Review

1. Review the Third Commandment.

2. Review the difference between the Sabbath and the Lord's Day. Why do we worship on Sunday? (Sunday is the day of the Resurrection of our Lord.)

3. What is the Sunday obligation? How should we participate in the Mass? Why is receiving the Eucharist a great blessing and joy for us?

4. Review the Holy Days of Obligation: What are they? What do we celebrate with each one of them?
- Nativity
- Epiphany
- Ascension
- Corpus Christi
- Mary, Mother of God
- Immaculate Conception
- Assumption
- Saint Joseph
- Saints Peter and Paul
- All Saints

5. What else are we called to do on Sunday? How can we grow in holiness?

Name: _____

The Lord's Day — Quiz 10

"This is the day, which the Lord has made; let us rejoice and be glad in it" (Psalm 118:24).

Word Bank

| holy | happiness | Days | Christmas |
| serious | Mass | offer | Son |

Fill in the blanks with the correct words from the Word Bank.

1. The Third Commandment is "Remember to keep **holy** the Lord's Day."

2. The greatest gift that we can offer to God on His day is to participate in the **Mass** faithfully.

3. At every Mass, we are able to **offer** ourselves to God and join ourselves with Christ's gift of Himself to God the Father.

4. In the Mass, the Father gives us His own **Son** as "the Bread of Life" in Holy Communion.

5. The Church teaches that there is a **serious** obligation for us to participate in the Mass on Saturday evening or Sunday each week unless we are unable to because of sickness, lack of transportation, or other reasons.

6. Sunday is a special day for family and a time for spreading **happiness** to others.

7. Holy **Days** of Obligation are special holy days, besides Sunday, which God wants us to keep holy by participating in the Mass.

8. The Holy Day of Obligation we celebrate on December 25 is: **Christmas**

9. Write out the Scripture verse shown at the top of this page.

Assess

1. Distribute the quizzes and read through them with the students to be sure they understand the questions.

2. Administer the quiz. As they hand in their work, you may orally quiz them on the Memorization Questions for this chapter.

3. After all the quizzes have been handed in, you may wish to review the correct answers with the class.

Conclude

1. End class by praying the Acts of Faith, Hope, and Love.

2. Sing "On this day, the first of days," *Adoremus Hymnal*, #610.

CHAPTER ELEVEN
OBEDIENCE AND LOVE

Catechism of the Catholic Church References

Fourth Commandment: 2197–57
  Family in God's Plan: 2201–6, 2249
  Duties of Children: 2214–20, 2251
  Authorities in Civil Society: 2234–46, 2254–57
  Jesus as our Teacher and Model of Holiness: 468–69, 516, 519–21, 561

Sacrifice: 2099–100
Fifth Commandment: 2258–30
  Respect for Human Life: 2259–83, 2319–25
  Respect for the Dignity of Persons: 2284–301, 2326

Scripture References

The Fourth Commandment: Ex 20:12

The Fifth Commandment: Ex 20:13

Background Reading: *The Fundamentals of Catholicism* by Fr. Kenneth Baker, S.J.

Volume 1:
"Honor Your Father and Mother," pp. 182–84
"Love for One's Relatives," 185–87
"He Who Spares the Rod Hates His Son," pp. 188–90
"Caesar and God," pp. 191–93

"Man's Unalienable Right to Life," pp. 194–96
"Stewards of Life," pp. 196–99
"Innocent Human Life," pp. 203–5
"Adequate Care of One's Health," pp. 212–15

Summary of Lesson Content

Lesson 1

The Fourth Commandment is "Honor your father and your mother."

God chose our families and has a special plan for them.

Within the family, there are roles for the parents and the children. Both of these roles demand love and respect.

Lesson 2

The Holy Family is a model for all families.

Obedience and love are due to parents.

Lesson 3

The Fourth Commandment also demands that we love and obey our authorities.

Lesson 4

The Fifth Commandment is "You shall not kill."

This Commandment teaches the value of all human life.

God wants us to respect all human life around us, from the moment of conception to natural death.

The Good Samaritan is an example of how to love our neighbor.

LESSON ONE: FAMILY

Aims

The students will learn that the Fourth Commandment is "Honor your father and your mother."

They will learn that God chose our families and that He has a special plan for them. Within the family, there are roles for the parents and the children, both of which demand love and respect.

Materials

- *Activity Book*, p. 40
- Pencils, markers
- Construction paper, scissors; or if possible, foam board and picture frames

Optional:
- "O Lord, the Giver of all life," *Adoremus Hymnal*, #609

Begin

Review the first three Commandments, noting especially Honor the Lord's Day. We must go to church because that is where we show our love for God and receive His love for us. We must behave and be respectful in church because it is a holy place. God gave us a special gift called the "domestic church." This is our family. We can love God through our parents, brothers, and sisters. He loves us through them, too. Just as in church we must behave properly, according to our different roles, so, too, we must live according to our role in the family. Our families should bring us closer to God.

---

11 Obedience and Love

"Lord, now lettest thou thy servant depart in peace, according to thy word. . . ."
Luke 2:29

We bring happiness to our home when we live up to God's Fourth Commandment: "Honor your father and your mother."

To **honor** means to love, respect, and obey. To **obey** means to do as we are told. God wants us to honor our parents because He brought us into the world through them. Once we were born, they gave us very much. Ever since we were tiny babies, our parents have loved, protected, and guided us. God entrusted us especially to them for that reason. They work and make sacrifices for us. They care for us every day. They give us all we need, whether it is a good meal to eat, new clothes as we grow, or surprises for our birthday.

Above all, they care for our souls. They want us to be good, so that we will be happy not only in this world but also for all eternity in Heaven. That is why they had us baptized and want us to receive the sacraments and learn about our faith.

When the Christ Child was growing up in Nazareth, He had many chances to love and obey His mother and foster father, Joseph. Joseph was a carpenter and Jesus helped him carry the wood and hammer the nails. He surely also helped His mother Mary. We can picture Jesus doing these things kindly and cheerfully. Even though He was God, He respected His parents enough to obey and listen to them.

We discover the secret of the Holy Family's happiness every time we obey and offer to help. Some days it is hard to obey our parents because we would really rather play outside or go somewhere with

---

Develop

1. Read paragraphs 1–3 with the students. They may take turns reading sentences aloud.

2. God loves us very much. He knows us even better than we know ourselves because He created us. God took special care in choosing our parents, as well as our brothers and sisters. Therefore, He wants us to love and obey our parents because He has given them authority over us. We should also love our brothers and sisters because He has given them to us as part of our family, which is the domestic church.

3. How have your parents shown their love for you?
- *They give us meals to eat*
- *They give us clothes to wear*
- *They give us a home*
- *They celebrate our birthdays*
- *They help us to grow in our faith*
- *They do things with us, etc.*

4. Your parents know that you are God's special gift. At your Baptism, you became a child of God. Your parents have been given the job of caring for God's child—what a responsibility. They should do everything they can to care for you, protect you, and make sure you grow up well. This is why they give you rules and make great sacrifices to take care of your needs. They want to do everything they can so that you can grow closer to God and be happy and united with Him forever.

5. Because God has given you your parents to help you grow closer to God, how should you treat your parents? They are God's helpers. You should love, respect, obey, help, and pray for them.

6. What is a church? A church is a house of God and of His family. How can you make your family and home more of a domestic church? Pray together, celebrate feasts, and love each other.

Name:_____

God's Plan For My Family

Glue a picture of your family in the box below.

[ ]

1. Who did God choose for my family?
   Answers will vary.

2. What ways do my parents show that they love me?

3. What ways do I show my parents that I love them?

4. How have my parents helped me to grow as a child of God?

40 Faith and Life Series • Grade 3 • Chapter 11 • Lesson 1

MARRIED SAINTS

While many of the most famous saints were called to the single life, there are many married saints and blesseds, honored by the Church for their lives of holiness and charity. Here are just a few:
- Saint Mary and Saint Joseph
- Saint Anne and Saint Joachim
- Saint Clotilde and Clovis
- Saint Matilda and Henry I
- Saint Elizabeth of Hungary and Louis
- Saint Thomas More and Jane Colt
- Saint Philip Howard and Anne
- Saint Ceferino Giménez Malla and Teresa Giménez Castro

Reinforce

1. Have the students work on *Activity Book*, p. 40. They may make presentations based upon their completed work.

2. Teach the children to sing "O Lord, the Giver of all life," *Adoremus Hymnal*, #609.

Conclude

Lead the children in praying for their intentions, especially in thanksgiving for their families.

Preview

In the next lesson, the students will learn about the Holy Family so that they may have a role-model of family life.

NOTES

LESSON TWO: HOLY FAMILY

Aims

The students will learn that the Holy Family is a model for all families.

The students will learn about the virtues of obedience and love, and that these virtues are due to parents.

Materials

- *Activity Book*, p. 41
- Children's Bible
- Paper and markers

Optional:
- "The Boy Jesus in the Temple," video;
- Jesus: A Kingdom without Frontiers, available through Ignatius Press
- "O Lord, the Giver of all life," *Adoremus Hymnal*, #609

Begin

Begin class by reviewing the Fourth Commandment. What is the domestic church? How do our parents show their love for us? How do we show our love for them?

What is the ultimate goal of the family? The ultimate goal of the family is to grow closer to God, so that the family can be with Him forever.

How do parents work toward this goal of the family? They have their children baptized, take them to Mass, and instruct them in the faith.

---

our friends. When this happens, just remember that making sacrifices of love makes us happiest of all in the end. Doing the right thing can be hard sometimes, but it will make us happy. Doing the wrong thing leaves a feeling of sadness inside us. This is part of our human nature because God made us to love Him, and we can only be happy when we obey the Commandments.

God wants us to respect and obey, not only our parents, but others who have lawful authority to protect us. For example, if we are at school and our teacher asks us to put away our artwork, listen without talking, or help a classmate who is in trouble we obey, and by doing so we please God.

In the Fourth Commandment God tells us to honor our father and mother, whom He gave us.

In the Fifth Commandment, God asks us to respect all human life. "You shall not kill," He tells us. The life of every person, no matter how poor, old, weak, or small, belongs to God and is precious. When you were inside your mother's womb and small enough to fit in the palm of a hand, God loved you and had a plan for your life. That is why the life of every baby inside of his mother is sacred and we respect it.

God wants us to respect the lives of people around us. In the Gospel, Jesus told the story of a man who was attacked by robbers when he was going down the road. They took his money and clothes and left him half dead. Three people passed the wounded man. The first two ignored him. The third one stopped to clean and bandage the man's wounds. Then he took the man to an inn and paid for his care and shelter. Jesus said that this Good Samaritan acted the way He wants us to act, especially toward the suffering and the poor. God will reward us if we show a readiness to make sacrifices for others and **good will**: always wanting to do what is right. He will bless us whenever we value, protect, or save the lives of others.

55

Develop

1. Read paragraphs 4 and 5 from the student text with the children. They may take turns reading sentences aloud.

2. You may read from the children's Bible the story of the finding of the child Jesus in the Temple (Lk 2:41–52). Using this story, point out that Mary and Joseph took Jesus to Jerusalem to worship according to their faith. Also let the children see how Jesus was obedient to His parents. If the Son of God can be obedient to Mary and Joseph, then surely we can learn to be obedient to our parents.

3. What are some of the ways that Jesus helped Mary and Joseph? How can we love and help our parents?

4. What does the student text say about the secret to happiness? Whenever we obey and offer help, we will be happy. These are sacrifices of love. Can the children think of different sacrifices of love? The example in the student text states that we should obey our parents when we would prefer to be outside or with our friends. Have each of the children think of an example of a sacrifice of love. Write each idea on the board.

5. Review the virtues of love and obedience:
Love is a theological virtue. It is a gift from God that directs us toward Him. When we love our neighbor, we love God. When we love our family, we love God. We can express this love through acts of charity—doing good for another person. Charity is another name for sacrifices of love. Obedience is a virtue by which we do what our authorities tell us to do out of concern for our good. We should be cheerfully obedient because we are doing a good thing, although it may seem hard at the time. Have the children think of people they can love and ways they can show their love. Also have them think of people to whom they should be obedient and ways of being obedient.

Name: _____

The Fourth Commandment

1. What is the Fourth Commandment?
   Honor your father and your mother
2. Why should we honor our parents?
   We honor our parents because they gave us life and care for us.
3. What should our parents do to honor the Fourth Commandment?
   Our parents should care for all our needs, especially the needs or our souls, so that we will be happy.
4. What family can we use as a model for the Fourth Commandment?
   The Holy Family
5. What did Jesus do for Joseph and Mary?
   Jesus loved and obeyed Joseph and Mary.
6. How can you honor the Fourth Commandment? What can you do?
   Answers will vary.
7. Who else should you honor according to the Fourth Commandment?
   We honor those with lawful authority to protect us.

Faith and Life Series • Grade 3 • Chapter 11 • Lesson 2

THE HOLY FAMILY

Mary and Joseph were married according to Jewish custom and were recognized by their community as a legitimately married couple, with Jesus as their son. Though Joseph was actually the foster-father of Jesus, he raised Jesus as his own son, instructing him in the Jewish faith and very likely in his trade, as well. Mary, as the natural mother of Jesus and the wife of Joseph, maintained the home and cared for her family.

The Holy Family is a model for all families. The calling of Joseph and Mary in raising the Son of God was a greater task than anything to which we will be called; nonetheless, we are similarly called to holiness through our families.

Reinforce

1. Have the children work on *Activity Book*, p. 41.

2. They may draw pictures showing Jesus being obedient to His parents out of love.

3. Show the video, "The Boy Jesus in the Temple," from the Jesus: A Kingdom without Frontiers series (available through Ignatius Press; 30 minutes).

4. Have the students work on Memorization Question 45, regarding the Fourth Commandment.

Conclude

1. Lead the children in praying for their families and their intentions.

2. Sing "O Lord, the Giver of all life," *Adoremus Hymnal*, #609.

Preview

In the next lesson, the students will learn that the Fourth Commandment requires obedience to all our authorities.

NOTES

LESSON THREE: OBEDIENCE

Aims

The students will learn that the Fourth Commandment also demands love of and obedience to our authorities.

The students will spend time learning about respect and the "golden rule."

Materials

- Children's Bible
- *Activity Book*, p. 42
- Posterboard, markers/crayons, construction paper, scissors, glue, etc.

Optional:
- "O Lord, the Giver of all life," *Adoremus Hymnal*, #609

Begin

Who are our authorities? They are people to whom God has given the job of caring for us in one way or another. They are looking out for our good, helping our parents bring us closer to God, and protecting us from harm.

Who are some of our authorities?
- *Policemen*
- *The president*
- *The Pope & clergy*
- *Teachers*
- *Coaches*
- *Relatives*

How must we obey them?

Develop

1. *Read paragraph 6 with the children.*

2. Ask the children if we must obey people who want to harm us. No. For example, if someone told you to steal something for him or to take drugs, you would not need to obey. Our true authorities are those who seek our good.

3. Read Mt 17:24–27 from the children's Bible. Even Jesus and Peter paid taxes out of obedience. Why? Their authorities demanded that they, too, pay taxes, and Jesus saw these authorities as appointed by God. He knew that in obeying, He would please God and be a good example for others.

You may also remind the children that Jesus was obedient to Mary and Joseph, and to the will of God the Father. We can see then that obedience is a very important virtue.

4. Play a round of "Jesus Says," which is similar to "Simon Says." There is one leader, who gives commands to the others. If the command is "Jesus says . . ." then the students must obey; if it simply is "do this . . ." then they should not. This game teaches the children about obedience.

5. *The Fourth Commandment tells us to love and obey our parents and authorities, but it also tells us to respect them. What does respect mean? It means to treat others as they deserve to be treated. Some call this the "golden rule." It says "Do unto others as you would have them do unto you." We have to respect people and things. For example, if your parents tell you to do something, you should obey them. You should also be respectful—obey cheerfully and use good manners. Respect requires saying "Please" and "Thank you." If we are respectful, we use proper titles for people, such as "Mr.," "Mrs.," "Father," and "Officer." To be disrespectful would be to "talk back" or not to give care to a person, thing, or situation.*

Jesus said: "Truly, I say to you, as you did it to one of the least of these my brethren, you did it to me" (Matthew 25:40).

On the other hand, it saddens God when we say mean things in anger, or refuse to make up with a friend after a fight. He wants us to be forgiving, loving, and generous. In our lifetime, He will give us many chances to be kind. We are kind when we help someone who is sick or disabled. We are kind when we hug a little brother or sister after he or she has fallen down. We are kind when we pray for people we do not like.

God wants us to respect our own lives, too. Our lives are a gift we must protect. When we try to eat the right foods to stay healthy or when we cross the street only when it is safe, we show God that we value His gift of life.

Words to Know:

honor   obey   good will

> **Q. 45** *What does the Fourth Commandment, "Honor your father and your mother," tell us to do?*
> The Fourth Commandment tells us to love, respect, and obey our parents and our superiors (CCC 2197).

Name:_____

Honor Your Mother and Father Respect and Obey Authorities

Color the pictures below.

Faith and Life Series • Grade 3 • Chapter 11 • Lesson 3

RESPECT

- **People:** Use proper titles: Mr. Jones, Officer Bob, Miss Black, Fr. Brown. We should use proper manners and a friendly tone of voice. We must not be rude or inconsiderate. We try to be helpful and always remember with whom we are speaking.
- **Things:** We treat others' property as we would want our own property to be treated, and we return it promptly; e.g., we should not write in another's book.
- **Situations:** We must be respectful in church and other holy places. Sometimes places demand respect. For example, if we are visiting a sick person in the hospital, we must behave, keep our hands to ourselves, and be quiet.

Reinforce

1. Make posters showing how we can obey various authorities; e.g., obeying the crossing guard at the intersection, obeying a coach or teacher, listening to a priest or religious, etc. They may also make a poster on respect of persons, places, and situations.

2. Have the students work on *Activity Book*, p. 42.

3. Have the students work on their Memorization Questions.

Conclude

1. Lead the children in praying for their authorities. Have each child name an authority and his special intention; e.g., one student might pray, "God, please bless Fr. O'Brien, and make him a faithful priest." Lead the students in replying, "Lord hear our prayer." Another might pray, "God, please bless Ranger Doug, and keep him safe on the job." Again lead the response, "Lord hear our prayer," etc.

2. Lead the children in singing "O Lord, the Giver of all life," *Adoremus Hymnal*, #609.

Preview

In the next lesson, the students will learn about the Fifth Commandment.

NOTES

LESSON FOUR: LOVE LIFE

Aims

The students will learn the Fifth Commandment, "You shall not kill."

They will learn that this Commandment teaches the value of all human life. God wants us to respect all human life around us, from the moment of conception to natural death.

The parable of the Good Samaritan is an example of how to love and respect human life.

Materials

- *Activity Book*, p. 43
- Children's Bible

Optional:
- "The Story of the Good Samaritan," video; The Beginner's Bible, available through Ignatius Press
- "Lord, the Giver of all life," *Adoremus Hymnal*, #609

Begin

Begin this lesson with the story of the Good Samaritan. You can find it in the children's Bible (Lk 10:30–36) or watch a video on this story.

Did the Samaritan fail to love the man because he was of a different race? Did he fail to love him because he was weak, poor, and injured? Did he fail to love him even though he was near death? What does this story teach us about love—especially love for human life?

Q. 46 *What does the Fifth Commandment, "You shall not kill," tell us to do?*
The Fifth Commandment tells us to be of good will toward all, including our enemies, and to mend any bodily or spiritual wrong we do to our neighbor (CCC 2302–3).

Q. 47 *What does the Fifth Commandment tell us not to do?*
The Fifth Commandment tells us not to harm the life of anyone. This means that murder, suicide, fighting (out of anger), cursing, and giving scandal are wrong (CCC 2261–62).

"Even these may forget, yet I will not forget you. Behold, I have graven you on the palms of my hands."

Isaiah 49:15–16

Develop

1. Read the rest of the chapter with the children.

2. Ask the children Who gave us life. Only God can give us life and keep us alive. He alone can decide when our time on earth is through and He will take us to Heaven the way He has planned. No one else can do this. Life is a sacred gift from God. While we are alive, we should be reminded of God's nearness to each of us because He holds us in existence.

3. The Fifth Commandment is "You shall not kill." We are made up of a body and a soul. This Commandment protects both. We can kill someone physically by taking his life. However, this Commandment means more than that. We should not even harm another. We can kill or harm someone spiritually by causing him to sin or by giving him an example of sin. We can also harm someone spiritually by being mean to him or by causing harm to his reputation through gossip or speaking poorly about him. It is important that we never kill a person physically or spiritually.

4. Sins of killing someone physically include:
- *Murder: purposely taking an innocent life*
- *Suicide: purposely taking your own life*
- *Abortion: purposely taking the life of an unborn baby*
- *Euthanasia: purposely taking the life of an elderly or sick person*
- *Fighting: causing bodily harm to another out of anger*

5. Sins of killing someone spiritually:
- *Ruining someone's reputation: either telling lies or speaking a truth that makes someone look bad in the eyes of another*
- *Causing or leading someone to sin*
- *Cursing someone: wishing ill upon another*

Name:_____

Respect Life

Use these pictures to reflect on the value of human life.

Faith and Life Series • Grade 3 • Chapter 11 • Lesson 4

43

Reinforce

1. Have the students work on a pro-life project.

2. Have the students color *Activity Book*, p. 43.

3. Have the students work on their Memorization Questions.

Conclude

1. Lead the children in praying for life issues: e.g., for an aunt who is with child, for the homeless, for the elderly, or for the sick, etc.

2. Lead the children in singing "O Lord, the Giver of all life," *Adoremus Hymnal*, #609.

Preview

In the next lesson, the students' knowledge of the material covered this week will be reviewed and assessed.

PRO-LIFE PROJECTS

- Throw a baby-shower and donate supplies to a crisis pregnancy center
- Visit the elderly and sick
- Collect necessities for the homeless or poor; e.g., shampoos and soaps from hotels; hold clothing drive or socks drive, etc.
- Write cards to parents thanking them for giving all that is needed to live
- Have a "healthy lifestyles" on-going project (proper diet and exercise); have a guest speaker come in and teach about this
- Have an anti-drug speaker come in

NOTES
_____
_____
_____
_____
_____
_____
_____
_____
_____
_____
_____

CHAPTER ELEVEN
REVIEW AND ASSESSMENT

Aims

The students' knowledge of the material covered this week will be reviewed and assessed.

Materials

- Quiz 11, Appendix, p. A-15
- "O Lord, the Giver of all life," *Adoremus Hymnal*, #609

Review

1. Review the Fourth Commandment. Review with the children how their parents make sacrifices of love. Review what honoring our parents means. We should love, respect, and obey them, as well as our authorities. We, too, should make sacrifices of love for them. We can show our love through acts of charity. Have the students give concrete examples of acts of charity.

2. The children should be able to explain what a domestic church is and how our families should bring us closer to God, so that we can be happy with Him forever. Parents must care for our souls, as well as our bodies.

3. The Holy Family is a model for all families. Mary and Joseph brought Jesus to the Temple so that he might grow closer to God and learn to practice their faith. Jesus was obedient and respectful of Mary and Joseph. This is demonstrated in the story of the finding of the Child Jesus in the Temple.

4. The students should know the virtues of love, obedience, and charity. They should show respect for others.

5. Review the Fifth Commandment. Review that we have a physical and spiritual life. Discuss sins against both and how we can protect and respect both.

Name: _____

Obedience and Love   Quiz 11

"Children, obey your parents in everything, for this pleases the Lord" (Colossians 3:20)

Word Bank

others	helped	sacred	difficult	respect
God	kind	obey	happiness	

Fill in the blanks with the correct words from the Word Bank.

1. The Fourth Commandment is "Honor your father and your mother." Honor means to love, respect, and **obey**.

2. We bring **happiness** to our home when we live up to God's Fourth Commandment.

3. Some days it is **difficult** to obey our parents because we would rather play outside or go somewhere with our friends.

4. We must **respect** and obey our parents and teachers, and not talk back to them.

5. Jesus wants us to act the way the Good Samaritan did when he **helped** the man who had been attacked by robbers.

6. God will reward us if we show a readiness to make sacrifices for **others** and show good will by always wanting to do what is right.

7. The Fifth Commandment is "You shall not kill." The life of every person, no matter how poor, old, weak, or small, belongs to **God** and is precious.

8. The life of every baby inside of his mother is **sacred** and we must respect it.

9. We must be **kind**. We must not argue, fight, hurt others, say mean things to others, or refuse to make up with someone after a fight.

10. Write out the Scripture verse shown at the top of this page.

_____

Faith and Life • Grade 3 • Appendix A   A - 15

Assess

1. Distribute the quizzes and read through them with the students to be sure they understand the questions.

2. Administer the quiz. As they hand in their work, you may orally quiz them on the Memorization Questions for this chapter.

3. After all the quizzes have been handed in, you may wish to review the correct answers with the class.

Conclude

1. End class with prayers for our families and for human life.

2. Sing "O Lord, the Giver of all life," *Adoremus Hymnal*, #609.

CHAPTER TWELVE
PURITY AND TRUTH

Catechism of the Catholic Church References

Sixth Commandment: 2331–400
- Chastity: 1832
- Fidelity: 736, 1644–45, 1832
- Love and Fidelity of Spouses: 2360–65, 2397
- Modesty: 1832, 2521–24
- Vocation to Chastity: 2337–59, 2394–95

Seventh Commandment: 2401–63
- Love for the Poor: 2443–49, 2462–63
- Respect for Persons and Their Goods: 2407–18, 2453–57

Eighth Commandment: 2464–2513
- Bearing Witness to the Truth: 2471–74, 2506

Jesus as Our Teacher and Model of Holiness: 468–69, 516, 519–21, 561
- Living in the Truth: 2464–70, 2505
- Offenses Against Truth: 2475–87, 2507–9

Ninth Commandment: 2514–27, 2528–33
- Purity of Heart: 2513, 2517–19
- Struggle for Purity: 2520–27, 2530, 2532–33

Tenth Commandment: 2534–57
- Disorder of Covetous Desires: 2535–40, 2552–53
- Desire of the Spirit: 2541–43, 2554–55
- Desire to See God: 2548–50, 2557
- Poverty of Heart: 2544–47, 2556

Scripture References

The Sixth Commandment: Ex 20:14
The Seventh Commandment: Ex 20:15
The Eighth Commandment: Ex 20:16
The Ninth Commandment: Ex 20:17
The Tenth Commandment: Ex 20:17

Background Reading: *The Fundamentals of Catholicism* by Fr. Kenneth Baker, S.J.

Volume 1:
On the Sixth through Ninth Commandments, pp. 215–82

Summary of Lesson Content

Lesson 1

The body is a gift from God. We are to enjoy it and the world around us with the gifts of the senses and our talents.

The body is holy: it is the temple of the Holy Spirit.

The Sixth and Ninth Commandments tell us to respect our bodies and those of others.

Lesson 2

The Sixth and Ninth Commandments call us to faithful relationships.

In marriage, we must be faithful to the vows we make.

God will help us and bless us in living our vocations.

Lesson 3

The Seventh and Tenth Commandments teach us to be fair with property.

We must be satisfied with the things we have, taking care of them and sharing them.

We must also respect other people's belongings.

Lesson 4

The Eighth Commandment tells us to be honest: "You shall not bear false witness against your neighbor."

LESSON ONE: THE BODY

Aims

The students will learn that the body is a gift from God. We are to enjoy it and the world around us with the gifts of the senses and our talents.

The body is holy: it is the temple of the Holy Spirit.

The Sixth and Ninth Commandments tell us to respect our bodies and those of others.

Materials

- Something to test each of the senses
- *Activity Book*, p. 44

Optional:
- "God Father, praise and glory," *Adoremus Hymnal*, #464

Begin

Begin the class by telling the children to close their eyes and test their senses. Have the children smell perfume or something fragrant. Test their hearing with beautiful music or funny sounds. Have them touch things with different textures—soft, rough, etc. Show them brilliant colors and beautiful pictures to dazzle the eyes. Have them taste a sweet candy or something salty or bitter. Make sure that they enjoy their senses.

Develop

1. Read the first two paragraphs with the children.

2. Have the children think of ways that they use their senses to give glory to God. We can appreciate God in the world around us or use our talents to glorify Him in our works and hobbies.

3. Ask the children why God gave them their voices, eyes, and hands. To do the work of God—to spread His love and reach all of His children.

4. Our bodies are holy because, on the day of our Baptisms, we became temples of the Holy Spirit. What does this mean? With the Holy Spirit in us, the work we do is really God working through us.

5. We must respect our bodies and those of others. This means that we should take care of our bodies and protect them. We learned from the Fifth Commandment that we must be healthy by exercising and maintaining a good diet. We must also care for our soul. We must keep both our bodies and our souls pure. The Sixth Commandment is "You shall not commit adultery." This means that we must be pure in our actions. The Ninth Commandment is "You shall not covet your neighbor's wife." This means we must be pure in our thoughts.

6. In order to stay pure and modest we must avoid that which may lead us to sin. We must stay away from movies, books, pictures, video games, etc., that are not good examples for us since they may lead us to use our bodies in ways that are not pleasing to God. What are other things that may give us bad examples?

7. How should we clothe our bodies? Modestly and with respect for ourselves and others. How should we respect each other? We should not hit each other, etc.

---

12 Purity and Truth

> The commandments, "You shall not commit adultery, You shall not kill, You shall not steal, You shall not covet," and any other commandment, are summed up in this sentence, "You shall love your neighbor as yourself."
>
> Romans 13:9

Have you ever thought about how important your body is? You speak with your body. You run, walk, and stand up to help someone with your body. With your five senses of touch, taste, sight, smell, and hearing, you are able to enjoy and learn about the world, and bring your talents to it.

God gave you your voice, your eyes, your hands, and all of your body for many wonderful reasons. Your body is holy because on the day of your Baptism, the Holy Spirit came to live inside of it. In the Sixth and Ninth Commandments, God told us to respect our bodies and the bodies of other people. He wants us to keep our bodies pure and pleasing to Him. We can have **purity** if we are clean in what we think, say, and do. He wants us to be modest and to stay away from movies, books, and pictures that are not good examples for us.

God also wants us to be faithful in our relationships with other people. For example, someday we may marry a person we love. God will expect us to be faithful to the love and promises we vow on our wedding. If we make ourselves strong to live up to that love, God will reward us richly.

The Seventh Commandment and the Tenth Commandment tell us to be fair with property. God wants us to be satisfied with what

Name:_____

Your Body, a Gift from God

1. What can you do that makes you special?
   Answers will vary.

2. What do you enjoy most with your sense of:

   Touch: *Answers will vary.*

   Sight:

   Smell:

   Hearing:

   Taste:

4. Your body is a temple of the Holy Spirit Who came to live there on the day of your Baptism. How does God work through you?
   Answers will vary.

5. How can you use your body in a way that is pleasing to God?
   Answers will vary.

Faith and Life Series • Grade 3 • Chapter 12 • Lesson 1

Reinforce

1. Have the children work on *Activity Book*, p. 44.

2. Teach the children to sing "God Father, praise and glory," *Adoremus Hymnal*, #464.

3. Have the children start working on the Memorization Questions.

Conclude

Lead the children in praying for their intentions.

Preview

In the next lesson, the students will learn about the sacredness of marriage and the virtue of fidelity, or faithfulness.

SAINT AUGUSTINE AND GRACE

Sometimes a life without grace and filled with sin is dramatically altered by God. In the history of the Church, one of the most striking stories of God's grace and redemption can be found in the person of Saint Augustine. Born into privilege in the twilight years of the Western Roman Empire, Augustine lived a life that was focused upon pleasure, greed, and pagan philosophy. Throughout his youth and young adulthood, he had nothing but contempt for the Christian Church. He thought the Gospels and Letters of Paul to be nothing but badly written rhetoric, undeserving of his attention. Augustine's way of living made his mother very sad, for she knew God had other plans for her son. Augustine became frustrated with his life and prayed for guidance.

Fed up with his life of sin and dissipation, Augustine threw himself to the earth and begged for God's help. Just then, he heard a child singing "*Tolle Lege*" ("Take up and read"). Taking the child's song as a sign from God, Augustine began reading the Scriptures. He decided to follow Paul's admonition to live as Christ lived. To his mother's great joy, Augustine was baptized and began a life of dedication to Jesus. Not only was his once sin-filled life now filled with God's own life, but he was so dedicated that he became a bishop, a defender of the Church against heresy, and a saint. Augustine wrote of his conversion in his autobiographical masterpiece, the *Confessions*.

LESSON TWO: FAITHFULNESS

Aims

The students will learn that the Sixth and Ninth Commandments call us to faithful relationships.

In marriage, we must be faithful to the vows we make. God will help us and bless us in living our vocations.

Materials

- *Activity Book*, p. 45
- If possible, arrange a visit by a religious, a priest, and a married person to discuss vocations
- Lined paper and pencils

Optional:
- "God Father, praise and glory," *Adoremus Hymnal*, #464

Begin

Begin class by having your guest speakers talk about their vocations.

Help the guests to explain the different vocations: marriage, holy orders, religious life, and single life.

---

we have, not to covet what others have. To **covet** is to wrongfully want something that does not belong to you. We are also to respect other people's things. God told us, "You shall not steal." If someone takes a snack or a toy or money that belongs to someone else, he is breaking God's Law. Cheating on tests, borrowing things and not returning them, or being dishonest in a store breaks the same Law.

We can obey the Seventh and Tenth Commandments by being satisfied with the things we have, by taking care of them, and by sharing them. It pleases God when we give or share a snack, a toy, or money that belongs to us.

God also wants us to take special care of other people's things. If we borrow a book from the library, we should take good care of it and return it on time. If we accidentally break something that belongs to someone else, God wants us to make up for it, either by paying for it or replacing it. This is called justice or fairness.

If four children are playing ball on the front lawn and by mistake their ball smashes a neighbor's window, they have some choices. They can run away and pretend it did not happen. They can lie and say that someone else broke the window. They can keep playing ball and not worry about it. Or they can go to the neighbor, tell him what really happened, then help pay for the damage. Which choice do you think obeys the Seventh and Tenth Commandments?

The Eighth Commandment tells us to be honest: "You shall not **bear false witness** against your neighbor" (tell a lie). This means that we should always speak the truth. The **truth** means how things really are. God loves the truth. When Jesus was on earth He spoke the truth in all things, even when it did not make Him popular. He wants us to do the same.

Sometimes we are afraid to tell the truth or we want to blame someone else for something we did. But God asks that we be honest with ourselves and others. **Honesty** means telling the truth. If we are honest and keep our promises, we will be like Jesus Who is the Truth.

60

Develop

1. After the presentations of the various vocations, read paragraph 3 from the student text.

2. God calls us to faithful relationships. Whether we are single, married, priests, or religious, we need to have good and healthy friendships. We need to grow in holiness ourselves in order to have holy friendships. Someday, we will find God's call in our lives to a particular vocation, and then we will have to live our lives according to it. As a married person, we live in love with a husband or wife. As a religious, priest, or single person, we love according to our state. This means that we will never be married and must express our love in a different way—a way that allows us to love everyone in Christ.

3. We must do all we can to prepare ourselves to live according to our vocation. We must guard our hearts and our bodies so that we can love the way God wants us to love. We must become disciplined. For example, if we marry, we must only have a married love for our husband or wife. This means that we must learn to love only one person that way. In order to prepare our hearts to love according to God's plan, we must be sure we have good examples before us. Often television and movies show us bad examples. If we are influenced by these, we must not watch them.

4. In order to prepare our hearts, we must pray often. The more familiar we are with God and the more we listen to Him, the more certain we will be of what God is asking of us.

5. Lastly, we must have good and holy friendships and develop all the virtues we need to live our vocation: love, joy, peace, patience, kindness, goodness, faithfulness, gentleness, and self-control. Explain each of these and other virtues and have the children give examples appropriate to their age.

Name:_____

Purity

Purifying Our Thoughts, Words, and Deeds

1. What can you do to show that you respect your body?
   Answers will vary.

2. What can you do to show that you respect other people's bodies?
   Answers will vary.

3. How can we live the virtue of purity?
   Answers will vary.

4. What things can we do to help us grow in purity?
   Answers will vary.

5. How should we live our relationships with other people?
   We should always be respectful.

6. Why is purity pleasing to God? (Remember we are made in His image!)
   Purity is pleasing to God because God made our bodies good.

7. What does the Sixth Commandment tell us not to do?
   The Sixth Commandment tells us not to be impure. This means that it is wrong to use immoral words or view books, pictures, and shows that are bad examples for us.

8. What does the Ninth Commandment forbid?
   The Ninth Commandment tells us not to have impure thoughts and desires.

Faith and Life Series • Grade 3 • Chapter 12 • Lesson 2   45

VIRTUES FOR HOLY FRIENDSHIPS AND VOCATIONS

In his letter to the Galations, Saint Paul writes of the fruits of the Spirit that should characterize the Christian, and likewise his friendships and vocation.

". . . the fruit of the Spirit is love, joy, peace, patience, kindness, goodness, faithfulness, gentleness, self-control . . . If we live by the Spirit, let us also walk by the Spirit. Let us have no self-conceit, no provoking of one another, no envy of one another" (Gal 5:22–26).

Use this quotation and the text which follows as background material for the class discussion suggested in the develop section.

Reinforce

1. Have the children write prayers asking God to show his will in their lives and to help them fulfill their vocations.

2. Have the students work on *Activity Book*, p. 45.

3. Have the students work on their Memorization Questions.

Conclude

1. Lead the children in praying for their vocations. They may take turns reading the prayers they have written.

2. Sing "God Father, praise and glory," *Adoremus Hymnal*, #464.

Preview

In the next lesson, the students will learn about fairness with property.

NOTES

_____
_____
_____
_____
_____
_____
_____
_____
_____
_____

LESSON THREE: PROPERTY

Aims

The students will learn that the Seventh and Tenth Commandments teach us to be fair with property.

We must be satisfied with the things we have, by taking care of them and sharing them. We must respect other people's belongings.

Materials

- *Activity Book*, p. 46
- Have the students bring in an item for "show and tell." Tell each to bring in his favorite thing.
- Lined paper and pencils
- Snack to share with class

Optional:
- "God Father, praise and glory," *Adoremus Hymnal*, #464.

Begin

Begin the class by having a session of "show and tell." Have each student bring in his favorite thing and present it to the class. Have him explain what it is and why it is his favorite thing. Ask all of them if they want to have their favorite things taken away or destroyed. Why not? Because these things are theirs and to take them away would be an injustice. Explain the importance of respecting property, both our own and that belonging to others, for we should treat the property of others as though it is our own while it is in our care.

"Blessed are the pure in heart, for they shall see God."

Matthew 5:8

Many holy people have even died for the truth. Saint Thomas More is one example. He was a special friend and helper of King Henry the Eighth in England during the sixteenth century. One day the king decided to disobey God and make himself head of the Church. He asked Thomas More to agree with him. But Thomas refused because this was not right. The king's judges tried to force Thomas to lie. When they could not succeed, they put him to death. Thomas told the English people, "I die the king's good servant, but God's first." Thomas More had integrity, which means he was true to himself and to God. His honesty helped him get to Heaven.

Can you think of any other saints or holy people who have suffered to witness to the truth?

Words to Know:

purity	covet	bear false witness
	truth	honesty

Q. 48 *What does the Eighth Commandment, "You shall not lie," tell us to do?*
The Eighth Commandment tells us to speak the truth carefully and to think the best of our neighbor (CCC 2469, 2478).

Develop

1. Read paragraphs 4–7 with the children.

2. What are the Seventh and Tenth Commandments?
   - Seventh: You shall not steal
   - Tenth: You shall not covet your neighbor's goods
   These are much like the sixth and ninth, because one deals with actions and the other with our thoughts.

3. What are some ways we break the Seventh Commandment, "You shall not steal"?
   - Taking something that belongs to another
   - Breaking or destroying another's property
   - Purposely not returning something you borrowed because you want to keep it for yourself
   - Cheating on a test: you are taking someone else's work
   Have the children give more examples like these.

4. What are some ways we break the Tenth Commandment, "You shall not covet your neighbor's goods"?
   - Being jealous of others
   - Wanting something so badly that if we cannot have it, we do not want anyone else to have it either
   - Being unhappy with what we have

5. Respecting property also means that we must take care of the things we have. This may mean picking up your toys and not writing on your books. It may also mean taking care of a pet.

6. We should also share our things with others. Can the students give examples? It's much nicer to share your snack than to hoard it all for yourself. What other things can be shared?

7. Justice demands replacing or repairing someone's goods if you damage them.

Name:_____

Fairness with Property

1. What is the Seventh Commandment?

   <u>You shall not steal.</u>

2. What is the Tenth Commandment?

   <u>You shall not covet your neighbor's goods.</u>

3. Why should we not steal or want what others have?

   <u>God wants us to respect other people's things and be satisfied with what we have.</u>

4. How can we show respect for our possessions?

   <u>We can show respect for our possessions by taking care of them.</u>

5. How can we please God with our possessions?

   <u>We can please God with our possessions by sharing them.</u>

6. How should we treat other people's things?

   <u>We should treat other people's things respectfully.</u>

7. If we break or steal someone else's property, what must we do as Christians?

   <u>We should help repair the damage or return the property.</u>

Faith and Life Series • Grade 3 • Chapter 12 • Lesson 3

Reinforce

1. Have every student write a paragraph about his favorite thing and how he cares for it.

2. Have the students work on *Activity Book*, p. 46.

3. The students may put on skits with various endings. The example from the student text about breaking a window while playing would be a suitable situation for a skit. Discuss the possible endings to the skit to determine the best and moral ending. Some suggestions are provided in the culture box at the bottom of this page.

4. Have a snack to share with the children.

Conclude

1. Lead the children in praying for their intentions.

2. Sing with the children "God Father, praise and glory," *Adoremus Hymnal*, #464.

Preview

In the next lesson, the students will learn about honesty, or truthfulness.

SCENARIOS FOR SKITS

1) A boy breaks a window while playing ball; he can:
   - Run away and not take responsibility
   - Lie and say he did not do it
   - Tell the owner he did it, and try to help pay for it.
2) John has a birthday and Bob sees John receive a toy that Bob really wanted; Bob can:
   - Steal the toy
   - Break the toy because if he can't have it, then neither should John
   - Ask John to share his toy
3) Sue dares Anne to steal a candy bar; Anne can:
   - Steal it
   - Tell Sue it is wrong to steal

NOTES

LESSON FOUR: HONESTY

Aims

The students will learn that the Eighth Commandment, "You shall not bear false witness against your neighbor," tells us to be honest.

Materials

- *Activity Book*, p. 47

Optional:
- "God Father, praise and glory," *Adoremus Hymnal*, #464

Begin

Explain to the children why telling the truth is so important. If we want to understand each other, we must speak the truth. Sometimes we lie so we can look better than we are or to get out of trouble. Sometimes it is so easy to lie that we do not even know we did it! There are different ways to be dishonest: by not telling the whole truth, by telling a lie, or by exaggerating the truth; e.g., "If I told you once, I told you a thousand times" or "Sue *always* gets more presents than me." When we do not speak the truth, we deceive people and this is harmful to us and them.

Q. 49 *What does the Eighth Commandment tell us not to do?*
The Eighth Commandment tells us not to harm another person's reputation. This includes false witness, lies, flattery, unfounded suspicion, and rash judgment (CCC 2477–78).

Q. 50 *What must a person do, who has damaged his neighbor's good name by falsely accusing him or speaking wickedly of him?*
He who has damaged his neighbor's good name by false accusation or wicked talk, must repair the damage he has done, so far as he is able (CCC 2487).

Q. 51 *What does the Sixth Commandment, "You shall not commit adultery," tell us not to do?*
The Sixth Commandment tells us not to be impure. This means that it is wrong to use immoral words or view books, pictures, and shows that are bad examples for us (CCC 2339).

Q. 52 *What does the Ninth Commandment, "You shall not covet your neighbor's wife," tell us not to do?*
The Ninth Commandment tells us not to have impure thoughts and desires (CCC 2514–15).

Q. 53 *What does the Seventh Commandment, "You shall not steal," tell us to do?*
The Seventh Commandment tells us to give back property belonging to others, to fix

---

Develop

1. Finish reading the chapter with the children.

2. Have the children imagine a world in which everything they say is false. You could ask them questions (yes or no) and have them all give false answers. We could figure out what they meant by reversing the answers, right? Well, what if sometimes they spoke the truth and sometimes they didn't. That would be very confusing. We might end up doing the wrong thing or harming people because of misunderstandings. It would be mean to purposely cause harm like this.

3. Play a game of "truth or dare." Give each of the children three cards. You may ask questions—not too personal—and the students must tell the truth. If they do not, take away a card. Let them see that not telling the truth has consequences.

4. Show the children how one lie can lead to another, like a chain. Often we have to continue lying in order to cover up our first lie. Help the children understand that it is much better to be honest, for lying leads to a chain of sins that is difficult to break.

5. Explain that the Eighth Commandment also tells us to think the best of the actions of our neighbors. We should not gossip or cause harm to another's reputation ever.

6. In order to avoid bearing false witness against our neighbor, we should not gossip or speak of another's faults without a very good reason (e.g., to protect someone from danger), even if they are the truth! We should always strive to look for the best in people and speak well of them.

damages that we cause, and to pay our debts (CCC 2412, 2454).

Q. 54 *What does the Seventh Commandment tell us not to do?*
The Seventh Commandment tells us not to damage our neighbor's property. This includes theft and damaging actions. It is wrong to help those who do such damages (CCC 2401).

Q. 55 *If we have stolen or damaged our neighbor's property, should we try to make restitution?*
Yes, if we have stolen or damaged our neighbor's property, we should try to make restitution (CCC 2412).

Q. 56 *What does the Tenth Commandment, "You shall not covet your neighbor's goods," tell us to do?*
The Tenth Commandment tells us to be just in the desire to improve our lives, and to suffer with patience the hardships and other sufferings permitted by the Lord for our own good (CCC 2544).

Q. 57 *What does the Tenth Commandment tell us not to do?*
The Tenth Commandment tells us not to have an unhealthy desire for riches, which would make us forget the rights and welfare of our neighbors (CCC 2534, 2536).

Reinforce

1. Have the students work on *Activity Book*, p. 47 (not shown).

2. Have the students discuss the life of Saint Thomas More as described in the student text. They should value his truthfulness.

3. Have the students work on their Memorization Questions and prepare for their quiz and unit test.

Conclude

1. Lead the children in prayer, asking God to help them grow in holiness and to follow the Commandments.

2. Sing "God Father, praise and glory," *Adoremus Hymnal*, #464.

Preview

In the next lesson, the students' knowledge of the material covered this week will be reviewed and assessed.

HOLY SCRIPTURE ON TRUTH

The Bible has a great deal to say about the truth. Following are two good examples:

"If you continue in my word, you are truly my disciples, and you will know the truth, and the truth will make you free" (Jn 8:31–32).

"Hear, for I will speak noble things, and from my lips will come what is right; for my mouth will utter truth; wickedness is an abomination to my lips. All the words of my mouth are righteous; there is nothing twisted or crooked in them" (Prov 8:6–8).

NOTES

CHAPTER TWELVE
REVIEW AND ASSESSMENT

Aims

The students' knowledge of the material covered this week will be reviewed and assessed.

Materials

- Quiz 12, Appendix, p. A-16
- Unit 3 Quiz, Appendix, A-17 and A-18

Optional:
- "God Father, praise and glory," *Adoremus Hymnal*, #464

Review

1. Review the Sixth through Tenth Commandments: what do they mean and how do they inspire us to live?

2. Review the sacredness of the body (because it is a temple of the Holy Spirit) and how we must respect both other people's bodies and our own.

3. Review the sacredness of vocations and how we must prepare to live the call God has for us, according to our state in life.

4. The students should discuss fairness with property. What does this mean?

5. The students should be able to discuss the value of honesty.

6. The students should have memorized the Ten Commandments in their correct order. They should be able to discuss what the Commandments mean, using concrete examples.

7. You may review the Memorization Questions for Chapters 9–12.

Name: _____

Purity and Truth　　　　　　　　　　　　Quiz 12

"Blessed are the pure in heart, for they shall see God" (Matthew 5:8).

Word Bank

satisfied	Law	false	truth
want	respect	day	Commandment

Fill in the blanks with the correct words from the Word Bank.

1. The Sixth commandment is "You shall not commit adultery. The Ninth Commandment is "You shall not covet your neighbor's wife." Covet means to **want** what is not yours.

2. In the Sixth and Ninth Commandments, God told us to **respect** our bodies and the bodies of other people.

3. Your body is holy because on the **day** of your Baptism the Holy Spirit came to live inside of it.

4. The Seventh **Commandment** is "You shall not steal." The Tenth Commandment is "You shall not covet your neighbor's goods."

5. The Seventh and Tenth Commandments tell us not to want what others have. We should be **satisfied** with the things we have and share them.

6. If someone takes money or other property that belongs to someone else, he is breaking God's **Law** and must make up for it in order to receive forgiveness.

7. The Eighth Commandment is "You shall not bear **false** witness against your neighbor." This commandment tells us not to tell a lie about our neighbor.

8. Sometimes we are afraid to tell the **truth,** or we want to blame someone else for something we did. God asks us to be honest.

9. Write out the Scripture verse shown at the top of this page.

_____

A - 16　　　　　　　　　　　　　Faith and Life • Grade 3 • Appendix A

Assess

1. Distribute the quizzes and read through them with the students to be sure they understand the questions.

2. Administer the quiz. As they hand in their work, you may orally quiz them on the Memorization Questions for this chapter.

3. After all the quizzes have been handed in, you may wish to review the correct answers with the class.

4. Repeat steps 1 and 3 for the Unit 3 Quiz.

Conclude

Sing "God Father, praise and glory," *Adoremus Hymnal*, #464.

CHAPTER THIRTEEN
GOD'S TENDER MERCY

Catechism of the Catholic Church References

Confession: 615, 984, 1424, 1441, 1444–45, 1708
Contrition: 1451–54, 1492
Definition of Sin: 1849–51, 1871
Different Kinds of Sin: 1852–58, 1861–63, 1873
Different Names for the Sacrament of Penance: 1423–24
Effects of the Sacrament of Penance: 1468–70, 1496
Forgiveness: 1856, 2842–45, 2862
God Alone Forgives Sin: 1441–42
God Does Not Abandon Us in Sin: 410, 1609, 1870

Grace: 1848, 1996–2005, 2021–24
Gravity of Sin: Mortal and Venial: 1854–64, 1874–75
Mercy and Sin: 1846–48
Minister of the Sacrament of Penance: 1461–67, 1495
Need for a Sacrament of Reconciliation after Baptism: 1425–26, 1486–89
Priest: 1461–7, 1548, 1552–53
Sacrament of Penance as Sacrament of Forgiveness: 1446–49

Scripture References

Good Shepherd: Jn 10:10–21; Mt 18: 12–14; Lk 15:1–10
Jesus Anointed with Oil: Mt 26:6–13; Jn 12:1–8
Forgiveness of Dimas (the penitent thief): Luke 23:39–43

Forgiveness of Peter: Jn 21:1–19
Institution of Penance: Jn 20:19–23

Background Reading: *The Fundamentals of Catholicism* by Fr. Kenneth Baker, S.J.

Volume 3:
"Importance of Confession," pp. 292–94

Summary of Lesson Content

Lesson 1

God's merciful love is endless. It is greater than any sin man can commit. God can forgive any sin and wants to reconcile man to Himself.

When man repents of his sins, God will forgive him in the Sacrament of Penance.

Jesus is the Good Shepherd.

Lesson 2

Jesus taught man about the forgiveness of sins through healings, stories, and through the forgiving example of His life.

Perfect contrition is inspired by love and acceptance of God's mercy. Peter and Mary Magdalene are examples of repentant sinners who showed mercy and compassion.

Lesson 3

Only God can forgive sins.

Jesus instituted the Sacrament of Penance for the forgiveness of sins. He gave the power to forgive sins to the Apostles. The Apostles have handed on this power through their successors, the bishops and priests, to the present day.

Lesson 4

In the Sacrament of Penance, Christ forgives man's sins (both mortal and venial) through the priest.

The Sacrament of Penance also restores the life of grace to man's soul.

LESSON ONE: GOD'S MERCIFUL LOVE

Aims

The students will learn that God's merciful love is endless. It is greater than any sin man can commit. God can forgive any sin and wants man's reconciliation with Himself.

The students will learn that God will forgive them for their sins if they are truly repentant.

They will learn that Jesus is the Good Shepherd.

Materials

- *Activity Book*, p. 48
- Children's Bible
- "Lord Jesus, think on me," *Adoremus Hymnal*, #364
- Coloring pencils
- Pictures of your local bishop and pastor

Begin

Discuss the work of a shepherd. Ask the children what they know of shepherds. If you have pictures of shepherds and their work, these would be helpful. Discuss:
- *Shepherds leading their sheep to green pastures*
- *Shepherds protecting their sheep from wolves*
- *Shepherds caring for weak or injured sheep*
- *Shepherds looking for lost sheep*
- *They know the sounds of their sheep, and the sheep know their master's voice*
- *They stay with them always*

Develop

1. Read paragraphs 1 and 2 from the student text.

2. Read from a children's Bible the following passages on the Good Shepherd: Jn 10:10–21; Mt 18:12–14; Lk 15:1–10; Ps 23. You may tell the students that the bishop (and his helper the pastor of the parish) are shepherds of the diocese.

3. Using the chart on p. 3, show the parallel between the Good Shepherd with his sheep and Jesus with sinners.

4. Tell the children that God never stops loving us. No matter how grave our sin, God will not turn away from us. He is always waiting for us and loving us. However, when we sin we choose to turn away from God. Have two children stand at the front of the class. One should stand with his arms outstretched as if to welcome a person. He represents God. The second child should turn slightly away from the first to represent venial sin. He should then turn completely away from the first child to represent mortal sin. Continue by explaining that it is we who turn away from God in sin. We have free will, and we can choose to reject God through sinning, but He is still there, waiting for us to return to Him (but He will not force us to return to Him). Ask the children how we can return to God when we sin:
- Go to Confession (necessary for mortal sin)
- Tell God we are sorry (for venial sins)
- Pray
- Change our sinful behavior

5. You may need to review mortal vs. venial sin:
MORTAL SIN: grave matter, full knowledge, and free choice to commit sin
VENIAL SIN: may be a grave object but without full knowledge or freedom, or may be less grave, with full knowledge and freedom
Note: Sin and accident are not the same!

Name:_____

God's Love and Mercy

1. Does God love us even if we sin? How do we know?
Yes. Jesus told us that God will always love us.
2. What example did Jesus give to tell us about God's love for us?
The Good Shepherd
3. How is Jesus like a "good shepherd?"
Jesus protects us and cares for us. When we are sorry for our sins, he forgives us.
4. How can we be "good sheep?"
We can be "good sheep" by following Jesus, the Good Shepherd.

Draw a picture of Jesus as the Good Shepherd.

48   Faith and Life Series • Grade 3 • Chapter 13 • Lesson 1

JESUS: THE GOOD SHEPHERD

Shepherd with Sheep

- Finds lost sheep
- Feeds his sheep
- Leads his sheep
- Protects his sheep
- Cares for his sheep

Jesus with Sinners

- Seeks out sinners
- Feeds Christians in the Eucharist
- Is the Invisible Head of the Church
- Protects sinners from satan

Reinforce

1. Have the students work on *Activity Book*, p. 48.

2. Teach the children to sing "Lord Jesus, think on me," *Adoremus Hymnal*, #364.

3. Have the students write paragraphs on "How I can be a good sheep for Jesus."

Conclude

1. Pray with the children, thanking Jesus for being the Good Shepherd. Have the children name specific examples of His care for us.

2. Pray the Act of Contrition:
O my God, I am heartily sorry for having offended You. I detest all my sins because of Your just punishments, but most of all because they offend You, my God, Who are all-good and deserving of all my love. I firmly resolve, with the help of Your grace, to confess my sins, to do penance, and to amend my life. *Amen*.

Preview

In the next lesson, the students will learn more about Jesus' forgiveness through the examples of Peter and Mary Magdalene.

NOTES

LESSON TWO: FORGIVENESS

Aims

The students will learn that Jesus taught man about the forgiveness of sins through healings, stories, and the forgiving example of His life.

They will learn that perfect contrition is inspired by love and acceptance of God's mercy. Peter and Mary Magdalene are examples of repentant sinners who showed mercy and compassion.

Materials

- *Activity Book*, p. 49
- Children's Bible
- Costumes and props to act out the stories of Peter and Mary Magdalene

Optional:
- "Lord Jesus, think on me," *Adoremus Hymnal*, #364

Begin

Ask the children why we need forgiveness. Because our sins harm our relationship with God and our neighbors, we need God's forgiveness. Review the definitions of mortal and venial sin. Ask the children how they request forgiveness at home. We use words like "I'm sorry" or "Please forgive me." We know that we are forgiven when we hear words like "I forgive you" or "It's okay." People can forgive each other for the harm others have done them, but only God can forgive a sin against God. Jesus is God. He forgave sins and gave this power to his priests. We will learn more about this soon. Today we will learn how Jesus forgave.

---

13 God's Tender Mercy

My enemies say of me in malice:
"When will he die, and his name perish?"

Psalms 41:5

Jesus told many stories to show us how deep God's love is. God's love follows us wherever we go. Even when we commit sins, God does not stop loving us. He waits and watches for us to return. The moment we say we are sorry, He welcomes us back with open arms. No sin on earth will ever be greater than His mercy and love.

Jesus told the story about a shepherd who loved his sheep. The shepherd gave his flock fresh water and food. He protected it from wolves. He knew all of His lambs by name and was willing to lay down His life for them to protect them from danger. One day a lamb got lost and the shepherd did not rest until he found it. When the lamb came back, the shepherd said, "Rejoice with me, because I have found my lost sheep." Then Jesus told us He was the Good Shepherd and we were His sheep. He compared the story to His love for us: "In the same way, there is great joy in Heaven whenever anyone is sorry for his sins."

Jesus did more than tell stories about **forgiveness**. He forgave many sinners. Some of the sinners were among His own friends. Peter the Apostle denied Jesus three times on the night He was betrayed. After Peter realized what he had done and wept with sorrow, Jesus forgave him completely.

Jesus' love and mercy gave hope to people with very bad sins. It invited them to be good. Mary Magdalen was a great sinner, but she believed in Jesus and the Good News of God's love. One night she came up to Jesus, poured precious oil on His feet, and wept for forgiveness. That was all Mary had to do. Jesus told everyone, "This woman's sins are forgiven because she has loved much."

Develop

1. Read paragraphs 3 and 4 from the student text.

2. From the children's Bible, read Peter's denial of Jesus found in Lk 22:54–63 and Jn 18:15–27, and Jesus' forgiveness of Peter found in Jn 21:1–19. Also read the story of Mary Magdalene pouring oil on Jesus' feet in Mt 26:6–13 and John 12:1–8.

3. Discuss these two stories:
- What were the sins of Peter and Mary Magdelene?
- Were they sins against God, man, or both?
- Why did Jesus forgive them?
- How did they show that they wanted God's forgiveness?
- How did Jesus show that they were forgiven?
- Did Jesus' forgiveness change them?
- Was Jesus angry? How did He receive them as sinners?

4. The children may act out these two stories. Have them take parts from the story, sharing how their characters may have felt. This may be done as a television interview between commentator and character after the dramatization of each story.

5. Ask the children how they can approach Jesus for forgiveness of their sins. Do they know the five steps to a good Sacrament of Penance? Should they fear approaching Jesus in Penance? Why or why not? How do they feel when they come out of Confession after being forgiven?

6. Ask the children how love and forgiveness are related. Use the stories of Peter and Mary Magdalene to exemplify this. How much does God love us? Remind them that Jesus showed His love for us by dying on the Cross and rising from the dead. How can we show God that we love Him?

Name:_____

God Forgives Sins

1. What is mortal sin?
   A mortal sin is a serious sin done on purpose, with full knowledge that it is wrong.

2. What is venial sin?
   A venial sin is a less serious sin or a wrong that we do without knowing that it is wrong.

3. Are all sins equal?
   No. Some sins are more harmful than others.

4. How are love and forgiveness related? You may use the example of Peter and Mary Magdalen to explain.
   Answers will vary based on the student text.

Faith and Life Series • Grade 3 • Chapter 13 • Lesson 2

Reinforce

1. Have the students work on *Activity Book*, p. 49.

2. Have the students work on the Memorization Questions for this chapter.

3. The children may be given time for an examination of conscience and to think of people from whom they may need to ask forgiveness. They can write cards or letters of apology for their sins.

Conclude

1. Lead the children in singing "Lord Jesus, think on me," *Adoremus Hymnal*, #364.

2. End class by praying the Act of Contrition.

Preview

In the next lesson, the students will learn how Jesus instituted the Sacrament of Penance.

FIVE STEPS TO A GOOD SACRAMENT OF PENANCE

1) Examination of conscience

2) Have sorrow for sin

3) Resolve to not sin again

4) Confess to a priest in the Sacrament of Penance

5) Do the penance given by the priest

NOTES

LESSON THREE: PENANCE

Aims

The students will learn that only God can forgive sins. Jesus showed that He is God by forgiving sins.

Jesus instituted the Sacrament of Penance for the forgiveness of sins. He gave the power to forgive sins to the Apostles. The Apostles have handed on this power through their successors, the bishops and priests, to the present day.

Materials

- *Activity Book*, p. 50
- Children's Bible

Optional:
- "Lord Jesus, think on me," *Adoremus Hymnal*, #364

Begin

Remind the children of God's merciful love for us. Through sin we turn away from God. Review the definitions of mortal and venial sin. Also review that we can show forgiveness in our families, but for sins against God, we must go to the Sacrament of Penance. Penance is the ordinary means of forgiveness of sins.

Develop

1. Read paragraph 5 aloud from the student text.

2. Read from the children's Bible the story of Jesus healing the paralytic from Luke 5:17–26. The importance in this passage is that Jesus gave a physical sign to show that He has the power to forgive sins—and only God can forgive sin. Therefore, this passage clearly teaches that Jesus is God and has the authority and power to forgive sins.

3. Explain that the Sacrament of Penance is a sacrament of healing. Using the chalk talk diagram on the the facing page, demonstrate the healing power of the Sacrament of Penance.

4. Review how the various names for the Sacrament of Penance relate to its parts and effects:

Only God can forgive sins. But on the first Easter Sunday night, Jesus gave His Apostles the power to forgive sins in His name. This was a great gift of grace to the world. Jesus breathed on the Apostles and said, "Peace be with you. Receive the Holy Spirit; if you forgive men's sins, they are forgiven."

The Apostles were the early priests of the Church. Our priests today carry the same power to forgive sins. They do this through the Sacrament of Penance. This sacrament frees our souls of any **mortal sins**, which are very serious and remove God's life of **grace** from our souls. It also frees us of less serious, **venial sins** that make a soul weak and less pleasing to God. When we go to a priest for this sacrament, we can be sure that Christ Himself is present, and He washes away all our sins. He will never turn us away when we are truly sorry for our sins, but He will only hold us closer to His Heart.

Remember, Jesus was crucified on a Cross between two thieves. The thief on Jesus' left had no sorrow for his crimes. But the thief on Jesus' right cried out that he was sorry. Jesus forgave him and said to him, "Today you will be with me in Paradise" (Luke 23:43).

Words to Know:

forgiveness   mortal sin   grace   venial sin

> **Q. 58** *In how many ways is sin committed?*
> Sin is committed in four ways, in *thoughts*, in *words*, in *deeds*, and in *omissions*, things we fail to do (CCC 1849).
>
> **Q. 59** *How many kinds of sin are there?*
> Sin is of two kinds: *mortal* and *venial* (CCC 1854).

- Penance—the work prescribed by the priest to aid us in changing our sinful ways and making up for the damage done by our sin.
- Confession—the act of confessing our sins
- Reconciliation—the effect of the Sacrament of Penance, to be restored to relationship with God and neighbor in the Church through the absolution said by the priest, speaking on behalf of Christ

5. Teach the children that Jesus Himself gave us this precious sacrament. Again, read John 20:19–23 from the children's Bible. Tell the students that Jesus gave the Apostles and their successors, the bishops and priests, the power to forgive sins. This power is extended to the priests and bishops at their ordination by the laying on of hands and the passing on of the gifts of the Holy Spirit.

Name:_____

Confession

Color the picture below.

Only God can forgive sins. But on the first Easter Sunday night, Jesus gave His Apostles the power to forgive sins in His name. This was a gift of grace to the world. Jesus breathed on the Apostles and said, "Peace be with you. Receive the Holy Spirit; if you forgive men's sins, they are forgiven."

The Apostles were the early priests of the Church. Our priests today carry the same power to forgive sins. They do this through the Sacrament of Penance.

50   Faith and Life Series • Grade 3 • Chapter 13 • Lesson 3

Reinforce

1. Have the students work on *Activity Book*, p. 50.

2. Have the students work on the Memorization Questions.

3. The students should also work on memorizing the Scripture quotation, John 20:23.

Conclude

1. Sing "Lord Jesus, think on me," *Adoremus Hymnal*, #364.

2. End class by praying the Act of Contrition.

Preview

In the next lesson, the students will learn more about the effects of the Sacrament of Penance.

CHALK TALK: SIN AND FORGIVENESS

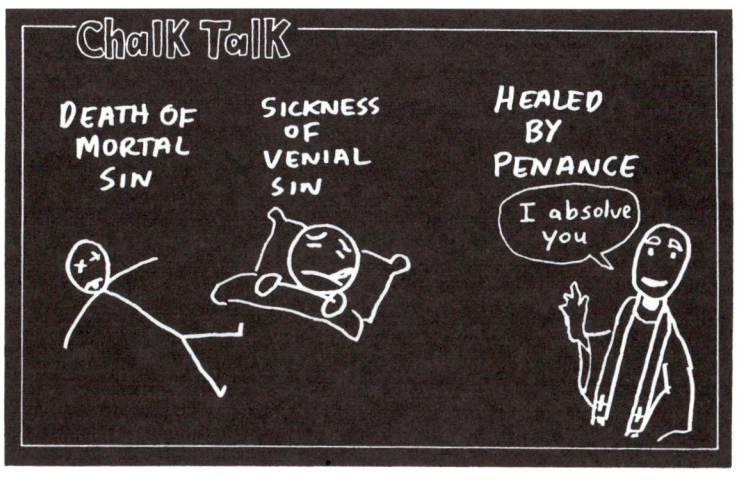

NOTES
_____
_____
_____
_____
_____
_____
_____
_____
_____

LESSON FOUR: EFFECTS OF PENANCE

Aims

The students will learn that in the Sacrament of Penance, Christ forgives man's sins (both mortal and venial) through the priest.

They will also learn that the Sacrament of Penance also restores the life of grace to man's soul.

Materials

- *Activity Book*, p. 51
- Children's Bible

Optional:
- "Lord Jesus, think on me," *Adoremus Hymnal*, #364

Begin

Begin this class with an overview of the Sacrament of Penance. What are the different names by which this sacrament is known? Who gave priests the power to forgive sins? Why is it a sacrament of healing? Review the matter and form of the Sacrament of Penance: confess sins to a priest, who says, "I absolve you from your sins in the Name of the Father and of the Son and of the Holy Spirit. *Amen.*"

Q. 60 *What is mortal sin?*
Mortal sin is a serious wrong done on purpose with full knowledge that it is wrong (CCC 1857).

Q. 61 *What is venial sin?*
Venial sin is a less serious sin, or a wrong that we do without knowing that it is wrong (CCC 1862).

Q. 62 *Are all sins equal?*
No, sins are not all equal. Just as some venial sins are less light than others, some mortal sins are more serious and harmful than others (CCC 1854).

Q. 63 *What is Confession?*
Confession is the sacrament instituted by Jesus Christ to forgive the sins committed after Baptism. Confession is also called the Sacrament of Penance or Reconciliation (CCC 1446).

Q. 64 *When was the Sacrament of Confession instituted by Jesus Christ?*
The Sacrament of Confession was instituted by Jesus Christ when He said to the Apostles, "Receive the Holy Spirit. If you forgive the sins of any, they are forgiven; if you retain the sins of any, they are retained" (John 20:22–23, CCC 1441).

Develop

1. Finish reading the chapter with the children.

2. Teach the students that the Sacrament of Penance has many effects including:

a) Forgiveness of mortal and venial sins. Whatever sins we confess—and we must confess our mortal sins—are forgiven. We cannot withhold wilfully any mortal sins.

b) Grace is restored to the soul. Because of sin, we lose grace. Mortal sin kills the life of grace in the soul, while venial sin lessens or weakens it. Sacrament of Penance restores the life of grace to our soul so that we can go to Heaven.

c) Healing. The sacrament brings healing to the person who wants forgiveness. It takes away our sins, restores grace, and gives us a penance to heal the damage caused by our sins.

d) Helps us to overcome our sins. The sacrament is so powerful that God gives us extra graces to overcome our sins through the practice of virtues. It also gives us the grace to desire to overcome our sins and the ability to overcome them with grace.

e) Reconciliation with God and neighbor through the Church. The priest, who is the representative of Christ and His Church, absolves us from our sins and restores our relationship with God and the Church.

f) Meeting with Christ. In every sacrament, we meet with Christ. He forgives our sins, welcomes us back into union with Him, and shows us His love in the Sacrament of Penance.

Name:_____

God's Tender Mercy

Match up the two columns according to the example.

__E__ God A. poured precious oil on Jesus' feet and wept for forgiveness.

__C__ Peter B. was known by name and was precious to the shepherd.

__B__ The lost sheep C. denied Jesus three times on the night He was betrayed. He wept with sorrow.

__G__ No sin on earth D. have the same power as the Apostles to forgive sins.

__H__ Jesus gave E. the One who forgives our sins.

__J__ Sins F. are two kinds of actual sin.

__A__ Mary Magdalene G. is greater than God's love and mercy.

__I__ Sacrament of Penance H. the power to forgive sins in His name.

__F__ Mortal and venial sins I. frees us from our sins.

__D__ Our priests today J. are not all equal. Some are more serious than others.

Faith and Life Series • Grade 3 • Chapter 13 • Lesson 4   51

SAINT PETER FACTS

In the Gospels we learn that Saint Peter:

- Walked on water, then sank when his faith weakened
- Proposed to build three tabernacles at the Transfiguration, when Jesus was with Moses and Elijah
- Cut off the ear of the high priest's slave
- Denied Christ three times
- Told Jesus that he loved Him three times
- Was forgiven by Jesus
- Was made head of the Church by Jesus

Reinforce

1. Have the students make posters of the effects of the Sacrament of Penance.

2. Have the students work on *Activity Book*, p. 51.

3. Have the students work on their Memorization Questions and begin reviewing for the quiz.

Conclude

1. Sing "Lord Jesus, think on me," *Adoremus Hymnal*, #364.

2. End class by praying the Act of Contrition.

Preview

In the next lesson, the students' knowledge of the material covered this week will be reviewed and assessed.

NOTES

CHAPTER THIRTEEN
REVIEW AND ASSESSMENT

Aims

The students' knowledge and understanding of the material covered this week will be reviewed and assessed.

Materials

- Quiz 13, Appendix, p. A-19

Optional:
- "Lord Jesus, think on me," *Adoremus Hymnal*, #364.

Review

1. Review God's love for man. Remind the students that He always loves us. We are the ones who turn away from God when we sin. God is always waiting for us to return to Him in the Sacrament of Penance.

2. Jesus is the Good Shepherd. Review this image of Christ and draw the parallel between a shepherd with his sheep and Christ with sinners.

3. Review the stories of God's forgiveness of Peter and Mary Magdalene.

4. Only God can forgive sins. Exemplify that Christ is God and has the power to forgive sins, as shown in His healing of the paralytic.

5. Review how Jesus instituted the Sacrament of Penance. Also, remind the students of the matter and form of the sacrament.

6. Review the definitions of mortal and venial sins.

Name: _____

God's Tender Mercy   Quiz 13

"Blessed are the merciful, for they shall obtain mercy" (Matthew 5:7).

Word Bank

sheep	Christ	sins	priests	forgiven
venial	Easter	go	grace	

Fill in the blanks with the correct words from the Word Bank.

1. God's love follows us wherever we *go*.

2. Jesus told us that He is the Good Shepherd and we are His *sheep*.

3. Only God can forgive sins. On that first *Easter* Sunday night, Jesus gave His Apostles the power to forgive sins in His Name.

4. Jesus breathed on the Apostles and said, "Peace be with you. Receive the Holy Spirit; if you forgive men's sins, they are *forgiven*."

5. The Apostles were the early *priests* of the Church. Our priests today have the same power to forgive sins through the Sacrament of Penance.

6. The Sacrament of Penance frees our souls of any mortal sins that remove God's life of *grace* from our souls.

7. The Sacrament of Penance or Reconciliation frees us of less serious, *venial* sins that weaken our love toward God and our neighbor.

8. When we go to a priest in the Sacrament of Penance, we can be sure that *Christ* Himself is present and He washes away all our sins.

9. God will never turn us away when we are truly sorry for our *sins*.

10. Write out the Scripture verse shown at the top of this page.

_____

Faith and Life • Grade 3 • Appendix A   A - 19

Assess

1. Distribute the quizzes and read through them with the students to be sure they understand the questions.

2. Administer the quiz. As they hand in their work, you may orally quiz them on the Memorization Questions for this chapter.

3. After all the quizzes have been handed in, you may wish to review the correct answers with the class.

Conclude

1. Sing "Lord Jesus, think on me," *Adoremus Hymnal*, #364.

2. End class by praying the Act of Contrition.

CHAPTER FOURTEEN
MEETING JESUS IN CONFESSION

Catechism of the Catholic Church References

Confession of Sins: 1455–58, 1493
Contrition: 1451–54, 1492
Minister of the Sacrament of Penance: 1461–67, 1495

Penance: 1422–98
Satisfaction for Sin: 1459–60, 1494

Scripture References

Parable of the Prodigal Son: Lk 15:11–32

Background Reading: *The Fundamentals of Catholicism* by Fr. Kenneth Baker, S.J.

Volume 3:
"Punishment Is Not Popular," pp. 298–300
"Reconciliation with God," pp. 301–3
"Who Can Hear Confessions?" pp. 304–6

Summary of Lesson Content

Lesson 1

When we are sorry for offending someone, we should say we are sorry. This is true in friendships and also in our relationship with God and His Church.

In the Sacrament of Penance, we repent of our sins against God and man (His Church), accept forgiveness, and are reconciled with God and man.

With God's grace, we strive to avoid sin in the future.

Lesson 2

Man must prepare to receive the Sacrament of Penance.

With the aid of the Holy Spirit, man first examines his conscience.

Man must be sorry for his sins (perfect or imperfect contrition.) Man must resolve to amend his life.

Next, he confesses his sins to a priest in the Sacrament of Penance.

Lesson 3

The steps to follow in the confessional include:
1) Receive a welcome and make the Sign of the Cross.
2) Tell the priest how long it has been since our last confession.
3) Confess our sins.
4) Receive our penance.
5) Say an Act of Contrition.
6) Receive absolution by saying "Amen."
7) Dismissal.

Lesson 4

The Sacrament of Penance is a sacrament of healing.

Communal penance services have large groups of people prepare for the Sacrament of Penance together. After this preparation, each person confesses individually.

General absolution is possible where individual confessions are not possible; however, one is obliged to confess individually at the first possible opportunity.

LESSON ONE: RECONCILIATION

Aims

When we are sorry for offending someone, we should say that we are sorry. This is true in our friendships, and also in our relationship with God and His Church.

The students will understand that in the Sacrament of Penance we repent of our sins against God and man (His Church), accept forgiveness, and are reconciled to God and man.

With God's grace, we strive to avoid sin in the future.

Materials

- *Activity Book*, p. 52
- Children's Bible

Optional:
- "Jesus, Lover of my soul," *Adoremus Hymnal*, #604
- "The Prodigal Son," video; Jesus: A Kingdom without Frontiers, available through Ignatius Press

Begin

Begin the class with the story of the Prodigal Son. If you have the video, "The Prodigal Son," from the Jesus: A Kingdom without Frontiers series (available through Ignatius Press; 30 minutes), you may show it. You may also dramatize this story. It is found in the children's Bible in Luke 15:11–32.

---

14   Meeting Jesus In Confession

"If you forgive the sins of any, they are forgiven; if you retain the sins of any, they are retained."

John 20:23

If you know you have hurt someone you love, what should you do? The best thing to do is to go to that person and say you are sorry. It is not enough just to think about how sorry you are. A good friendship calls for more. A true friend will go to the person he has hurt, say he is sorry, and make up and be friends again.

In the **Sacrament of Penance**, that is what we do with Jesus. We go to Him, tell Him we are sorry, resolve not to sin again, accept His forgiveness, and keep our friendship with Him alive and strong.

To prepare ourselves for this sacrament, there are certain things we must do. First we ask God the Holy Spirit, Who lives inside us, to help us remember our sins. We think about what we have done wrong and how many times we have done it. This is called **examination of conscience**.

Next, we think about how our sins offend Jesus and how we are sorry for them. This is called **sorrow for sins**. We make up our minds not to commit the same sins again, and we say an Act of Contrition. **Contrition** means sorrow. An Act of Contrition is a prayer telling God we are sorry and we hate our sins. In the Act of Contrition we say we hate sin because we know it can keep us from Heaven, but much more importantly, because it offends God. We

69

Develop

1. Read paragraphs 1 and 2 from the student text.

2. Using the example of the Prodigal Son, discuss how we should be reconciled in our relationships.
   - Why did the son leave?
   - How did he offend his father?
   - What did the son do with his inheritance?
   - What happened to the son?
   - Why did the son want to return?
   - Did the son know he did something wrong?
   - Did the father stop loving the son? How do we know this?
   - Did the father reject the son when he returned?
   - What did the son say to the father?
   - Did the son decide not to sin again?
   - Did the father forgive the son?
   - Was their relationship restored?

3. Reread paragraph two from the student text. Using the story of the Prodigal Son, demonstrate the steps to the

Sacrament of Penance:
1. The son knew he offended the father
2. The son was sorry for his sins
3. The son decided to not sin again and accepted the mercy and penance of the father.
4. The son went to the father to ask forgiveness
5. The father forgave his son and restored him to relationship with the father.

4. Discuss how sinning against someone here on earth offends God. Because all people are God's children, it saddens him to see us offend one another. Also, when we sin, we break God's laws. Jesus, as God and Man, died to reconcile us with God and neighbor. To help us to be sorry for our sins, we can look upon the Crucifix. In the Crucifix, we see the sacrifice Jesus made to save us from our sins. He made this sacrifice because He loves us. When we sin, we are not loving God or neighbor. Seeing this example of love may remind us of how we should love one another and God.

Name:_____

Word Find

Use your student text to find these words and use them in a sentence.

Examination of Conscience: _____
Answers will vary.
_____

Penance: _____
_____

Sorrow for sins: _____
_____

Contrition: _____
_____

Sacrament of Penance: _____
_____

Forgiveness: _____
_____

Grace: _____
_____

Sacrament: _____
_____

Sin: _____
_____

Mortal Sin: _____
_____

Venial Sin: _____
_____

52   Faith and Life Series • Grade 3 • Chapter 14 • Lesson 1

Reinforce

1. Have the students work on *Activity Book*, p. 52. Note: This will help them with the rest of the chapter.

2. Have the students dramatize scenarios of sinning against a person and then reconciling; e.g., start an argument with a sibling, then tell him you're sorry.

3. Teach the students to sing "Jesus, Lover of my soul," *Adoremus Hymnal*, #604.

Conclude

Lead the children in praying the Prayer before a Crucifix and the Act of Contrition.

Preview

In the next lesson, the students will begin learning the steps to a good Sacrament of Penance.

PRAYER BEFORE A CRUCIFIX

Behold, O Kind and most sweet Jesus, before Thy face I humbly kneel, and with the most fervent desire of soul, I pray and beseech Thee to impress upon my heart lively sentiments of faith, hope and charity, true contrition for my sins and a firm purpose of amendment. With deep affliction and grief of soul, I ponder within myself, mentally contemplating Thy five wounds, having before my eyes the words which David the Prophet spoke concerning Thee: "They have pierced my hands and my feet, they have numbered all my bones. *Amen*.

NOTES

LESSON TWO: PREPARING FOR CONFESSION

Aims

We must prepare to receive the Sacrament of Penance:

First, we must examines our consciences.

Second, we must be sorry for our sins (perfect or imperfect contrition) and decide not to sin again.

Third, we confess our sins to a priest in the Sacrament of Penance.

Materials

- *Activity Book*, p. 53
- Age-appropriate examinations of conscience
- Posterboard/markers

Optional:
- "Jesus, Lover of my soul," *Adoremus Hymnal*, #604.

Begin

Begin the class by asking the children a question: if they were to go on a long trip, would they simply go to the airport/bus station, buy a ticket, and go? No, they would have to plan their trip. What must they do before they can go?
- Decide where they want to go
- Buy a ticket
- Apply for a passport
- Prepare for a place to stay at your destination
- Decide what should be packed
- Pack

---

tell God that He is all good and deserving of all our love. We ask for His grace to do better in the future.

After our Act of Contrition, it is time to receive the sacrament. We go into the confessional or reconciliation room where the priest welcomes us. Together we make the Sign of the Cross. The priest may read to us from the Bible. Usually he says words about God's mercy and love.

We tell the priest how long it has been since our last confession, then we confess our sins since that time. After we are all finished, the priest talks to us about what we have told him. Then he gives us a **penance**, which can be some prayers or action that helps to make up for the wrong we have done to God and to others. (We will do the penance after our confession is over.) Then we say the Act of Contrition out loud.

Before we leave the confessional, the priest will absolve us. This means that he uses his Christ-given power to forgive all our sins. When we hear the words of absolution, we know that Jesus Himself is forgiving us through the priest. He says, "I absolve you from your sins in the Name of the Father, and of the Son, and of the Holy Spirit." We accept the absolution by answering, "Amen." This is a beautiful moment, because God has completely forgiven us. He is giving us a fresh start.

Every time we receive the Sacrament of Penance, Jesus is with us, healing our hearts. We always confess our sins privately to a priest, usually in the confessional. Sometimes, at a communal Penance service, all the people in the church prepare together for Confession and then confess and receive absolution individually. In cases of necessity where to hear individual confessions of large numbers of people is impossible, a priest may give general absolution to all the people. But those people then have to make a private, individual confession as soon as they are able.

Develop

1. Read paragraphs 3–4 with the students. Write the steps to preparing for the Sacrament of Penance on the board:
   - *Examination of conscience*
   - *Sorrow for sin*
   - *Decide not to sin again*
   - *Confess sins*

2. Walk the children through these steps:

- Examination of conscience:
  Using the Ten Commandments and the virtues they have already learned, have the children silently reflect on which Commandments they have broken and how many times (since their last confession). They may write down their sins, but they must keep this page to themselves—instruct them not to write their names on it.

- Sorrow for sin:
  Guide the students through a meditation to help them have sorrow for sin, both perfect contrition (being sorry because our sins offend God) and imperfect contrition (being sorry because we fear the consequences of our sins). You may have them look upon a Crucifix. They may also pray the Prayer before the Crucifix.

- Decide to not sin again:
  Ask the children to think of why they do not want to sin again, and ways to avoid sinning again. Lead the children in an Act of Contrition.

- Confess sins:
  Ask the children to whom they must confess and where. It is important to stress that they must confess to a priest (not just pray) and do this in the Sacrament of Penance; e.g., they may not merely approach a priest and say, "Guess what I did last week?"

Name:_____

Preparing for Penance

1. How many things are required to make a good confession?
There are 5 steps to a good confession: examination of conscience, sorrow for sins, intention of not committing sin again, the accusation of our sin, and satisfaction or penance.

2. How is the examination of conscience done?
It is done by remembering the sins committed in thought, words, deeds, and omissions against the Commandments of God beginning from the last confession.

3. What is sorrow?
Sorrow is a sadness and hatred for the sins we have committed, which makes us decide not to sin again.

Write out the Act of Contrition.
O my God, I am heartily sorry for having offended You. I detest all my sins because of Your just punishments, but most of all because they offend You, my God, Who are all good and deserving of all my love. I firmly resolve, with the help of Your grace, to confess my sins, to do penance, and to amend my life. Amen.

Faith and Life Series • Grade 3 • Chapter 14 • Lesson 2

Reinforce

1. Have the students work on *Activity Book*, p. 53.

2. Have the students make posters of the steps to prepare for a good Sacrament of Penance.

3. Give the children time to pray before the Blessed Sacrament to help them prepare for the Sacrament of Penance.

Conclude

1. Sing together "Jesus, Lover of my soul," *Adoremus Hymnal*, #604.

2. Pray the Prayer before a Crucifix and the Act of Contrition.

Preview

In the next lesson the students will learn the steps to confessing their sins.

EXAMINATION OF CONSCIENCE

We all make mistakes sometimes. Guide the children through an examination of conscience. The students should use the knowledge they gained about the Ten Commandments and the virtues to judge their own actions.

Go through each of the Ten Commandments with the children, and tell them to review their actions and recall where they have failed to live the Commandments. Remind them that God loves them and wants them to live by His Commandments, but He will forgive them in the Sacrament of Penance when they make a mistake and sin.

NOTES

LESSON THREE: CONFESSION

Aims

The students will learn the proper steps to follow in receiving the Sacrament of Penance.

Materials

- *Activity Book*, p. 54
- Paper and pencils
- Scripts for practicing a confession

Optional:
- "Jesus, Lover of my soul," *Adoremus Hymnal*, #604

Begin

Review with the students the steps to preparing for the Sacrament of Penance.
- Examination of conscience
- Sorrow for sin
- Decide not to sin again
- Confess sins to a priest in the Sacrament of Penance

Ask the children to explain each step.

Jesus waits for us in this sacrament because He has so much merciful love and grace to give us. Let us try to go to Him often.

ACT OF CONTRITION

O my God, I am heartily sorry for having offended You. I detest all my sins because of Your just punishments, but most of all because they offend You, my God, Who are all-good and deserving of all my love. I firmly resolve, with the help of Your grace, to confess my sins, to do penance, and to amend my life. *Amen*.

THE WORDS OF ABSOLUTION

God, the Father of mercies, through the death and Resurrection of His Son, has reconciled the world to Himself and sent the Holy Spirit among us for the forgiveness of sins; through the ministry of the Church, may God give you pardon and peace, and I absolve you from your sins in the name of the Father, and of the Son, and of the Holy Spirit.

Words to Know:

Sacrament of Penance   examination of conscience
sorrow for sins   contrition   penance

Develop

1. Read paragraphs 5–7 in the student text.

2. On the board, write the steps to confessing our sins:
   - *The priest welcomes*
   - *Make the Sign of the Cross*
   - *Tell the priest how long it has been since your last confession*
   - *Tell the priest your sins (mortal and venial—for mortal sins tell the number or frequency)*
   - *Listen to the priest*
   - *Receive your penance*
   - *Say the Act of Contrition*
   - *Receive absolution*
   - *Dismissal*
   - *Do your penance*

3. Teach the children about the sacramental seal. The priest cannot tell anyone anything you say in the Sacrament of Penance. It is important to know this, so we can be honest in confessing our sins.

4. Copy the chalk talk (at right) onto the board. Have the students copy it onto paper.

5. Have the students rehearse confessing. Allow them to make up one mortal and one venial sin to confess. Parent helpers would be great "priests" for this exercise. If need be, you can call each child back while they work on their chalk-talk diagrams.

6. *If possible, tour the confessionals.*

7. Give the children time to pray in order to prepare themselves to receive the Sacrament of Penance.

Name:_____

Confessing Our Sins

Steps to Confessing Sins	Give an example
1. Welcome and Sign of the Cross (Note: this may include reading a passage from Scripture.)	The Sign of the Cross is: In the Name of the Father and of the Son and of the Holy Spirit
2. Tell the priest how long it has been since your last confession.	"Bless me father, for I have sinned. It has been _____ days/months since my last confession."
3. Confess your sins.	An example of a mortal sin is: Answers will vary. An example of a venial sin is:
4. Receive your penance.	A penance may be some prayers, such as: Or a work of charity, such as:
5. Say an act of contrition	Write out an act of contrition on a separate piece of paper.
6. Receive absolution from the priest.	"I absolve you from your sins in the Name of the Father and of the Son and of the Holy Spirit."
7. Dismissal	"Your sins are forgiven. Go in peace to love and serve the Lord."

54   Faith and Life Series • Grade 3 • Chapter 14 • Lesson 3

Reinforce

1. Have the students work on *Activity Book*, p. 54.

2. Give all the children time to practice going to the Sacrament of Penance.

Conclude

1. Sing "Jesus, Lover of my soul," *Adoremus Hymnal*, #604.

2. Pray the Prayer before the Crucifix and the Act of Contrition.

Preview

In the next class, the students will learn about communal penance services. If possible, they will experience one and have a chance to receive the Sacrament of Penance.

Note: This must be arranged with a priest.

CHALK TALK: A GOOD CONFESSION

NOTES

LESSON FOUR: HEALING

Aims

The Sacrament of Penance is a sacrament of healing.

Communal penance services let people prepare for the Sacrament of Penance together. After this preparation, each person confesses individually.

General absolution is only permissible in the event that individual confessions are not possible; however, one is obliged to confess individually at the first possible opportunity after receiving general absolution.

Materials

- *Activity Book*, p. 55

Optional:
- "Jesus, Lover of my soul," *Adoremus Hymnal*, #604
- Arrange for a priest to preside over a communal penance service and hear confessions.

Begin

Begin the class by reviewing the definitions of mortal and venial sin, and the steps to making a good Sacrament of Penance.

Briefly walk with the children through an age-appropriate examination of conscience. They should have already done a thorough examination of conscience in the previous days.

Q. 65 *How many things are required to make a good confession?*
To make a good confession five things are required: 1) examination of conscience; 2) sorrow for sins; 3) the intention of not committing sin again; 4) the accusation of our sin; 5) satisfaction or penance (CCC 1450, 1454, 1456, 1459).

Q. 66 *How is the examination of conscience done?*
The examination of conscience is done by remembering the sins we have committed in thoughts, words, deeds, and omissions against the Commandments of God, beginning from our last good confession (CCC 1454).

Q. 67 *What is sorrow?*
Sorrow is a sadness and hatred for the sins we have committed, which makes us decide not to sin again (CCC 1451).

Develop

1. Read the remainder of the text from the chapter aloud.

2. Bring the students to the church or a communal penance service. Encourage the students to bring with them:
   - Their examinations of conscience
   - *Activity Book*, p. 55
   - Act of Contrition

Note: This service will likely take the entire class.

3. Celebrate with a treat, such as cookies and punch, in imitation of the story of the Prodigal Son, in which the father celebrates his son's repentance with a great feast.

4. If a communal penance service cannot be arranged, explain general absolution to the children. In cases of emergency (e.g., on the battlefield, on a sinking ship, or in a natural disaster) or when it is not possible for individual confessions to be heard (e.g., when there are too many people), a priest may give general absolution; however, when possible, the people must go to an individual confession as soon as possible. So, for example, if general absolution is given to a group of fire-fighters entering a dangerous fire, and they all come out alive, then they must still go to individual confessions at the earliest opportunity.

5. Explain the importance of the Sacrament of Penance. Although sometimes we become nervous before receiving the Sacrament of Penance, it is very important that we go, and we often feel better after we confess. Using the example of Saint John Vianney (Curé of Ars), show how priests want us to receive the Sacrament of Penance. They are very happy to have people come to the Sacrament of Penance, so that they can receive the Sacrament of the Eucharist worthily. Priests want to help us to get to Heaven—this is their vocation.

Name:_____

Forgiving Sins

1. If you have hurt someone you love, what should you do?
You should go to that person and say you are sorry.

2. What do we do in the Sacrament of Penance?
We tell Jesus that we are sorry, resolve not to sin again, accept His forgiveness, and keep our friendship with Him alive and strong.

3. What are the five steps to a good confession?
   1. Examination of conscience
   2. Sorrow for sins
   3. The intention of not sinning again
   4. The accusation of our sins
   5. Satisfaction or penance

4. What is contrition?
Contrition is sorrow for sins.

5. What is penance?
Prayers or actions that help to make up for the wrong that we have done to God and to others

6. What does it mean to say that the priest will absolve you?
This means that he uses his Christ-given power to forgive all our sins.

7. What are the words of absolution?
"I absolve you from your sins in the Name of the Father and of the Son and of the Holy Spirit."

8. What does Jesus give us in the Sacrament of Penance?
Jesus gives us a fresh start.

Faith and Life Series • Grade 3 • Chapter 14 • Lesson 4   55

Reinforce

1. If possible, have the students go to a communal penance service and receive the Sacrament of Penance.

2. Have the students work on *Activity Book*, p. 55.

Conclude

1. Sing "Jesus, Lover of my soul," *Adoremus Hymnal*, #604.

2. Pray the Prayer before the Crucifix and the Act of Contrition.

Preview

In the next lesson, the students' knowledge of the material covered this week will be reviewed and assessed.

THE CURÉ OF ARS

Jean-Marie Vianney was a humble servant who almost wasn't ordained because of his slowness in studies. After being ordained in 1815, he was sent to Ars, where there was little or no faith left in the community. Jean-Marie Vianney was sent to bring them back to pious devotion to God. His bishop told him, "There is not much love of God in that parish, you will put some there." Soon, his reputation for saintliness and an ability to read souls in confession drew tens of thousands to his parish each year. People came because they recognized the opportunity to see a model of true godliness and, by this meeting, move closer to God, themselves.

NOTES

CHAPTER FOURTEEN
REVIEW AND ASSESSMENT

Aims

The students' knowledge and understanding of the material covered this week will be reviewed and assessed.

Materials

- Quiz 14, Appendix, p. A-20

Optional:
- "Jesus, Lover of my soul," *Adoremus Hymnal*, #604

Review

1. Review the need for the Sacrament of Penance. The students should know the story of the Prodigal Son.

2. Review the steps to preparing for a good Sacrament of Penance. Have the students explain each of the steps.

3. Review the steps to confessing our sins. Have the students explain each of the steps. This may be demonstrated with a "confession" dramatized by two students.

4. The students should know what general absolution is, and the need to receive individual confession as soon as the recipients of general absolution are able.

5. The students should understand the great gift of the Sacrament of Penance. They should know the effects (from the previous chapter) and that even the priests want us to receive this sacrament.

6. The students should know about the sacramental seal.

Name: _____

Meeting Jesus in Confession   Quiz 14

"If you forgive the sins of any, they are forgiven" (John 20:23).

Word Bank

forgiving	receive	sorry	Jesus
penance	sins	absolution	offend

Fill in the blanks with the correct words from the Word Bank.

1. If we hurt someone, we tell that person that we are **sorry**.

2. In the Sacrament of Penance we tell **Jesus** that we are sorry.

3. We prepare to **receive** the sacrament by making an examination of conscience. We think about what we have done wrong and about how many times we have done it.

4. Next, we think about how our sins **offend** Jesus and how we are sorry for them. We make up our mind not to commit the same sins again. We say the Act of Contrition.

5. We go into the confessional or reconciliation room and tell our **sins** to the priest. After we are finished, the priest talks to us about what we have told him.

6. The priest then gives us a **penance** which can be prayers or things to do to make up for the wrong we have done to God and others. Then we say the Act of Contrition.

7. We receive **absolution**, the forgiveness of our sins, when the priest says, "I absolve you from your sins in the Name of the Father and of the Son and of the Holy Spirit."

8. Every time we hear the words of absolution, we know that Jesus Himself is **forgiving** us through the priest.

9. Write out the Scripture verse shown at the top of this page.

_____

A - 20   Faith and Life • Grade 3 • Appendix A

Assess

1. Distribute the quizzes and read through them with the students to be sure they understand the questions.

2. Administer the quiz. As they hand in their work, you may orally quiz them on the Memorization Questions for this chapter.

3. After all the quizzes have been handed in, you may wish to review the correct answers with the class.

Conclude

1. End class by singing "Jesus, Lover of my soul," *Adoremus Hymnal*, #604.

2. Pray the Prayer before the Crucifix and the Act of Contrition

CHAPTER FIFTEEN
THE CHRIST CHILD IS BORN

Catechism of the Catholic Church References

Christ: At the Heart of Catechesis: 426–29
Christmas Mystery: 525–26
God Forms His People, Israel: 62–64, 72, 218, 2077
Good News: God Sent His Son: 422–29
Immaculate Conception: 490–93, 508
Incarnation: 461–79, 483
Jesus as Messiah: 436–40, 453
Jesus as True God and True Man: 464–70, 480–83
Jesus' Human Nature: 470–78, 482
Jesus' Mission of Salvation: 456–60

Mary's Consent: 494–511
Mary's Divine Motherhood: 495–509
Mary, Ever-Virgin: 496–507, 510
Mary's Predestination: 488–89
Mysteries of Jesus' Infancy: 527–30, 563
Nativity: 437, 525
Obedience of Mary's Faith: 148–49
Preparations for Christ's Coming: 522–24
Promise of a Redeemer: 410–12, 420–21
Why the Son of God Became Flesh: 456–60

Scripture References

Prophecies: Is 7:14, 11:1–3
Annunciation: Lk 1:26–38
Visitation: Lk 1:38–56
Nativity: Lk 2:1–20; Mt 1:18–23

Adoration of the Three Wise Men: Mt 2:1–12
Presentation in the Temple: Lk 2:22–40
Flight into Egypt: Lk 2:13–23

Background Reading: *The Fundamentals of Catholicism* by Fr. Kenneth Baker, S.J.

Volume 2:
"Jesus Christ Is True God," pp. 197–99
"Jesus' Divine Knowledge and Power," pp. 200–3

"Jesus Christ Is Truly Human," pp. 210–13
"The Perfect Man," pp. 213–16

Summary of Lesson Content

Lesson 1

The people of Israel waited for thousands of years for the coming of the Savior, Jesus, the light of the world.

God sent His Son, the Second Person of the Trinity, to redeem humanity. The Son of God became Man and was born of the virgin named Mary.

Lesson 2

God sent the angel Gabriel to Mary to invite her to be the mother of His Son, and she said "Yes." This event is called the Annunciation.

Mary conceived by the power of the Holy Spirit and remained a virgin.

Jesus will save His people from their sins so they can be united with Him forever.

Lesson 3

God predestined Mary to be the Mother of God.

From the very first moment of her life (conception), Mary was free from Original Sin. We call this gift from God to Mary the Immaculate Conception.

Lesson 4

Joseph is the foster-father of Jesus. Joseph took Mary to Bethlehem, where Jesus was born.

Because there was no room in the inn, Jesus was born in a stable, wrapped in swaddling clothes, and laid in a manger.

Jesus' birth was announced first to shepherds by angels.

Later, three wise men came to pay homage to Jesus.

LESSON ONE: INCARNATION

Aims

The children will learn that the people of Israel waited for thousands of years for the coming of the Savior, Jesus, the light of the world.

They will learn that God sent His Son, the Second Person of the Trinity, to earth. The Son of God became Man and was born of a virgin named Mary.

Materials

- *Activity Book*, p. 56
- Children's Bible
- Nativity set
- Candle, matches, and votive candles
- Advent wreath, advent calendar, and Jesse Tree

Optional:
- "Once in royal David's city," *Adoremus Hymnal*, #328

Begin

Begin the class in darkness. Make the room as dark as possible and read the following prophecies: Is 9:2, 42:6, 51:4, 60:19.

Then light a single candle and read the following Bible quotes: Mt 4:16; Lk 2:32; Jn 8:12.

Have each child light a votive candle from the main candle and read Mt 5:16.

---

15 The Christ Child Is Born

"Behold, a virgin shall conceive and bear a son, and his name shall be called Emmanuel. . . ."

Matthew 1:23

How would you feel if you and your family sat for a long time in a cold, dark room with no light? That is how the people of Israel might sometimes have felt during their long wait for the Messiah. They waited in darkness for two thousand years. At last God kept His promise. He sent the world a Savior Who shattered the darkness with a great light. Jesus is the Light of the World.

God did not send a rich king or strong warrior to be the Light of the World. He sent a little child. This child was His own Son, the Second Person of the Holy Trinity. Jesus is God, but He was born into the world as a man like us. God the Father invited Mary to be a part of this special plan to save His people. Jesus came to the world because Mary answered "Yes."

Mary was a young woman of Nazareth. She was in her simple, village home one day when the angel Gabriel appeared before her to bring God's message:

"Hail, full of grace, the Lord is with you! Blessed are you among women! You will bear a son and call His name Jesus, for He shall save His people from their sins. The Holy Spirit will come upon you and the power of the Most High will overshadow you, and so the holy Child to be born shall be called the Son of God."

Develop

1. Read paragraph 1 from the student text.

2. Read some prophecies from a children's Bible about the coming of Jesus into the world, so the children will know that the Jewish people were awaiting the coming of the Messiah. Suggested readings are Isaiah 7:14 and Isaiah 11:1–3.

3. Read paragraph 2 from the student text.

4. Discuss the role of Mary as the Mother of God. God prepared Mary for this role by her Immaculate Conception. This means she was full of grace and without the stain of Original Sin from the first moment of her life, though she still had free will. She freely accepted God's invitation to be the Mother of Jesus Christ.

5. You may display a Nativity set, but do not put out the baby Jesus yet. Let the children anticipate His coming.

6. God has a plan for each of us, and we can freely choose to accept or deny it. One way to deny His plan is to sin (because God wants all of us to go to Heaven and to be holy). But God has a specific plan for each of us. In this way, we bring Christ into the world. Refer back to the lighting of the candle. The one candle represents Christ. We were all able to light our candle from this one candle, which symbolizes the life of Christ that we received in Baptism. We may choose what we do with this light of grace. We may blow it out (mortal sin), or let it shine to spread the Good News and bring the light of Christ to others through good works. Have the students think of ways that they can say "Yes" to God and follow Mary's example.

7. Ask the students to share traditions they have in their family to prepare for Christmas, the celebration of the birth of Jesus.

Name:_____

Mary's "Yes!"

Color the picture below.

God did not send a rich king or strong warrior to be the Light of the World. He sent a little child who was His own Son. Jesus is God, but He was born into the world as a man like us. God the Father invited Mary to be a part of this special plan to save His people. Jesus came into the world because Mary answered "yes."

56 Faith and Life Series • Grade 3 • Chapter 15 • Lesson 1

ADVENT: A TIME OF WAITING

Each year the Church has a special time of waiting before Christmas called Advent (from the Latin "Advenire" meaning "to come"). As an Advent activity, prepare a classroom manger using pieces of straw. Tell the children that when Advent begins they should try very hard to do acts of sacrifice, obedience, and love each day. Explain that an act of sacrifice means giving up something they like for love of Jesus (candy, TV, etc.). Each time they do an act of sacrifice, obedience, or love, they can place a piece of straw in the manger for baby Jesus. When Christmas day comes, the students' good deeds will cushion the Savior's bed.

Reinforce

1. Have the students work on *Activity Book*, p. 56.

2. Have the children share their advent traditions with the class. You may teach the children about the Advent wreath, Advent calendars, and the Jesse Tree.

3. Teach the children to sing "Once in royal David's city," *Adoremus Hymnal*, #328.

Conclude

1. Gather the children around the Nativity set and pray together the Hail Mary.

2. You may have each child think of something he will do this night to say "Yes" to God.

Preview

In the next class the students will learn about the Annunciation.

NOTES

_____
_____
_____
_____
_____
_____
_____
_____
_____

LESSON TWO: ANNUNCIATION

Aims

The students will learn that God sent the angel Gabriel to Mary to invite her to be the mother of His Son, and she said "Yes." This event is called the Annunciation.

They will also learn about the Visitation.

Materials

- *Activity Book*, p. 57
- Pieces of straw

Optional:
- "Once in Royal David's City," *Adoremus Hymnal*, #328
- "The Announcement to Mary," video; Jesus: a Kingdom without Frontiers, available through Ignatius Press

Begin

Begin the class by having the students recall the ways that they said "Yes" to God since the previous class. For every good work or prayer they said, have the children put a piece of straw in the manger to make a soft bed for Baby Jesus when He comes.

Tell the students that the straw will be available throughout the week. They may add a piece of straw whenever they do a good work or say a prayer.

Mary knew if she said "Yes" it might mean great sorrows as well as great joys. But she wanted to do whatever God asked. She bowed her head and told the angel: "Behold the handmaid of the Lord, let it be done to me according to your word." Mary's quiet "Yes" was still a secret to God's people, but it was the beginning of His loving plan to save them from sin.

An ordinary girl might have been afraid. But Mary was special. God prepared her to be the mother of the Savior even before she was born. He had given her a gift which we call Mary's Immaculate Conception. This means that Mary was created free from Original Sin. From the moment she was conceived in her mother's womb, her soul was filled with sanctifying grace. Mary did not need to be baptized because she always had God's life in her soul. This is why she was worthy to be the mother of Jesus. God also chose a good man named Joseph to marry her and be the foster father of Jesus. A **foster father** is a man who takes the place of the real father.

On the night of Jesus' birth, Mary and Joseph walked from inn to inn looking for shelter. They were in the town of **Bethlehem** because the Roman governor made all people return to their hometowns. The little town of Bethlehem was full. Every innkeeper told Joseph, "Sorry, there is no room for you in this inn."

At last, Joseph found a **stable** under the stars. Animals were sheltered beneath its roof. Jesus was born that night among the gentle oxen, donkeys, and lambs. Mary wrapped Him tenderly in soft cloth and laid Him in a **manger**, a box that held food for the animals. The Son of God spent His first earthly hours on a **humble** bed of straw.

An angel appeared to shepherds on the hillsides near Bethlehem and proclaimed, "Behold, I bring you Good News of great joy! Today, in the town of David, has been born to you a Savior, Who is Christ the Lord. You will find Him lying in a manger." Full of

75

Develop

1. Read paragraphs 3–4 aloud.

2. You may read the story of the Annunciation from the children's Bible: Luke 1:26–35. If you have the video "The Announcement to Mary," from the Jesus: a Kingdom without Frontiers series (available through Ignatius Press; 30 minutes), you may show it at this time.

3. You may discuss the story of the Annunciation and let the children act it out. How would Mary have felt when the angel suddenly appeared to her? How would the children have felt? Would she have been scared to be asked to be the Mother of God? Would she have been confused? Would she have been excited? Let the children tell you how they understand the Annunciation. You may let them know that for Mary to become the mother of Jesus a miracle had to happen, for she was a virgin.

4. Read the story of the Visitation found in Luke 1:38–56.

Show how the Hail Mary is found in the two stories of the Annunciation and the Visitation.

5. Discuss how Mary found joy in serving others. Mary even served Elizabeth after she knew she was with child. Serving others is a great way to love as Jesus loved.

6. You may lead the children in praying the first two Joyful Mysteries of the Rosary.

7. How do they think Mary would have prepared for the coming of Jesus? Would she have made clothes for him? Would she have prayed for his safe arrival? Would she have prayed that Joseph would be understanding? Did she learn from Elizabeth how to prepare for the coming of her baby?

8. How can we prepare to say "Yes" to God? Do we need to work on certain virtues? Can we practice being good and obeying God's laws?

Name:_____

Hail Mary!

Color the picture below.

Hail Mary, full of grace, the Lord is with you. Blessed are you among women, and blessed is the fruit of your womb, Jesus. Holy Mary, Mother of God, pray for us sinners, now and at the hour of our death. Amen.

Faith and Life Series • Grade 3 • Chapter 15 • Lesson 2   57

Reinforce

1. Have the students work on *Activity Book*, p. 57.

2. Have the students dramatize the Annunciation and the Visitation.

3. Begin working on the Memorization Questions.

Conclude

1. Sing "Once in royal David's city," *Adoremus Hymnal*, #328.

2. Pray the Hail Mary.

Preview

In the next lesson, the students will focus more on the Immaculate Conception and the holy family.

SAINT NICHOLAS AND SANTA CLAUS

Though one of the most popular saints in the Church, little is known about Saint Nicholas except that he was born in Parara, a city of Lycia in Asia Minor, and he was the bishop of Myra in the fourth century. His relics are preserved today in the church of San Nicola in Bari, Italy. He is the patron saint of mariners, merchants, bakers, travelers, and children, and his feast day is December 6. Tradition asserts that he became well-known during his life for giving generous gifts to many people, including the poor. In the United States he is identified with Santa Claus, the jolly man in a red suit who brings presents to children every Christmas Eve.

NOTES

LESSON THREE: MARY

Aims

God predestined Mary to be the Mother of God.

From the very first moment of her life (conception), Mary was free from Original Sin. We call this gift from God the Immaculate Conception.

Materials

- *Activity Book*, p. 58
- Construction paper and markers

Optional:
- "Once in royal David's city," *Adoremus Hymnal*, #328

Begin

Begin the class by inviting the children to come forward to add straw to the manger of Jesus, as they did in the previous class.

You may review the mysteries of the Annunciation and Visitation.

Stress the importance and beauty of Mary's "Yes" to God, by which she accepted her role as the Mother of Jesus, the Savior of the world.

Develop

1. Read paragraphs 5 and 6 with the children.

2. Discuss the Immaculate Conception. You may use the chalk talk diagram at the right to assist you in this lesson. Remind the students that the Immaculate Conception means that Mary was without sin and was filled with grace from the moment of her conception (the very start of her life). Mary did not need to be baptized. This was a great gift from God.

3. Discuss how Mary was helped by Joseph, her husband. He did his best to take care of Mary and Jesus. When they had to go to Bethlehem for the census, he tried very hard to find a good place for them to stay. How must he have felt to know that there was no room for them at the inn?

4. Discuss the Holy Family. Mary was the Mother of Jesus, and, therefore, may be called the Mother of God. She was without sin (Immaculate Conception) and freely said "Yes" to being the Mother of Jesus. She would have made clothes for him, cooked for him, kept home for the family, and done all the wonderful things that mothers do. Have the children think of things that Mary likely would have done for Jesus. Joseph is the foster-father of Jesus. He was not the natural father of Jesus because God was His father. However, everyone thought that Joseph was His father. Joseph was a carpenter. He probably taught Jesus about carpentry and the Scriptures. He would have cared for Mary, his wife, and for Jesus as though He were his own son. Jesus would have been faithful and obedient to Mary and Joseph, and loved them very much.

5. Have the students think of ways that they can imitate the Holy Family in their homes.

6. Have the students think of ways to give straw to Jesus.

---

wonder, the shepherds ran to be the first to adore Him. Later three wise men followed a great star to find the Child. They brought Him precious gifts for a King: gold, frankincense, and myrrh. We can bring the Christ Child our hearts, as our Gifts for Him.

Christmas is Jesus' birthday. Every year we sing carols to celebrate. This carol was written over a hundred years ago:

WE THREE KINGS OF ORIENT ARE

We three kings of Orient are,
Bearing gifts we traverse afar,
Field and fountain, Moor and mountain,
Following yonder star.

O star of wonder star of night,
Star with royal beauty bright;
Westward leading, still proceeding,
Guide us to thy perfect light.

Born a King on Bethlehem's plain,
Gold I bring to crown Him again,
King for ever, ceasing never
Over us all to reign.

Words to Know:

foster father   Bethlehem   stable   manger   humble

"Glory to God in the highest, and on earth peace among men with whom he is well pleased!"

Luke 2:14

Name:_____

*Behold the Handmaid of the Lord,
Let it Be Done to Me According to Your Word.*

Color the picture below.

An ordinary girl might have been afraid. But Mary was special. God prepared her to be the mother of the Savior even before she was born. He had given her a gift which we call Mary's Immaculate Conception. This means that Mary was always free from Original Sin even before she was born. From the moment she was conceived in her mother's womb, her soul was filled with sanctifying grace. Mary did not need to be baptized because she always had God's life in her soul. This is why she was worthy to be the Mother of Jesus.

Faith and Life Series • Grade 3 • Chapter 15 • Lesson 3

Reinforce

1. Have the students work on *Activity Book*, p. 58.

2. Have the students think about the stable where Jesus was born. It was cold, it smelled badly, it was drafty and damp. There was no place for him to lay his head. There are many reasons to give straw to Jesus to warm and cushion His manger.

3. Have the students create invitations for the Holy Family, welcoming them into their hearts, which are warm, loving places for the baby Jesus.

4. Students may work on the Memorization Questions.

Conclude

1. Lead the children in singing "Once in royal David's city," *Adoremus Hymnal*, #328.

2. Pray the Hail Mary.

3. You may lead the children in praying the first three Joyful Mysteries of the Rosary.

Preview

In the next lesson, the students will learn about the Nativity of Jesus.

CHALK TALK: GRACE

NOTES

LESSON FOUR: NATIVITY

Aims

The students will learn that because there was no room at the inn, Jesus was born in a stable, wrapped in swaddling clothes, and laid in a manger.

They will learn that Jesus' birth was announced by angels first to the shepherds. Later, three wise men came to pay homage to the Christ child.

Materials

- *Activity Book*, p. 59
- Baby Jesus for the Nativity set
- Samples of gold, frankincense, and myrrh
- Party favors
- Children's Bible

Optional:
- "Once in royal David's city," *Adoremus Hymnal*, #328
- "The King Is Born," video; Jesus: a Kingdom without Frontiers, available through Ignatius Press

Begin

Begin the class by having the students place their straw offerings to the child Jesus in the manger.

After all the straw offerings are made, you may place the baby Jesus in the manger. Have the children sing "Once in royal David's city," *Adoremus Hymnal*, #328.

Q. 68 *Did Jesus Christ always exist?*
As God, Jesus Christ has always existed; as man, He began to exist from the moment of the Incarnation (CCC 461, 470).

Q. 69 *From whom was Jesus Christ born?*
Jesus Christ was born of Mary ever-virgin, who therefore is the Mother of God (CCC 485, 495–96, 499).

Q. 70 *Was Saint Joseph the father of Jesus Christ?*
Saint Joseph was not the *true* father of Jesus Christ; as the spouse of Mary and the guardian of Jesus, he was the foster father of Jesus (CCC 532).

Q. 71 *Where was Jesus Christ born?*
Jesus Christ was born at Bethlehem, in a stable, and He was placed in a manger (CCC 525).

Q. 72 *Why did Jesus Christ wish to be poor?*
Jesus Christ wished to be poor in order to teach us to be humble and not to place our happiness in the riches and the pleasures of this world (CCC 526).

Q. 73 *What is the Epiphany?*
The Epiphany is a feast celebrated to remember how the wise men followed a star to Bethlehem to adore Jesus, bringing Him gifts fit for a king. This event shows that Jesus is Savior of the whole world (CCC 528).

Develop

1. Finish reading the chapter with the students.

2. You may read the story of the Nativity, found in Matthew 1:18–23 and Luke 2:1–7, from the children's Bible. If you have the video, "The King Is Born," from the Jesus: a Kingdom Without Frontiers series (available through Ignatius Press; 30 minutes), you may show it to the class.

3. Discuss the people who visited the Baby Jesus:

Shepherds: Lk 2:8–20. Why were they the first to receive the announcement? Why did they receive it from angels?
- They were poor and faithful men
- They were overlooked by society (as they were always with their sheep)
- Jesus is the Good Shepherd

Wise Men: Mt 2:1-12. Why did they come? What does their coming tell us about Jesus?

- They were not Jews, but foreigners. God came to save all men, not just the people of Israel. This also showed that non-Jewish people could know God.
- They brought gifts fit for a king. You may discuss these gifts as noted in the box at right.

4. Teach the children about Epiphany. It is the feast that celebrates the adoration of the wise men, who found Jesus by following the great star. It is a reminder that Jesus is the light of the world.

5. Host a Christmas party for the children. You may have a snack and some drinks. You may also give them a small gift, such as a prayer card and holy medal. Try to keep a Christian theme. You may sing Christian Christmas carols to Jesus in the manger. The children may dramatize the Nativity. Use costumes and props for more fun.

Reinforce

1. Have the students work on *Activity Book*, p. 59.

2. Celebrate Christmas with a party.

3. Pray the third Joyful Mystery of the Rosary.

4. Have the students work on their Memorization Questions.

Conclude

1. Sing "Once in royal David's city," *Adoremus Hymnal*, #328.

2. Pray the Hail Mary.

Preview

In the next lesson, the students' knowledge of the material covered this week will be reviewed and assessed.

Name:_____

Annunciation (Lk 1:26–38)	Visitation (Lk 1:39-56)
Nativity (Lk 2:1–20)	Visit of the Magi (Mt 2:1–12)
Presentation (Lk 2:22–40)	Flight into Egypt (Mt 2:13–23)

Choose one or more of the events surrounding the birth of Christ above and read the Gospel text indicated. Then either draw a picture or write beautifully some words from the Gospel story. You may also decorate the boxed-in areas.

Faith and Life Series • Grade 3 • Chapter 15 • Lesson 4   59

THE GIFTS OF THE WISE MEN

The gifts brought to the newborn Savior by wise men from the East were not only valuable items—each had a special significance in identifying Jesus as Priest, Prophet, and King.

- Gold: wealth and money for a King and his Kingdom

- Frankincense: a burnt offering of the royal priesthood

- Myrrh: an oil used to prepare a body for death—Jesus would die on the cross

---

NOTES

CHAPTER FIFTEEN
REVIEW AND ASSESSMENT

Aims

The students' knowledge and understanding of the material covered this week will be reviewed and assessed.

Materials

- Quiz 15, Appendix, p. A-21

Optional:
- "Once in royal David's city," *Adoremus Hymnal*, #328

Review

1. Review that the people of Israel were preparing for the coming of the Savior for many years. The prophets let them know how they could recognize Him when he came.

2. Review the Annunciation and the Visitation.

3. Review Mary's Immaculate Conception.

4. Review the members of the Holy Family and their different roles.

5. Review the story of the Nativity and the special guests that came to pay homage to Jesus: the shepherds and the wise men.

6. Review the offerings or gifts that the children can give to Jesus.

7. You may review Advent and Christmas traditions with the children.

Name: _____

The Christ Child Is Born Quiz 15

"Glory to God in the highest, and on earth peace among men with whom he is pleased! (Luke 2:14).

Word Bank

| gifts | Jesus | Savior | Bethlehem |
| word | News | Mary | Joseph |

Fill in the blanks with the correct words from the Word Bank.

1. Angel Gabriel said to Mary: "Hail, full of grace, the Lord is with you! Blessed are you among women! You will bear a son and call His name Jesus."

2. Mary told the angel, "Behold the handmaid of the Lord, let it be done to me according to your _word_."

3. God prepared _Mary_ to be the mother of the Savior. From the first moment of her life, she was full of grace, without Original Sin. This is called Mary's Immaculate Conception.

4. God chose a good man named _Joseph_ to be the foster father of Jesus.

5. Jesus was born in poverty in a stable at _Bethlehem_.

6. An angel appeared to shepherds and said "Behold, I bring you Good _News_ of great joy."

7. "Today, in the town of David has been born to you a _Savior_ Who is Christ the Lord. You will find Him lying in a manger."

8. The shepherds ran to adore Him. Later, three Wise Men brought him precious gifts. We can bring the Christ child our hearts as our _gifts_ for Him.

9. Write out the Scripture verse shown at the top of this page.

_____

_____

Faith and Life • Grade 3 • Appendix A   A - 21

Assess

1. Distribute the quizzes and read through them with the students to be sure they understand the questions.

2. Administer the quiz. As they hand in their work, you may orally quiz them on the Memorization Questions for this chapter.

3. After all the quizzes have been handed in, you may wish to review the correct answers with the class.

Conclude

1. Sing "Once in royal David's city," *Adoremus Hymnal*, #328.

2. Pray the Hail Mary.

CHAPTER SIXTEEN
JESUS GROWS IN AGE AND WISDOM

Catechism of the Catholic Church References

Baptism of Jesus: 535–37, 565
Holy Spirit: 683–86, 742
    In Baptism: 1266
        Names, Titles and Symbols of Holy Spirit: 691–701
Jesus: the only Son of God: 441–45, 454
Jesus and the Holy Spirit: 727–30, 746
Jesus as our Teacher and Model of Holiness: 468–69, 516, 519–21, 561
Jesus as True God and True Man: 464–70, 480–83
Jesus' Mission of Salvation: 456–60
John: Forerunner, Prophet, and Baptizer: 523, 717–20
Mysteries of Jesus' Hidden Life: 531–34, 564
Sacrifice: 2099–100

Scripture References

Presentation of Jesus in the Temple: Lk 2:21–40
Finding in the Temple: Lk 2:41–52
Baptism of Jesus: Lk 3:1–22, 4:1

Background Reading: *The Fundamentals of Catholicism* by Fr. Kenneth Baker, S.J.

Volume 2:
Jesus Christ Is True God, pp. 197–99
Jesus Christ Is Truly Human, pp. 210–13
Jesus Is a Divine Person, pp. 216–19
Talking about Jesus, pp. 240–43

Summary of Lesson Content

Lesson 1

The first thirty years of Jesus' life are referred to as Jesus' "hidden life."

Jesus led an ordinary life. He was likely trained in carpentry by Joseph.

The Holy Family is an example for all families.

Lesson 2

The Holy Family is a model for all families.

The Holy Family models the virtues found in daily life.

God the Father sees all and is all knowing.

Lesson 3

At age thirty Jesus, though He was sinless, was baptized by John the Baptist and began his public life.

At the Baptism of Jesus, God the Holy Spirit descended upon Jesus, God the Son. With this, God the Father was heard, saying "This is my beloved Son."

Jesus was anointed by the Spirit and was prepared for His mission of salvation.

Lesson 4

When man is baptized, the Holy Spirit descends upon him, too. The Spirit of God brings the life of God, sanctifying grace, to the soul of man.

Like Jesus, our Baptism prepares us for our mission: to love God and neighbor and to reach our final goal of Heaven.

LESSON ONE: HIDDEN LIFE

Aims

The students will learn about the first thirty years of Jesus' life, referred to as the "hidden life."

Jesus led an ordinary life. The students will learn about the Jewish traditions in which Jesus would have taken part

The students will learn about the possible daily routine of the Holy Family.

Materials

- Appendix pp. B-18–B-20
- Children's Bible
- Scissors, string, and markers

Optional:
- "Hail to the Lord's Anointed!" *Adoremus Hymnal,* #354
- If possible, have a Jewish person visit to explain Jewish feasts

Begin

Set up the materials needed to make the mobile.

Ask the children what their daily lives are like. They get up for breakfast, go to school, maybe play a sport or musical instrument, do homework, eat supper as a family, and go to bed. What traditions do their families have? What do they celebrate every year? They celebrate birthdays, Advent, Christmas, Lent, Easter, saints' feast days, anniversaries, etc. The same would be true with Jesus and the Holy Family, except the traditions of the Holy Family were based on the Jewish faith.

Develop

1. Read the first two paragraphs with the children.

2. From a children's Bible, read the Presentation of Jesus in the Temple: Lk 2:21–40. This is a Jewish Tradition of recognizing the first born son as a gift from God and committing to raising him in the faith. It is similar to Baptism in that it is a religious rite done early in the life of the baby.

3. Explain that Jesus would have had many different religious traditions because He was Jewish. He did not celebrate Christmas as we do. He did not celebrate Easter because before He died on the Cross and rose from the dead, there was no Easter to celebrate. Jewish people have their own religious traditions and feasts, based on the great events of the Old Testament. Today, we will learn more about these great feasts. You may have a guest speaker.

4. The feasts to be presented are:
- *Passover—feast of unleavened bread celebrated ever year to commemorate the Exodus of the Israelites from slavery in Egypt and the "passing over" of the angel of death.*
- *Weeks—also called Pentecost or First Fruits, this feast commemorates God's gift of the Torah to Moses on Mt. Sinai, fifty days after the first Sunday in Passover.*
- *Trumpets—feast upon which the blowing of trumpets signaled the end of the Jewish religious year. The feast of Trumpets was a time for repentance, mercy, and judgment.*
- *Tabernacles or Booths—week-long harvest festival commemorating God's care for the Israelites during the Exodus. In Jerusalem, pilgrims would live throughout the week in booths made of branches.*

5. Explain that these celebrations would have been part of the life of Christ and the Holy Family as they shared their faith.

Reinforce

1. Work on creating the mobile found on pp. B-18–B-20 in the Appendix.

2. Have the children dramatize the Jewish feasts or the great events that lead to the Jewish feasts. The children can also dramatize the daily routine of a Jewish family 2000 years ago.

3. Teach the children to sing "Hail to the Lord's Anointed!" *Adoremus Hymnal*, #354.

Conclude

End class by praying the fourth Joyful Mystery of the Rosary, the Presentation in the Temple.

Preview

In the next lesson, the students will learn more about the shared life of the Holy Family.

THE DAILY ROUTINE OF JESUS' CHILDHOOD

Little is known of Jesus' childhood in Nazareth. We learn from the Gospel that Jesus was obedient and brilliant, but as to His daily life, we can only make an educated guess, based upon the culture in which He was raised.

Like other Jewish children, Jesus would have had to do chores around the home and assist his mother. He would likely have been trained by Joseph in the trade of carpentry.

It is interesting to imagine the boy Jesus in Nazareth. Who were his friends? What would it have been like to see the Son of God as a little boy?

NOTES

LESSON TWO: HOLY FAMILY LIFE

Aims

The students will learn that the Holy Family is a model for all families, exemplifying virtues for all families.

They will also learn that God the Father sees all and is all knowing.

Materials

- *Activity Book*, p. 60
- Paper, pencils

Optional:
- "Hail to the Lord's Anointed!" *Adoremus Hymnal*, #354

Begin

Begin by reviewing that God is the Father of all people. He loves us very much. He is very interested in our lives. He knows all, sees all, and even knows what is in our hearts.

Jesus lived a hidden life (review His first 30 years, including religious feasts of Jews in Jesus' life). We, too, have a hidden life—in childhood we are not yet doing our "public" work. God, nonetheless, sees and knows all that we do. We can choose to do it well and in love, or not to do it well. How we live each moment, can be a "Yes" or "No" to God.

---

16 Jesus Grows in Age and Wisdom

"And Jesus increased in wisdom and in stature, and in favor with God and man."
                                                               Luke 2:52

As a boy growing up in Nazareth, Jesus led an ordinary life. He ate, slept, laughed, played, worked, and studied. Even though He was God, He was truly a human and He grew up and learned things just as we do. Since Jesus was Jewish, He learned all the Jewish customs and traditions of His time.

Joseph, a skilled carpenter, probably taught Jesus how to make fine things from wood. As a tiny boy, Jesus could only watch and pick up the wood chips as they fell. The neighbors of the Holy Family must have loved Jesus very much, but they had no idea that He was God's own Son. Only Mary and Joseph knew that. It was still hidden from the rest of the world. That is why we call the first thirty years of Jesus' time on earth His "hidden life."

Even though Jesus was living a "hidden" life, none of it was hidden from God the Father. God watched every moment of it. God sees every moment of *our* hidden lives too. He sees all the times we sacrifice something we would rather do to obey our parents. For example, you might want to play with a friend, but your mother needs you to set the table. Or you might want to finish a book, but your father needs you to help him rake the lawn. When we offer up our little disappointments or boredom and obey our parents with love, God sees it all. He blesses us for acting as Jesus did when He was growing up.

Develop

1. Read paragraphs 3 and 4 with the students.

2. Have the students recall events that would have occurred in the daily life of Jesus. Review the roles of Mary, the Mother of Jesus, and Joseph, his foster-father.

3. From the children's Bible, read the story of the Finding of the Child Jesus in the Temple: Lk 2:41–52.

4. Review the various virtues that each of the persons of the Holy Family would have exemplified. For example, Mary would have been gentle and humble. Jesus would have been obedient and loving. Joseph would have been patient and honorable, etc. Have the children think of many different virtues, and examples of these virtues.

5. Relate these virtues to the lives of the students. How can they see them in their families? How could they live them in their families?

6. Explain that Jesus' hidden life was the first 30 years of His life. It was a time to prepare Him for His public life. He entered His public life at the age of thirty to complete God's plan of salvation. Do the children know what Jesus' mission was?
   - *Preach the good news*
   - *Heal people*
   - *Tell people about the Kingdom of God*
   - *Establish the Church, and give Her the Sacraments*
   - *Die on the Cross for our sins and rise again so that we may have eternal life*

7. God is working in our hidden lives, too. What may He be preparing us for? Ask the children how they feel called to serve God in His plan of salvation. Let each child take a turn.

Name:_____

Imitating Jesus

1. Where did Jesus grow up?
<u>Nazareth</u>
2. With whom did Jesus grow up?
<u>His parents, Mary and Joseph</u>
3. How did Jesus help Mary and Joseph?
<u>Answers will vary.</u>
4. Did God the Father of Jesus see all of His "hidden life?"
<u>Yes. God watched every moment of it.</u>
5. Does God see all our "hidden life?"
<u>Yes. When we offer up our little disappointments or boredom and obey our parents with love, God sees it all.</u>
6. If we act like Jesus, God will bless us. Can you think of some examples of things you can do?
<u>Answers will vary.</u>
7. When did Jesus receive the Holy Spirit?
<u>At His Baptism</u>
8. When did you receive the Holy Spirit? Is this Spirit the same as the one Jesus received?
<u>We receive the Holy Spirit at our Baptism. This is the same Spirit Jesus received.</u>

60   Faith and Life Series • Grade 3 • Chapter 16 • Lesson 2

Reinforce

1. Have the students work on a virtue chart. An example of this is found at the bottom of this page.

2. Have the students work on *Activity Book*, p. 60.

3. Have the students work on their Memorization Questions.

4. The students may draw pictures of, or write about, the Finding of the Child Jesus in the Temple.

Conclude

1. Sing "Hail to the Lord's Anointed!" *Adoremus Hymnal*, #354.

2. You may lead the students in praying the fourth and fifth Joyful Mysteries of the Rosary.

Preview

In the next lesson, the students will learn about the Baptism of Jesus.

VIRTUE CHART

Virtue	How lived by Holy Family	How I Can Live this Virtue
obedience	Jesus obeyed	I can obey my parents
prudence	Jesus learned	I can study
temperance	Jesus did not fuss or fight	I can be well behaved
justice	Jesus was fair	I can be fair
fortitude	Jesus worked	I can work

NOTES

LESSON THREE: BAPTISM OF JESUS

Aims

The students will learn about John the Baptist and the Baptism of Jesus.

They will know that Jesus was anointed by the Spirit and was prepared for His mission of salvation.

The students will learn different titles for Jesus.

Materials

- *Activity Book*, p. 61
- Children's BIble

Optional:
- "Hail to the Lord's Anointed!" *Adoremus Hymnal*, #354
- "The Baptism of Jesus," video; Jesus: A Kingdom without Frontiers, available through Ignatius Press

Begin

Explain to the children that God had been preparing for the public life of Jesus in many ways. Can the children think of some of them?
- By the good home with Mary and Joseph
- By the gifts the wise men brought to Jesus
- By his Presentation in the Temple
- By his Jewish religion

As the time drew nearer for the public life of Jesus, God sent John the Baptist (the cousin of Jesus and son of Mary's cousin Elizabeth) to prepare the way for Jesus. He was the last and greatest of the prophets.

When the time came, Jesus left His quiet life in Nazareth. He put away the tools of a carpenter and started working to fulfill God's plan of salvation.

God sent a prophet to prepare the way for Jesus. This prophet told people in a loud, clear voice, "Get ready! The Promised One is coming! Be sorry for your sins." This holy man was named **John the Baptist**. He baptized with a baptism of repentance and all the people who listened and were sorry for their sins.

One day Jesus Himself came to John to be baptized in the waters of the Jordan River. As Jesus came out of the water, God gave a wonderful sign. The Holy Spirit came down upon Him in the form of a dove, and the voice of His Father called from Heaven: "This is My Beloved Son with Whom I am well pleased." Now Jesus was ready to begin His public life in His mission as the Savior of the world.

At your own Baptism, the Holy Spirit came upon you, too. He came inside your soul and filled it with God's life of grace. On that happy day, God silently told you, "You are My beloved child, and I love you." Just as with Jesus, our Baptism has prepared us for a mission. Our mission on earth is to love God with all our hearts and to love each other.

Words to Know:

John the Baptist

80

Develop

1. Read paragraphs 5 and 6 with the students.

2. Using a children's Bible, read more about John the Baptist and the Baptism of Jesus from Luke 3:1–22, 4:1. If you have the video, "The Baptism of Jesus," from the Jesus: A kingdom without Frontiers series (available through Ignatius Press; 30 minutes), you may watch it.

3. Note that John the Baptist was a man of God. He wore camel skins for clothes and ate only wild honey and locusts. He was a very pure man. Have a class discussion about John. "What did he tell the people to do?" (He told them to be sorry for their sins and have contrition.) "What did John the Baptist announce?" (He announced the coming of the Promised One.) "Who is the Promised One?" (His other names include: Savior, Messiah, Redeemer, Son of God, Jesus.) "When/why was He promised?" (He was promised after the fall of Adam and Eve.) "How did John the Baptist announce the Promised One?" (Refer back to Lk 3:16.) Tell the story of John the Baptist pointing to Jesus and announcing: "Behold the Lamb of God Who takes away the sin of the world" (Jn 1:29). "What did he mean by these words?" (He was announcing that Jesus was the Savior Who would save the people from their sins. He would sacrifice himself like a lamb. He would die for us.) Ask the students if any of them have heard these words before. (The priest says them at Mass: "Behold the Lamb of God . . .")

4. Explain the importance of the Baptism of Christ. God revealed Himself as a Trinity. God the Father spoke from Heaven and said: "This is my beloved Son, in Whom I am well pleased." Also, God the Holy Spirit came down upon Jesus in the form of a dove. Jesus was anointed with the Spirit, and prepared for His public life.

5. Emphasize that Jesus was without sin and did not need a Baptism of repentance. Jesus' Baptism was a model for us so that we would see that Baptism is pleasing to God.

Name:_____

John the Baptist

Color the picture below.

God sent a prophet to prepare the way for Jesus. He cried out, "Get ready! The Promised One is coming! Be sorry for your sins." This holy man was named John the Baptist. He baptized all the people who were sorry for their sins. One day, Jesus Himself came to be baptized by John. When Jesus came out to the water, the Holy Spirit came down upon Him, and God the Father in Heaven called down from Heaven saying, "This is My beloved Son, with Whom I am well pleased."

Faith and Life Series • Grade 3 • Chapter 16 • Lesson 3   61

THE VISITATION AND SAINT ELIZABETH

When Saint Elizabeth heard Mary's greeting, her baby – filled, like his mother, with the Holy Spirit – "leaped for joy" in her womb, as if to acknowledge the presence of his Lord. At this moment the prophecy was fulfilled that the child should "be filled with the Holy Spirit, even from his mother's womb." Since the presence of sin is incompatible with the indwelling of the Holy Spirit in the soul, it follows that at this moment John was cleansed from the stain of Original Sin. Thus Saint John the Baptist was conceived with, but born without, Original Sin.

Reinforce

1. Have the students work on *Activity Book*, p. 61.

2. The students may dramatize the Baptism of Jesus based upon the Gospel accounts.

3. Have the students work on their Memorization Questions.

Conclude

1. Together, sing "Hail to the Lord's Anointed!" *Adoremus Hymnal*, #354.

2. Lead the children in praying the Joyful Mysteries of the Rosary.

Preview

In the next lesson, the students will learn more about their own Baptisms.

NOTES

LESSON FOUR: BAPTISM

Aims

The children will learn that when they were baptized, the Holy Spirit came upon them and they became children of God.

Like that of Jesus, our Baptism prepares us for our mission: to love God and neighbor, and to reach our final goal of Heaven.

Materials

- *Activity Book*, p. 62
- Rite of Baptism, doll, water, basin, candle, white garment, chrism, and oil of catechumens

Optional:
- "Hail to the Lord's Anointed," *Adoremus Hymnal*, #354

Q. 74 *Who is John the Baptist?*
John the Baptist is the last of the prophets. He prepared the way for Jesus and baptized Him in the Jordan River (CCC 523).

Q. 75 *What special event happened at Jesus' Baptism in the Jordan?*
When Jesus was baptized in the Jordan, the Holy Spirit came down upon Him in the form of a dove and God the Father spoke from Heaven, saying, "This is my Beloved Son, in Whom I am well pleased (CCC 535).

Q. 76 *How is your Baptism like the Baptism of Jesus?*
At my Baptism, the Holy Spirit came upon me to bring God's Life of grace into my soul and to prepare me for the work God has planned for me to do (CCC 1265, 1268, 1270).

Begin

Review the Baptism of Jesus. What special events happened at Jesus' Baptism?
- *John identified Him as the Savior, the Lamb of God*
- *God the Father spoke and said that Jesus was His beloved Son*
- *God the Holy Spirit came down in the form of a dove and anointed Jesus*
- *Jesus was prepared for His public life*

Develop

1. Finish reading the chapter.

2. Review the rite of Baptism by dramatizing a Baptism with a doll. You may have students play the roles of the parents and godparents. Be sure to explain all the symbols used during this rite to explain the great effects of Baptism:

- Water: washes away all sin, original and actual. This is the matter of the sacrament.

- Words: "I baptize you in the Name of the Father and of the Son and of the Holy Spirit. Amen." These words mean that we are claimed for the one God in three Persons. The words are the form of the sacrament.

- White garment: reminds us that our souls are clean and filled with grace. We must work at keeping them clean and pure, just as we must work hard at keeping a white garment clean and white.

- Oil of Catechumens: this oil is blessed to make us strong in our faith and to protect us from the temptations of the devil.

- Oil of chrism: this oil is consecrated by the bishop. It is a sign that we share in the ministry of Christ as prophet (to speak the truth), priest (to worship) and king (to inherit the Kingdom of Heaven). We are sealed with chrism in the Sign of the Cross, the sign of our faith in Jesus, Who died for our sins. Also, it places an invisible and indelible (permanent) mark on our soul, which claims us as God's children. Therefore, we are to love one another as sisters and brothers in Christ, and God as our Father. We are to live as His faithful and obedient children.

- Candle: we receive the light of Christ in our hearts.

Name:_____

Jesus Crossword Puzzle

Across

1. The first thirty years of Christ's life is sometimes called His _____ life.
3. _____ is true God and true man.
6. Jesus learned all the _____ customs and traditions of His time.
7. God sees every moment of our hidden _____, too.
9. The name of the town where Jesus grew up is _____.
10. Our mission on earth is most of all to love _____ with all our heart, mind, soul, and strength.
11. Jesus was _____ in the Jordan River.
12. Next to loving God, our work on earth is to love each _____ as we love ourselves.

Down

2. The Holy Spirit descended upon Jesus in the form of a _____.
3. _____ the Baptist baptized Jesus.
4. The Holy _____ comes to us at our Baptism, too.
5. Our Baptism has prepared us for a special _____.
6. _____ is Jesus' foster-father.
8. Joseph worked as a _____.

Answers filled in:
- 1 Across: hidden
- 3 Across: Jesus
- 6 Across: Jewish
- 7 Across: lives
- 9 Across: Nazareth
- 2 Across (lower): dove
- 10 Across: God
- 11 Across: baptized
- 12 Across: other
- 3 Down: John
- 4 Down: spirit
- 5 Down: mission
- 6 Down: Joseph
- 8 Down: carpenter

Faith and Life Series • Grade 3 • Chapter 16 • Lesson 4

Reinforce

1. Have the students work on *Activity Book*, p. 62.

2. Have the students work on their Memorization Questions and review for the unit quiz.

Conclude

1. Sing "Hail to the Lord's Anointed!" *Adoremus Hymnal*, #354.

2. Lead the children in the renewal of their baptismal promises, found below.

3. End class by praying a decade of the Rosary.

Preview

In the next lesson, the students' knowledge of the material covered this week will be reviewed and assessed.

BAPTISMAL PROMISES

- Do you reject Satan?
- And all his works?
- And all his empty promises?
- Do you believe in God, the Father almighty, Creator of Heaven and earth?
- Do you believe in Jesus Christ, His only Son, our Lord, Who was born of the Virgin Mary, was crucified, died, and was buried, rose from the dead, and is now seated at the right hand of the Father?
- Do you believe in the Holy Spirit, the holy Catholic Church, the communion of saints, the forgiveness of sins, the resurrection of the body, and life everlasting?

NOTES

CHAPTER SIXTEEN
REVIEW AND ASSESSMENT

Aims

The students' knowledge and understanding of the material covered this week will be reviewed and assessed.

Materials

- Quiz 16, Appendix, p. A-22
- Unit 4 Quiz, Appendix, pp. A-23 and A-24

Optional:
- "Hail to the Lord's Anointed!" *Adoremus Hymnal*, #354

Review

1. Review the Jewish feasts that were a part of Jesus' life on earth.

2. Review life in the Holy Family and discuss what the Hidden Life of Jesus would have been like.

3. Review some of the virtues exemplified by the Holy Family, and have the students give concrete examples as to how they could live these virtues within their own families.

4. Review that Jesus entered His public life at age thirty.

5. Review that John the Baptist announced that Jesus was the Savior, the Lamb of God.

6. Review the events of the Baptism of Jesus:
   - John the Baptist baptized Jesus in the Jordan
   - God the Father spoke from Heaven
   - God the Holy Spirit descended upon Jesus in the form of a dove and anointed Him

7. Review the Sacrament of Baptism:
   - Matter and form
   - Symbols
   - Effects

Name: _____

Jesus Grows In Age and Wisdom   Quiz 16

"*Thou art my beloved Son; with thee I am well pleased*" (Luke 3:22).

Word Bank

baptized	Jewish	thirty	prophets	Nazareth
carpenter	Joseph	dove	blesses	

Fill in the blanks with the correct words from the Word Bank.

1. As a boy growing up in _Nazareth_, Jesus led an ordinary life. He ate, slept, laughed, played, worked, and studied.

2. Since Jesus was _Jewish_, He learned all the Jewish customs and traditions of His time.

3. Joseph, a skilled _carpenter_, probably taught Jesus how to make fine things from wood.

4. No one knew He was God's own Son except Mary and _Joseph_.

5. We call the first _thirty_ years of Jesus' time on earth "His hidden life."

6. God _blesses_ us for acting as Jesus did when He was growing up.

7. John the Baptist was the last of the _prophets_ to prepare the way for Jesus.

8. Jesus was _baptized_ by John the Baptist in the River Jordan.

9. At His Baptism, the Holy Spirit came down upon Jesus in the form of a _dove_. The voice of His Father called from Heaven: "Thou art my beloved Son; with thee I am well pleased."

10. Write out the Scripture verse shown at the top of this page.

_____

Assess

1. Distribute the quizzes and read through them with the students to be sure they understand the questions.

2. Administer the quiz. As they hand in their work, you may orally quiz them on the Memorization Questions for this chapter.

3. After all the quizzes have been handed in, you may wish to review the correct answers with the class.

4. Repeat steps 1–3 for the Unit 4 Quiz.

Conclude

Sing "Hail to the Lord's Anointed!" *Adoremus Hymnal*, #354.

CHAPTER SEVENTEEN
SIGNS AND WONDERS

Catechism of the Catholic Church References

"The Kingdom of God is at hand": 541–42, 567
Christ the Physician: 1503–5
Jesus: The Only Son of God: 441–45, 454
Jesus as True God and True Man: 464–70, 480–83

Jesus' Mission of Salvation: 456–60
Miracles and Other Signs of the Kingdom: 547–50, 567
Proclamation of the Kingdom of God: 543–46

Scripture References

Wedding at Cana: Jn 2:1–12
Gospel: Jn 3:22—4:3; 4:43–45; Mt 4:12–17, 5:1—7:29
Multiplication of Loaves and Fish: Mt 14:13–21
Healing of the Blind, Sick and Lame: Mt 9:27–31, 9:32–34, 12:15–21, 15:2–31

Centurion: Mt 8:5–13
Lazarus: Jn 10:40—11:44
Kingdom Parable: Mt 12:46–50, 13:1–52

Background Reading: *The Fundamentals of Catholicism* by Fr. Kenneth Baker, S.J.

Volume 2:
"The Divine Teacher," pp. 279–82

"The Power of Christ," pp. 263–66

Summary of Lesson Content

Lesson 1

Jesus began His public ministry at age thirty, when He started preaching the Good News of the Kingdom of God.

Jesus performed many miracles to show that He is the Savior of the world.

His first miracle was the transformation of water into wine at the wedding at Cana.

Lesson 2

Jesus performed the miracle of the multiplication of loaves and fish.

Jesus performed many healing miracles (as prophesied by Isaiah 35:5–6).

Jesus healed the centurion's servant

Lesson 3

Jesus raised Lazarus from the dead.

Jesus healed souls by teaching people to love and forgive.

Many of Jesus' miracles were to prepare man for the Sacrament of the Eucharist.

Lesson 4

Jesus preached parables to foster conversion.

Many people did not love Jesus and could not accept His message because of their pride.

Many of Jesus' parables were to prepare man for the celebration of the Eucharist.

LESSON ONE: MIRACLES

Aims

The children will learn that Jesus began His public ministry at age thirty, when He began preaching the Good News of the Kingdom of God.

They will learn that Jesus performed many miracles to show that He is the Savior of the world.

They will learn about Jesus' first miracle: the transformation of water into wine at the wedding at Cana

Materials

- *Activity Book*, p. 63
- Children's Bible
- Pitcher of water, koolaid crystals, cups
- Magic trick

Optional:
- "O God of loveliness," *Adoremus Hymnal*, #608

Begin

Gather the children around and perform a magic trick. Ask them if this is a miracle. No. A magic trick simply fools people. You can show them how your magic trick worked. A miracle is something that only God can do. What are some examples of miracles? Could the children do any of them? No. How could Jesus do them? He is God the Son, the Savior of the wold.

---

17   Signs and Wonders

When the people saw the sign which he had done, they said, "This is indeed the prophet who is to come into the world!"

John 6:14

When He was about thirty years old, Jesus the Savior began making His presence clear to the people of God. He started preaching the Good News of the Kingdom of God in the area called Galilee. Crowds came from all over to hear Him speak. They were fascinated because Jesus was telling them things they had never heard before. He told them, "I am the Way, the Truth, and the Life."

Jesus performed many miracles to prove He was the Savior and the Son of God. A **miracle** is something wonderful that is done by the power of God. It is something only God can do. Once a bride and groom in Cana ran out of wine at their wedding feast. Jesus solved their problem by changing the water in six stone jars into good wine.

Another time, Jesus fed a crowd of five thousand on five loaves of bread and two fish! People had crowded the hillsides all day to hear Him preach, and Jesus knew they were hungry. The Apostles warned Him there was not enough food. Jesus blessed the handful

83

Develop

1. Read the first two paragraphs from the student text with the children.

2. Remind the children that Jesus lived a hidden life up to age thirty. When He began preaching and performing miracles, the public life of Jesus began.

3. Why do the children think that Jesus was so popular? What do they think Jesus looked like? How would His voice have sounded? Would He have been friendly or distant from people? How would He have made people feel?

4. What is the Good News? What is the Kingdom?
   - God loves us
   - God wants us to be with Him forever in Heaven
   - God gave us Jesus to lead us to Heaven.

5. Read from a children's Bible the story of the Wedding at Cana found in John 2:1–12.

6. Review what wine is and how it is usually made—it takes a lot of time! You need to pick grapes, get the juice from them, add the ingredients, and store it for months in the dark. It is a lengthy process. If you have a barrel of water and leave it alone for months, will it become wine? No. You must have the correct ingredients. You may demonstrate by making juice. You may start with a pitcher of water, but you must add flavor crystals or concentrated juice. Share and enjoy your beverages.

7. Why did Jesus perform the miracle at Cana?
   - *His mother asked Him to*
   - *The bride and bridegroom would have been embarrassed*
   - *To show that He is the Savior*
   - *What was the response of the steward? the servants? the disciples? Mary? What would the children's response have been?*

Name:_____

I am the Way, the Truth, and the Life!

Color the picture below.

Faith and Life Series • Grade 3 • Chapter 17 • Lesson 1

63

Reinforce

1. You may continue the discussion on miracles and their qualities (and how they contrast from magic).

2. Have the children work on *Activity Book,* p. 63. Discuss what it means for Jesus to be "the way, the truth, and the life."

3. Teach the children to sing "O God of loveliness," *Adoremus Hymnal,* #608.

Conclude

Pray with the children, thanking God for His many miracles, including the life of each of the children.

Preview

In the next lesson, the students will learn more of Jesus' miracles, and why they prove He is the Savior of the world.

INSTRUCTIONS FOR A SIMPLE MAGIC TRICK

Materials: two paper clips and a sheet of paper

1. Fold the sheet of paper in three.

2. Fasten a paper clip at the two places indicated.

3. Pull the ends of the paper outward and the two paper clips will be interlocked.

LESSON TWO: PROPHECIES FULFILLED

Aims

The children will learn that Jesus performed the miracle of the multiplication of loaves and fish.

They will learn that Jesus also performed many healing miracles, as prophesied by Isaiah 35:5–6.

They will read about many of Jesus' miracles, including the healing of the centurion's servant.

Materials

- *Activity Book*, p. 64
- Children's Bible
- Paper/poster board or white paper table cloths and crayons/markers

Optional:
- "O God of loveliness," *Adoremus Hymnal*, #608
- "The Miracles of Jesus," video; Hannah-Barbera's Greatest Adventure: Stories from the Bible, available through Ignatius Press

Begin

Begin the class by reviewing the miracle of Cana about which the children learned in the previous lesson. Also review how only God can perform miracles. How do we know this? It was prophesied in the Old Testament (see Is 35:5–6). The people knew that the Messiah would do such miracles.

---

of loaves and fishes and suddenly there was enough food for everyone. All five thousand people were amazed to get a delicious dinner in the hills that day.

Most of the time, Jesus performed miracles to heal the suffering. At His word or touch, the blind could see, the lame walked, and the sick got well. All of this gave people great faith in Jesus.

Once a Roman soldier trusted in Jesus' power so much that he asked Jesus to heal his sick servant. When Jesus said, "I will go to heal him," the soldier said, "Lord, I am not worthy that You should come under my roof. Only say the word, and I know my servant will be healed." Jesus marveled at this man's trust and belief. He said, "Go your way. Because you have believed, your servant is cured." Later the Roman soldier learned that his servant had been cured at that very instant.

> The Roman centurion's trust in Jesus' power to heal is remembered every time we go to Holy Mass. Right before Holy Communion we tell Jesus, "Lord, I am not worthy to receive You, but only say the word and I shall be healed."

Jesus' power to perform miracles was even stronger than death. He brought back to life a man named Lazarus who had been buried for four days. All hope seemed lost, but Jesus promised Lazarus' good sisters, "Your brother will rise." Then He ordered the stone to be rolled back from the tomb, and He called to Lazarus. Lazarus arose, alive and well, and all the people rejoiced in amazement.

Develop

1. Read paragraphs 3–5 and the box about the Roman centurion's trust in Jesus repeated from Matthew 8:8 in the Mass.

2. From a children's Bible, read about some of Jesus' miracles. Some appropriate references include:
Multiplication of loaves and fish: Mt 14:13–21
Healing of the Blind, Sick, and Lame: Mt 9:27–31, 9:32–34, 12:9–14, 12:15–21, 15:2–31
Healing of centurion's servant: Mt 8:5–13

3. You may have the students act out these miracles or play charades, having the students guess which miracles are being acted out.

4. Show the video "The Miracles of Jesus," from Hanna-Barbera's Greatest Adventure: Stories from the Bible series (available through Ignatius Press; 30 minutes).

5. Ask the children if they know of any of Jesus' other miracles. This may include the Incarnation, the Resurrection, the Ascension, etc. Only let them discuss what they already know.

6. Discuss the virtues of faith, hope, and trust:
   - Faith: to believe in what God has revealed, even if we do not have full knowledge.
   - Hope: to await the fulfillment of something promised
   - Trust: to believe or know that something is possible

How are these virtues exemplified in the various miracle stories?

7. Ask the children what they can learn from Jesus' miracles.

Name:_____

Jesus' Ministry

1. Where did Jesus preach, and what did Jesus preach?
Jesus preached the Good News of the Kingdom of God in the area called Galilee.

2. Why did Jesus perform miracles?
Jesus performed miracles to show that He is God and the Kingdom is present in Him. His miracles were to gather people into the Kingdom of God.

3. What miracles did Jesus perform?
Answers will vary.

4. How strong was Jesus' power?
Stronger than death.

5. Why did Jesus come?
Jesus came to heal people's souls.

6. Did everyone love Jesus?
No. He had enemies too.

7. Who is Jesus? Is He God or man?
Jesus is true God and true Man.

8. What can we learn from Jesus' teaching and miracles?
We can learn to love God the Father, to stop sinning, and to be holy.

Faith and Life Series • Grade 3 • Chapter 17 • Lesson 2

Reinforce

1. Have the students work on *Activity Book*, p. 64.

2. Have the students draw pictures or make a mural of the many miracles of Jesus.

3. Have the children create skits of the miracles of Jesus, or do "interviews" of people for whom Jesus worked miracles, emphasizing their responses to Jesus and the virtues of faith, hope, and charity.

Conclude

1. Lead the students in singing "O God of loveliness," *Adoremus Hymnal*, #608.

2. Ask the children to pray in faith for the miracles they want in their lives (prayers of petition).

Preview

In the next lesson, the students will learn the great power of Jesus' miracles and Jesus' ability to heal people's souls.

MIRACLE PROPHECIES IN THE OLD TESTAMENT

Many of Jesus' miracles were predicted in the Hebrew Scriptures. Even His miraculous birth was predicted in the pages of Isaiah (Is 7:14). In Jeremiah, Jesus' miracles of healing are predicted:

"Behold, I will bring them from the north country, and gather them from the farthest parts of the earth, among them the blind and the lame...With weeping they shall come, and with consolations I will lead them back, I will make them walk by brooks of water, in a straight path in which they shall not stumble; for I am a father to Israel . . ." (Jer 31:8–9).

NOTES

LESSON THREE:
THE GREATEST MIRACLE

Aims

The students will learn that Jesus raised Lazarus from the dead.

They will learn that Jesus healed souls by teaching people to love and forgive.

They will learn that Jesus still works miracles today through the sacraments.

Materials

- *Activity Book*, p. 65
- Children's BIble
- Mustard seed and picture of mustard plant
- Paper and markers

Optional:
- "O God of loveliness," *Adoremus Hymnal*, #608

Begin

Review some of Jesus' miracles:
- Multiplication of loaves and fish
- Healing the blind, lame, and sick
- Changing water into wine

Review faith, hope, and charity. Have the children explain these virtues to you using examples.

Jesus came to heal people's souls. He taught them to love God the Father, to stop sinning, and to be holy. He gave them **parables**, or stories, that explained the Kingdom of God. One parable was about a mustard seed. A mustard seed is very tiny, but when planted in the ground it grows to be a huge tree. Jesus compared the mustard seed to His own Kingdom. It had small beginnings, but would cover the whole world.

He told another parable about a farmer sowing seeds. Some of the seeds fell on good ground and they yielded a rich harvest. Other seeds fell on rocks and thorns and they yielded nothing. Jesus said the seeds were like the Word of God falling on the ears of good men and bad men. If it falls on the good soil of a faithful heart, it yields many good things. If it falls on the poor soil of a stubborn heart, it can yield nothing at all.

Jesus found both friends and enemies on earth. His friends were the Apostles and disciples who followed Him. His enemies were the ones who doubted and made fun of Him. These enemies could not understand a Savior Who ate with sinners and Who loved the poor. Many of the Jewish leaders, such as the Pharisees, were jealous of Jesus. They hated Him because He pointed out their faults. They were too proud to follow Jesus' teachings of love because it would mean changing their lives. They did not have the courage to become humble, forgiving, and loving like Jesus.

Words to Know:

miracle   parable

Develop

1. Read paragraphs 6–8 with the children.

2. Discuss the raising of Lazarus. You may read the full story found in John 10:40—11:44 from the children's Bible. Questions you may ask include:
   - How long was Lazarus dead?
   - What expression of faith did Lazarus' sisters make?
   - Did they trust in Jesus?
   - Did they believe that He could raise Lazarus from the dead?
   - Is this a greater miracle than healing a person or multiplying loaves and fish? What does it say of Jesus' power?

3. Discuss what a parable is. It is a short story that people can understand, which teaches a lesson. What are the two parables found in this chapter?
   - *The mustard seed* (show size of mustard seed and picture of mustard bush so they better understand)
   - *The sower*

You may read parables from a children's Bible: Mt 12:46–50, 13:1–52.
Questions:
- What do these parables teach about the Kingdom of God?
- What do these parables teach about man's openness to God's word?
- How can they prepare our hearts for God's word?

4. Have the children tell modern day parables using these same themes. The children may draw upon the biblical parables using modern day examples.

5. Explain that Jesus was able to show that He is the Savior both by His miracles and by His teachings.

6. Show how the miracles of Jesus prepare us for the sacraments, through which Jesus still works miracles today.

Name:_____

Parables

1. Explain the parable of the Kingdom of God being like a mustard seed. <u>A mustard seed is very tiny, but when planted in the ground it grows to be a huge tree. In the same way, the Kingdom of God has small beginnings, but it will cover the whole world.</u>
2. Explain the parable about a farmer sowing seed, which taught us about the word of God. <u>The seeds are like the word of God falling on the ears of good men and bad men. If it falls on the good soil of a faithful heart, it yields many good things. If it falls on the poor soil of a stubborn heart, it can yield nothing at all.</u>

Draw one of these parables and explain what you have drawn.

Faith and Life Series • Grade 3 • Chapter 17 • Lesson 3

Reinforce

1. Have the students work on *Activity Book*, p. 65.

2. Have the students present their parables.

3. Have the students work on the Memorization Questions.

Conclude

1. Lead the students in singing "O God of loveliness," *Adoremus Hymnal*, #608.

2. Pray with the children, asking God to make their hearts open to His word.

Preview

In the next lesson, the students will learn about different groups of people in the time of Jesus and how they responded to Jesus.

JESUS WORKS MIRACLES TODAY

Jesus works miracles even today. We can see Jesus' miraculous work in the sacraments of the Church:

- Penance: God forgives sins and restores grace

- Eucharist: God feeds our souls

- Anointing of Sick: God spiritually and sometimes physically heals people

- Matrimony: God joins two people into one flesh

- Holy Orders: the gifts of the Holy Spirit make a man a priest

NOTES

LESSON FOUR: RECEIVING GOD'S WORD

Aims

The students will learn that many people did not love Jesus and could not accept His message out of pride.

They will learn that we can choose to open our hearts to Jesus and His teachings, but we can also choose not to.

They will learn that following Jesus is courageous.

Materials

- *Activity Book*, p. 66
- Optional:
  - "O, God of all loveliness," Adoremus Hymnal, #608

Q. 77 *What is the mystery of the Son of God made man called?*
The mystery of the Son of God made man is called the Incarnation (CCC 461).

Q. 78 *Who is Jesus Christ?*
Jesus Christ is the Second Person of the Most Holy Trinity, the Son of God made man (CCC 470).

Q. 79 *Is Jesus Christ God and man?*
Yes, Jesus Christ is true God and true man (CCC 470).

Q. 80 *Why did Jesus work miracles?*
Jesus worked miracles to show that He is God and the Kingdom is present in Him. His miracles were to gather people into the Kingdom of God (CCC 542, 547).

Q. 81 *Why did Jesus tell parables?*
Jesus told parables to teach people about the Kingdom of God and invite them into it (CCC 546).

Begin

Begin the class by inviting the children to do something hard, such as solving a difficult long division problem. See if anyone wants to come forward to answer it. Some will choose to, some will choose not to. Guide them through the problem, to come to the correct answer. Explain that this is like Jesus' call to follow Him. Some will choose to, some will choose not to. It is really only possible with Jesus' guidance and help.

Develop

1. Review Jesus' call to each of us.
   - Love one another
   - Follow God's Commandments
   - Follow Jesus' example
   - Have faith and live by it

2. Next, read the last paragraph with the children.

3. Explain the different groups of people in the time of Jesus:
Pharisees: Jews who lived the letter of the law, but not the spirit of the law (rules without love).
Saducees: were less strict about rules, but didn't have faith in God's promises.
Essenes: separated themselves from others to be "faithful." This was not love.
Gentiles: anyone who was not a Jew, e.g., the Centurions, the Samaritans, etc.

4. Explain that Jesus called all people to believe and change their lives. This is called conversion. Conversion is not a one-time event, such as Baptism. It is an everyday decision to follow Jesus even when it is difficult to follow Him. Ask the children why they choose to follow Jesus. What are some of the choices they have had to make to be faithful to Jesus' call? (E.g., not sleeping at a friend's house on Saturday night so you can go to Mass giving up something for Lent, etc.)

5. Discuss the virtues mentioned at the end of the chapter that are necessary to follow Jesus: courage (doing what is right, even when it is difficult); humility (seeing and living the truth, without pride); forgiving (loving as Jesus loved, not holding grudges or being mean); loving (even making sacrifices for others because we care about them).
   - Discuss how these virtues were exemplified in the miraculous stories learned this week.
   - Discuss ways the students can live these virtues.

Name:_____

Jesus Came For All of Us

1. How did Jesus show us that God cares for our needs?
With the miracles of the wedding at Cana and the feeding of the five thousand

2. How did Jesus show us that God cares for the sick and suffering?
By making the blind see the lame walk, and by healing the sick

3. How did Jesus show us that God's love for us is stronger than death?
By raising Lazarus from the dead

4. How did Jesus show us that He wants us to learn about God and His Kingdom?
He taught us about God and His Kingdom.

5. How did Jesus show us that He loves sinners and the poor?
Jesus showed us that He loves sinners and the poor by spending time with them and even eating with them.

Faith and Life Series • Grade 3 • Chapter 17 • Lesson 4

Reinforce

1. The students may act out scenarios in which people accept or reject Jesus' call.

2. Have the students work on *Activity Book*, p. 66.

3. Have the students work on their Memorization Questions and prepare for the quiz.

Conclude

1. Lead the students in singing "O God of loveliness," *Adoremus Hymnal*, #608.

2. Have the children ask God for the virtues necessary to follow His call.

Preview

In the next lesson, the students' knowledge of the material covered this week will be reviewed and assessed.

SAINT PHILOMENA: THE WONDER WORKER

Saint Philomena was a young girl of fourteen, martyred in the early days of the Church. Her remains were discovered in Italy in the catacomb of Saint Priscilla in 1802. Saint Philomena was identified by the words, "Peace be with thee, Philomena," and she was buried with a vial of her blood and other symbols that identified her as a Christian martyr. It was not until several years later that Canon Francis de Lucia discovered her relics in the Vatican and moved them to a separate chapel. It was then that the miracles of Saint Philomena occurred in rapid succession. Among those cured through her intercession were Pope Pius IX and Venerable Pauline Jaricot.

NOTES

CHAPTER SEVENTEEN
REVIEW AND ASSESSMENT

Aims

The students' knowledge and understanding of the material covered this week will be reviewed and assessed.

Materials

- Quiz 17, Appendix, p. A-25

Optional:
- "O God of loveliness," *Adoremus Hymnal,* #608

Review

1. Review that Jesus was thirty years old when He began His public life.

2. Jesus said that He is "the way, the truth, and the life."

3. The first miracle of Jesus was changing water into wine at the wedding at Cana.

4. Jesus also multiplied 5 loaves and 2 fish to make food for 5000 men. He healed the blind, lame, and sick. Jesus healed the centurion's servant without even being near him. Jesus raised Lazarus from the dead.

5. The children should know the difference between miracles and magic.

6. The students should know what parables are. They should be able to explain the parable of the mustard seed and the parable of the sower.

7. The children should understand that we are all called to follow Jesus. We will need the virtues of faith, hope, trust, courage, humility, forgiveness, and love. They should be able to explain each virtue and give an example of each.

Name: _____

Signs and Wonders — Quiz 17

"I am with you always, to the close of the age" (Matthew 28:20).

Word Bank

Lazarus	man	miracles	cured	parables
fish	wine	faith	Galilee	seed

Fill in the blanks with the correct words from the Word Bank.

1. When Jesus was about thirty years old, He began teaching in a place called **Galilee**.

2. Jesus performed many **miracles** to prove that He was the Savior and the Son of God.

3. When a bride and groom ran out of wine at their wedding feast in Cana, Jesus changed the water in six stone jars into good **wine**.

4. Jesus fed a crowd of over five thousand with five loaves of bread and two **fish**.

5. At the word of Jesus, the blind saw, the lame walked, and the sick were cured. All of this gave people great **faith** in Jesus.

6. Jesus **cured** a Roman soldier's servant from a distance because of the soldier's belief in Jesus.

7. Jesus raised **Lazarus** from the dead.

8. Jesus used ordinary stories, called **parables**, to teach about God and Heaven.

9. He compared the tiny mustard **seed** with His own Kingdom, which had small beginnings but would cover the whole world.

10. Jesus Christ is true God and true **man**.

11. Write out the Scripture verse shown at the top of this page.

_____

Faith and Life • Grade 3 • Appendix A   A - 25

Assess

1. Distribute the quizzes and read through them with the students to be sure they understand the questions.

2. Administer the quiz. As they hand in their work, you may orally quiz them on the Memorization Questions for this chapter.

3. After all the quizzes have been handed in, you may wish to review the correct answers with the class.

Conclude

1. Lead the students in singing "O God of loveliness," *Adoremus Hymnal,* #608.

2. End class with a prayer.

CHAPTER EIGHTEEN
THE LAST SUPPER, OUR FIRST MASS

Catechism of the Catholic Church References

Effects of Holy Communion: 1391–1405, 1416–17, 1436–46
Holy Communion: 1382–90, 1415
Institution of the Eucharist: 1333–44, 1373–77, 1411–17
Last Supper: 610–11, 621, 1323
Passover: 1164

Passover in Relation to the Holy Eucharist: 1334, 1362–65, 1409
Presence of Christ in the Eucharist: 1373–81, 1410, 1418
Signs of Bread and Wine in the Eucharist: 1333–36, 1412

Scripture References

Last Supper:
Mt 26:26–29; Mk 14:22–25; Lk 22:15–20; Jn 13:1–20

1 Cor 11:23—26

Background Reading: *The Fundamentals of Catholicism* by Fr. Kenneth Baker, S.J.

Volume 3:
"Jesus Gave Thanks," pp. 226–28
"The Catholic Doctrine of the Real Presence," pp. 229–31
"My Flesh Is Real Food and My Blood Is Real Drink," pp. 232–35

"Water into Wine, Wine into Blood," pp. 235–38
"A Wonderful Change," pp. 238–40
"Presence of the Whole Christ," pp. 241–43
More on the Eucharist, pp. 244–56

Summary of Lesson Content

Lesson 1

On the night before Jesus died, He celebrated the Passover with His Apostles. This is referred to as the Last Supper.

Jesus anticipated His death on the Cross through the gift of His Body and Blood at the Last Supper.

Lesson 2

At the Last Supper, Jesus taught His Apostles a lesson in service and humility by washing His Apostles' feet.

Lesson 3

At the Last Supper, Jesus instituted the Sacrament of the Eucharist. From the story of the Last Supper, we learn of the matter and form of this sacrament.

The change from bread and wine into the Body and Blood of Jesus is called transubstantiation. After the Consecration there is no longer bread and wine present, only the Body and Blood of Jesus Christ, although the appearance of bread and wine remains. Jesus gave the power to consecrate the Eucharist to His Apostles at the Last Supper.

Lesson 4

Jesus gives Himself to man in Holy Communion.

This gift of Himself is made possible through the celebration of the Mass, wherein the priest consecrates the Holy Eucharist.

In Holy Communion, man is intimately united with Christ through the Eucharist.

LESSON ONE: SELF-GIFT

Aims

The students will learn that on the night before Jesus died, He celebrated the Passover with His Apostles. This is referred to as the Last Supper.

Jesus anticipated His death on the Cross through the gift of His Body and Blood at the Last Supper

The children will review the Passover.

Materials

- *Activity Book*, p. 67
- Children's Bible
- Construction paper, scissors, glue, markers
- Preparations for a seder meal

Optional:
- "O Thou, who at thy Eucharist didst pray," *Adoremus Hymnal*, #521
- "Moses," video; Hanna-Barbera's Greatest Adventure: Stories from the Bible, available through Ignatius Press

Begin

Begin today's class by showing the segment of the video "Moses," from the series Hanna-Barbera's Greatest Adventure: Stories from the Bible (available through Ignatius Press; 30 minutes), that shows the Passover, or read Exodus 12:1–14 from a children's Bible. It is very important that the children know and understand this story.

---

18   The Last Supper, Our First Mass

"This is my body which is for you. Do this in remembrance of me."
                           1 Corinthians 11:24

The night before Jesus died, He and the Apostles gathered to celebrate the feast of Passover. This Jewish feast was a holy dinner held once a year. It honored the sacred memory of the time when God saved Moses and His Chosen People from slavery in Egypt.

On the Passover night that Jesus and His Apostles gathered, God was about to save His people again. This time He would save them from the darkness of sin and death. He would unlock the gates of Heaven and make it possible for them to live with Him in joy for ever.

Jesus, Our Savior, was about to pay a great price to win this grace. He was about to lay down His own life so that we could go to Heaven. Jesus knew His death was very near. Sitting at the Passover table that night, Jesus felt tender sadness at the thought of leaving His friends. He wanted them to be strong and holy when He was gone.

> "Little children, yet a little while I am with you. . . . A new commandment I give to you, that you love one another; even as I have loved you, that you also love one another. By this all men will know that you are my disciples, if you have love for one another."
>   John 13:33–35

87

Develop

1. Read with the children the first three paragraphs from the student text.

2. As you explain how Jesus celebrated the Passover on the night before He died, lay out the Passover feast on a table, and have the children gather around (like the Apostles). Explain the parts of the seder meal; e.g., the reading of the Passover/Exodus story, the significance of the foods, and the fact that everybody had to sit to eat as though they were ready to leave in a moment's time. This meal is a great example of trust in God's deliverance.

3. Using the chart at right, compare the Passover sacrifice and meal with Jesus and His institution of the Eucharist. Jesus is the Lamb, sacrificed and eaten.

4. Discuss the night of the Passover:
- If Jesus was celebrating a holy dinner with his friends, why was He sad?
- Why was Jesus going to pay such a great price?
- How would He pay this price?
- For whom would Jesus pay this great price?
- How did Jesus lay down His life?
- We can say that Jesus completely gave Himself up for our sins. How can we imitate Jesus in our daily life?
- What did Jesus want for His disciples? What does He want for each of us?
- Does God give us help to be followers of Jesus?

5. Ask the children what they would do if they knew that Jesus would be coming to their house for dinner. What would they serve Him? What would they wear? How would they prepare? What would they want to give Him? What would they want to talk about or receive from Him? How would they act in His presence? Have the children make an invitation for Jesus.

Name:_____

The Last Supper, Our First Mass

Color the picture below.

Faith and Life Series • Grade 3 • Chapter 18 • Lesson 1

67

Reinforce

1. Have the children make invitations for Jesus.

2. Have the students work on *Activity Book*, p. 67.

3. Teach the children to sing "O Thou, who at thy Eucharist didst pray," *Adoremus Hymnal*, #521.

Conclude

Lead the children in praying the Agnus Dei from Mass:
Lamb of God, you take away the sins of the world, have mercy on us.
Lamb of God, you take away the sins of the world, have mercy on us.
Lamb of God, you take away the sins of the world, grant us peace.

Preview

In the next lesson, the students will learn about the humility of Jesus and the need for us to serve others.

PASSOVER AND THE LAST SUPPER

Passover

- Slaves to Pharaoh
- Needed spotless lamb
- Killed the lamb
- Ate the lamb
- Sprinkled blood on doorposts
- Prepared to go to the Promised Land

Last Supper

- We were slaves to sin
- Jesus, the lamb of God
- Jesus died on Cross
- Jesus in Eucharist
- We are marked by the Blood of Jesus
- Prepared to go to the Promised Land of Heaven

NOTES
_____
_____
_____
_____
_____
_____
_____
_____
_____

LESSON TWO: SERVICE

Aims

The students will learn how at the Last Supper, Jesus taught His Apostles a lesson in service and humility by washing His Apostles' feet.

Materials

- Appendix, pp. B-21 and B-22
- Holy cards of each of the Apostles. You will also need summaries of their lives.
- Basin, towel(s), water

Optional:
- "O Thou, who at thy Eucharist didst pray," *Adoremus Hymnal*, #521

Begin

Begin this lesson by reading Chapter 4 from the student text with the children. You may dramatize this by washing the feet of the students.
Questions to follow:
- Who was the servant?
- How did this make the students feel?
- How can a teacher also be a servant? (Note: Teaching is service.)

Explain what humility and service are:
- **Humility**: not to be proud, to see things as they really are and to act upon them
- **Service**: to recognize Christ in your neighbor and love him. Service may involve words, deeds, or prayers. Have the students give examples.

First Jesus gave them a lesson in holiness. He knelt down to wash their feet. Peter told Him, "Master, You will never wash my feet." However, Jesus told Peter that friends love and serve one another without shame. He told the Twelve Apostles, "If I, the Lord and Master, have washed your feet, you also ought to wash the feet of one another. For I have given you an example; that as I have done to you, so you also should do."

Later, while they were eating, a very important moment came. Jesus took bread, blessed and broke it, and gave it to His disciples saying, "This is My Body, which will be given up for you."

Then He took a cup of wine. He gave thanks and gave it to them saying, "This is the Cup of My Blood, the Blood of the new and everlasting Covenant. It will be shed for you, and for all, so that sins may be forgiven."

When Jesus spoke those words, the bread and wine were changed into His Body and Blood. It still looked and tasted like ordinary food, but it was Jesus. When the Apostles ate it, Jesus came into their souls. They were the first ones ever to receive Holy Communion.

Jesus told the Apostles, "Do this in **remembrance** of Me." With these words, Jesus gave the Apostles the power to change bread and wine into the Body and Blood of Jesus from that night on.

> The **Last Supper** was actually the first Mass. It took place on a Thursday, the night before Jesus died. Every year on **Holy Thursday** we especially remember the first Mass and Jesus' gift of the Holy Eucharist and of the priesthood.

89

Develop

1. Discuss the Apostles; who they were and how they served Christ.
- Peter was the head of the Apostles. He was the son of John, brother of Andrew. He was a fisherman. He walked on water with Jesus and was present for the Transfiguration. Though he denied Jesus three times, he later professed his love for Jesus three times. Jesus named him "Rock," the head of the Church. He gave up family and friends to serve the Church, for which he ultimately died, crucified upside down as witness to his faith (and because he thought he was unworthy to die in the same manner as His Lord).
- Philip was from Bethsaida in Galilee. He was called to follow Jesus the day after Peter and Andrew.
- James the Less is the author of the first Catholic epistle. His mother was a close family relative of Mary, the Mother of Jesus, so he was sometimes called the brother of our Lord. The first bishop of Jerusalem, he was martyred.
- Bartholomew, also called Nathaniel, preached the Gospel in the East, traveling as far as India. He was martyred for the faith.
- Simon was a zealot, who originally followed Christ hoping for political victories. He was martyred in Persia.
- Jude, also called Thaddeus, is the patron of hopeless causes. He was the brother of James the Less. He preached the gospel in Judea, Mesopotamia, and Lybia. He is the author of an epistle. He was martyred in Armenia.
- Thomas is known as the doubter. He was given the gift of placing his hands in the wound of Christ after the Resurrection, so that he (and others) might believe. He, too, was martyred in the East.
- James the Greater was the brother of John. Together they were known as the Sons of Thunder. He was present at the Transfiguration and the agony in the garden with Peter and John. He preached the Gospel in Spain.

The Twelve Apostles.

I followed Jesus after John the Baptist pointed him out.	Philip	I was a tax collector.	Matthew
I was Jesus' first follower. I met Him at the Sea of Galilee.	Andrew	I was the youngest Apostle.	John
Jesus nicknamed me "Rock." I ruled the Church from Rome.	Peter	My brother John was also an Apostle. I went as far as Spain to preach the Gospel.	James the Greater
My friend Philip brought me to Jesus.	Bartholomew	At the Last Supper, I asked Jesus to tell us where He was going.	Thomas
My brother Peter was also an Apostle.	Andrew	My brother Jude and I were cousins of Jesus	James the Less
I first followed Jesus because I hoped He would help us to overthrow the Romans.	Simon	My brothers James and Simon and I were cousins of Jesus.	Thaddeus (Jude)
I was the Apostle in charge of the group's money	Judas	At the Last Supper, I asked Jesus to "show us the Father."	Philip
I am the patron saint of impossible causes	Thaddeus (Jude)	Because I had the same name as another Apostle, I was nicknamed "the Greater."	James the Greater
I doubted that Jesus had risen because I had not seen Him with my own eyes.	Thomas	Because I was afraid, I denied that I even knew Jesus—three times!	Peter
I betrayed Jesus for thirty pieces of silver.	Judas	Besides John, I was the other Apostle who wrote a Gospel account of Jesus' life.	Matthew
I was bishop of Jerusalem. I was martyred by being thrown off a high tower.	James the Less	I am often referred to as the "beloved disciple."	John
James and Jude were my brothers. I preached the Gospel in Arabia, where I was martyred.	Simon	I preached the Gospel in Arabia, India, and Armenia. I suffered a martyr's death.	Bartholomew

Faith and Life • Grade 3 • Appendix B   B - 21

INTERESTING APOSTLE FACTS

- Andrew was the first follower of Jesus and the brother of Peter.
- Matthew was a tax collector, a "publican" named Levi. He is the author of the first Gospel. Much of his work took place in Palestine.
- John, known as the Beloved Disciple, was the brother of James the Greater. He stood by the foot of the Cross during the Passion of Jesus and was made guardian of the Blessed Virgin Mary. He spent the rest of his life in Ephesus, where he wrote the fourth Gospel and three epistles.
- Judas is the Apostle who betrayed Jesus. He received thirty pieces of silver for assisting in Jesus' arrest. He took his own life soon after.

Reinforce

1. Play the game in Appendix, pp. B-21 and B-22.

2. The students may draw pictures of the Apostles or make a book in which to identify them. They should place a picture of an Apostle on each page and write a brief summary of his life. Also, they should write a description of the ways each Apostle can be an example for them.

3. Begin working on the Memorization Questions for this chapter.

Conclude

1. Lead the students in singing "O Thou, who at thy Eucharist didst pray," *Adoremus Hymnal*, #521.

2. Pray a Litany of the Apostles, e.g., "Saint Jude, pray for us."

Preview

In the next lesson, the students will learn about the institution of the Eucharist.

NOTES

LESSON THREE: EUCHARIST

Aims

The students will learn that at the Last Supper, Jesus instituted the Sacrament of the Eucharist.

They will review that the change from bread and wine into the Body, Blood, Soul, and Divinity of Jesus is called transubstantiation. There is no longer bread and wine present, only the Body, Blood, Soul, and Divinity of Jesus Christ, although the appearance of bread and wine remains.

They will review that Jesus gave the power to consecrate the Eucharist to His Apostles at the Last Supper.

Materials

- *Activity Book*, p. 68
- Children's Bible

Optional:
- "O Thou, who at thy Eucharist didst pray," *Adoremus Hymnal*, #521

Begin

Review the miracles of the multiplication of loaves and fish and of the changing of water into wine at Cana. Emphasize that Jesus had the power to multiply matter and change its substance. These are important elements to understanding the Consecration of the Eucharist.

Also review that the Twelve Apostles were present at the Last Supper.

Holy Communion was not meant just for the Apostles. It was meant for all of Jesus' followers until the end of time. At every Holy Mass the priest says the same words over bread and wine, and they become the Body and Blood of Jesus. We call this the sacrament of the Holy Eucharist. Whenever we receive it, Jesus comes into our hearts, alive and full of love.

Words to Know:

remembrance   Last Supper   Holy Thursday

"I am the bread of life; he who comes to me shall not hunger, and he who believes in me shall never thirst."

John 6:35

Q. 82 *When was the first Mass celebrated?*
Jesus celebrated the first Mass with his Apostles on Holy Thursday, the night before he died (CCC 1340).

Develop

1. As a class, read paragraphs 5–8 from this chapter.

2. From a children's Bible, you can read accounts of the Last Supper: Mt 26:26–29; Mk 4:22–25; Lk 22:15; Jn 13:1–20; 1 Cor 11:23–26.

3. Review with the children the teachings on the Eucharist:
- Matter: bread and wine
- Form: "This is my body," "This is the cup of my blood."
- Minister: ordained priest (Power conferred to Apostles, and through them to their successors when Jesus said: "Do this in remembrance of Me")

The change from bread and wine to the Body and Blood of Jesus is called transubstantiation. The parts of the word give its meaning:
- "trans-" (change or action e.g., transit, transfer, transition)
- "-substanti" (substance, what it is)
- "-ation" (a suffix that forms a noun from an action; e.g., participation, accommodation, identification)

Also: Jesus is wholly present in each of the Eucharistic Hosts, Body, Blood, Soul, and Divinity; further, He is present in each part of each Host. Jesus is also wholly present, Body, Blood, Soul, and Divinity, in the consecrated wine.

4. Review that the Blessed Sacrament is reserved in the tabernacle in the church. Take the children to the tabernacle for silent prayer. Remind them to be silent, to genuflect, and to be aware of Jesus truly present in the Eucharist.

5. Review: "This is the cup of my Blood, the Blood of the new and everlasting covenant." A covenant is an oath that makes us family. After the Passover, Moses led the Israelites to Mt. Sinai, where they received God's Laws and made a covenant. Jesus offers us the perfect covenant that we entered at Baptism and renew in the Eucharist.

Name:_____

I am the Bread of Life

**This is My Body,
which will be given up for you.**

Color the picture.

This is the cup of My Blood, the Blood of the new and everlasting covenant. It will be shed for you and for all so that sins will be forgiven.

68   *Faith and Life Series • Grade 3 • Chapter 18 • Lesson 3*

DO THIS IN REMEMBRANCE: TO MAKE PRESENT

When the priest acts in the person of Christ, uses the matter Jesus used, and says the words Jesus said, God makes present the mysteries that were celebrated at the Last Supper, the gift of Christ on the Cross and the triumph of the Resurrection. We are called to be united with Jesus as we receive Him in the Blessed Sacrament. During the Mass, we offer ourselves (with Jesus, the perfect sacrifice) to the Father and receive from Him many graces and blessings. Our participation in the Mass is more than a Sunday duty, it is a renewal of our covenant (the new and everlasting covenant) with God. Now, that's something to meditate on . . . and to inspire us to come to Mass in love.

Reinforce

1. Have the students work on *Activity Book*, p. 68.

2. The students may continue working on their Memorization Questions.

3. Take time to pray before the Blessed Sacrament; if possible, arrange for an Adoration and Benediction service.

4. You may discuss with the children the way they feel or what they pray when they have just received Jesus and He is united with them so closely through Communion.

Conclude

1. Lead the students in singing "O Thou, who at thy Eucharist didst pray," *Adoremus Hymnal*, #521.

2. Lead the children in praying prayers of Adoration with the response: "Jesus, in the Blessed Sacrament, have mercy on us. Jesus I love you, save souls."

Most Holy Trinity, Father, Son, and Holy Spirit, I adore Thee profoundly. I offer Thee the Most Precious Blood, Body, Soul, and Divinity of our Lord, Jesus Christ, present in all the tabernacles throughout the world, in reparation for the outrages, sacrileges, and indifferences by which He Himself is offended. And through the infinite merits of His Most Sacred Heart, and those of the Immaculate Heart of Mary, I beg of thee the conversion of all poor sinners. *Amen.*

O My Jesus, forgive us our sins, save us from the fires of hell. Lead all souls to Heaven, especially those most in need of Thy mercy. *Amen.*

Preview

In the next lesson, the students will learn more about Holy Communion.

NOTES
_____
_____
_____
_____
_____

LESSON FOUR: COMMUNION

Aims

The children will learn that Jesus gives Himself to man in Holy Communion. In Holy Communion, man is intimately united with Christ through the Eucharist.

The children will learn the effects of Holy Communion.

Materials

- *Activity Book*, p. 69
- Dominos

Optional:
- "O Thou, who at thy Eucharist didst pray," *Adoremus Hymnal*, #521

Begin

Before the class comes in, arrange the dominos, standing on end, in a line (so that if you knock one down, it will knock down all the others). Demonstrate the theory of cause and effect. Pushing over one domino causes all of the others to be knocked down, one at a time. Be sure they understand this theory.

Questions:
- Do I have to knock down the first domino?
- What happens if I do? What is the effect?
- What was the cause of this mess?
- What did I have to do with all of this?

Q. 83 *What is the Sacrament of the Holy Eucharist?*
The Holy Eucharist is the sacrament in which Jesus is present under the appearance of bread and wine (CCC 1337, 1374).

Q. 84 *What does the priest say over the bread and wine?*
The priest says the same words Jesus said at the Last Supper. Over the bread he says, "This is my Body, which is given up for you." Over the wine he says, "This is the cup of my Blood, the Blood of the new and everlasting covenant. It will be shed for you and for all so that sins may be forgiven" (CCC 1333, 1339, 1375).

Q. 85 *What happens to the bread and wine when the priest says the words of Jesus?*
When the priest says the words of Jesus over the bread and wine, by the power of the Holy Spirit, the bread and wine change entirely into the Body, Blood, Soul, and Divinity of Jesus. The appearances of bread and wine remain, but Jesus is truly present (CCC 1374–75).

Q. 86 *What is Holy Communion?*
Holy Communion is the way we unite ourselves to Jesus by receiving Him into ourselves. He comes into us and gives us His life and grace. By Holy Communion, Jesus makes us sharers in His Body and Blood to form one single Body in Christ (CCC 1331).

Develop

1. Read the last paragraph with the children.

2. Let them share their First Communion experiences with you: what they wore, how they celebrated, etc. Wasn't it a great day?

3. Explain that every time the we receive Holy Communion, certain things happen:
- *We are cleansed and separated from venial sin (Note: however, if they receive in mortal sin, they commit sacrilege)*
- *We become more loving and committed to serving the poor (like the Apostles learned in the washing of feet)*
- *We are in union with Jesus in the Blessed Sacrament and, because Jesus is God, we are in union with the whole Trinity*
- *We are united with the whole Church (militant, suffering, and triumphant)*
- *We have a foretaste of Heaven (to be with Jesus and God forever)*
- *We grow in the Christian life and receive an increase in the life of grace, God's life in us*
- *We have a source of conversion (turning toward God and His will for us) and penance (making up for our sins and their consequences)*
- *Our souls are fed with spiritual food; our souls need the Eucharist, just as our bodies need food.*
- *We become more like Jesus, Who lives in us*
- *We participate in the sacrifice of Christ, being united with Him and offering ourselves to the Father*
- *We are united in the Heavenly liturgy. In fact at every Mass, the angels and the saints are gathered around the altar*

4. Explain that the effects listed above always take place; however, how much we experience them depends on our disposition or how open we are to them. For example, we can't enjoy the beach if we don't bring a towel and a bathing suit, but if we are prepared, we will enjoy ourselves.

Name:_____

Holy Communion

Color the pictures.

At every Holy Mass, the bread and wine become the Body and Blood of Jesus. We call this the Sacrament of the Holy Eucharist. Whenever we receive it, Jesus comes into our hearts, alive and full of love.

Faith and Life Series • Grade 3 • Chapter 18 • Lesson 4   69

Reinforce

1. Have the students work on *Activity Book*, p. 69.

2. Have the students work on their Memorization Questions and prepare for the quiz.

Conclude

1. Lead the students in singing "O Thou, who at thy Eucharist didst pray, *Adoremus Hymnal*," #521.

2. Pray, asking God to help the children receive all the graces and benefits of Holy Communion. Pray that they be open to receiving all of the effects (you may list the effects as a review).

Preview

In the next lesson, the students' knowledge of the material covered this week will be reviewed and assessed.

SAINT POPE PIUS X

In 1835, the man who would become Pope Pius X, and then Saint Pope Pius X, was born in Italy. A humble man, he wrote in his will, "I was born poor, I have lived in poverty, and I wish to die poor."

Saint Pope Pius X strengthened and united the Church during the early years of the twentieth century. He exposed the evils of the heresy of modernism that was sweeping the world and damaging the souls of Christians everywhere. He re-established the tradition in the Church of Holy Communion for young children. He was canonized in 1957 and his feast day is August 21.

NOTES

CHAPTER EIGHTEEN
REVIEW AND ASSESSMENT

Aims

The students' knowledge and understanding of the material covered this week will be reviewed and assessed.

Materials

- Quiz 18, Appendix, p. A-26

Optional:
- "O Thou, who at thy Eucharist didst pray," *Adoremus Hymnal*, #521

Review

1. On the night before Jesus died, He celebrated the Passover with His Apostles. The children should be able to parallel the Passover with Jesus' Sacrifice and the Last Supper.

2. Jesus taught His Apostles a lesson in humility and service by washing their feet. The students should be able to define and give examples of humility.

3. Jesus instituted the Eucharist at the Last Supper and gave the power to consecrate the Eucharist to His Apostles (and through them to all priests).

4. The children should know the following about the Eucharist: matter, form, and minister. They should also be able to define transubstantiation.

5. The students should know about Jesus' presence in the Holy Eucharist. They should know that we receive Jesus in Holy Communion.

6. The students should be able to describe the effects of Holy Communion. They should know that their disposition is important to receiving all the possible graces offered in this sacrament.

Name: _____

The Last Supper, Our First Mass — Quiz 18

"Love one another as I have loved you" (John 15:12).

Word Bank

Mass	wash	bread	Passover
wine	changed	Jesus	Sacrament

Fill in the blanks with the correct words from the Word Bank.

1. On Holy Thursday, the night before He died, Jesus and His Apostles gathered to celebrate the feast of the **Passover**, a holy dinner in memory of the time God saved the Israelites from slavery in Egypt.

2. That night, Jesus knelt down to **wash** the feet of His Apostles, telling them that He had given them an example that they should follow.

3. During the meal, Jesus took **bread**, blessed and broke it, and gave it to His Apostles saying "This is My Body which will be given up for you."

4. Then He took a cup of **wine**. He gave thanks and gave it to them saying, "This is the cup of My Blood, the Blood of the new and everlasting covenant. It will be shed for you and for all, so that sins may be forgiven."

5. At the moment Jesus spoke the words, the bread and wine were **changed** into His Body and Blood. It looked and tasted like bread and wine, but it was now Jesus.

6. Jesus told the Apostles, "Do this in remembrance of Me." With these words, **Jesus** gave the Apostles the power to do the same.

7. At every Holy **Mass**, the priest says the same words over bread and wine, and they become the Body and Blood of Jesus.

8. We call this the **Sacrament** of the Holy Eucharist. When we receive this sacrament, Jesus comes into our hearts alive and full of love.

9. Write out the Scripture verse shown at the top of this page.

_____

A - 26 — Faith and Life • Grade 3 • Appendix A

Assess

1. Distribute the quizzes and read through them with the students to be sure they understand the questions.

2. Administer the quiz. As they hand in their work, you may orally quiz them on the Memorization Questions of this chapter.

3. After all the quizzes have been handed in, you may wish to review the correct answers with the class.

Conclude

1. Lead the students in singing "O Thou, who at thy Eucharist didst pray," *Adoremus Hymnal*, #521.

2. End class by saying a prayer.

CHAPTER NINETEEN
JESUS GIVES HIS LIFE FOR US

Catechism of the Catholic Church References

Agony at Gethsemane: 572–60, 612
Arrest and Passion: 457, 517, 561–2, 606–7, 1067
Christ's Redemptive Death in the Divine Plan of Salvation: 599–605, 619–20
Christ's Whole Life as a Self Offering to the Father: 606–18, 621–23
Death of Christ as the Unique and Definitive Sacrifice: 613–14
Jesus as True God and True Man: 464–70, 480–83
Jesus Freely Embraces the Father's Redemptive Love: 609

Jesus' Human Nature: 470–78, 482
Jesus' Mission of Salvation: 456–60
Last Supper: 610–11
Mary as our Mother: 963–70, 973–75
On the Cross, Jesus Consummates His Sacrifice: 616–17
Our Participation in Christ's Sacrifice: 618
Redemption: 571, 601, 669
Sacrifice: 2099–2100
Satisfaction for Sin: 1459–60, 1494
Why the Son of God Became Flesh: 456–60

Scripture References

Passion of Jesus: Mt 26:30—27:54

Background Reading: *The Fundamentals of Catholicism* by Fr. Kenneth Baker, S.J.

Volume 2:
"Jesus' Sacrifice on the Cross," 289–92
"What Do We Mean by "Redemption,"" 292–95

"Jesus Died Not for Himself but for All Men," pp. 295–98
"Jesus Merited Grace for Us," pp. 298–301

Summary of Lesson Content

Lesson 1

After the Last Supper, Jesus went to the Garden of Gethsemane.

His agony in the garden included seeing all of man's sins, knowing the price He must pay for them, and reconciling His will with the Father's.

Jesus was arrested and stood trial, facing death.

Lesson 2

The Jews sought the permission of Pontius Pilate to put Jesus to death. Pilate gave in to public outcry and sentenced Jesus to death.

Jesus was treated like a criminal and was beaten.

Lesson 3

Jesus died by crucifixion. This is commemorated by the Stations of the Cross.

Jesus suffered in love, forgiving the sins of the thief and the soldiers.

Mary and John were present with Jesus when He died upon the Cross.

Jesus chose to suffer and die to redeem the world.

Lesson 4

Jesus' sacrifice was so perfect and complete that it conquered death forever. It healed the wounds of Original Sin and restored grace and friendship between God and man.

Jesus' Passion taught man the value of suffering and sacrifice.

LESSON ONE: GETHSEMANE

Aims

After the Last Supper, Jesus went to the Garden of Gethsemane.

His agony in the garden included seeing all of man's sins, knowing the price He must pay for them, and reconciling His will with the Father's.

Jesus was arrested and stood trial, facing death.

Materials

- *Activity Book*, p. 70
- Olives
- Picture of the Agony in the Garden
- Children's Bible
- Paper, markers

Optional:
- "Ah, holy Jesus," *Adoremus Hymnal*, #402

Begin

Show some olives to the class. If they are already pickled, let the children taste them. Explain that olives are used for making oil, for cooking, and for eating. In the Church, olive oil is used to make Sacred Chrism by mixing it with fragrant balsam and having it consecrated by the bishop. Olives are a sign of eternal life because an olive tree will not die, unless it is killed purposely or by disease. In today's lesson, we will learn about the Garden of Olives, where Jesus prayed. If you were to go there today, you could pray under the same tree Jesus prayed under!

---

19 Jesus Gives His Life for Us

"Greater love has no man than this, that a man lay down his life for his friends."
John 15:13

After the Last Supper, Jesus went out to pray in the Garden of Olives. He asked His disciples to stay awake with Him for a little while, but they fell asleep. Jesus was alone in His great suffering.

Jesus saw all of our sins that night and it saddened Him. He thought of all the suffering He would accept to make up for our sins. Remember, Jesus was both God and man. As a man, He felt deep emotions. That night He felt sadness and fear. He asked God the Father, "If it is possible, take this suffering away from Me." But then He told Him, "Your will, not Mine, be done." God the Father sent an angel to comfort Him.

Later in the night, soldiers came to arrest Jesus. These soldiers were cruel, but Jesus was gentle and went with them. He knew He was about to fulfill His Father's plan for our salvation. Jesus bravely went before the high priest and Jewish leaders. He was silent when they wrongly accused Him and wanted Him to be put to death.

By law, the Jewish leaders could not put Jesus to death. They had to have the permission of Pontius Pilate, the Roman governor of Judea. He also had the power to set Jesus free. He knew Jesus was innocent. But Pilate was too afraid of not being popular. When an angry crowd kept yelling out, "Crucify Him!" Pilate gave in. He did not protect Jesus. He sentenced Him to death as His enemies wanted.

Develop

1. Read the first three paragraphs from this chapter aloud.

2. You may read the Agony in the Garden from the children's Bible, Matthew 26:30–58. Note that this passage is found immediately after the Last Supper.
You may ask the children questions to be sure they understand the passage:
- *When did Jesus and the Apostles go to the Mount of Olives?*
- *What did Jesus do there? What did the Apostles do there?*
- *Why was Jesus upset with the Apostles?*
- *What did Jesus say to the Father?*
- *Who consoled Him?*
- *What happened when He finished praying?*

3. Ask the children in what other story do we find a garden? The story of Adam and Eve. Did they choose to do God's will? No. How do we know this? They ate the fruit of the tree of knowledge of good and evil. What happened because of this? They had to leave Eden. They committed Original Sin, and the gates of Heaven were closed. Who could undo these sad things? Only the Savior, Who was promised by God, could undo them. Now, in this Garden of Olives (a sign of eternal life), does Jesus do the Father's will? Yes, even though it is hard, He prays "Your will, not mine, be done." What is God's will? That Jesus give his life for our salvation. After this, the gates of Heaven could be opened again. Teach the children that Jesus is the New Adam because in Jesus we find the life of grace, and all the effects of Adam's sin are repaired.

4. In the Garden of Olives, Jesus suffered because He saw all of our sins; every sin by every person, throughout time—even our sins. Jesus loves each of us so much that He would have died for just one of us.

Name:_____

The Passion of Jesus

Write sentences using these words.

Garden of Olives: **Answers will vary.**

Your will: _____

Salvation: _____

Soldiers: _____

Pontius Pilate: _____

Thorns: _____

Cross: _____

Calvary: _____

Mary: _____

Sacrifice: _____

Stations of the Cross: _____

70   *Faith and Life Series • Grade 3 • Chapter 19 • Lesson 1*

ADAM AND JESUS

Adam:
- Adam
- Garden of Eden
- Did not do will of God
- Caused man to be cast from Eden
- Brought death to world
- Bound man to sin
- Closed gates of Heaven

Jesus:
- New Adam
- Garden of Olives
- Did will of God
- Reunited man with God
- Brought eternal life to world
- Freed man from sin
- Opened gates of Heaven

Reinforce

1. Have the students research the words on *Activity Book*, p. 70 and write sentences using them.

2. Have the students draw posters of Christ, the New Adam.

3. Teach the children to sing "Ah, holy Jesus," *Adoremus Hymnal*, #402.

Conclude

End class by saying a prayer for all the people whom the children know who are in need prayers. Let them say their intentions and have the class respond with "Lord, hear our prayer."

Preview

In the next lesson, the students will learn about the trial of Jesus and how He was treated.

NOTES

LESSON TWO: ON TRIAL

Aims

The Jews sought the permission of Pontius Pilate to put Jesus to death. Pilate gave in to the public outcry and sentenced Jesus to death.

Jesus was treated like a criminal and was beaten.

Materials

- *Activity Book*, p. 71
- List of Stations of the Cross and pictures of them (you may take children to church)
- Cards to sign, or paper and markers

Optional:
- "Jesus Dies on the Cross," video; Jesus: A Kingdom without Frontiers, available through Ignatius Press
- "Ah, holy Jesus," *Adoremus Hymnal*, #402

Begin

Ask the students if they know what the Stations of the Cross are. Many may know from their previous year of study. It is a way that we can follow Jesus on His way to suffer and die for our sins, so that we can be united with Him. In this prayer, we can walk (literally from one Station to the next) and learn to imitate Jesus. Today, we will learn about Jesus' journey from the time He was arrested to the time He was crucified. We will then learn the Stations of the Cross, and think about ways we can imitate Jesus and His faithfulness to the Father.

The soldiers grabbed Jesus and treated Him like a criminal. They beat Him with whips. They pushed a crown of sharp thorns on His head. They made fun of Him by saying in disrespectful voices, "Hail, King of the Jews."

Now Jesus was very weak, but the soldiers hurt Him even more. They made Him carry a heavy Cross. They gave Him no rest or water. Jesus fell down three times, but they made Him go on. When Jesus reached the top of Mount **Calvary**, they nailed His hands and feet to the wood of the Cross, raised the Cross upright, and left Him to die in pain.

Even in the midst of great suffering, Jesus was full of love. He asked His Father to forgive the cruel soldiers. He gave hope and forgiveness to a thief hanging by His side. He told His mother Mary to be the mother of His beloved Apostle John, and of the whole world.

Some of the people laughed at Jesus and said, "He heals others, but He cannot save Himself!" Jesus was God, and He had full power to escape the pain of the Cross. But He stayed on the Cross. He freely chose to suffer and die because He loved us so much. He wanted to make up for our sins. He wanted to **redeem** us, or buy our freedom, so we could go to Heaven.

A **sacrifice** is something that is offered to God. Jesus' sacrifice was so complete and so perfect that it conquered death for ever. It healed the wounds of Adam's Original Sin. It restored full friendship between man and God.

Jesus' great victory taught us the value of sacrifice. His **Passion** and death saved the world. When we offer up things out of love, we are part of Jesus' great Sacrifice. We make up for our sins and the sins of others. In some way we help Him in saving the world. Small acts of self-denial can be as simple as giving up a piece of candy we want to keep or helping our mother when we are tired. These acts

94

Develop

1. Read aloud paragraphs 4–6 from the student text.

2. You may read the story of Jesus' Passion from a children's Bible (Mt 26:58—27:54).

3. Discuss how Jesus was treated as a criminal, even though He was sinless. He suffered greatly. They beat Him, pressed a crown of thorns into His head, teased Him, spat on Him, made Him carry His Cross, and nailed Him to it, leaving Him to suffocate.

4. Jesus suffered because He loved us, and we can learn much from His sufferings. If the Son of God came and suffered, then our sufferings must have value if we unite them with the sufferings of Our Lord.

5. Teach the children to pray the Stations of the Cross. You may have age-appropriate prayer aides to help you. Take the

children to the church to pray the Stations or provide images of the Stations and pray them in class.

6. After praying the Stations, ask the children what they could learn from Jesus in each of the Stations. Write a chart on the board, using the children's examples. A sample chart is found at right.

7. If your classroom has a Crucifix, take it down and pass it around to all the children. Let them reverence the Cross in silence. Lead them in thanking Jesus for His gift of Himself and His great love for each child. In your prayer, name each child in the class (including those not present).

Name:_____

Stations of the Cross

Put the Stations of the Cross in the right order.

Number	Station
4	Jesus meets his Mother.
11	Jesus is nailed to the Cross.
6	Veronica wipes the face of Jesus.
14	Jesus is placed in the tomb.
1	Jesus is condemned to death.
9	Jesus falls a third time.
2	Jesus carries His Cross.
12	Jesus dies on the Cross.
3	Jesus falls the first time.
8	Jesus speaks to the women.
13	Jesus is taken down from the Cross.
7	Jesus falls the second time.
5	Jesus is helped by Simon.
10	Jesus is stripped of His clothes.

Faith and Life Series • Grade 3 • Chapter 19 • Lesson 2

Reinforce

1. Take the children to the church to pray the Stations of the Cross.

2. Have the students work on *Activity Book*, p. 71. They may do this in the church, using the Stations as a reference.

3. Have the children make cards for prisoners or groups of oppressed people.

4. Show the video, "Jesus Dies on the Cross," from the *Jesus: A Kingdom without Frontiers* series (available through Ignatius Press; 30 minutes).

Conclude

1. Lead the students in singing "Ah, holy Jesus," *Adoremus Hymnal*, #402.

2. Lead the children in praying to Jesus, thanking Him for the gift of His life on the Cross and for His great love of each student in your class. Name each child during the prayer. As you pray in thanksgiving for Jesus' love of each child, you may allow that child to hold a Crucifix.

Preview

In the next lesson, the students will learn about the final moments of Jesus' life on the Cross.

STATIONS OF THE CROSS: OUR IMITATION OF CHRIST

Stn. 1 We can be obedient to our authorities
Stn. 2 We can suffer gladly
Stn. 3 Every time we fall, we turn to Jesus for help
Stn. 4 We can ask the Mother of God for help
Stn. 5 We can accept help/give to others
Stn. 6 We can console others, and be consoled
Stn. 7 We should persevere in our trials
Stn. 8 We should put others before ourselves
Stn. 9 We should not give up hope
Stn. 10 We should be humble
Stn. 11 We should die to our sin
Stn. 12 We should place our lives in God's hands
Stn. 13 We should receive the Body of Christ
Stn. 14 We should visit Jesus in the Tabernacle

NOTES

LESSON THREE: CRUCIFY HIM

Aims

Jesus died by crucifixion.

Jesus suffered in love, forgiving the sins of the thief and the soldiers.

Mary and John were present with Jesus when He died upon the Cross.

Jesus chose to suffer and die to redeem the world.

Materials

- *Activity Book*, p. 72
- Appendix, pp. B-23–B-25
- Children's Bible

Optional:
- "Ah, holy Jesus," *Adoremus Hymnal*, #402

Begin

You may begin the class by praying (and thereby reviewing) the Stations of the Cross.

Ask the children the following questions:
- During the suffering of Jesus, how was He feeling? How would you have felt?
- If you had seen Jesus on His Way of the Cross, what would you have liked to do for Him?
- How do you feel about your sins, knowing what Jesus suffered for them?
- Why do we wear crucifixes? (As a sign of our love and thankfulness for Jesus and our faith)

of love become part of Jesus' Sacrifice and help bring grace into the world.

The next time you go to Mass, find the Stations of the Cross in your church. Look at all fourteen images. Remember that Jesus loved you so much He suffered and died for you. You must be very precious to Him. Tell Him that you will love Him for ever.

STATIONS OF THE CROSS
1. Jesus is condemned to death.
2. Jesus carries His Cross.
3. Jesus falls the first time.
4. Jesus meets His Mother.
5. Jesus is helped by Simon.
6. Veronica wipes the face of Jesus.
7. Jesus falls a second time.
8. Jesus speaks to the women.
9. Jesus falls a third time.
10. Jesus is stripped of His clothes.
11. Jesus is nailed to the Cross.
12. Jesus dies on the Cross.
13. Jesus is taken down from the Cross.
14. Jesus is placed in the tomb.

Words to Know:

Calvary   redeem   sacrifice   Passion

Develop

1. Read paragraphs 7 and 8 from the student text.

2. Using a children's Bible, read the last minutes of the life of Jesus from the Gospel of John (Jn 19:18–30).
- *Note how people were angered that He was called King of the Jews*
- *Jesus was crucified between two thieves*
- *Mary and John were there at the foot of the Cross*
- *Jesus loved even from the Cross.*

3. Discuss the important roles of Mary and John. They were there to mourn and comfort our Lord in His suffering. Sometimes it is harder to watch another suffer than it is to suffer yourself. Mary, the Mother of Jesus, must have suffered greatly watching her Son die this way. John was Jesus' beloved disciple. He was faithful to Christ, never abandoning Him. Jesus gave Mary to John, since Joseph had already passed away and Jesus would no longer be able to care for His mother. What a great honor to receive the mother of your Lord! John represents all of us who are faithful to Jesus. She was given to each of us by Christ on the Cross that day. In turn, we were also given to her, for her to care for. She still does this by interceding for us with her Son. We can turn to Mary for a good example and to ask her to pray for us. What are some Marian prayers and songs?
- *Hail Mary*
- *Hail Holy Queen*
- *Memorare*
- *Sing of Mary, Immaculate Mary, etc.*

4. Jesus, as God, could have come down from the Cross. Because He loved us so much, He stayed on the Cross to give Himself so we could live with Him forever. It is said that Jesus didn't need nails to keep Him on the Cross, for His love for us would have held Him there.

Name:_____

Jesus' Passion

1. Where did Jesus go after the Last Supper? What did He do there?
Jesus went to the Garden of Olives to pray.
2. What did Jesus ask the Father in the Garden of Gethsemane?
"If it is possible, take this suffering away from me."
3. What happened later that night?
Soldiers came to arrest Jesus. They took Him before the high priests and Jewish leaders.
4. How was Jesus sentenced to death?
The Jewish leaders sent Jesus to Pontius Pilate. He knew that Jesus was innocent, but the crowd kept shouting, "Crucify Him" so Pilate gave in.
5. How did the soldiers treat Jesus?
Like a criminal. They beat Him with whips, put a crown of thorns on His head, and made fun of Him by saying, "Hail, King of the Jews."
6. How did Jesus and the Cross get to Calvary?
Jesus carried the Cross to Calvary.
7. What special role did Jesus give to Mary?
He told Mary to be the mother of the whole world.
8. How did Jesus die?
Jesus died on the Cross by crucifixion.
9. What was special about Jesus' sacrifice?
His sacrifice was so complete and so perfect that it conquered death forever. It healed the wounds of Adam's Original Sin. It restored full friendship between God and man.

Faith and Life Series • Grade 3 • Chapter 19 • Lesson 3

Reinforce

1. Have the children work on *Activity Book*, p. 72.

2. You may teach the children about Jesus' love for us as shown by the Sacred Heart. You will need to turn to Appendix, pp. B-23 and B-24.

3. Have the students work on their Memorization Questions.

Conclude

1. Lead the students in singing "Ah, holy Jesus," *Adoremus Hymnal*, #402.

2. You may lead the students in praying Marian prayers.

Preview

In the next lesson, the students will learn about the perfection of Jesus' sacrifice and the value of penance.

SAINT MARGARET MARY ALACOQUE

Holy from her childhood, Saint Margaret Mary Alacoque is an example of penance and devotion to God. Growing up in a prosperous family, she shunned the pleasures of the world, imposing numerous sufferings upon her body. She decided to take the habit and enter a convent. Even among nuns, Saint Margaret Mary Alacoque experienced great suffering, which she welcomed with patience and faith. As she grew older, so did her devotion to the Sacred Heart. She wrote spiritual maxims and prayers, initiated the Holy Hour, and received the call from Jesus to first Friday devotions. This holy woman was canonized by Pope Benedict XV in 1920. Her feast day is October 17.

NOTES

LESSON FOUR: THE PASSION

Aims

The students will learn that Jesus' sacrifice was so perfect and complete that it conquered death forever. It healed the wounds of Original Sin and restored grace and friendship between God and man.

Jesus' Passion taught man the value of suffering and sacrifice.

Materials

- *Activity Book*, p. 73
- "The Day the Sun Danced," from CCC of America Video; available through Ignatius Press

Optional:
- "Ah, holy Jesus," *Adoremus Hymnal*, #402

Begin

Review the Memorization Questions. Focus on sacrifice. What other people in the Bible, aside from Jesus, offered sacrifices to the Father? (Abel, Noah, Abraham, Moses, David) Did their sacrifices reconcile God and Man? No. Why not? Because they were not perfect sacrifices, nor were the people who offered the sacrifices perfect. Why is the Sacrifice of Jesus different? He was the priest and the victim. Jesus offered Himself to the Father; Jesus was sinless and perfect; therefore, He was the perfect Sacrifice of redemption.

Q. 87 *Why did the Son of God become man?*
The Son of God became man to save us, that is, to redeem us from sin and to regain Heaven for us (CCC 461).

Q. 88 *What did Jesus Christ do to save us?*
To save us, Jesus Christ paid for our sins by suffering and sacrificing Himself on the Cross, and He taught us how to live according to God (CCC 571, 580).

Q. 89 *What is a sacrifice?*
Sacrifice is the public offering to God of something to show that God is the Creator and Supreme Master to Whom everything belongs (CCC 606).

Q. 90 *What are the Stations of the Cross?*
The Stations of the Cross are a devotional prayer in which we think about the suffering and death of Jesus (CCC 1674, 1676).

"Let not your hearts be troubled. . . . And when I go and prepare a place for you, I will come again and will take you to myself, that where I am you may be also."

John 14:1–3

Develop

1. Read the rest of the chapter aloud.

2. Review the wounds of Adam's sin, and how Jesus healed them:

Adam	Jesus
Sickness and death	Eternal life
Exiled us from Eden	Reconciled us with the Father
Enslaved us to sin	Freed us from sin
Lost grace	Restored grace
Gates of Heaven closed	Opened gates of Heaven

3. Discuss the value of suffering and sacrifice. Any suffering we have can be a sacrifice to God, be it illness, a wound, a humiliation, an act of obedience, etc. God gives us many opportunities to suffer and gain the merits of suffering by offering them to God. We can see the value of sacrifice in Jesus' Passion and death. Jesus did not have to suffer and die this way. He chose to. We, too, can choose to make sacrifices to God. They may be small acts of self-denial, or penance. Have the children give ideas for each of the following and write them on the board:

- *Fasting:* giving up something, e.g., candy, meat
- *Almsgiving:* giving to the poor
- *Works of charity:* do something out of love for another
- *Penance:* offer up sufferings to God
- *Prayers:* dialogue with God (intercessory prayer is to pray on behalf of another)

4. If you have the video "The Day the Sun Danced" (available through Ignatius Press; 30 minutes), or another video on Fatima, or a video that touches on the value of sacrifices, you may watch it with the children. You may also read the story of Fatima to the children.

5. Have the students think of works of sacrifice they will promise to offer God the Father over the coming week.

Name:_____

The Crucifixion

Color the picture below.

Jesus' sacrifice was so perfect that it conquered death forever and healed the wounds of Adam's sin. It restored full friendship between man and God. His Passion and death saved the world. When we offer up things out of love, we are part of Jesus' great sacrifice.

Faith and Life Series • Grade 3 • Chapter 19 • Lesson 4   73

PENANCE

We have in the Church two penitential seasons, Advent and Lent, during which the priest wears purple. Penance prepares us for very important things: the coming of Jesus, and Jesus' death and Resurrection.

There are different ways to do penance. We receive a penance when we go to Confession. We may abstain from meat on Fridays. Penance includes: prayers, fasting and abstinence, works of charity, and almsgiving.

At Fatima, Mary asked the children to do penance. If Jesus suffered and died to redeem the world, there must be value in our suffering and penance, if we unite it with Jesus and offer it to Him.

Reinforce

1. Have the students work on selecting works of sacrifice to offer to God the Father during the next week.

2. Have the students work on *Activity Book*, p. 73.

3. Have the students review their Memorization Questions and prepare for the quiz.

Conclude

1. Lead the students in singing "Ah, holy Jesus," *Adoremus Hymnal*, #402.

2. Offer up your sacrifices to the Father, through Jesus Christ, in the Holy Spirit.

Preview

In the next lesson, the students' knowledge of the material covered this week will be reviewed and assessed.

NOTES

CHAPTER NINETEEN
REVIEW AND ASSESSMENT

Aims

The students' knowledge and understanding of the material covered this week will be reviewed and assessed.

Materials

- Quiz 19, Appendix, p. A-27

Optional:
- "Ah, holy Jesus," *Adoremus Hymnal*, #402

Name: _____

Jesus Gives His Life for Us Quiz 19

"Could you not watch with me one hour?" (Matthew 26:40).

Word Bank

| forgive | unpopular | Heaven | Calvary | sacrifice |
| Passion | head | Cross | John | pray |

Fill in the blanks with the correct words from the Word Bank.

1. After the supper, Jesus went to the Garden of Olives to *pray*. In His Agony in the Garden, He asked His Apostles, "Could you not watch with Me one hour?"

2. Pilate knew Jesus was innocent, but he was afraid of being *unpopular*.

3. The soldiers beat Jesus with whips and pushed a crown of sharp thorns on his *head*.

4. They made Him carry a heavy *Cross*. He fell three times.

5. When Jesus reached the top of Mount *Calvary*, the soldiers nailed His hands and feet to the wood of the Cross, raised the Cross upright, and left Him to die in pain.

6. Jesus asked His Father to *forgive* the cruel soldiers.

7. He gave His Mother to be the Mother of His Apostle *John* and of all people.

8. Jesus wanted to redeem us and to buy our freedom, so we could go to *Heaven*.

9. A *sacrifice* is something that is offered to God. Jesus offered Himself as a sacrifice to God so we could receive God's life within us and become His children.

10. The *Passion* and death of Jesus saved the world.

11. Write out the Scripture verse shown at the top of this page.

_____

Faith and Life • Grade 3 • Appendix A   A - 27

Review

1. Review Jesus' Passion and death. You may do this with the Stations of the Cross.

2. Remind the children that Jesus loves each of them; review that He would suffer and die for each and every one of them individually.

3. Review that Jesus gave Mary to all of us to be our Mother.

4. Review that we can offer our sufferings and penances to God as sacrifices, united with Jesus.

Assess

1. Distribute the quizzes and read through them with the students to be sure they understand the questions.

2. Administer the quiz. As they hand in their work, you may orally quiz them on the Memorization Questions for this chapter.

3. After all the quizzes have been handed in, you may wish to review the correct answers with the class.

Conclude

1. Lead the students in singing "Ah, holy Jesus," *Adoremus Hymnal*, #402.

2. End class by leading the children in prayer.

CHAPTER TWENTY
OFFERING GIFTS OF LOVE

Catechism of the Catholic Church References

Eucharist as Sacrifice: 1356–81, 1414
Eucharist as Thanksgiving and Praise to the Father: 1359–61
Eucharist as Sacrificial Memorial of Christians: 1362–72, 1408, 1414
Mass: 1347, 1356–57, 1408, 2177–79
Our Participation in Christ's Sacrifice: 618
Presence of Christ in the Eucharist: 1373–81, 1410, 1418
Priests: 1539–66
Sacrifice: 1365–72, 1410, 2099–2100

Scripture References

Christ's Saving Blood: Heb 9:11–28
Cup of Blessing and Bread: 1 Cor 10:16
Living Bread: Jn 6:48–58

Background Reading: *The Fundamentals of Catholicism* by Fr. Kenneth Baker, S.J.

Volume 3:
"The Mass and the Cross," pp. 262–64
"Where Is the Sacrifice?" pp. 265–67
"Power of the Mass," pp. 268–70
"Each Mass Benefits All," pp. 271–73

Summary of Lesson Content

Lesson 1

Sacrifices in the Old Testament were burnt offerings or offerings of oblation to God. They showed that God was more valuable than His gifts.

Examples of such sacrifices were given by Abraham and Old Testament priests.

Lesson 2

In the time of Jesus, Temple worship was celebrated with sacrificial offerings to God.

Jesus was the perfect gift from God and the perfect offering to God.

Jesus offered Himself to the Father by dying on the Cross. As the perfect Sacrifice, He opened the Father's heart and the gates of Heaven.

Lesson 3

Men throughout time want to share in this sacrifice. Therefore His Body and Blood are offered continually in the one perfect Sacrifice of Christ through the Mass.

The Sacrifice of the Cross and the Sacrifice of the Mass are one and the same sacrifice.

We share in this sacrifice by actively participating in the Mass.

Lesson 4

The Sacrifice of the Mass is the continual offering of Christ in an unbloody manner.

Through the Mass Jesus' Sacrifice is made present in a real and sacramental way.

Together, with the priest, uniting ourselves to Jesus, we offer Jesus, the perfect Sacrifice, to the Father as the most pleasing and powerful offering.

LESSON ONE: SACRIFICES

Aims

The students will review that sacrifices in the Old Testament were burnt offerings or offerings of oblation to God. They showed that God was more valuable than His gifts. Examples of such sacrifices were given by Abraham and Old Testament priests.

Materials

- *Activity Book*, p. 74

  Optional:
  - "Jesus, my Lord, my God, my all!" *Adoremus Hymnal*, #516

Begin

Begin by asking the children what kinds of things they could sacrifice to show God how much they love Him. These may be sacrifices that they have already been making. Ask them why they chose these sacrifices. Were they things that were hard to give up? Have them think of the sacrifices their parents have made: sacrifice of sleep, comfort, doing things they may not like (such as cleaning up after a sick child), etc. Ask the children why their parents make these sacrifices. They make them out of love. All sacrifices should be made out of love.

---

20 Offering Gifts of Love

"This cup which is poured out for you is the new covenant in my blood."

Luke 22:20

All through the ages, God's children have offered sacrifices to Him as a sign of their worship and love. During the Old Testament days, before Jesus came to earth, the people of God offered up many things that were dear to them. In this way they told God that they loved His gifts, but they loved Him even more.

Whenever a person offered up something in sacrifice, he burned or destroyed it. This showed that he was giving it completely back to God. Farmers thanked God for their crops by sacrificing the first fruits of their harvest. It was a way of saying, "We believe that these gifts are from You. Thank You. Please keep blessing us."

So men made a present to the Heavenly Father of the very things that nourished them and kept them alive. Healthful grains like barley, wheat, and oats were baked into unleavened bread and cakes. Grapes were pressed into wine. Then the good grain and wine were given to God as gifts.

People of the Old Testament also offered up the bloody sacrifice of animals. They used cows, sheep, and doves. During an animal sacrifice, the priest placed the victim on an altar and put his hands on it. Then he killed the animal, shed its blood, and burned it.

Holy men of the Old Testament were generous in these sacrifices. Abel, who was a shepherd, offered up his best lamb. The first thing Noah did after the rains stopped was to build a stone altar and sacrifice some animals from the ark. Abraham was even willing to obey God's request that he sacrifice his own beloved son, Isaac. God was only testing Abraham's trust and love. He rewarded

---

Develop

1. Read paragraphs 1–7 with the children. They may take turns reading aloud.

2. Explain that in the Old Testament, God's people offered three types of sacrifices:
   - Offerings in which man recognized Almighty God's gifts to him, rejoicing in God's power and rule. Each man showed his gratitude and respect for God's "strong hand and outstretched arm" (Deut 26)
   - Offerings of atonement (Lev 16), in which whatever man sacrificed on the outside was more and more in accord with his inside: for instance, as a result of sorrow for sin, one might demonstrate a heart filled with contrition, saying "My sacrifice, O God, is a contrite spirit" (Ps 51:19)
   - Peace offerings, in which the people all gathered and shared a feast in joy and communion with God. The covenant at Mt. Sinai was sealed in this way (Ex 24)

3. Have the children recount the various sacrifices in the Old Testament and discuss into which of the three categories their sacrifices fit.

4. Ask the children to think of an offering for each of these categories in our time, something to which they can relate.

5. Discuss the reasons that none of the Old Testament sacrifices could restore God's friendship with man. Man was sinful. Man could not offer a perfect sacrifice. Man could not offer a sacrifice on behalf of all men.

6. Discuss how the Old Testament sacrifices helped to prepare for the New Testament Sacrifice of Christ. Are there parallels? Are there typologies?

Name:_____

Old Testament Sacrifices

1. What is a sacrifice?
A sacrifice is a sign of worship and love offered to God.

2. What does a sacrifice show God?
It shows God that we love His gifts, but we love Him even more.

3. What kinds of things were sacrificed during Old Testament times?
Animals like cows, sheep, and doves

4. Name some people from the Old Testament who offered up sacrifices.
Abel, Noah, and Abraham

5. Which men were appointed to offer sacrifice by Moses?
Moses appointed priests to offer sacrifice.

6. What was the goal of Old Testament sacrifice?
Old Testament sacrifice wanted to make up for Adam's sin.

7. Where did people in the Old Testament offer their sacrifices?
At the Temple

Reinforce

1. Have the children work on *Activity Book*, p. 74.

2. Have the students make posters of the various Old Testament sacrifices (and the ways they point to Jesus's perfect Sacrifice).

3. Teach the children to sing "Jesus, my Lord, my God, my all!" *Adoremus Hymnal*, #516.

Conclude

End class by saying prayers of thanksgiving, contrition, and peace. The children may say their own prayers and intentions.

Preview

In the next lesson, the students will learn about the perfection of the Sacrifice of Jesus.

OLD TESTAMENT SACRIFICES PREFIGURING CHRIST

- Abel: a sacrifice of love and of his best

- Noah: a sacrifice of thanksgiving (for finally getting off the boat)

- Abraham: sacrifice of dearly beloved son

- Moses: sacrifices of atonement and covenant

- David: many sacrifices of thanksgiving

- Temple worship: sacrifices of atonement, covenant, and thanksgiving

NOTES

LESSON TWO: THE PERFECT SACRIFICE

Aims

The students will learn that Jesus was the perfect gift from God and the perfect offering to God.

Jesus offered Himself to the Father by dying on the Cross. He opened the Father's heart and the gates of Heaven.

Materials

- *Activity Book*, p. 75
- Picture of the Temple in Jerusalem.
- Paper and colored pencils

Optional:
- "Jesus, my Lord, my God, my all!" *Adoremus Hymnal*, #516

Begin

Teach the children about Temple worship. Families went to the Temple to offer sacrifices of lambs, doves, and food. Why would God allow the sacrifice of animals? We are to take care of our pets and must respect the environment as stewards of creation. However, when the Israelites were among foreign people they strayed from the one true God and adopted customs from local religions, including some that worshiped animals (remember the golden calf at Mt. Sinai). The sacrifice of animals was God's way of having the people demonstrate that they worshiped the one true God and not mere creatures.

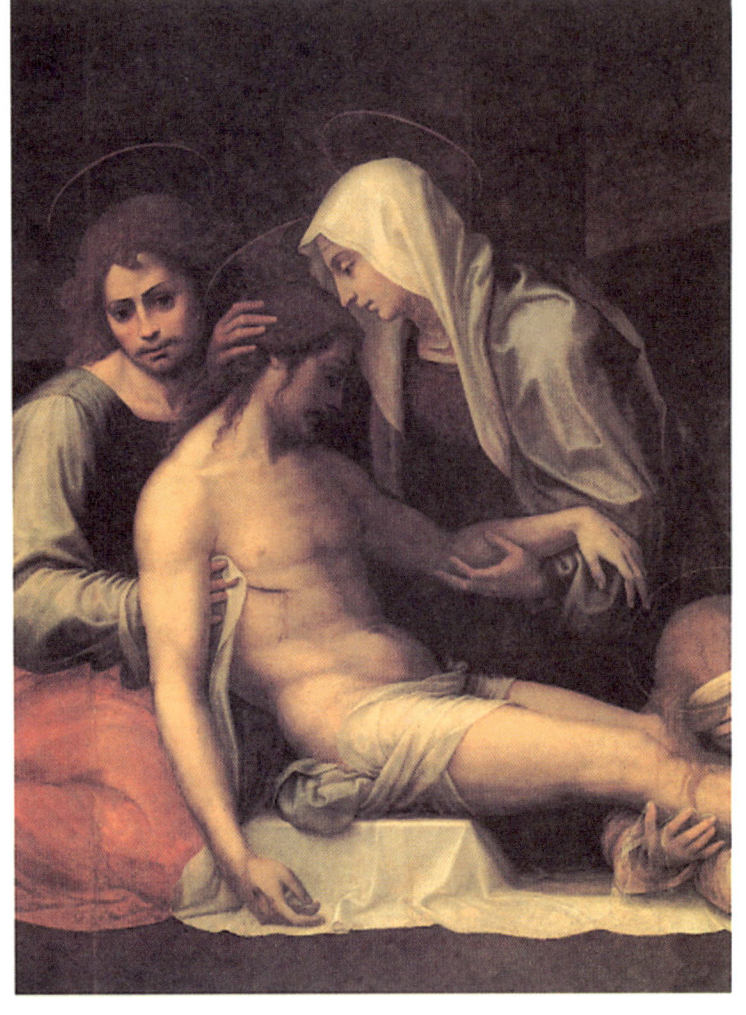

98

Develop

1. Read paragraphs 8 and 9 aloud from the student text.

2. Ask the children why Jesus was the perfect Sacrifice
   - He was God the Son
   - He was Man
   - He was sinless
   - He loved perfectly
   - He freely gave up His life

3. Using the Chalk Talk at right, show how the sin of Adam had caused a great divide between God and man. For that separation to be bridged, it would take a gift from God (the sending of His Son) and the gift of Man (the "Yes" of Mary). With these two gifts, God was made Man in the Divine Person of Jesus Christ.

4. Using the Cross, show the children the vertical bar and say: "This beam of the Cross reminds us of our love for God and His love for us." Show them the horizontal bar, and say: "This beam of the Cross reminds us that we should love our neighbors and Christ in them." The Cross reminds us of God and man. Drawing a Cross into Chalk Talk A as a bridge of the separation between God and Man, show that by the Cross, Jesus won reconciliation between God and man.

5. Ask the children what kinds of crosses they have in their lives. How can they offer them to God? Can they suffer their crosses in a way that will help their neighbors? Ask them to think of ways they can see Christ in their crosses or imitate Christ in carrying their crosses.

6. Review that Jesus died once, for all our sins. His Sacrifice is good for all eternity. Although we may sin over and over again, He has died once for all. We celebrate this in the Mass, which is a continuation of His Sacrifice of the Cross made present on the altar.

Name:_____

Old and New Testaments

Use Chapter 20 to help you fill in the blanks.

1. C O M P L E T E L Y
2.   S H E D
3.   P R I E S T S
4.   T E M P L E
5.   G A V E
6.   M A S S
7.   O F F E R E D
8.   N E W
9.   A L T A R

1. In the Old Testament, whenever a person offered up something in sacrifice, he burned or destroyed it, thereby showing that he was giving it _____ back to God.
2. In the Old Testament, the priest would kill the animal, _____ its blood, and then burn it.
3. God had Moses appoint a few men to offer up gifts for all the people. These men were called _____.
4. In the Old Testament, families went to the _____ in Jerusalem to offer up gifts of lambs, doves, and food to God.
5. When Jesus, God's beloved Son, shed His Blood, died on the Cross, and rose from the dead, He _____ us the perfect gift that would unite us with Him to the end of time.
6. On the night before He died, Jesus gave His apostles the power to change bread and wine into His Body and Blood. This act was the Sacrifice of the _____.
7. Jesus is the Lamb of God being _____ continually to save our world.
8. Can you see the wonderful preparation of the Old Testament for the _____ Testament?
9. The Holy Mass is the Sacrifice of the Body and Blood of Jesus Christ, which is offered on the _____ by the priest of God.

Faith and Life Series • Grade 3 • Chapter 20 • Lesson 2   75

Reinforce

1. Have the children work on *Activity Book*, p. 75.

2. Have the children draw and explain the Chalk Talk they learned today.

3. Have the students begin working on the Memorization Questions and reviewing the unit.

Conclude

1. Lead the children in singing "Jesus, my Lord, my God, my all!" *Adoremus Hymnal*, #516.

2. Lead the children in praying the Prayer before the Crucifix.

Preview

In the next lesson, the students will learn about the Sacrifice of the Mass.

CHALK TALK: SEPARATION BETWEEN GOD AND MAN

NOTES

LESSON THREE: SACRIFICE OF THE MASS

Aims

The children will learn that in the Mass, we can share in Jesus' Sacrifice. At Mass, His Body and Blood are offered continually in the one perfect Sacrifice of Christ through the Mass.

The Sacrifice of the Cross and the Sacrifice of the Mass are one and the same sacrifice.

Materials

- *Activity Book*, p. 76
- Missals for the children

Optional:
- "Jesus, my Lord, my God, my all!"
- *Adoremus Hymnal*, #516
- Arrange for a Mass, in which the priest can explain all the parts to the children. Have the children participate.

Begin

Explain that the Mass is a continuation of the one Sacrifice of Christ on the Cross. It is the Sacrifice of the Body and Blood of Jesus, offered by Jesus to the Father. It has the same priest and the same sacrifice; only the manner is different. When we go to Mass, it is as though we are at the Last Supper, the Crucifixion, and the Resurrection. We should actively participate at Mass.

Abraham by stopping him and showing him a ram he could sacrifice instead.

In time, God had Moses anoint a few men to offer up gifts for all the people. These men were called priests. The people joined the priests in praying to God. Some of these prayers were cries for help or sorrow for sin. Others were gifts of praise or thanks.

Every Old Testament sacrifice had one great goal in common. Man deeply longed to make up for Adam's sin. Man wanted to restore his friendship with God.

When Jesus came into the world, people were still trying to restore friendship with God. Jewish families went to worship God at the **Temple** in Jerusalem. They offered up lambs, doves, and food. God was pleased with these sacrifices. But He wanted to give His people a far greater gift to offer. He wanted to give them one gift that would unite them with Him to the end of time. And He wanted to give them a perfect gift.

Jesus, God's beloved Son, was that perfect gift. When He shed His blood and died on the Cross, He gave God that perfect gift, as a sacrifice on our behalf. The Sacrifice of Himself was so perfect and true that it was the best gift ever given to God. It was so powerful that it washed away Adam's sin and saved the whole human race. It opened the Father's heart and the gates of Heaven.

Jesus knew that men and women in all of history would want to share in this perfect gift to God, too. So He made it possible for the perfect gift of His Body and Blood to be offered continually. On the night before He died, Jesus gave His Apostles the power to change bread and wine into His Body and Blood. This act was the Sacrifice of the **Mass**.

Today all over the world the Sacrifice of the Mass continues in the same way. Listen to the words of the priest. "Take this, all of you, and eat it: this is My Body. . . . Take this, all of you, and drink

99

Develop

1. Before taking your class to Mass, prepare the readers and the gift bearers. Review the songs that will be sung at Mass. You will also want to review church etiquette. It will be helpful to have parent volunteers come in to assist with overseeing the group at Mass.

If you cannot attend Mass, go through the Mass parts with the children, explaining them.

2. Read paragraphs 10 and 11. If your class Mass takes up the entire class time, save this lesson and combine it with the next.

3. Ask the children if God needed the Mass. No, but we do. We need the Mass so we can share in the Sacrifice of Christ, and show God how much we love Him. It should not be a chore to go to Mass, but a great joy. Ask the children what they like most about the Mass.

4. Review the parts of the Mass. You may list them on the board. If you have them on cards, let the children place them in order. Review the words of the Mass and what they mean. Also, help the children to memorize the proper responses at Mass.

5. *Teach what it means to participate at Mass. We should listen attentively, and not disturb people around us. We should say all the responses, and sing the songs. Also, we should think about the priest's homily and how we can live his message. We should offer ourselves to the Father united with Jesus on the altar. We should worthily receive our Lord in Holy Communion and make thanksgiving. Review proper church etiquette, genuflecting to the tabernacle (or in churches without the tabernacle in the church, bowing to the altar). They should be silent. If your church has candles, you may teach the children how to light them. They should always walk in church. They should dress well as a sign of respect.*

Name:_____

The Perfect Sacrifice

1. In Jesus' time, were people still offering sacrifices? What kind? Where?

   In Jesus' time, people offered sacrifices of lambs, doves, and food at the Temple in Jerusalem

2. Was God pleased with these sacrifices?

   Yes

3. What did God want to give His people?

   He wanted to give them a gift that would unite them with Him to the end of time.

4. Who gave us the perfect gift? What was it?

   God gave us Jesus, the perfect gift.

5. What did this gift do?

   Jesus offered Himself as a perfect gift and sacrifice to God.

6. Because Jesus knew that we would want to offer gifts to God, what did He do?

   He gave us the Sacrifice of the Mass.

7. What is the Sacrifice of the Mass?

   It is the Sacrifice of the Body and Blood of Jesus. It is offered on the altar by the priest of God, under the appearances of bread and wine, in memory of the Sacrifice of the Cross.

8. Is the Sacrifice of the Mass the same as the sacrifice of the Cross?

   Yes. The only difference is in the manner of performing it.

76 Faith and Life Series • Grade 3 • Chapter 20 • Lesson 3

Reinforce

1. Take the children to Mass. If a Mass is not possible, take them to the church, read through the parts of the Mass, and review etiquette in the church. If the church is not available, do this review in the classroom.

2. Have the students work on *Activity Book*, p. 76.

3. Have the students work on the Memorization Questions and on memorizing the parts of the Mass.

Conclude

1. Lead the children in singing "Jesus, my Lord, my God, my all!" *Adoremus Hymnal*, #516.

2. End class by saying a prayer.

Preview

In the next lesson, the students will learn more about the Sacrifice of the Mass.

PADRE PIO AND THE STIGMATA

The saintly confessor, Padre Pio, was canonized in 2002 as Saint Pio of Pietrelcina. His life was marked by remarkable devotion to God, physically demonstrated in his reception of the stigmata, the marks of which lasted until his death. When he died, all sign of the wounds disappeared completely. Padre Pio is best remembered as a confessor who knew exactly how to bring each penitent sinner closer to God. To accommodate the thousands who came to him to receive the Sacrament of Penance, Padre Pio spent the better part of every day in the confessional, sometimes for as many as twelve hours at a time. Padre Pio died in 1968.

NOTES

LESSON FOUR: OUR OFFERING

Aims

The students will learn that the Sacrifice of the Mass is the continual offering of Christ in an unbloody manner. Through the Mass, Jesus' Sacrifice is made present in a real and sacramental way.

Together with the priest, we offer Jesus, the perfect Sacrifice and the most pleasing and powerful offering, to the Father.

Materials

- *Activity Book*, p. 77
- Pencils
- "Jesus, my Lord, my God, my all!" *Adoremus Hymnal*, #516
- Mass parts written on cards and Mass responses written on cards

Begin

Begin by reviewing the parts and the responses to the Mass. Ask the children how they can fully participate in the Mass and how they can offer themselves in union with Christ to the Father.

You may play a review game, having the children put the Mass parts in order. Play a matching game to put the responses together, e.g.,
You: "The Lord be with you."
Students: "And also with you."

---

from it: this is the Cup of My Blood. . . ." Every time we go to Holy Mass, we offer up Christ Himself to the Father. It is the very same Sacrifice as the one on Calvary.

On the Cross Jesus offered Himself, shedding His Blood for our redemption. Through the ministry of the priest Jesus is offered on the altar again without shedding His Blood. At Mass we not only remember Jesus' Sacrifice of Himself to the Father, we continue it. Each time, Jesus brings His Sacrifice before us in a real but sacramental way. He is the Lamb of God being offered continually to save our world. We can share in this perfect gift to God at each Mass. Together with the priest we offer Jesus to the Father. This is the most pleasing and powerful gift we can ever give God. It is our most wonderful offering. It unites us with God and fills our world with His life and love.

Words to Know:

Temple   Mass

> **Q. 91** What is the Holy Mass?
> The Holy Mass is the Sacrifice of the Body and Blood of Jesus Christ. The Holy Mass is offered on the altar by the priest of God, under the appearances of bread and wine, in memory of the Sacrifice of the Cross (CCC 1364–65).
>
> **Q. 92** Is the Sacrifice of the Mass the same sacrifice as the Sacrifice of the Cross?
> The Sacrifice of the Mass is the Sacrifice of the Cross; the only difference is in the manner of performing it (CCC 1366–67).

Develop

1. Finish reading the chapter in the student text. If the students attended Mass during the previous lesson, you may need to begin on paragraph 10. You may want to combine the previous and the current lesson. This lesson will continue with the presumption that you have already covered the content of the previous lesson.

2. What is redemption? To redeem something means to purchase or buy it back. For example, if you redeem a coupon, you get money back. When we are talking about Jesus redeeming our souls, we mean that Jesus paid the price of sin with His Blood, so that we could be freed from sin.

3. What do we mean by salvation? Salvation means that we are saved from something for something else. We are saved from sin for union with God.

4. What is atonement? Atonement means to put together again, much like reconciliation.

5. Jesus' Sacrifice is perfect. It is a Sacrifice praising the Father for His gifts, asking pardon for sins, and bringing peace through a covenant. It redeems us for salvation and atonement with God. It not only forgives our sins, but also frees us, so we can choose to be united with God in this Sacrifice.

6. At Mass, the Sacrifice of Christ on the Cross is made present on the altar. We can be there with Jesus, offering Jesus (and ourselves in union with Him) to the Father, as part of this perfect Sacrifice.

7. Review the effects of Holy Communion, focusing on man's union with God through this sacrament.

8. Take the children to pray before the Blessed Sacrament.

Name:_____

Write about how all of these events are connected.
Answers will vary.

_____
_____
_____
_____
_____
_____
_____
_____
_____
_____
_____
_____
_____
_____
_____
_____

Faith and Life Series • Grade 3 • Chapter 20 • Lesson 4   77

PARTS OF THE MASS

Introductory Rites
- Entrance song and greeting
- Penitential Rite and Kyrie Eleison
- Opening Prayer

Liturgy of the Word
- Readings from the Old Testament, the Psalms, and the New Testament
- Reading from the Gospel
- Homily

Liturgy of the Eucharist
- Preparation of the Gifts
- Eucharistic Prayer
- Consecration
- Holy Communion

Reinforce

1. Have the children work on *Activity Book*, p. 77.

2. Have the students work on their Memorization Questions and review for the Chapter 20 Quiz and the Unit 5 Quiz.

3. Take the children to pray before the Blessed Sacrament.

Conclude

1. Lead the students in singing "Jesus, my Lord, my God, my all!" *Adoremus Hymnal*, #516.

2. End class by saying a prayer.

Preview

In the next lesson, the students' knowledge of the material covered this week will be reviewed and assessed.

NOTES

CHAPTER TWENTY
REVIEW AND ASSESSMENT

Aims

The students' knowledge and understanding of the material covered this week will be reviewed and assessed.

Materials

- Chapter 20 Quiz, Appendix p. A-28
- Unit 5 Quiz, Appendix, pp. A-29 and A-30

Optional:
- "Jesus, my Lord, my God, my all!" *Adoremus Hymnal*, #516

Review

1. The students should know why Old Testament sacrifices were made. They should also be able to recount many stories (or the history) of Old Testament sacrifices.

2. The students should know that Jesus is the perfect Sacrifice and why He is the perfect Sacrifice.

3. They should know that we can share in the perfect Sacrifice of Christ in the Mass when the Sacrifice of the Cross is made present on the altar.

4. The students should know that Jesus is not being sacrificed over and over again, but that in the Mass, that one same Sacrifice of Jesus is made present sacramentally.

5. The students should know the parts of the Mass and the responses for the Mass.

Name: _____

Offering Gifts of Love   Quiz 20

"I am the living bread which came down from heaven" (John 6:51).

Word Bank

| Son | destroyed | Temple | Blood |
| Christ | offered | Apostles | Sacrifice |

Fill in the blanks with the correct words from the Word Bank.

1. All through the ages, God's children have **offered** sacrifices to Him as a sign of their worship and love.

2. Whenever a person offered up something in sacrifice, he burned or **destroyed** it. This showed that he was giving it completely back to God.

3. Jewish families went to worship God at the **Temple** in Jerusalem. They offered up lambs, doves, and food.

4. When Jesus shed His **Blood** on the Cross, He gave God the perfect gift: the Sacrifice of Himself on the Cross.

5. Jesus made it possible for the perfect gift of His Body and Blood to be offered continually. At the Last Supper, Jesus gave His **Apostles** the power to change bread and wine into His Body and Blood.

6. Today, all over the world the Sacrifice of the Mass continues in the same way. Every time we go to Holy Mass, we offer **Christ** Himself to the Father.

7. Mass is the very same **Sacrifice** as the one that took place on Calvary.

8. Jesus, the **Son** of God, is being offered continually to save our world. With the priest we offer Jesus to the Father—the best gift we can give.

9. Write out the Scripture verse shown at the top of this page.

_____

Assess

1. Distribute the quizzes and read through them with the students to be sure they understand the questions.

2. Administer the quiz. As they hand in their work, you may orally quiz them on the Memorization Questions for this chapter.

3. After all the quizzes have been handed in, you may wish to review the correct answers with the class.

4. Repeat steps 1–3 with Unit 5 Quiz.

Conclude

End class by singing with the children "Jesus, my Lord, my God, my all!" *Adoremus Hymnal*, #516.

CHAPTER TWENTY-ONE
THE HOLY MASS

Catechism of the Catholic Church References

Apostolic Succession: 75–79, 96
Creeds: 185–97
"Do This in Memory of Me": 1341–44, 1409
Homily: 2033
Institution of the Eucharist: 1337–40
Liturgical Celebration of the Eucharist
    Celebration through the Ages: 1345–47

Movement of the Celebration: 1348–66, 1408
Mass: 1341–44
Must Participate: 389
Sacrifice: 1365–72, 1410
Scripture in the Life of the Church: 131–33, 141
Sunday Eucharist: 2177–79

Scripture References

Paul Describes Holy Eucharist: 1 Cor 11:23–34

Background Reading: *The Fundamentals of Catholicism* by Fr. Kenneth Baker, S.J

Volume 3:
"A Wonderful Change," pp. 238–40
"Presence of the Whole Christ," pp. 241–43
"The Eucharist: A Pledge of Future Glory," pp. 247–50
"Ministers of the Eucharist" pp. 250–53

"The Mass is a True Sacrifice," pp. 259–61
"The Mass and the Cross," pp. 262–64
"Power of the Mass," pp. 268–70

Summary of Lesson Content

Lesson 1

The Sacrifice of Christ on the Cross reconciled man with God.

At the Last Supper, Jesus gave us a way to share in His Sacrifice to the Father for all time.

Jesus gave His Apostles—and through them, all priests—the power to consecrate the Eucharist.

We share in the Sacrifice of Christ at Mass.

Lesson 2

As Catholics we are obliged to participate in Mass every Sunday and on Holy Days of Obligation.

The Mass begins with the Sign of the Cross, the Kyrie, and the Gloria.

Lesson 3

The Liturgy of the Word includes readings from the Scriptures, the word of God.

The Gospel contains Jesus' own words; therefore, when the priest reads the Gospel, we stand to show our respect.

The priest explains the Gospel during a homily.

Lesson 4

After the homily, we stand to profess our faith by saying the Creed.

Jesus comes into our hearts at Mass. He teaches us through the readings.

The Mass is the greatest prayer.

LESSON ONE: HIS SACRIFICE

Aims

The students will learn of the effects of the Sacrifice of Christ on the Cross which reconciled man with God.

They will learn that, at the Last Supper, Jesus gave us a way to share in His Sacrifice to the Father for all time. He perpetuated His Sacrifice in the Eucharist and through the work of the priesthood.

Materials

- *Activity Book*, p. 78
- Crucifix, children's Bible, children's missal

Optional:
- "Father, we thank thee who hast planted," *Adoremus Hymnal*, #515

Begin

Begin the class by reviewing what a sacrifice is: giving something of our own to God for the purpose of worship. Sacrifices may be for the forgiveness of sin, for thanksgiving, to establish a covenant, or for other reasons. You may give examples from the Old Testament.
Review what is needed for a sacrifice: a priest, a victim, and an altar.

---

21   The Holy Mass

Then they told what had happened on the road, and how he was known to them in the breaking of the bread.

Luke 24:35

Jesus' Sacrifice on the Cross healed a great wound. It reunited man and God in full friendship for the first time since the disobedience of Adam and Eve. This Sacrifice paid the price of our sins. It opened the gates of Heaven. It was the most perfect gift a man ever gave to God. Jesus became a man for this very purpose. The gift of His life was so powerful that He wants us to continue offering it to the Father until the end of time.

At the Last Supper, Jesus gave us a way to do that. He passed on to the Apostles and through them to all priests His power to bless and change the bread and wine. Now at every Mass this miracle happens. The priest turns the bread and wine into Christ's own Body and Blood. Then the priest lifts up the Sacred Host and Cup of salvation and offers them to the Father. Christ, the Lamb of God, is sacrificed on the altar at Mass just as He was on Calvary. It is in a different way, but it is the very same Sacrifice.

We go to Mass every Sunday, and other days as well, to offer this gift to the Father. We also offer up our hearts and lives to Him. We offer all our joys and sufferings for His glory. We **worship** and adore Him. Sometimes we sing joyous songs of praise that voice our love.

At the beginning of the Mass, we make the Sign of the Cross. The priest asks us to call to mind our sins, and to ask for God's forgiveness. All together we say, "Lord have mercy, Christ have

---

Develop

1. Read paragraph 1 with the children.

2. On the chalkboard, list the results of Jesus' Sacrifice:
   - Paid the price for our sins
   - Reunited God and man
   - Opened the gates of Heaven

3. Hold up a Crucifix so the children can visualize the Sacrifice of Christ. Jesus died on the Cross because He loves them so much and because He wants to save each of them from sin. He is the priest and victim

4. Read paragraph 2 with the children.

5. Using a children's Bible, read the account of the Last Supper from Luke 22:7–20. Note that at the Last Supper, Jesus gave the Apostles (and through them, all priests) the power to consecrate the Eucharist.

6. *Compare the words of Jesus at the Last Supper to those of the priest in a children's missal. They are the same words, using the same matter: bread and wine. Explain that at Mass, the priest acts in the person of Christ. Jesus is working through the priest. Therefore, the priest and the victim of the Sacrifice of the Mass are the same as the priest and victim of the Sacrifice of the Cross. The only difference is the manner in which the Sacrifice is made: on the Cross, Jesus was sacrificed in a bloody manner; on the altar, Jesus is sacrificed in an unbloody manner. The Sacrifice of the Mass, however, is not a new sacrifice every time, but Christ's one Sacrifice.*

7. If you have a video on the Mass, show it to the children.

8. Have the children explain the Sacrifice of the Cross (and how it is connected to the Last Supper) and the Sacrifice of the Mass in their own words.

Name:_____

The Sacrifice of the Mass

1. What did Jesus do at the Last Supper to make sure that we can continue this sacrifice to the Father?
Jesus gave the Apostles the power to turn bread and wine into His own Body and Blood.

2. What happens at every Mass?
Jesus is sacrificed to the Father, just as He was on Calvary, when the priest turns the bread and wine into the Body and Blood of Jesus.

3. What are the parts of the Mass listed in the student text?
The Sign of the Cross, "Lord, have mercy," "Glory to God," the readings, the Gospel, the homily, and the Creed

4. What is the Gospel?
Gospel means Good News. The Good News of Christ's miracles, parables, stories, and teachings is meant for us today.

5. What happens during Communion?
Jesus unites us to Himself.

6. What is the greatest prayer on earth?
The Mass

Faith and Life Series • Grade 3 • Chapter 21 • Lesson 1

Reinforce

1. Have the students work on *Activity Book*, p. 78.

2. Teach the children to sing "Father, we thank thee who hast planted," *Adoremus Hymnal*, #515.

3. Have the students begin working on the Memorization Questions. They should also begin memorizing the Nicene Creed.

Conclude

Pray the Nicene Creed with the students. You may have them copy out this prayer as part of their efforts to memorize it.

Preview

In the next lesson, the students will work on the introductory rites of the Mass.

THE SACRIFICE OF THE MASS IS THE SACRIFICE OF THE CROSS

The Sacrifice of Jesus is truly the Sacrifice of the Cross, anticipated at the Last Supper and completed in the Offering of Jesus' Body and Blood for our sins on the Cross. At the Consecration of the Mass, we are truly present at the Last Supper, the Crucifixion, and the Resurrection of Christ. According to the *Catechism of the Catholic Church*, "since in this divine sacrifice which is celebrated in the Mass, the same Christ who offered himself once in a bloody manner on the altar of the cross is contained and offered in an unbloody manner . . ." (*CCC* #1367).

NOTES

LESSON TWO: WE GO TO MASS

Aims

The students will learn that as Catholics we are obliged to participate in Mass every Sunday and on Holy Days of Obligation.

The children will learn the introductory rites of the Mass.

Materials

- *Activity Book*, p. 79
- Children's missals
- Flash cards of the introductory rites

Optional:
- "Father, we thank thee who hast planted," *Adoremus Hymnal*, #515

Begin

Begin the class by reviewing our Mass obligations: Sunday Mass and Holy Days of Obligation. Have the children memorize the Holy Days of Obligation in the United States. You may quiz the children. Also note that they are not bound to receive Holy Communion at Mass and, in fact, they should not receive it unworthily.

---

mercy." We thank God for His goodness in another prayer which begins "Glory to God. . . ."

Next we listen to readings from the Bible. On Sundays the first reading is usually taken from the Old Testament, the second from an Epistle, or letter, that one of the Apostles wrote after Jesus returned to Heaven. These readings are messages of faith, hope, and love. They give us things to think about in our everyday lives.

After that, the priest reads to us from the Gospel. We stand during the Gospel reading because we are hearing Jesus' own words to us. For example, we might hear one of Jesus' parables, or stories, such as the Good Shepherd. At another Mass we may hear about one of Jesus' wonderful miracles. Every Sunday the **Gospel** gives us another message of love and hope. Remember, "Gospel" means Good News. The Good News of Christ's miracles, parables, and teachings is meant for us today, just as it was for His friends on earth two thousand years ago. The priest explains the Gospel message in a short talk called a homily. During the Gospel reading and the homily, it is very important to listen carefully.

After the homily, we stand with the priest to say the Creed. **Creed** means belief. Our Creed is a prayer that professes our faith. We say out loud that we believe in God the Father, the Creator of all things. We believe He sent His Son Jesus to save us from our sins. We believe God the Holy Spirit is alive among us. We say the Creed together at Mass because our faith is what binds us together as a Church.

Jesus comes into our hearts and lives at Mass. He teaches us through the readings. He offers Himself for us to God Our Father. He unites Himself to us in Holy Communion. Truly, the Holy Mass is our greatest prayer on earth.

Develop

1. Read paragraphs 3 and 4 with the children.

2. Have the students open their children's missals. Review the introductory rites, all the possible responses, and the gestures.

3. Give the various options and have the children read the appropriate responses. Have the children read along. If the children own these books, you may have them write in when to stand and when to sit. Help them to recognize the dialogue between the priest and the congregation.

4. Have the students memorize the Sign of the Cross (and be able to explain that it is a witness to our faith in the Trinity and that our salvation was by Jesus Christ).

5. Have the students memorize the Confiteor. They should also have memorized the "Lord have mercy/Christ have mercy/Lord have mercy." If your parish sings these parts of the Mass, teach them according to your parish traditions. Remind them that they should be aware of their sins and their need for God's mercy. How should they say this prayer? How should they feel?

5. Read the Gloria and discuss all the parts of this great prayer. Explain that it is not said during certain times of the year (e.g., Lent). How should the children feel when they say this prayer? What is their favorite part of the Gloria?

6. Finish reviewing the introductory rites. You may quiz the children with flash cards. The students should put the parts of the introductory rites in order. In a variation upon this, have the students match the card showing the words of the prayer with the card showing its title.

Name:_____

The Mass

1. For what ends is the Sacrifice of the Mass offered?
The Mass is offered as it was at Calvary: as a gift to the Father to pay the price for our sins.

2. Are we obliged to attend Mass?
Yes. We are obliged to attend Mass on Sundays and Holy Days of Obligation.

3. What is the most proper way of attending Mass?
To offer the Mass to God in union with the priest, remember the life and sacrifice of Jesus Christ, and receive Holy Communion

Faith and Life Series • Grade 3 • Chapter 21 • Lesson 2

Reinforce

1. Have the students work on *Activity Book*, p. 79.

2. Have the students work on memorizing the parts of the introductory rites. The students should be able to put the introductory rites in order. They should also know the responses and prayers. You may teach the children to sing the prayers and responses, if this is customary in your parish.

3. Have the students work on their Memorization Questions and on memorizing the Nicene Creed.

Conclude

1. Lead the children in singing "Father, we thank thee who hast planted," *Adoremus Hymnal*, #515.

2. Lead the children in reciting the Nicene Creed.

Preview

In the next lesson, the students will learn about the Liturgy of the Word.

HOLY DAYS OF OBLIGATION

The Holy Days of Obligation in the United States are:
- January 1: the solemnity of Mary, Mother of God
- Thursday of the Sixth Week of Easter: the solemnity of the Ascension;
- August 15: the solemnity of the Assumption of the Blessed Virgin Mary
- November 1: the solemnity of All Saints
- December 8: the solemnity of the Immaculate Conception
- December 25: the solemnity of the Nativity of Our Lord Jesus Christ.

NOTES

LESSON THREE: LITURGY OF THE WORD

Aims

The students will learn about the Liturgy of the Word, which includes readings from the Scriptures, the word of God.

They will learn the importance of the Gospel, which contains Jesus' own words.

They will learn that the priest explains the Gospel during a homily.

Materials

- *Activity Book*, p. 80
- Children's Bible
- Children's missal

Optional:
- "Father, we thank thee who hast planted," *Adoremus Hymnal*, #515

Begin

Begin the class by reviewing the introductory rites of the Mass, so that the children may see the context for the Liturgy of the Word. The students may put the parts of the introductory rites in order and review the correct responses.

THE NICENE CREED

We believe in one God, the Father, the Almighty, maker of heaven and earth, of all that is, seen and unseen.

We believe in one Lord, Jesus Christ, the only Son of God eternally begotten of the Father, God from God, Light from Light, true God from true God, begotten, not made, one in Being with the Father. Through him all things were made. For us men and for our salvation he came down from heaven:

by the power of the Holy Spirit he was born of the Virgin Mary, and became man.

For our sake he was crucified under Pontius Pilate; he suffered, died, and was buried.

On the third day he rose again in fulfillment of the Scriptures;

he ascended into heaven and is seated at the right hand of the Father. He will come again in glory to judge the living and the dead, and his Kingdom will have no end.

We believe in the Holy Spirit, the Lord, the giver of life, who proceeds from the Father and the Son. With the Father and the Son he is worshipped and glorified. He has spoken through the Prophets. We believe in one holy catholic and apostolic Church. We acknowledge one baptism for he forgiveness of sins. We look for the resurrection of the dead, and the life of the world to come. *Amen.*

Develop

1. Read paragraphs 5 and 6 with the children.

2. Have the children look through their missals. They will recognize the first reading, the Psalm, the second reading, and the Gospel.

3. *Using a current missal, find the readings in a Bible. Show the children that the readings for the Mass come directly out of the Bible (even though they are read from a different book called a Lectionary).*

4. Have a children's Liturgy of the Word in class. Teach the children the responses to the readings. Also, teach the children to sing the responsory psalm. Have the students do the readings.

5. Have the students memorize the correct responses to the readings; e.g., "The word of the Lord," "Thanks be to God." "The Lord be with you," "And also with you." "A reading from the holy Gospel according to ___," "Glory to you Lord." "The Gospel of the Lord," "Praise to You, Lord Jesus Christ."

6. Teach the children the correct gestures. Teach the children that we stand during the Gospel because it is the word of Jesus. Also teach the children to trace a small cross on their foreheads, lips, and hearts, while silently saying: "May the Lord be on my mind, on my lips, and in my heart." Teach them that they should do this while saying "Glory to you O Lord." These gestures are important for the children to understand. Often, children cannot hear exactly what is being said in the responses.

7. Teach the children about the homily. They should pay special attention to the homily because the priest is explaining what the readings mean to us today and how we can live in a manner that is pleasing to Jesus.

Name:_____

Word Search

Sacrifices	Doves	Wine	Listen
Sheep	Praise	Altar	Crops
Thanks	Cross	Sunday	Cows
Bread	Reunited	Communion	Prayers
Homily	Father	Priests	Jerusalem
Offer	Bible	Temple	Mass
Unleavened	Creed	Blood	Miracle
Bread	Worship	Heaven	Gospel

```
A J P R A I S E G W O R S H I P X C M P
Z E S T R X Y T S I C R O P S E G S A R
J R B L O O D R C T P L R J E S R O S A
O O U N L E A V E N E D B R E A D A S Y
X S P O G E S S J M J O O S B D I A L E
D A T R A W I N E P O D W U R N C O R R
T L Y D N I G S T L P Y F S E E D R R S
Z E S H I N N P D E L C O M M U N I O N
S M L A F N E F G O D O R S B N L F T W
T H E V A Y F A C F O W S A T I Y I S W
A O S E L R T B R F V S I F J T S C G T
V M O M S S H I E E E B N R R E L E O D
E I F E E L E B E R S L O I E D I S H S
R L A R P O C L D E P R I E S T S O T T
T Y T C S A R E S T R N P N R O T O H A
Y S H Y Q L O D Y T O V O Q T L E D E X
B R E A D T S E T H C R O S S E N S A E
J E R S U A S H E E P C R H E G O B V C
P R A Y E R G O S P E L M I R A C L E Q
S U N D A Y E T H A N K S P E E D O N D
```

80   Faith and Life Series • Grade 3 • Chapter 21 • Lesson 3

Reinforce

1. Have the students work on memorizing all the parts of the introductory rites and the Liturgy of the Word. They should know the prayers, responses, and gestures.

2. Have the students work on their Memorization Questions.

3. As the children finish their individual memorization work, they may work on *Activity Book*, p. 80.

Conclude

1. Lead the children in singing "Father, we thank thee who hast planted," *Adoremus Hymnal*, #515.

2. Pray the Nicene Creed together.

Preview

In the next lesson, the students will learn about the Creed and the importance of the Liturgy of the Word.

SAINT DOMINIC

Born to a prominent and devout Spanish family, circa 1170, Saint Dominic was destined for sainthood. After studying and receiving ordination to the priesthood in Palencia, he entered the monastery at Osma. When his bishop went north to preach against the Cathars —the Albigensian heretics—Dominic accompanied him. When Pope Innocent III called for a crusade against the Albigensians, Saint Dominic followed the army, preaching to the heretics. Soon, Saint Dominic was widely known for his holiness and powerful preaching. He was given a castle by a Spanish nobleman, where he founded the Order of Preachers. The Feast of Saint Dominic is August 8.

NOTES

LESSON FOUR: WE BELIEVE

Aims

The students will learn about the Creed and its importance.

They will learn that Jesus comes into our hearts at Mass. He teaches us through the readings.

They will learn that the Mass is the greatest prayer on earth.

Words to Know:

worship   Gospel   Creed

Q. 93 *Are we obliged to go to Mass?*
We are obliged to go to Mass on Sunday and on the Holy Days of Obligation. (CCC 2176–77).

Q. 94 *What is the most proper way of taking part in Mass?*
The most proper way of taking part in Mass is to offer it to God in union with the priest. We should remember the Sacrifice of Jesus, His life, death, and Resurrection. We should receive Holy Communion (CCC 1391, 2180).

Materials

- *Activity Book*, p. 81

Optional:
- "Father, we thank thee who hast planted," *Adoremus Hymnal*, #515

Begin

Begin by reviewing the introductory rites and the Liturgy of the Word. They should know the correct order of the parts of the Mass: the prayers, responses, and gestures.

Develop

1. You may play review games with the children to cover the content learned on the introductory rites and the Liturgy of the Word.

2. Read paragraphs 7 and 8 with the children.

3. Explain that the Creed is a summary of what we believe as Catholics. It is very important because all Catholics believe these things. That is why the Creed begins with "We believe." What we believe is very important. It determines who we are. In the Catholic Church, there are two great creeds: the Apostles' Creed and the Nicene Creed. We say the Apostles' Creed in the Rosary and we say the Nicene Creed at Mass.

4. Saint Augustine said that the Creed is the summary of Scripture and the key to reading Scripture. Using the Nicene Creed, think of biblical passages that reveal these truths. For example:

- *We believe in One God, the Father Almighty, Maker of Heaven and Earth* . . . The Creation stories in Genesis.
- *By the power of the Holy Spirit, He was born of the Virgin Mary and became man* . . . The Annunciation
- *For our sake* . . . The Crucifixion
- *On the third day* . . . The Resurrection
- *He ascended into Heaven* . . . The Ascension
- *He will come again in glory* . . . Angels at Ascension
- *We believe in the Holy Spirit* . . . Baptism of Jesus, Pentecost
- *He has spoken through the prophets* (name some)
- *We believe in one*—only one Church was founded by Christ; *holy*—life of the Church is the Holy Spirit, with the one holy Sacrifice of Christ; *catholic*—for all people, even gentiles; *apostolic*—12 Apostles taught others and, through them, the Sacrament of Holy Orders has been passed on.
We acknowledge one Baptism for the forgiveness of sins . . . the resurrection of the dead, and the life of the world to come.

Name: _____

The Nicene Creed

Fill in the blanks with the correct words.

We believe in <u>one</u> God, the <u>Father</u>, the Almighty, <u>maker</u> of Heaven and earth, of all that is seen and unseen. We believe in one Lord, <u>Jesus Christ</u>, the only <u>Son</u> of God, eternally <u>begotten</u> of the <u>Father</u>, God from <u>God</u>, Light from <u>Light</u>, true God from <u>true God</u>, begotten, not <u>made</u>, one in being with the Father. Through Him all things were made. For us men and for our <u>salvation</u> He came down from heaven: by the power of the <u>Holy Spirit</u> He was born of the <u>Virgin Mary</u>, and became man. For our sake He was <u>crucified</u> under Pontius Pilate; He <u>suffered</u>, <u>died</u> and was <u>buried</u>. On the <u>third</u> day He <u>rose</u> again in fulfillment of the Scriptures; He <u>ascended</u> into <u>Heaven</u> and is seated at the right hand of the <u>Father</u>. He will come again in <u>glory</u> to judge the <u>living</u> and the <u>dead</u>, and His <u>Kingdom</u> will have no end. We <u>believe</u> in the <u>Holy Spirit</u>, the Lord, the giver of life, Who <u>proceeds</u> from the <u>Father</u> and the <u>Son</u>. With the <u>Father</u> and the <u>Son</u> He is worshiped and glorified. He has spoken through the <u>prophets</u>. We believe in <u>one</u>, <u>holy</u>, <u>catholic</u>, and <u>apostolic</u> Church. We acknowledge one <u>baptism</u> for the <u>forgiveness</u> of sins. We look for the <u>resurrection</u> of the dead, and the life of the world to come. <u>Amen</u>.

Faith and Life Series • Grade 3 • Chapter 21 • Lesson 4   81

Reinforce

1. Have the students work on *Activity Book*, p. 81.

2. Have the students work on memorizing the parts of the Mass, the prayers, responses, and gestures.

3. Have the students work on their Memorization Questions and prepare for their quiz.

Conclude

1. Lead the children in singing "Father, we thank thee who hast planted," *Adoremus Hymnal*, #515.

2. Lead the children in the Nicene Creed.

Preview

In the next lesson, the students' knowledge of the material covered this week will be reviewed and assessed.

WHY DO WE CALL THEM CREEDS?

Both of the accepted professions of faith in the Catholic Church are called *creeds*: the Apostolic Creed and the Nicene Creed. These professions begin with similar words:

- Apostolic: "I believe in God . . ."

- Nicene: "We believe in one God . . ."

In Latin, the word for "I believe" is *credo*. It is from this Latin word that the English word creed is derived.

NOTES

_____
_____
_____
_____
_____
_____
_____
_____
_____
_____

CHAPTER TWENTY-ONE
REVIEW AND ASSESSMENT

Aims

The students' knowledge and understanding of the material covered this week will be reviewed and assessed.

Materials

- Quiz 21, Appendix, p. A-31

Optional:
- "Father, we thank thee who hast planted," *Adoremus Hymnal,* #515

Review

1. Quiz the children on the parts, prayers, responses, and gestures of the introductory rites and the Liturgy of the Word.

2. The students should know the results of the Sacrifice of Christ, including:
   - Reunited man and God
   - Paid the price for our sins
   - Opened the gates of Heaven

3. The students should know that Jesus gave us two great gifts at the Last Supper so that we may continue offering Jesus to the Father until the end of time:
   - The Eucharist
   - The priesthood (who has the power to consecrate the Eucharist)

Note: They should also know that we participate in this Sacrifice and join ourselves to it by means of the Mass, the greatest prayer.

4. The students should know their Mass obligations: Sundays and Holy Days of Obligation. (They should also know the specific Holy Days of Obligation in the United States).

5. The students should know that the readings for the Mass come from the Bible and are found in a book called the Lectionary. We follow along in a book called a missal.

Name: _____

The Holy Mass   **Quiz 21**

"I am the living bread, which came down from heaven" (John 6:51).

Word Bank

Father	God	priest	Calvary	News
belief	adore	Cross	Gospel	Mass

Fill in the blanks with the correct words from the Word Bank.

1. At every Mass a miracle happens. Through the **priest**, God changes the bread and wine into Christ's own Body and Blood.

2. The priest lifts up the Sacred Host and the Cup of Salvation and offers them to the **Father**.

3. Christ, the Lamb of God, is sacrificed on the altar at Mass, just as He was on **Calvary**. It is in a different way, but it is the very same Sacrifice.

4. We are obliged to go to Mass every Sunday and on Holy Days of Obligation to offer Jesus to the Father with the priest. We are to worship and **adore** Him.

5. At the beginning of Mass, we make the Sign of the **Cross**. We call to mind our sins and ask God's forgiveness.

6. We listen to the readings from the Old and New Testament. We stand for the **Gospel** reading because we are hearing Jesus' own words.

7. The Gospel means Good **News**. The Good News of Christ's miracles, parables, and teachings are meant for us today, as it was meant for those who lived two thousand years ago.

8. After the homily, we stand and say the Creed. The word Creed means **belief**. We say out loud that we believe in God, the Father, Son, and Holy Spirit.

9. Jesus comes into our hearts and lives at Mass. He teaches us through the readings. He offers Himself for us to **God** our Father.

10. Jesus unites Himself to us in Holy Communion. The Holy **Mass** is the greatest prayer.

Faith and Life • Grade 3 • Appendix A   A - 31

Assess

1. Distribute the quizzes, and read through them with the students to be sure they understand the questions.

2. Administer the quiz. As they hand in their work, you may orally quiz them on the Memorization Questions for this chapter.

3. After all the quizzes have been handed in, take up the correct answers as a final review.

Conclude

1. Lead the children in singing "Father, we thank thee who hast planted," *Adoremus Hymnal,* #515.

2. Pray the Nicene Creed.

CHAPTER TWENTY-TWO
OFFERING JESUS TO THE FATHER

Catechism of the Catholic Church References

Christ's Whole Life as a Self-Offering to the Father: 606–18, 621–23

Liturgical Celebration of the Eucharist:
　　Celebration through the Ages: 1345–47
　　Movement of the Celebration: 1348–55, 1408

Presence of Christ in the Eucharist: 1088, 1373–81, 1410, 1418

Signs of Bread and Wine in the Eucharist: 1333–36, 1412

Transubstantiation: 1373–77, 1413

Scripture References

Paul's Description of the Eucharist: 1 Cor 11:23–34
Breaking of Bread in the Early Church: Acts 2:41–42, 20:7

Participation in the Body and Blood of Christ: 1 Cor 16–17

Background Reading: *The Fundamentals of Catholicism* by Fr. Kenneth Baker, S.J

Volume 3:
"The Catholic Doctrine of the Real Presence," pp. 229–31
"My Flesh Is Real Food and My Blood Is Real Drink," pp. 232–35

"Water into Wine, Wine into Blood," pp. 235–38
"How Long Is the Lord Present in the Eucharist?" pp. 244–47

Summary of Lesson Content

Lesson 1

The Liturgy of the Eucharist comes after the Liturgy of the Word.

During the Offertory the gifts are brought forward to the altar.

Lesson 2

At Mass, we unite our prayers with the angels and the saints, who are present around the altar.

We sing or say the Sanctus.

During the Consecration, Jesus is made present on the altar by the power of the priest.

Jesus is present under the appearance of bread and wine.

Lesson 3

The Body and Blood of Christ are offered up to the Father as the one perfect Sacrifice.

We are called to unite ourselves with Christ in this offering to the Father.

Lesson 4

Jesus present in the Eucharist is our greatest treasure. He is truly present Body, Blood, Soul, and Divinity.

Jesus is entirely present in every part of the Eucharist (even in broken parts).

The Eucharist is reserved for adoration and ministry to the sick.

LESSON ONE: OFFERTORY

Aims

The children will learn that the Liturgy of the Eucharist comes after the Liturgy of the Word.

They will learn that during the Offertory the gifts are brought forward to the altar.

Materials

- *Activity Book*, p. 82
- Missal
- Show and tell (some of the children's gifts or talents they can use for God)
- Paper, pencils, box for "offertory"

Optional:
- "O saving Victim," *Adoremus Hymnal*, #519 or #520

Begin

Review the Introductory Rites and the Liturgy of the Word. Explain that God is present in His word, but most perfectly in the Sacrament of the Eucharist. The next part of the Mass is called the Liturgy of the Eucharist. It is during this part of the Mass that Jesus is offered to the Father. We, too, can unite ourselves to the Father as a sacrifice.

---

22 Offering Jesus To the Father

> He has no need, like those high priests, to offer sacrifices daily, first for his own sins and then for those of the people; he did this once for all when he offered up himself.
>
> Hebrews 7:27

After we listen to God's word and pray the Creed and the Prayers of the Faithful, we prepare our hearts for the most important part of the Mass. This is the moment when Jesus will offer His life to the Father once more through the hands of the priest.

First, we must prepare the gifts that go to the altar of God. We call this preparation time the **Offertory** of the Mass. During the Offertory, bread and wine are taken to the priest. These foods nourish us and keep us alive. By giving them to God, we show that we offer our very lives to Him. We offer Him our hearts. We offer Him all that we think, say, and do. We also offer money in the collection as a sign of our love for His people. All of these gifts are soon to be joined with Jesus, our best gift of all.

Honoring the coming of Jesus, we join with the angels in praising Him: "Holy, holy, holy Lord, God of power and might. Heaven and earth are full of Your glory. Hosanna in the highest. Blessed is He Who comes in the name of the Lord. Hosanna in the highest."

Jesus is now about to come into our midst. Over the gifts of bread and wine, the priest says the words of Jesus at the Last Supper. "This is My Body," . . . "This is the Cup of My Blood." This praying over the gifts is called the **Consecration**. At the moment of Consecration,

107

Develop

1. Read paragraphs 1 and 2 with the students.

2. The Offertory procession is usually done on Sundays and feast days. It continues a practice begun in the early Church. Certain lay people carry bread, wine, and other gifts like money collected, etc. to the altar. With these gifts, the faithful symbolically offer themselves to God.

3. Have the students do a "show and tell" of the gifts and talents that they want to offer to God through the sacrifice of their lives. They may offer gifts or talents, such as drawing or dance. As each student makes his presentation, write each talent or gift on a piece of paper and have the student fold it up and put it in the "offertory box." You will use this in a procession later.

4. The offering of the gifts of bread and wine are very important. Why? They are important because they nourish us. Bread and wine are universal nutrients. Offering bread and wine to God is a symbol of offering our very lives to God. During the preparation of the gifts, the priest raises the bread on a paten and says "Blessed are you Lord God of all creation, through your goodness we have this bread to offer, which earth has given and human hands have made, it will become for us the bread of life." Next, the priest mixes water and wine in the chalice and the priest offers them to the Father saying: "Blessed are you Lord God of all creation, through your goodness we have this wine to offer, fruit of the vine and work of human hands, it will become our spiritual drink." To each of these blessings, we respond "Blessed be God forever." Just as the water is lost in the wine, so we are absorbed in the majesty of Christ. Our union with Him is so great that nothing can separate us. We are like the grain broken to make bread; we are like the water mixed with the wine. We are united in Christ as an offering to the Father.

Name:_____

Jesus in Holy Communion

Find these words in your textbook and use them in sentences.

Eucharist: **Answers will vary.**
_____

Offertory: _____
_____

Consecration: _____
_____

Divinity: _____
_____

Appearance: _____
_____

Host: _____

Miracle: _____

82   Faith and Life Series • Grade 3 • Chapter 22 • Lesson 1

AN OFFERTORY BOX

Have the children carefully decorate an offertory box. Every day, add slips of paper upon which you have written the children's gifts—their talents and achievements.

Celebrate your own offertory procession, with the box full of gifts and talents to offer to God. In a solemn procession, take this box to the Church, and offer each gift to God, reading the talent or achievement aloud. Lead the children in responding, "We offer this gift to the Lord," after each gift is read.

Reinforce

1. Have the students work on *Activity Book*, p. 82.

2. Have the students celebrate their Offertory procession

3. Teach the children to sing "O saving Victim," *Adoremus Hymnal*, using one of the two versions offered, #519 or #520.

Conclude

1. End with a prayer, such as the Our Father.

2. If possible, take the children to the reservation chapel to pray before the Blessed Sacrament in silence. Review reverent behavior with the children.

Preview

In the next lesson, the student will learn more about the Consecration of the Eucharist.

NOTES

LESSON TWO: CONSECRATION

Aims

The children will learn that at Mass, we unite our prayers with the angels and the saints, who are present around the altar.

They will learn that during the Consecration, Jesus is made present on the altar, in our midst, by the power of the priest. Jesus is present under the appearance of bread and wine.

Materials

- *Activity Book*, p. 83
- Palms or green construction paper cut out to be "palms"
- Children's Bible

Optional:
- "O saving Victim," *Adoremus Hymnal*, #519 or #520

Begin

From a children's Bible, read the story of Jesus' triumphant entry into Jerusalem on Palm Sunday. Explain that the people were celebrating the coming of Jesus. They waved palms in the air and laid them on the street. Help the children understand the great joy and excitement that the presence of Jesus in our midst should bring. Allow the children to sing and dance and put on a parade with their palms, while one child plays the part of Jesus coming into Jerusalem.

---

the bread and wine change into Jesus' Body and Blood. The Precious Body of Jesus still looks, tastes, and feels like ordinary bread, but it is really and truly Jesus, Our Savior. The Precious Blood still looks and tastes like ordinary wine, but it too is Jesus.

The priest takes the Sacred **Host** and lifts it up toward Heaven. We bow our heads because Our Lord is really present before us. The priest then lifts up the chalice. We bow our heads again. God the Father accepts our offering held up by the priest. As He accepted both the earthly wheat and wine—the work of human hands—now He accepts the consecrated Body and Blood of His own Son, Jesus.

This Holy Eucharist is not only the best gift for the Father, it is the greatest treasure we have on earth. It is Jesus Himself among us. The **Eucharist** is not just a symbol of Jesus, but His real Body, Blood, Soul, and **Divinity**, the nature of God. Only the **appearance** of bread and wine remains. Appearance means how something looks. When the priest breaks the Host to eat it, Jesus is fully present in every broken part. If there are any extra consecrated Hosts after the Mass, the priest will treat them with special love and reverence. Once a Host is consecrated, anywhere in the world, it remains the Body, Blood, soul, and divinity of Jesus.

The Consecration of every Holy Mass renews Christ's gift on Calvary. Dying on the Cross, Jesus offered His life to the Father. Now at Mass, His life is offered to the Father through the priest and people of God. Through the Mass, Jesus keeps making up for our sins and uniting us with the Father just as He did in Jerusalem so long ago.

Words to Know:

Offertory   Consecration   Host
Eucharist   Divinity   appearance

Develop

1. Read paragraphs 3 and 4 with the children.

2. Explain that at Mass, we unite ourselves with all the other people in the Church. We are also united with the angels and the saints, who are invisibly present around the altar.

3. Review that the priest received the power to consecrate the Eucharist from Jesus at the Last Supper. That power has been passed down from Jesus through the Apostles to all our priests today.

4. The priest says the words of Jesus over the bread and wine during the part of the Mass called the Consecration. This is when the bread and wine become Jesus, truly present. The words of the Consecration are "This is My Body" and "This is the cup of My Blood." After these words are said, bread and wine are no longer present; only Jesus, Body, Blood, Soul, and Divinity, is present after the Consecration. This change from bread and wine to Jesus is called transubstantiation, which means change in substance (what something is). Jesus present in the Eucharist still looks, tastes, and smells like bread and wine, but we know by faith (because Jesus said so) that this is Jesus, truly present. In every consecrated Host, and in every part of a consecrated Host, Jesus is truly and entirely present.

5. Review the proper reverence required during the Mass. After the Sanctus ("Holy, Holy, Holy"), we kneel in reverence and awe of God in our midst. We should be joyful and thankful for Jesus coming among us. If your parish uses a bell during the Consecration, teach the children that the bell reminds us of Jesus' presence. Remind the children that this is the most sacred time in the Mass.

6. Tell the children what some saints taught about the Mass.

Name:_____

The Consecration

1. When does the most important part of the Mass occur?
   When the priest turns the bread and wine into the Body and Blood of Jesus Christ

2. What is the Offertory? What are we offering?
   Preparation of gifts that go to God's altar. We show we are offering our lives to Him

3. What do we say with the angels in praising Jesus, the Son of God?
   Holy, Holy, Holy Lord, God of power and might...

4. What is the prayer the priest, in the Divine Person of Jesus Christ, says to change the bread and wine into Jesus' Body and Blood? What does he say?
   This is my Body...
   This is my Blood...

5. What changes? What is the same?
   The bread and wine change into the Body, Blood, Soul, and Divinity of Jesus Christ. The appearance of bread and wine remain the same.

6. Is the Eucharist just a symbol?
   No. The Eucharist is really and truly the Body, Blood, Soul, and Divinity of Jesus Christ.

7. Once the Host is consecrated, what is it? Does it stay that way?
   Once it is consecrated, the Host is the Body, Blood, Soul, and Divinity of Jesus Christ. It remains that way.

Faith and Life Series • Grade 3 • Chapter 22 • Lesson 2   83

SAINT ANTHONY AND THE HOLY EUCHARIST

Saint Anthony became a holy Franciscan priest known for his miracles, especially in Padua, where he spent the last years of his life. In one incident of particular note, Saint Anthony was challenged by a Jewish merchant for his belief in the Holy Eucharist. The merchant held a donkey without food for three days, while Saint Anthony went out alone to pray for three days. At the end of the three days, the merchant brought out a sumptuous bail of hay and released the donkey; meanwhile, Saint Anthony went to the church for the Holy Eucharist and returned. As the donkey headed for the hay, Saint Anthony said, "Mule, in the name of the Lord our God, I command you to come here and adore your Creator!" The mule halted immediately, turned to Saint Anthony, and bowed his forelegs before the Holy Eucharist. The merchant converted.

Reinforce

1. Have the students work on *Activity Book*, p. 83.

2. Have them work on their Memorization Questions.

3. Have the students write prayers to Jesus in the Blessed Sacrament. You may take them to pray before the tabernacle. There, they may read their prayers to Jesus.

Conclude

1. Lead the children in singing "O saving Victim," *Adoremus Hymnal*, #519 or #520.

2. Have the student pray the Our Father, or another suitable prayer, such as the Anima Christi:
Soul of Christ, sanctify me.
Body of Christ, save me.
Blood of Christ, inebriate me.
Water from the side of Christ, wash me.
Passion of Christ, strengthen me.

O good Jesus, hear me.
Within Thy wounds, hide me.
Separated from Thee let me never be.
From the malignant enemy, defend me.

At the hour of death, call me.
To come to Thee, bid me,
That I may praise Thee in the company
Of Thy Saints, for all eternity. *Amen*.

Preview

In the next lesson, the students will better understand how the Eucharist is offered to the Father in the Mass.

NOTES

LESSON THREE: ELEVATION

Aims

The Body and Blood of Christ are offered up to the Father as the one perfect Sacrifice.

The students will learn that we are called to unite ourselves with Christ in this offering to the Father.

Materials

- *Activity Book*, p. 84
- Children's missals

Optional:
- "O saving Victim," *Adoremus Hymnal*, #519 or #520

Begin

Review yesterday's lesson. Remind the children of the meaning of the Consecration during Mass. The children should know that, after the Consecration, nothing remains of the bread and wine but the appearance of bread and wine. After the Consecration, the host becomes the Body, Blood, Soul, and Divinity of Jesus, truly and entirely present among us.

Q. 95 *What is the Eucharist?*
The Eucharist is the Sacrament which contains the Body, Blood, Soul, and Divinity of Our Lord Jesus Christ, really present under the appearances of bread and wine for the nourishment of souls (CCC 1323, 1333).

Q. 96 *When do the bread and wine become the Body and Blood of Jesus?*
The bread and wine become the Body and Blood of Jesus at the moment of the Consecration (CCC 1352–53).

Q. 97 *After the Consecration, is there nothing left of the bread and the wine?*
After the Consecration, neither bread nor wine is present any longer. Only the appearances of bread and wine, without their substance, remain (CCC 1375–76).

Develop

1. Read paragraphs 5 and 7 with the children.

2. Using a children's missal, teach the children the parts of the Liturgy of the Eucharist: the prayers, responses, and appropriate gestures.

Be sure the students know the responses, the Our Father, the sign of peace, the Agnus Dei, etc.

3. CCD: You may practice having the students receive unconsecrated hosts to be sure they know how to receive properly. Line up the children and ask each child a question about the Mass. If a student gives the correct answer, he may receive a host. Do not say "The Body of Christ." (It is not.) Rather, say "This is a host," to which they will respond "Amen."

4. Teach the students the importance of "Amen." This is said many times through the Mass. Have the children name different times it is said. What does it mean? It means "So be it" or "I believe this to be true." It is one of our greatest professions of faith. The "amen" is especially important when we receive Holy Communion and the priest or extraordinary minister of the Eucharist says "The Body of Christ." We are professing our faith that the Eucharist is Jesus, truly present.

5. Discuss how Jesus is offered to the Father during Mass and how we should unite ourselves with Jesus during this offering. When the priest holds up Jesus and says, "Through Him, with Him, in Him, in the unity of the Holy Spirit, all glory and honor are yours almighty Father, forever and ever" we should unite ourselves to Jesus as a gift to the Father. We can also do this in our morning offering.

6. Finish reading the Mass out of the missal.

Name:_____

The Body and Blood of Jesus

**This is My Body...
This is the cup of My Blood.**

Color the picture.

84 Faith and Life Series • Grade 3 • Chapter 22 • Lesson 3

Reinforce

1. Play a review game to go over all the parts and the responses of the Mass.

2. Have the students work on *Activity Book*, p. 84.

3. Have the students work on their Memorization Questions.

Conclude

1. Lead the children in singing "O saving Victim," *Adoremus Hymnal*, #519 or #520.

2. End with praying the Our Father and the Morning Offering.

Preview

In the next lesson, the students will learn that Jesus' presence remains in the Eucharist.

If possible, arrange for a priest or deacon to make a presentation on the vessels used during Mass. If a priest or deacon is not available, see if you can make the presentation.

MORNING OFFERING

O my Jesus, through the Immaculate Heart of Mary I offer Thee all my prayers, works, joys, and sufferings of this day for Thy greater honor and glory, the salvation of my soul, for the intentions of our Holy Father, and for the poor souls in Purgatory.

Eternal rest grant unto them, O Lord, and let perpetual light shine upon them. May they rest in peace. *Amen*.

NOTES

LESSON FOUR: JESUS PRESENT

Aims

The children will learn that Jesus' presence remains in the Eucharist, reserved in the Catholic churches.

They will learn that the Eucharist is reserved (or saved) for adoration and ministry to the sick.

If possible, a sacred vessels presentation should be made for the children.

Materials

- *Activity Book*, p. 85
- Sacred vessels presentation (and, if possible, a tour of the sacristy)

Optional:
- "O saving Victim," *Adoremus Hymnal*, #519 or #520

Begin

Begin today's class by reading paragraph 6 from the textbook. Discuss the real presence of Jesus in the Eucharist. Jesus remains with us and is reserved in the tabernacle of the Church. Tell the children that you will take time to visit the Blessed Sacrament today.

Q. 98 *When the Host is broken into several parts, is the Body of Jesus Christ broken?*
When the Host is broken into several parts, the Body of Jesus Christ is not broken, but only the appearances of the bread. The Body of Our Lord remains whole and entire in each of the parts (CCC 1377).

Q. 99 *Is Jesus Christ found present in all the consecrated Hosts of the world?*
Yes, Jesus Christ is present in all the consecrated Hosts of the world (CCC 1380).

"I will go to the altar of God, to God my exceeding joy."
Psalm 43:4

Develop

If a priest or deacon is available, have him make a presentation on the sacred vessels used during Mass. If possible, ask him to lead a tour of the sacristy and sanctuary. If a priest or deacon is not available, ask permission to make the presentation yourself. If you may not use the vessels, linens, etc., make cut-outs or take pictures, and show them to the children. Present the following items:

- **Chalice**: the sacred cup used during the Mass in which wine and water are mixed. After the Consecration, this cup holds the Blood (and Body) of our Lord. It is usually made of precious metals.
- **Paten**: the Sacred plate on which the host is placed. After the Consecration, this plate holds the Body (and Blood) of our Lord. Like the chalice, the paten is usually made of precious metal.
- **Ciborium**: the lidded chalice-like container that contains the consecrated hosts remaining after Holy Communion. Jesus is reserved in a ciborium in the tabernacle.
- **Monstrance**: a beautiful holder in which the Blessed Sacrament is displayed. It is used during a prayer service called Benediction and Adoration. Jesus is placed in the center of the monstrance for us to adore.
- **Cruets**: water and wine are kept in cruets which are used to pour the water and wine into the chalice.
- **Lavabo and fingercloth**: bowl and cloth used to wash the hands of the priest before Communion.
- **Corporal**: a sacred linen, upon which the Sacrifice of the Mass is offered. The corporal is laid on top of the altar so that the Holy Eucharist is on a sacred linen.
- **Purificator**: a linen used to clean the sacred vessels.
- **Pall**: a starched square used to cover the chalice during parts of the Mass.
- **Tabernacle**: a beautiful box made of wood or precious metal. It is solid and kept locked. The tabernacle should be a centerpiece of the church. Jesus is kept in the tabernacle—let's visit Him.

Name:_____

The Holy Eucharist

1. What is the Eucharist?
   <u>It is the sacrament of the Body, Blood, Soul, and Divinity of Jesus Christ.</u>
2. Is Jesus really and truly present in the Eucharist?
   <u>Jesus is really and truly present in the Eucharist.</u>
3. How should you love and revere the Eucharist?
   <u>Answers will vary.</u>
4. Where is the Eucharist kept after Mass?
   <u>The Eucharist is usually kept in the tabernacle.</u>
5. How can you show Jesus you love Him in the Eucharist?
   <u>Answers will vary.</u>
6. Is Jesus in every consecrated Host? In all its parts?
   <u>Jesus is present in every consecrated Host and in all its parts.</u>

Faith and Life Series • Grade 3 • Chapter 22 • Lesson 4   85

Reinforce

1. Have the students work on *Activity Book*, p. 85.

2. Visit Jesus in the tabernacle or, if possible, take part in a Benediction and Adoration service.

3. Have the students work on the Memorization Questions and prepare for the quiz.

Conclude

1. Lead the children in singing "O saving Victim," *Adoremus Hymnal*, #519 or #520.

2. End class by leading a prayer, such as the Our Father.

Preview

In the next lesson, the students' knowledge of the material covered this week will be reviewed and assessed.

NOTES

CHAPTER TWENTY-TWO
REVIEW AND ASSESSMENT

Aims

The students' knowledge and understanding of the material covered this week will be reviewed and assessed.

Materials

- Quiz 22, Appendix, p. A-32

Optional:
- "O saving Victim," *Adoremus Hymnal*, #519 or #520

Review

1. Review the parts of the Liturgy of the Eucharist, the responses, prayers, and gestures.

2. Review how we can offer ourselves, united with Jesus, to God the Father in the Mass.

3. Review that the Church—people on earth, angels, saints, and souls in Purgatory—are all united in the celebration of the Mass.

4. Review the definitions of the Consecration and transubstantiation. At the Consecration, transubstantiation takes place: the bread and wine change into the Body, Blood, Soul, and Divinity of Jesus Christ. Jesus is really and truly present in the Eucharist, in each part of the host. Jesus' presence remains after the Mass and is reserved in the tabernacle.

5. Review the sacred vessels and linens used during Mass and Benediction and Adoration services.

Name: _____

Offering Jesus to the Father   Quiz 22

Match the letter of the correct response on the right to the statement on the left.

WHAT THE PRIEST SAYS	WHAT WE SAY
1. Blessed are you, Lord, God of all creation. Through your goodness we have this bread to offer, which earth has given and human hands have made. It will become for us the bread of life. **E**	A. It is right to give Him thanks and praise.
2. Pray, brethren, that our sacrifice may be acceptable to God the Almighty Father. **F**	B. Christ has died, Christ is risen, Christ will come again.
3. The Lord be with you. **D**	C. Amen.
4. Lift up your hearts. **G**	D. And also with you.
5. Let us give thanks to the Lord our God. **A**	E. Blessed be God forever.
6. Let us proclaim the mystery of faith. **B**	F. May the Lord accept the sacrifice at your hands for the praise and glory of his Name, for our good, and the good of all His Church.
7. Through Him, with Him, in Him, in the unity of the Holy Spirit, all glory and honor is yours almighty Father, for ever and ever. **C**	G. We lift them up to the Lord.

Assess

1. Distribute the quizzes and read through them with the students to be sure they understand the questions.

2. Administer the quiz. As they hand in their work, you may orally quiz them on the Memorization Questions for this chapter.

3. After all the quizzes have been handed in, you may wish to review the correct answers with the children.

Conclude

1. Lead the children in singing "O saving Victim," *Adoremus Hymnal*, #519 or #520.

2. End class with a prayer.

CHAPTER TWENTY-THREE
THE BREAD OF LIFE

Catechism of the Catholic Church References

Eucharist as Sacrifice: 1356–81, 1414
Eucharist as thanksgiving and Praise to the Father: 1359–61
Eucharist as Sacrificial Memory of Christ and of His Body the Church: 1362–72, 1408, 1414
Presence of Christ in the Eucharist: 1373–81, 1410, 1418

Fruits of Communion: 1355, 1382–90, 1415, 1417
Holy Communion: 1355, 1382–96, 1415, 1417
Mystical Body: 1391–96, 1416
Sacrifice: 2099–2100

Scripture References

My Flesh Is Food Indeed: Jn 6:53–56

Background Reading: *The Fundamentals of Catholicism* by Fr. Kenneth Baker, S.J

Volume 3:
"Reception of Holy Communion," pp. 253–56

Summary of Lesson Content

Lesson 1

After the Consecration, God gives us the precious gift of Jesus in the Eucharist to come into us through Communion.

In the Old Testament, covenants were sealed with a sacrifice and a meal.

Lesson 2

In the New Covenant, Jesus is the Lamb of God, sacrificed and eaten as indicated by the Agnus Dei.

We are not worthy to receive Jesus in Communion; we receive Him by God's grace.

Lesson 3

The Eucharist is food for our souls.

Jesus is the Bread of Life.

Lesson 4

The Mass is the perfect prayer.

Jesus commanded that the Mass be celebrated when He said, "Do this in remembrance of Me."

LESSON ONE: COVENANT

Aims

After the Consecration, God gives us the precious gift of Jesus in the Eucharist.

In the Old Testament, covenants were sealed with a sacrifice and a meal.

Materials

- *Activity Book*, p. 86
- Loaf of bread and jar of jam or peanut butter (to be shared with entire class)

Optional:
- "Soul of my Savior," *Adoremus Hymnal*, #522

Begin

Discuss family meals. When do you celebrate them? Major holidays? Every night? Sundays? Why is it important to eat together? Who is invited? What do you eat? What does your family do to make these meals special? Have the children share their family traditions.

---

23   The Bread of Life

"Truly, truly, I say to you, unless you eat the flesh of the Son of man and drink his blood, you have no life in you. . . ."

John 6:53

Jesus is the precious gift we offer the Father at Mass. Then we receive Jesus into us as God's gift into our own souls. In this way, the Sacrifice of the Mass truly forms a bond between Heaven and earth.

As we remember, in the Old Testament, people offered gifts of value to God. A shepherd and his family might offer up a lamb. The shepherd placed his lamb on an altar and killed it. This was a sign that his gift was completely offered to God. But something else was needed to complete the act of love. The shepherd and his family sat together and ate the lamb as a sacred meal. This was an important sign of their covenant, or friendship, with God. They wanted to be closer to Him by eating something that He had been offered and had accepted.

Under the New Covenant, we lift up the Lamb of God. Then we share in this sacrificial gift by receiving God's own Son in Holy **Communion**. The priest holds Him before us and says, "This is the Lamb of God Who takes away the sins of the world. Happy are those who are called to His supper." We look at Jesus and answer, "Lord, I am not **worthy** to receive You, but only say the word and I shall be healed." To share fully in the New Covenant or the full friendship with God, we must share in Jesus' Sacrifice and the meal of the Sacrifice.

111

Develop

1. Read paragraphs 1 and 2 with the children.

2. Discuss how the sacred meal of the Mass brings us into communion with God. First, God receives the offering, then gives it back to us, so that we are united to God in this meal. Also, Jesus, Who is God, is present in the Eucharist. By receiving Communion, we are in union with God.

3. Discuss "communion." Even without a dictionary, we could figure out what the word "communion" means. "Com" means with. For example, combine (to mix one thing with another), comfort (with strength, we support someone), command (to give directions with authority). "Union" means joining together as one. Communion, then, is to join together as one with God! In Holy Communion, we become one with Jesus, the Bread of Life.

4. Referring to the matter of this sacrament, show how the grains are ground together to make one bread. Show how grapes are pressed together to make one wine. Likewise, we gather together to make one Church as an offering to God.

4. Sharing the sacred meal of Communion, we are placed in union with God, but also with His Body, the Church. The Church is called the Mystical Body of Christ; we all come together to form this Body. Each of us has a different role in this Body: some are priests, some are religious, some are parents, and some are children. Similarly, each of us has different gifts: some teach, some sing, some share the Scriptures, some console the sick, etc. These gifts are to be used for the glory of God and for His Church.

5. As we share in Communion, we are united. We all know the phrase "you are what you eat." By receiving Jesus, we become more like Him, in service to one another.

6. As a sign of your unity, share a meal as a class.

Name:_____

Sacred Meals

Meals are very important. Jesus shared His last meal with His Apostles.

1. Of what is a meal a sign?
   <u>Answers will vary.</u>
2. The Mass is a sacred meal.
   What is eaten at this meal?
   <u>Answers will vary. (Holy Communion, Lamb of God, etc.)</u>
   Of what is it a sign?
   <u>Answers will vary.</u>
   Why do we eat something offered to and received by God?
   <u>It helps us to be close to Him.</u>
   Does the Eucharist really nourish us? How?
   <u>Yes. It is food for our souls. It keeps the life of grace alive in our hearts and helps us to grow as good and loving children of God.</u>
   With whom does the sharing of the sacred meal of the Mass unite us?
   <u>Answers will vary.</u>
3. With whom do you normally share meals with? How is the Mass a meal shared with your eternal family?
   <u>We usually share meals with our family. Our faith in God makes us a family, so in Mass we share a meal with that eternal family.</u>

86   Faith and Life Series • Grade 3 • Chapter 23 • Lesson 1

Reinforce

1. Have the students work on *Activity Book*, p. 86.

2. Teach the children to sing "Soul of my Savior," *Adoremus Hymnal*, #522.

Conclude

1. End class by leading the students in praying the Our Father.

2. Focus on the "Our" of "Our Father" and explain how we are one family and one Body in Christ.

Preview

In the next lesson, the students will learn about the New Covenant.

SAINT PAUL ON THE MYSTICAL BODY OF CHRIST

"There is one body and one Spirit, just as you were called to the one hope that belongs to your call, one Lord, one faith, one baptism, one God and Father of us all, who is above all and through all and in all. But grace was given to each of us according to the measure of Christ's gift . . . .And his gifts were that some should be apostles, some prophets, some evangelists, some pastors and teachers, for the equipment of the saints, for the work of ministry, for the building up the body of Christ, until we all attain to the unity of the faith and of the knowledge of the Son of God, to mature manhood, to the measure of the stature of the fullness of Christ" (Eph 4:4–13).

NOTES

LESSON TWO: LAMB OF GOD

Aims

The students will learn how Jesus is the Sacrifice and meal of the New Covenant.

We are not worthy to receive Jesus in Communion; we receive Him by God's grace.

Materials

- *Activity Book*, p. 87
- Children's Bible

Optional:
- "Soul of my Savior," *Adoremus Hymnal*, #522

Begin

If you have a video on the Last Supper, watch it as a class (or read it from the children's Bible). *Discuss the following questions:*
- What was sacrificed and eaten?
- When would Jesus be sacrificed? (He offered the Sacrifice at the Last Supper and the Sacrifice was fulfilled at the Crucifixion)
- Was this Sacrifice accepted by God?
- Was it given to all men to share?
- What do we mean when we say Jesus is the Lamb of God? (See Jn 1:29).

Develop

1. Read paragraph 3 with the children.

2. Discuss the Old Covenant and the New Covenant. Make connections and distinctions between the two. In the Old Covenant, God delivered the Israelites from Pharaoh during the Exodus and bound them to Himself at Mt. Sinai. He gave them His Law in the Ten Commandments, and sealed the covenant with the sacrifice of oxen, the sharing of its blood in a sprinkling rite, and the eating of its flesh.
In the New Covenant, God delivered all people from slavery to sin by Jesus' death and Resurrection, and bound them to Himself by Holy Communion. He gave all people His Law of love, fulfilling the Commandments. He sealed this covenant in the Sacrifice of His Body and Blood on the Cross, shared in the Communion of His Body and Blood in the Eucharist. He is the Sacrifice and the meal of the New Covenant.

3. Review the Agnus Dei with the children. Also review the priest's words, "This is the Lamb of God Who takes away the sins of the world. Happy are those who are called to His Supper" and our response, "Lord, I am not worthy to receive You, but only say the word, and I shall be healed."

4. Teach the children to make a spiritual communion: Lord, as I cannot receive you now in the Most Holy and Blessed Sacrament of the Altar, I ask You to come, nevertheless, into my heart, and render it like unto Thine own." You may take the children to visit Jesus in the Blessed Sacrament. You may teach them appropriate prayers, such as: "Jesus in the Blessed Sacrament, have mercy on us."

5. Review all of the material taught in this lesson. Ask the children to explain why attending Mass and participating reverently are so important.

Name:_____

Jesus, the Lamb of God

Fill in the blanks.

In the <u>Old Testament</u>, people also offered gifts of value to God. A <u>shepherd</u> and his family might offer a <u>lamb</u>. The shepherd placed his lamb on an <u>altar</u> and killed it. This was a sign that his gift was <u>completely</u> offered to God. But something else was needed to complete the act of <u>love</u>. The shepherd and his family sat together and <u>ate</u> the lamb as a sacred <u>meal</u>. This was an important sign of their <u>covenant</u> with God. They wanted to be <u>closer</u> to Him by <u>eating</u> something that He had been <u>offered</u> and had <u>accepted</u>. Under the New <u>Testament</u>, we lift up the <u>Lamb of God</u>. Then we share in this <u>sacrificial</u> gift by <u>receiving</u> God's own Son in Holy <u>Communion</u>. The priest holds Him before us and says," <u>This is the Lamb of God Who takes away the sins of the world. Happy are those who are called to His supper</u>." We look at Jesus and answer, "<u>Lord, I am not worthy to receive you, but only say the word and I shall be healed</u>." Sharing this sacred banquet unites us in friendship with the Father. It also binds all of us together as one family.

Faith and Life Series • Grade 3 • Chapter 23 • Lesson 2

Reinforce

1. Have the students work on *Activity Book*, p. 87.

2. Take the students to pray before the Blessed Sacrament.

3. Have the children write letters to God, thanking Him for His New Covenant.

Conclude

1. Lead the children in singing "Soul of my Savior," *Adoremus Hymnal*, #522.

2. Review the Mass parts and responses with a review game, such as jeopardy.

3. End class by leading the students in a prayer, such as the Our Father.

Preview

In the next lesson, the students will learn how the Eucharist nourishes our souls.

LAMB OF GOD SCRIPTURE REFERENCES

- Exodus/Passover: Ex 12

- Covenant at Sinai: Ex 24:1–11

- Isaiah describes the Messiah: Is 53:7

- Last Supper: Mt 26; Mk 14; Lk 22

- John calls Jesus the Lamb of God: Jn 1:29

- Paul calls Jesus "a lamb without blemish or spot": 1 Pet 1:19

NOTES
_____
_____
_____
_____
_____
_____
_____
_____
_____
_____

LESSON THREE: FOOD FOR OUR SOULS

Aims

The students will learn that the Eucharist is food for our souls.

They will better understand that Jesus is the Bread of Life.

Materials

- *Activity Book*, p. 88
- Dietary chart

Optional:
- "Soul of my Savior," *Adoremus Hymnal*, #522

Begin

Ask the children what is necessary to make them strong and healthy physically. To be healthy, they must eat good foods from the various food groups: grains, fruits and vegetables, meats and proteins, dairy products, and water. Also, they must exercise, rest, and care for their bodies. Let the students discuss what they do to make sure they will be healthy and strong.

"As often as you eat this bread and drink the cup, you proclaim the Lord's death, until he comes."

1 Corinthians 11:26

The Eucharist really nourishes us. Just as we need food for our bodies to keep us alive, growing, and strong, so we need food for our souls. The Eucharist, the Bread of Life, does this. It keeps the life of grace alive in our hearts. It helps us to grow as good and loving children of God. Jesus said, "Whoever eats of this Bread will never hunger." He also told us that by eating this Bread we will never die; we shall live for ever.

Sharing this sacred banquet unites us in friendship with the Father. It also binds all of us together as one. Our faith in the one, true God makes us a family. All over the world, members of God's family gather to worship the way Jesus taught us at the Last Supper. Whenever we do this in memory of Him, we give joy to the Father. We become more and more like His beloved Son in Whom He is well pleased.

Words to Know:

Communion   worthy

> Because there is one bread, we who are many are one body, for we all partake of the one bread.
>
> 1 Corinthians 10:17

Develop

1. Read paragraph 4 with the children.

2. Ask the children what things we need to do to nourish our souls:
   - Prayer
   - Live the virtues
   - Acts of penance and charity
   - Read the Bible
   - Receive the Sacrament of Penance
   - Receive the Eucharist

3. Explain that receiving the Eucharist is the most perfect way to nourish our souls. All the other ways of prayer lead us to Jesus; however, receiving the Eucharist is receiving Jesus, really and truly present. Jesus is the giver of all graces, of all that nourishes our souls. It is very important to receive Jesus in Holy Communion, but we must receive Him worthily.

4. Explain that by the sacrament and its effects, Jesus is made present in the Eucharist. However, how much grace we receive depends upon our hearts and how open they are to receive God's graces.

5. Ask the students what they can do to open their hearts to receive God's grace:
   - Pray
   - Have faith
   - Go to Confession
   - Fast
   - Receive the Sacrament of Penance
   - Be thankful

6. From the children's Bible, read John 6:35–56. Have the students explain what it means to say that Jesus is the Bread of Life.

Name:_____

Bread From Heaven

Jesus said to them, "I am the bread of life; he who comes to me shall not hunger, and he who believes in me shall never thirst....I am the living bread which came down from heaven; if any one eats of this bread, he will live for ever; and the bread of which I shall give for the life of the world is my flesh" (Jn 6:35,51–56).

1. When Jesus told us that He is the Bread of Life, was He speaking in riddles?
   No
2. How did Jesus give us His Flesh and Blood?
   In Holy Communion
3. What are the rewards for eating His Body and Blood?
   We will live forever
4. If we eat the Bread of Life, will our souls be hungry again?
   No
5. Jesus says He is the Bread come down from Heaven. How did Jesus come from Heaven?
   Answers will vary.
6. Jesus refers to another bread, but that it does not give us life. What was that bread called?
   Bread from Heaven

88 Faith and Life Series • Grade 3 • Chapter 23 • Lesson 3

Reinforce

1. Have the students work on *Activity Book*, p. 88.

2. Have the students visit Jesus in the Blessed Sacrament.

3. Have the students make charts that depict how they should nourish their bodies and how they should nourish their souls.

Conclude

1. Lead the children in singing "Soul of my Savior," *Adoremus Hymnal*, #522.

2. End class by leading the students in making a spiritual communion.

Preview

In the next lesson, the students will learn about the importance of celebrating the Mass.

Steps to a Worthy Communion:
1. Be free of mortal sin
2. Fast for 1 hour (only water and medicine allowed)
3. Know Whom you are about to receive
4. Reverently receive our Lord
5. Offer thanksgiving in prayer

SAINT PASCHAL BABYLON

Born of a poor peasant family, Saint Paschal Babylon taught himself to read. He entered the Order of Friars Minor as a young man and lived a holy life of self-denial, prayer, and adoration of the Eucharist.

Though he was occupied primarily in the quiet and humble position of doorman for the priory, Saint Paschal Babylon had a moment of rhetorical brilliance in defending the real presence in the Holy Eucharist from angry Calvinists in France. He is the patron of all Eucharistic congresses and confraternities.

NOTES

_____
_____
_____
_____
_____
_____
_____
_____
_____
_____

LESSON FOUR: THE PERFECT PRAYER

Aims

The students will learn that the Mass is the perfect prayer.

They will learn that Jesus Himself commanded that the Mass be celebrated. The Mass is pleasing to God.

Materials

- *Activity Book*, p. 89
- Children's missals

Optional:
- "Soul of my Savior," *Adoremus Hymnal*, #522

Begin

Begin the class by reading the rest of the chapter. Discuss why the Mass is so pleasing to God.
The Mass is pleasing to God because:
- It unites His Family
- He gives Himself to us and accepts our sacrifices
- We are obedient to Jesus' command
- It is the perfect prayer

Q. 100 *What is the New Covenant?*
The New Covenant is the perfect and unbreakable friendship to which man is called by God. Jesus won the New Covenant for us. He is the Sacrifice and meal that seals the Covenant. We are called to share in the New Covenant through Holy Communion (CCC 610–11).

We Pray:

O Sacrament most holy, O Sacrament divine,
All praise and all thanksgiving be every moment Thine.

Develop

1. Discuss the forms of prayer:
   - *Blessing and Adoration:* We acknowledge God's gifts to us and give honor to God.
   - *Petition and Intercession:* We ask for our needs and the needs of others.
   - *Thanksgiving:* We thank God for His many gifts; the word "Eucharist" means thanksgiving.
   - *Praise:* We love God for being God and because of His divine attributes.

2. As you explain each form of prayer, have each child make up a sentence of prayer in that form:
   - *Blessing and Adoration:* Blessed are You, Lord, for you have given us Life!
   - *Petition and Intercession:* Lord, please make my grandmother well.
   - *Thanksgiving:* Thank You, Lord, for sunshine and rain.
   - *Praise:* We love You, Lord, for Your Mercy and Goodness.

3. Next, have the children use their missals to find parts of the Mass for each of the forms of prayer. They may work in groups. Have them write the parts of the Mass on paper or make posters for each of the forms of prayer (one per group).

4. Next, discuss that the Mass is the perfect prayer. It combines all the forms of prayer. The Mass is the prayer of Jesus, continued through His Body, the Church. It is the perfect sacrifice and covenant meal. It is the prayer of the Church on earth, the souls in Purgatory, and the angels and saints in Heaven.

5. Review that Jesus commanded us to worship at Mass when He said, "Do this in remembrance of Me" at the Last Supper.

6. Review how we should participate in the Mass—with attentiveness and reverence.

Name:_____

The Mass Is the Perfect Prayer

In the chart below, write out the parts of the Mass, which correspond to the forms of prayer.

Blessing and Adoration	Petition and Intercession
• For God's gifts and in receiving them • We honor God, our King **Answers will vary.**	• We pray for our needs and the needs of others
Thanksgiving	**Praise**
• We thank God for His many gifts • "Eucharist" means thanksgiving	• We recognize God and His attributes

How is the Mass the perfect prayer?

Faith and Life Series • Grade 3 • Chapter 23 • Lesson 4

Reinforce

1. Have the students make presentation on their findings of the forms of prayer in the Mass.

2. Have the students work on *Activity Book*, p. 89.

Conclude

1. Lead the children in singing "Soul of my Savior," *Adoremus Hymnal*, #522.

2. End class by leading the children in making a spiritual communion.

Preview

In the next lesson, the students' knowledge of the material covered this week will be reviewed and assessed.

FORMS OF PRAYER IN THE MASS

Here are some examples of the forms of prayer found in the Mass:

- Blessing and Adoration: Eucharistic prayer

- Petition and Intercession: Prayers of the people, Confession of sins, final blessing

- Thanksgiving: Post Eucharistic prayer of thanksgiving

- Praise: Gloria, Psalm

NOTES

CHAPTER TWENTY-THREE
REVIEW AND ASSESSMENT

Aims

The students' knowledge and understanding of the material covered this week will be reviewed and assessed.

Materials

- Quiz 23, Appendix, p. A-33

Optional:
- "Soul of my Savior," *Adoremus Hymnal*, #522

Review

1. The students should understand that Jesus is the precious gift given to the Father during Mass. It is Jesus Whom the Father receives and Whom we also receive in Holy Communion.

2. The students should understand what a sacred meal is—that it unites all who partake.

3. The students should know that in the New Covenant, Jesus is the Sacrifice and meal necessary for the binding of the covenant.

4. The Eucharist is food for our souls—it nourishes us.

5. The Mass is celebrated by the will of Jesus and it is pleasing to the Father. The Mass is the perfect prayer.

Name: _____

The Bread of Life   Quiz 23

"I am the bread of life; he who comes to me shall not hunger" (John 6:35).

Word Bank

| closer | God | supper | worthy | friendship |
| Lamb | unbreakable | family | Bread | |

Fill in the blanks with the correct words from the Word Bank.

1. In the Old Testament, the people would offer up a lamb. It was killed and the family would eat the lamb as a sacred meal and as a sign of their covenant and friendship with **God**.

2. They wanted to be **closer** to Him by eating something offered as a sacrifice to Him.

3. Under the New Covenant, we lift up the **Lamb** of God. Then we share in this Sacrifice by receiving God's own Son in Holy Communion.

4. The priest holds Jesus before us and says, "This is the Lamb of God who takes away the sins of the world. Happy are those who are called to His **supper**."

5. We look at Jesus and answer, "Lord, I am not **worthy** to receive You, but only say the word and I shall be healed."

6. To share fully in the New Covenant or full **friendship** with God, we must share in Jesus' Sacrifice and the meal of the Sacrifice.

7. The Eucharist, the **Bread** of Life, keeps the life of grace alive in our hearts.

8. Sharing this sacred banquet unites us in friendship with the Father. Our faith in the one, true God makes us a **family**.

9. The New Covenant is the perfect and **unbreakable** friendship with God. Jesus won the New Covenant for us.

10. Write out the Scripture verse shown at the top of this page.

Faith and Life • Grade 3 • Appendix A   A - 33

Assess

1. Distribute the quizzes and read through them with the students to be sure they understand the questions.

2. Administer the quiz. As they hand in their work, you may orally quiz the students on the Memorization Questions for this chapter.

3. After all the quizzes have been handed in, you may wish to review the correct answers with the class.

Conclude

1. Lead the children in singing "Soul of my Savior," *Adoremus Hymnal*, #522.

2. End class by leading the students in prayer.

CHAPTER TWENTY-FOUR
JESUS COMES TO US IN THE HOLY EUCHARIST

Catechism of the Catholic Church References

Charity: 1822–29, 1844
Forgiveness: 2839–45, 2862
Effects of Communion: 1000, 1325, 1370, 1391–95, 1405, 1416
Fruits of Communion: 1391–1401, 1416

Grace Conferred by the Sacraments: 1127–29, 1131
Holy Communion: 1355, 1382–90, 1415, 1417
Presence of Christ in the Eucharist: 1371–81, 1410, 1418
Preparing for Communion: 1385–87

Scripture References

Multiplication of Loaves and Fish: Mt 14:13–21
Bread of Life: Jn 6:22–71

Background Reading: *The Fundamentals of Catholicism* by Fr. Kenneth Baker, S.J

Volume 2:
"The Divinity of Jesus in St. John's Gospel," pp. 203–6

Volume 3: "Each Mass Benefits All," pp. 271–73

Summary of Lesson Content

Lesson 1

Jesus prepared us for the Eucharist by His miraculous multiplication of loaves and fish.

Jesus Himself told us that He is the Bread of Life.

Lesson 2

To prepare to receive Jesus in Holy Communion we must:

- Be free from mortal sin
- Fast from food or drink for one hour
- Know Whom we receive in the Eucharist.

Lesson 3

In Holy Communion we are united with Jesus and we should pray to Him.

We should offer thanksgiving to God.

Lesson 4

When we receive Holy Communion we receive grace and become more like Jesus.

Jesus gives us the strength to be generous, forgiving, and kind.

We should want to receive Communion because we love Jesus. The best way to be with Jesus is in Communion.

LESSON ONE: BREAD OF LIFE

Aims

The children will learn that Jesus prepared us for the Eucharist by His miraculous multiplication of loaves and fish.

They will learn that Jesus is the Bread of Life.

Materials

- *Activity Book*, p. 90
- Children's Bible
- Enough cookies for your students
- Construction paper circles

Optional:
- "O Lord, I am not worthy," *Adoremus Hymnal*, #512

Begin

Begin the class by telling the students that you have a treat for them. You have cookies that you would like to share. Ask the children how many students there are. Count out that many cookies. Share your cookies with the students. Explain that you have one for each of them, but you will have none left for yourself. If there were more people how would they share? They would have to break the cookies. With material things, if we give something away, it's gone. With spiritual things, when we give something away, we still have it, too. Examples: love, faith, hope, joy.

---

24 Jesus Comes to Us In the Holy Eucharist

Because there is one bread, we who are many are one body, for we all partake of the one bread.

1 Corinthians 10:17

Jesus once changed five loaves and two fishes into food for five thousand people. This miracle of love amazed His followers. But later, Jesus promised them a far more wonderful bread. He explained that this heavenly bread would satisfy the hungers of the heart. Then He told them: "I am the Bread of Life. He who eats My Flesh and drinks My Blood will live for ever."

The Holy Eucharist is the Bread of Life that Jesus promised. We are very fortunate because we can receive it at every Mass. Whenever we do, Jesus comes as a Guest into our hearts.

To prepare for our divine Guest, three things are necessary. We must believe in Him. We must be in His good graces, which means that if we have a grave sin on our soul, we must go to Confession before receiving the Eucharist. We must not eat or drink anything else (except water or medicine) for one hour before He comes to us. These things prepare us properly to receive Jesus in Holy Communion.

Once we receive Jesus, we kneel down to make a **thanksgiving**. Thanksgiving just means giving thanks. We may close our eyes to give Him our full attention. We silently pray to Him and He listens. Jesus already knows us completely, but He is pleased when we share our lives with Him. During Holy Communion we can tell Him our

---

Develop

1. Read paragraphs 1 and 2 with the students.

2. Read the story of the multiplication of loaves and fish from a children's Bible. It is found in John 6:1–14, 25–59.

3. Ask the children how five loaves of bread and two fish could feed five thousand people. It is not possible! Truly, this was a miracle of God.

4. How did the miracle of loaves and fish prepare people for the Eucharist?
   - It showed how spiritual goods are multiplied
   - It showed God's great love and care for man
   - It fed the hungry
   - The bread prepared the people for the Bread of Life
   - The fish is a symbol for Christ because, in Greek, the letters that spell the word for fish are the first letters of a creedal formula stating: Jesus, Son of God and Savior

5. Ask the children questions based upon the reading:
   - Did all people accept Jesus' teaching that He is the Bread of Life? Why not?
   - How is it possible to eat Jesus' Flesh and drink His Blood?
   - Why didn't the Apostles leave Jesus?
   - What is the Eucharist? How do we know it is Jesus?
   - What is the promise Jesus made for those who eat His Flesh and drink His Blood?

6. Discuss various symbols for Christ. Give the children large construction paper circles in white/neutral color. Have them design "hosts" using a symbol to represent Christ.

Name:_____

The Bread of Life

1. Jesus performed the Miracle of the Multiplication of the Loaves and Fish. Why were His followers amazed?
   Answers will vary.

2. Jesus promised a far more wonderful bread, what was that to be?
   The Holy Eucharist

3. How will this "Bread of Life" satisfy us, and nourish us?
   It preserves and increases grace. It also gives spiritual joy and consolation.

4. How can we receive His Bread of Life?
   We can receive it as Mass.

90 Faith and Life Series • Grade 3 • Chapter 24 • Lesson 1

VARIOUS SYMBOLS FOR CHRIST

- X: the Greek letter chi, X is the first letter of the Greek spelling of Christ; further, it resembles the Cross. For many years "X" was a scholarly abbreviation for Christ.
- Kairos: a moment of holy opportunity. This term is used throughout the New Testament as a symbol for the Spirit working through Christ.
- Alpha and Omega: first and last letters of the Greek alphabet. This is a way of saying that God is the first and the last, the beginning and the end.
- Ichthys: Greek acronym for "Jesus, Son of God and Savior." These letters spell "fish" in ancient Greek.

Reinforce

1. Have the students work on *Activity Book*, p. 90.

2. Teach the students to sing "O Lord, I am not worthy," *Adoremus Hymnal*, #512.

Conclude

1. Lead the children in praying for their intentions and making an act of spiritual communion.

2. You may visit Jesus in the Blessed Sacrament.

Preview

In the next lesson, the students will review the steps to making a good and worthy communion.

NOTES

_____
_____
_____
_____
_____
_____
_____
_____
_____
_____

LESSON TWO: RECEIVING JESUS

Aims

The students will review the steps to making a good Communion. To make a good Communion, they must:

• Be free from mortal sin
• Fast from food or drink for one hour
• Know Whom they receive in the Eucharist

Materials

• *Activity Book*, p. 91
• *Hymnal*, #512

Optional:
• "O Lord, I am not worthy," *Adoremus*
• If possible, arrange for your class to receive Penance

Begin

Discuss what preparations the students would make if the president, prime minister, or queen were coming over for dinner. They would:
• Set the table with their best dishes
• Prepare their best foods
• Wear their best clothes
• Clean thoroughly
• Arrange everything as perfectly as possible
Similarly, we must make proper preparations to receive God into ourselves. We must be sure we are ready to receive Jesus.

Develop

1. Read paragraph 3 with the children.

2. The First Step: we must believe that we are receiving Jesus in the Eucharist. Do the children believe? How do they know that it is Jesus they receive in the Eucharist?

3. Second Step: we must be free from mortal sin. This may require some children to go to Confession. Help the children do an examination of conscience. Review mortal and venial sin. Also review perfect and imperfect contrition.

4. Explain why it is wrong to receive Holy Communion in a state of mortal sin. It is an even greater sin called sacrilege. By receiving Jesus with mortal sin on our souls, we purposely receive Jesus unworthily. God made flesh is worthy of a holy dwelling place. When our souls are in mortal sin, they are displeasing to God. Although God still loves us and calls us to receive His mercy, we must receive the Sacrament of Penance to ask for His forgiveness and receive His grace.

5. You may take your class to the Sacrament of Penance.

6. The Third Step: we must fast for one hour before receiving Jesus in order to prepare our souls. This means no food or drink for one full hour before we receive Holy Communion. This way we will hunger for Jesus.

7. Review exceptions to the fast: we may receive water or medicine during the one hour before Holy Communion. Also, the elderly/sick and their caregivers need not take part in the Eucharistic fast.

8. Let the children know that when we receive Jesus in Holy Communion, He remains physically with us for about 15 minutes. During this time, we should pray and be united closely with Jesus without distractions.

Name:_____

Receiving Jesus in Communion

1. What is the first thing necessary in order to receive Holy Communion worthily?
   <u>We must be in a state of the grace of God, which means that if we have a grave sin on our soul, we must go to the Sacrament of Penance.</u>

2. What is the second thing necessary to receive Holy Communion worthily?
   <u>We must realize and consider Whom we are about to receive.</u>

3. What is the third thing necessary to receive Holy Communion worthily?
   <u>We must observe the Eucharistic fast.</u>

4. Is it a good and useful thing to receive Holy Communion frequently?
   <u>Yes. It is even useful to receive it every day, provided it is always done in the right way.</u>

5. What effects does the Eucharist produce in him who worthily receives it?
   <u>The Holy Eucharist preserves and increases grace. It takes away venial sins and preserves us from mortal sins. It gives spiritual joy and consolation by increasing charity and the hope of eternal life.</u>

Faith and Life Series • Grade 3 • Chapter 24 • Lesson 2   91

EXAMINATION OF CONSCIENCE

How have I acted toward God? Do I think of God and speak to Him by praying to Him each day?
Do I speak of God with reverence?
Do I go to Mass on Sunday?
Do I do all I can to make Sunday a day of rest and joy for my family?
Do I participate in Mass, or do I tease or distract others by laughing, talking, or playing?
Do I pay attention to my parents, priests, and teachers when they talk to me about God?
How have I acted toward others?

See back of student text for complete examination.

Reinforce

1. Have the students work on *Activity Book*, p. 91.

2. Have the students work on their Memorization Questions for this chapter.

3. If possible, have the students receive the Sacrament of Penance.

Conclude

1. Lead the children in singing "O Lord, I am not worthy," *Adoremus Hymnal*, #512.

2. Lead the students in making spiritual communion. Take them to pray before Jesus in the tabernacle.

Preview

In the next lesson, the students will learn of the effects of Communion.

NOTES

LESSON THREE: THANKSGIVING

Aims

The students will learn that in Holy Communion, we are united with Jesus and we should pray to Him.

They will review that we should offer thanksgiving to God.

Materials

- *Activity Book*, p. 92
- Unconsecrated hosts
- Posterboard, paper, pencils, markers

Optional:
- "O Lord, I am not worthy," *Adoremus Hymnal*, #512

Begin

Review the steps to worthily receiving Holy Communion. They must:
- Be free from mortal sin
- Fast for one hour
- Know Whom they are to receive

Review reverent behavior before the Blessed Sacrament, including:
- Genuflecting
- Remaining silent
- Not distracting others
- Paying attention

"My flesh is food indeed, and my blood is drink indeed. He who eats my flesh and drinks my blood, abides in me, and I in him."

John 6:56–57

disappointments and joys, our hopes and dreams. If we are having trouble being kind or good, Jesus understands. He will help us. If we want to be more obedient at home or school, we can ask Him to show us the way.

Every time Jesus comes to us, He fills our souls with His own life. We become more and more like Him. He gives us the strength to be generous, forgiving, and kind. We become the grace-filled persons God created us to be.

When we love someone, we never get tired of his company. We spend as much time with that person as we can. Think of how much more we want to enjoy the company of Jesus. The best way to stay close to Jesus is to go to Mass and receive Holy Communion, even every day if possible. He is the food and life of our souls. If we share in His life on earth, He will one day invite us to live with Him for ever in Heaven.

> "Your fathers ate the manna in the wilderness, and they died. This is the bread which comes down from heaven, that a man may eat of it and not die. I am the living bread which came down from heaven; if any one eats of this bread, he will live for ever; and the bread which I shall give for the life of the world is my flesh."
>
> John 6:49–51

Develop

1. Read paragraphs 5 and 6 with the students.

2. Have the students practice receiving unconsecrated hosts. Review the proper way to receive in the hand or on the tongue. Line them up and ask them review questions. If a child answers correctly, he may receive a host. Be sure the children:
   - Open their mouths and stick out their tongues far enough, or extend their hands, left cupped inside the right (left over right) as a throne or manger for Jesus
   - Listen for "The Body of Christ"
   - Say "Amen"
   - Receive the Host
   - Make the Sign of the Cross

3. Review that Jesus remains physically with us for about 15 minutes after we receive Him in the Eucharist.

4. Review the effects of Holy Communion with the students:
   - *Cleanses us from venial sin*
   - *Unites us with the poor*
   - *Shows us the unity of the three Persons of the Trinity (because we are united with Jesus in Communion)*
   - *Unites all the Church*
   - *Helps us to grow strong as Christians*
   - *Gives us an increase of grace*
   - *Helps us to do penance*
   - *Transforms us in Christ*
   - *Unites us with Jesus*
   - *Allows us to participate in the heavenly liturgy*
   - *Gives us a share in Jesus' Sacrifice to the Father*

   Have the students draw posters depicting these effects.

5. Help the students understand how Jesus hears their prayers when they receive Him.

Name:_____

Receiving Jesus in Communion

1. How should we prepare to receive Jesus in Holy Communion?
   We must believe in Him, be in a state of grace, and observe the Eucharistic fast.

2. What should we do once we receive Jesus in Holy Communion?
   We should kneel down and make a thanksgiving.

3. What can we tell Jesus once we have received Him?
   We can tell Jesus our disappointments and joys, as well as our hopes and dreams.

4. What gifts does Jesus bring into our souls every time we receive Him?
   Jesus fills our souls with His own life, helping us to become more like Him.

Faith and Life Series • Grade 3 • Chapter 24 • Lesson 3

Reinforce

1. Have the students work on *Activity Book*, p. 92.

2. Have the students complete and present their First Communion posters.

3. Have the students work on their Memorization Questions.

Conclude

1. Lead the children in singing "O Lord, I am not worthy," *Adoremus Hymnal*, #512.

2. Have the students make a spiritual communion and, if possible, take them to visit the Blessed Sacrament.

Preview

In the next lesson, the students will learn about adoration.

FIRST COMMUNION REPORT DISPLAY

Make a display of "Our First Communion" reports. Have the students include a photo of themselves on the day of the occasion.

The children may individually present their reports. They may tell the class how they prepared to receive Jesus. They may share their experiences, what they told God in their prayers after receiving the Holy Eucharist, or how they felt after they received first Communion.

NOTES

LESSON FOUR: ADORATION

Aims

The students will learn that we should want to receive Communion because we love Jesus. The best way to be with Jesus is in Communion.

The students will also learn about Eucharistic adoration.

Materials

- *Activity Book*, p. 93
- Pencils
- *Hymnal*, #512
- Monstrance

Optional:
- "O Lord, I am not worthy," *Adoremus*
- Arrange for Adoration and Benediction service

Begin

Ask the students to discuss their best friends. Who are they? What do they like doing with them? Do they ever get tired of one another? What about family? Do they ever get tired of spending time with their moms or dads? Of course not. Love draws us to people. It makes us want to be with them, even if we must give something up to be with them. Can the students think of examples of times they gave something up to be with a loved one? How did they feel? Did they miss what they gave up? Was it worth it?

Words to Know:

thanksgiving

Q. 101 *What things are necessary for the worthy reception of Holy Communion?*
For a worthy reception of Holy Communion three things are necessary: first, to be in the grace of God; second, to realize and to consider Whom we are about to receive; third, to observe the Eucharistic fast (CCC 1385–88).

Q. 102 *Is it a good and useful thing to receive Holy Communion frequently?*
It is a very good thing and most useful to receive Holy Communion frequently, even every day, provided it is done always in the right way (CCC 1391–92).

Q. 103 *What effects does the Eucharist produce in him who receives it worthily?*
In him who receives it worthily, the Holy Eucharist preserves and increases grace, which is the life of the soul, just as food does for the life of the body. The Holy Eucharist takes away venial sins and preserves us from mortal sins. It gives spiritual joy and consolation by increasing charity and the hope of eternal life, of which it is the pledge (CCC 1394–95).

Develop

1. Finish reading the chapter with the students.

2. Ask the students to reflect on the time they have spent with Jesus in the Eucharist, either at Mass or before the tabernacle. Have them share their experiences.

3. Discuss Adoration and Benediction. If you have a monstrance or a picture of one, show the students how Jesus is placed in the monstrance for all to come and adore Him. Ask the students:
   - Why would people come to adore a host in a monstrance?
   - Why would Jesus want to be put on display?
   - Does seeing Jesus help us to pray?
   - Why is the monstrance so beautiful?
   - How is praying before the monstrance different from praying before the tabernacle?
   - When the priest blesses us with Jesus in the monstrance, Who is blessing us?

4. Review an Adoration/Benediction service. If possible, take the students to one. They will need to review the hymns "Tantum ergo" and "O salutaris Hostia." They may also sing: "Holy God we praise thy Name," and "O Lord I am not worthy."

5. Ask the students what types of things they can discuss with Jesus. He wants to hear about everything. Even though He already knows all, He wants to hear it from us. He wants the students to turn to Him in thanksgiving and petition. He loves them very much.

6. Explain that by adoring Jesus now on earth, we are preparing for Heaven, where we will be gathered around the throne of God, singing His praises.

7. Discuss the life of Saint Clare and her love for Jesus in the Eucharist.

Name:_____

Thanking God

When you love someone, you want to spend as much time with that person as you can. We get to know Jesus through Holy Communion, by visiting Him in church, and by praying to Him.

Write a letter thanking Jesus for His love and the gift of Himself.

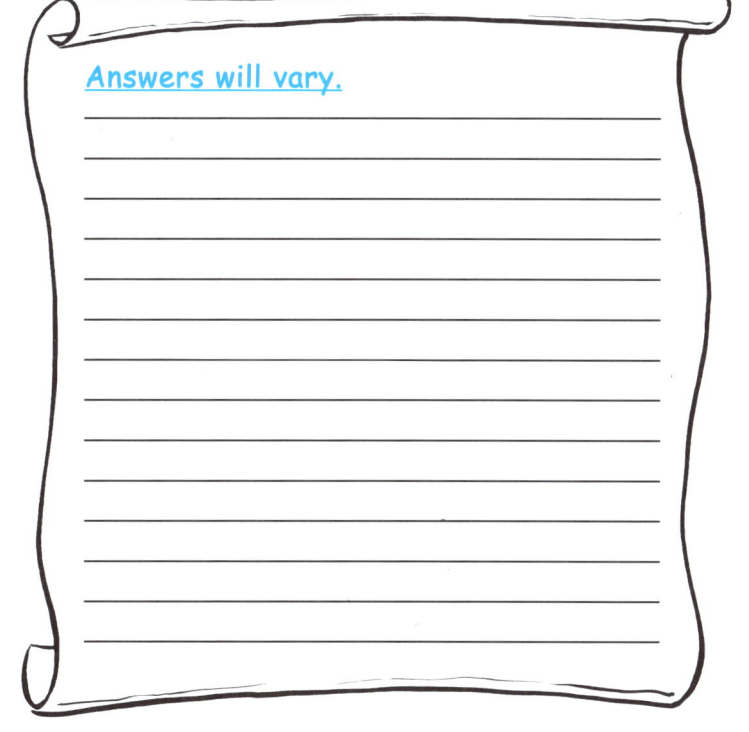

Answers will vary.

Faith and Life Series • Grade 3 • Chapter 24 • Lesson 4

Reinforce

1. Have the students work on *Activity Book*, p. 93.

2. Take the students to an Adoration and Benediction service.

3. Have the students work on their Memorization Questions and review for the quiz.

Conclude

1. Take the students to adoration, and lead them in singing "O Lord, I am not worthy," *Adoremus Hymnal*, #512.

2. Have the students take time for silent prayer. Lead them in offering up their petitions. Have them make a spiritual communion.

Preview

In the next lesson, the students' knowledge of the material covered this week will be reviewed and assessed.

SAINT CLARE AND THE EUCHARIST

The founder of the Poor Clares, Saint Clare was moved by Saint Francis to leave her comfortable noble home and take up the brown robes of the Franciscan.

Once, when her convent was about to be sacked by invaders attacking Assisi, Saint Clare placed the Holy Eucharist upon the top of the convent wall, praying to God to protect her helpless sisters. The invaders were frightened from their sacrilege and fled from the scene.

Today we can remember Clare's prayer of protection when we pray before the Holy Eucharist.

NOTES

CHAPTER TWENTY-FOUR
REVIEW AND ASSESSMENT

Aims

The students' knowledge and understanding of the material covered this week will be reviewed and assessed.

Materials

- Quiz 24, Appendix, p. A-34

Optional:
- "O Lord, I am not worthy," *Adoremus Hymnal*, #512

Review

1. The students should understand how the multiplication of loaves and fish and Jesus' Bread of Life discourse prepare us to better understand the Eucharist.

2. The students should know the steps to worthily receive Holy Communion. They must:
   - Be free from mortal sin
   - Fast for one hour
   - Know Whom they are to receive

3. The students should know the effects of Holy Communion upon the soul of the recipient.

4. The students should know about Adoration and Benediction.

5. They should know how to pray to Jesus in the Eucharist—that He is truly present, and therefore we may pray to Him and worship Him.

Name:

Jesus Comes to Us In the Holy Eucharist **Quiz 24**

"He who believes in me shall never thirst" (John 6:35).

Word Bank

bread	Life	5,000	Mass	God
close	listens	kind	grace	thanks

Fill in the blanks with the correct words from the Word Bank.

1. Jesus changed five loaves of bread and two fish into food for over **5,000** people.

2. He promised them a more wonderful bread when He said, "I am the **bread** of life; he who comes to me shall not hunger, and he who believes in me shall never thirst" (John 6:35).

3. The Holy Eucharist is the Bread of **Life** that Jesus promised.

4. We are so fortunate because we can receive the Holy Eucharist at every **Mass**.

5. For a worthy reception of Holy Communion, three things are necessary: to be in the grace of **God**, to realize and consider whom we are about to receive, and to observe the Eucharistic fast (CCC1385–88).

6. After we receive Jesus, we kneel down to make a thanksgiving. We give **thanks** to Jesus for being with us.

7. We silently pray to Him and He **listens**. If we are having trouble being kind or good, Jesus understands. He will help us.

8. Every time Jesus comes to us in Holy Communion, He fills our souls with His own life. God's life within us is called **grace**. Our venial sins are taken away.

9. When we receive the Holy Eucharist, our charity (our love for God and our neighbor) increases. We receive the strength to be generous, forgiving, and **kind**.

10. The best way to stay **close** to Jesus is to go to Mass and receive Holy Communion, even every day if possible.

11. Write out the Scripture verse shown at the top of this page.

A - 34   Faith and Life • Grade 3 • Appendix A

Assess

1. Distribute the quizzes and read through them with the students to be sure they understand the questions.

2. Administer the quiz. As they hand in their work, you may orally quiz the students on the Memorization Questions for this chapter.

3. After all the quizzes have been handed in, you may wish to review the correct answers with the class.

4. Repeat steps 1–3 with Unit 5 Quiz.

Conclude

End class by singing "O Lord, I am not worthy," *Adoremus Hymnal*, #512.

CHAPTER TWENTY-FIVE
JESUS RISES IN SPLENDOR

Catechism of the Catholic Church References

Ascension: 659–67
Easter as Central Christian Feast: 638, 1169
Historical and Transcendent Event of the Resurrection: 638–39, 656
Empty Tomb: 640, 657
Apparitions of the Risen One: 641–44
State of Christ's Risen Humanity: 645–46

Resurrection as Transcendent Event: 647
Peter as Pope: 881, 936
Prayer for the Dead: 1032, 1055
Presence of Christ in the Eucharist: 1373–81, 1410, 1418
Resurrection as a Work of the Holy Trinity: 648–55
Resurrection: Meaning and Consequences for Salvation: 658

Scripture References

Resurrection: Mt 29:1–10; Jn 20:19–29
Ascension: Acts 1

Peter as Pope: Mt 16:1–20

Background Reading: *The Fundamentals of Catholicism* by Fr. Kenneth Baker, S.J.

Volume 2:
"Jesus' Glorious Resurrection," pp. 304–7
"The Ascension of Jesus," pp. 308–11

Volume 3:
"The Primacy of St. Peter," pp. 107–10
"The Primacy of the Pope," pp. 110–13

Summary of Lesson Content

Lesson 1

On Easter Sunday some women went to Jesus' tomb to anoint His Body. They found the tomb empty. An angel announced that Jesus had risen.

The women announced to the Apostles that Jesus had risen. Peter and John ran to the tomb and found it empty.

Mary Magdalene was the first person to see Jesus risen.

Lesson 2

The disciples were gathered in an upper room when Jesus appeared among them.

Jesus said, "Peace be with you." He gave the Apostles the power to forgive sins.

Thomas said that in order to believe, he had to place his hand in Jesus' wounds.

Lesson 3

Jesus taught that His suffering and death leads to everlasting life.

On Easter Sunday, we celebrate the miracle of the Resurrection of Jesus, and rejoice because Jesus' death on the Cross destroyed death.

Lesson 4

Jesus stayed with His Apostles for 40 days.

Jesus forgave Peter and made him Pope.

Jesus taught the Apostles to go forth to baptize and teach all nations.

Jesus ascended into Heaven.

LESSON ONE: HE IS RISEN!

Aims

The students will become familiar with the biblical accounts of the risen Lord.

The students will learn about the reactions of Peter, John, and Mary Magdalene.

Materials

- *Activity Book*, p. 94
- Children's Bibles
- Craft supplies

Optional:
- "Christ the Lord is risen today," *Adoremus Hymnal*, #415

Begin

Ask what "Resurrection" means to the children. Resurrection is the act of rising from the dead. This means that one must die in order to be raised to new life. This is a great miracle! Only Jesus rose from the dead by His own power.

Have the children imagine what it would have been like to be Jesus' Apostles or friends on Good Friday. How sad they would have been to see Jesus on the Cross. How scared they would have been to see their Lord so mistreated. Do the children think they would have been confused? Did the Apostles doubt that Jesus was God? Imagine how they must have felt at finding the empty tomb.

---

25 Jesus Rises in Splendor

"In my Father's house are many rooms; if it were not so, would I have told you that I go to prepare a place for you? And when I go and prepare a place for you, I will come again and will take you to myself, that where I am you may be also."

John 14:2–3

Early on the Sunday morning after Jesus died, some women went to anoint His Sacred Body with spices and oils. But they arrived to find an empty tomb. The heavy stone that had sealed it was rolled away. And the body of Jesus was nowhere in sight. A beautiful angel told the women Jesus was no longer dead, but alive. "He is risen!" the angel said. "Rejoice and tell the others!"

The women ran to find the Apostles and tell them the news. Even though Jesus had told His friends that He would rise on the third day after His death, they were surprised. They wanted to see with their own eyes. Peter and John ran to the tomb and trembled with excitement to see that it was true. Only the burial cloths remained. Jesus had risen from the dead. He was alive!

We are told that the first person to whom Jesus appeared was Mary Magdalen, the holy woman, whose many sins He had forgiven. She was weeping in the garden near the tomb because she missed Him. Jesus softly called her by name. She looked up and cried, "Master!" Jesus also appeared to two disciples who were walking sadly in the country. Once the men realized it was Jesus, alive and well, they too raced to tell the Apostles.

Soon after, the **disciples** (followers of Jesus) were all gathered together in an upper room. The doors were locked. Suddenly Jesus

---

Develop

1. Begin by reading the first three paragraphs with the children.

2. Have the students dramatize the Easter story using a children's Bible as their guide: Mt 28:1–10; Mk 16:1–9; Lk 24:1–8; Jn 20:11–13.

3. After the students dramatize this play, ask each character the following questions:
   - What do you think your character felt before the Resurrection?
   - How do you think he felt after?
   - Do you think he doubted Jesus' Resurrection? Why or why not?
   - What did your character do once he learned of Jesus' Resurrection?

4. The students may make displays for each of their characters to illustrate how he responded to Jesus' Resurrection.

5. Discuss the importance of the Resurrection with the children. If Jesus rose from he dead, He is God. Through His death came new life, and through His suffering came great glory. Jesus died for our sakes and rose from the dead so that we, too, can rise with Him at the end of time. Jesus won eternal life for all of us. We can share in this by our Baptisms. When we go under the water we share in Jesus' death. When we come out of the water we share in Jesus' life. What a great mystery! Because of the glory of the Cross, we can find value in our sufferings. We can unite them with Jesus, crucified for the salvation of souls and to give God glory. Have the students give examples.

Name:_____

Jesus Christ is Risen Today

1. Who discovered that Jesus' tomb was empty?
   Some women. (Mary Magdalene, Mary the Mother of James, and Salome)

2. What did the angel say to the women?
   He told them, "He has risen! Rejoice and tell the others!"

3. What did the women do?
   They ran to the Apostles and told them.

4. Had Jesus told the Apostles that He would rise again?
   Yes. He had told them that He would rise again on the third day after His death.

5. Which Apostles first saw the empty tomb?
   Peter and John first saw the empty tomb.

6. To whom did Jesus first appear?
   Mary Magdalen

Faith and Life Series • Grade 3 • Chapter 25 • Lesson 1

Reinforce

1. Have the students work on *Activity Book*, p. 94.

2. Celebrate the Resurrection with a party.

3. Teach the students to sing "Christ the Lord is risen today," *Adoremus Hymnal*, #415.

Conclude

End class with the Prayer before the Crucifix, thanking Jesus for His death and Resurrection.

Preview

In the next lesson the students will lean about Jesus' appearance in the upper room.

Every suffering turns into glory	
My sufferings	My glory
Being made fun of	Reward in heaven
Being sick	Suffering with Christ
Being scolded by mistake	Gaining grace

NOTES

LESSON TWO: PEACE BE WITH YOU!

Aims

The students will learn that the disciples were gathered in an upper room when Jesus appeared among them.

They will learn that Jesus said, "Peace be with you!" and gave the Apostles the power to forgive sins.

They will learn how Thomas placed his hand in Jesus' wounds in order to believe.

Materials

- *Activity Book*, p. 95
- Children's Bible
- Box with some object inside

Optional:
- "Christ the Lord is risen today," *Adoremus Hymnal*, #415

Begin

Ask the children how the Apostles might have felt after the Resurrection of Jesus. Very likely people thought that they had stolen and hidden Jesus' body. The disciples must have wondered what Pilate would do to them, since he killed their leader. Remind the children that the Apostles did not stay with Jesus under the Cross. What would Jesus have to say to them after His Resurrection?

---

appeared among them! At first, the Apostles were afraid Jesus might be a ghost. But Jesus reassured them. "Peace be with you," He said. Then He ate with them. Their joy was great.

The Apostle named Thomas doubted Jesus. He was not with the others right after Jesus rose from the dead. He said, "Unless I see in His hands the print of the nails, touch them, and put my hand into His side, I will not believe."

When Jesus appeared in the upper room, He looked straight at Thomas. He said, "Put your finger here; look, here are My hands. Give me your hand; put it into My side, and believe." Thomas did so and then answered in awe, "My Lord and my God."

Jesus said: "Because you have seen Me, you believe. Blessed are those who have not seen, and yet have believed." Jesus was speaking about all of us. One day He will reward us for our faith.

Jesus taught us by His life that our suffering and death will be turned into glory and everlasting life. On **Good Friday**, He suffered and died on the Cross. But on Easter Sunday He arose from the dead in full splendor. Every **Easter**, we celebrate this miracle of the **Resurrection**: Jesus rising from the dead. We rejoice because Jesus' Sacrifice on the Cross destroyed death. Each of us will die one day, but our death will be only a doorway to Heaven. We will be alive for ever just like Jesus, Our Risen Lord.

121

Develop

1. Read paragraphs 4–7 with the students.

2. From a children's Bible, read John 20:19–31. What sacrament did Jesus institute in the upper room? Jesus gave His Apostles His peace and the Holy Spirit. He also gave them the power to forgive sins. This is called the Sacrament of Penance (also called reconciliation or confession). Why did Jesus say, "Peace be with you," to His Apostles? When we tell our sins to God and He forgives us through the ministry of the priest, we have peace in our souls again. What other effects are there to the Sacrament of Penance?
   - *Our sins are forgiven*
   - *We receive grace (God's life in us)*
   - *We are given the strength we need to overcome our sins*

3. Ask the students how the Apostles knew that Jesus was not a ghost after the Resurrection. *He ate and drank with them and Thomas put his finger in Jesus' wounds.*

4. Why would not Thomas believe? What proof did he need that Jesus rose from the dead? The students may dramatize this scene.

5. What did Jesus mean when he said, "Blessed are those who have not seen and yet believe" (Jn 20:29)?

6. Present a box to the children and tell them that there is something in it. Describe it to them and then ask them if they believe you. Some will while others will not. Open the box and show them the object. Ask them if they believe you now. Explain that if Thomas were here, he would need to see and feel what is in the box. If Thomas had told you what he had seen and felt, would we have believed him? Why? This is what happened to the Apostles. They have told us what happened at the Resurrection of Jesus and passed down their eye-witness accounts. These accounts have also been recorded in the Bible so we, too, can believe.

Name:_____

Resurrection Crossword Puzzle

Early on the Sunday morning after Jesus died, some women arrived at the tomb, but they found it (8 across). The heavy (3 down) that had sealed it was rolled (7 across). Jesus was no longer dead, but (11 across). "He is risen!" the angel said. "(17 down)! And go tell the others!" Jesus had told His friends that He would rise on the (2 down) day. In the Gospel accounts the first person to whom Jesus appeared was (5 down) Magdalene. She was weeping in the (6 across) near the tomb, when Jesus called her name. Later the disciples were all gathered together in an upper room with the doors (13 down). Suddenly (15 across) appeared! At first, the (11 down) were (12 across) Jesus might be a (9 across), but Jesus said, "Peace be with you..." On Good Friday, He had suffered and died on the (21 across), but on (8 down) Sunday He arose from the (22 across) in full splendor. "I will be with you (4 down), even to the end of time," He promised. No matter what happens to (20 down) on this earth, we can be full of (15 down) and (23 across). After His (16 across), Jesus Christ remained on earth (1 across) days. Then He (14 down) to (10 down) where He (3 across) (4 across) the right (18 across) of (19 down), the Father Almighty.

Faith and Life Series • Grade 3 • Chapter 25 • Lesson 2   95

Reinforce

1. Have the students put on a play about the Resurrection, using the various biblical Resurrection accounts. They may set the play in modern times or do a news interview with an Apostle, such as Thomas.

2. Have the students work on *Activity Book*, p. 95.

3. Have the students begin working on their Memorization Questions for this chapter.

Conclude

1. Lead the children in singing "Christ the Lord is risen today," *Adoremus Hymnal*, #415.

2. Lead the children in the Prayer before the Crucifix.

Preview

In the next lesson, the students will learn how we share in the resurrected life.

SAINT MARY MAGDALENE

Known as "The Penitent," Saint Mary Magdalene was a notorious Jewish sinner who lived among the gentiles. When she repented and showed her love for Jesus, He forgave her sins. She followed Christ and His Apostles after this and was present at the Crucifixion. She was the first to see the risen Jesus on Easter Sunday.

Not long after the Ascension, Saint Mary Magdalene was exiled, with several other early Christian saints, in a boat with no oars and no sails. She landed in France, where she lived as a holy hermit until her death.

NOTES

_____
_____
_____
_____
_____
_____
_____
_____
_____
_____

LESSON THREE: LIFE EVERLASTING

Aims

The students will learn that Jesus taught that His suffering and death leads to everlasting life.

They will learn that, on Easter Sunday, we celebrate the miracle of the Resurrection of Jesus and we rejoice because Jesus' death on the Cross destroyed death.

They will learn about the last things and the resurrected body.

Materials

- *Activity Book*, p. 96
- Children's Bible

Optional:
- "Christ the Lord is risen today," *Adoremus Hymnal*, #415

Begin

Read paragraph 8 with the children. Explain that death is the doorway to eternal life. It is not to be feared. The joys of Heaven are eternal, which means they will last forever. In Lesson 1 we learned that we receive God's life at Baptism. We need this life in order to go to Heaven. Today, we will learn more about the last things.

"Go therefore and make disciples of all nations, baptizing them in the name of the Father and of the Son and of the Holy Spirit . . . and lo, I am with you always, to the close of the age."

Matthew 28:19–20

After He rose from the dead, Jesus stayed among His disciples for forty days. He taught them more about the faith and their mission on earth. He told Peter, the first Pope, to "feed My sheep." He taught all of them to go out to teach and baptize. He promised He would send the Holy Spirit to help them.

Finally it was time for Jesus to go home to Heaven. "I will be with you always, even to the end of time," He promised. Then He rose up to Heaven and into glory. Jesus, the King of Heaven and earth, has prepared a place for us in Heaven, too. That is why, no matter what happens to us on this earth, we can be full of joy and hope.

Words to Know:

disciple   Good Friday   Easter   Resurrection

> **Q. 104** *What is the Resurrection?*
> The Resurrection is the fact that Christ is risen from the dead and has conquered death. Jesus rose from the dead on the first Easter Sunday, on the third day after his death on the Cross. The Resurrection is the crowning truth of our faith (CCC 638, 640–41).

Develop

1. Explain that death is when the body and the soul are separated. The soul lives forever! The body will die, but it will be raised to new life at the end of time.

2. Explain the particular judgment to the children. When we die, Jesus will judge all our thoughts, words, deeds, and omissions. If we have rejected God's love and mercy at the time of our deaths, then we will go to hell forever. Hell is a state of suffering because we are without God because of our sins. If we die in the friendship of God, but have not done enough penance in this life or still have to make up for some of our sins, we will be sent to a temporary state called Purgatory. The souls in Purgatory are purified and made perfectly pleasing to God so they can go to Heaven! If we die in perfect friendship with God and have made up for all our sins, then we will go to Heaven with the angels and the saints. There our souls will be perfectly happy forever with God.

3. At the end of time, when this world will end, Jesus will come again! At that time, Jesus will give a general judgment. All souls will be judged and given their eternal reward. Also, their bodies will be reunited with their souls because, as men, we have both bodies and souls. Our bodies will share in eternal life, just like Jesus, who rose body and soul into Heaven.

4. Our resurrected bodies will have special qualities. They will be beautiful spiritual bodies that will do whatever our wills desire, and there will be no temptation to sin. There will be no more suffering or death because our bodies, like our souls, will live forever. Compare these qualities with Jesus' resurrected body.

5. Read the story of Emmaus (Lk 24:13–48) aloud from a children's Bible. Point out that Jesus' Apostles did not recognize Him at first, but they did so in the Eucharist.

Name:_____

The Ascension

Color the picture.

Three days after His Crucifixion, Jesus rose from the dead. He appeared to His Apostles, and He was not a ghost! He had a resurrected and glorified body that could walk through walls and appear and disappear.

Faith and Life Series • Grade 3 • Chapter 25 • Lesson 3

JESUS' PRESENCE IN THE EUCHARIST:

- Same Jesus as was born of the Blessed Virgin Mary

- Body, Blood, Soul, and Divinity of Jesus

- Word made flesh

- Just as the disciples on the road to Emmaus did not recognize Jesus at first, we need faith to recognize Him in the Eucharist

- "Blessed are those who have not seen and yet believe" (Jn 20:29)

Reinforce

1. Have the students work on *Activity Book*, p. 96.

2. The students may draw pictures of the Resurrected Jesus and themselves in Heaven.

3. Have the students work on their Memorization Questions for this chapter.

Conclude

1. Lead the children in singing "Christ the Lord is risen today," *Adoremus Hymnal*, #415.

2. Have the students pray the Prayer before the Crucifix.

Preview

In the next lesson the students will learn about Jesus' time on earth between His Resurrection and Ascension into Heaven.

NOTES

_____
_____
_____
_____
_____
_____
_____
_____
_____
_____

LESSON FOUR: FORTY DAYS!

Aims

The students will learn that Jesus stayed with His Apostles for forty days after His Resurrection.

They will learn that during this time, Jesus forgave Peter, commissioned him to be Pope, and taught all the Apostles to go forth to baptize and teach all nations.

They will learn that Jesus then ascended into Heaven promising to send them the Holy Spirit.

Materials

- *Activity Book*, p. 97
- Children's Bible

Optional:
- "Christ the Lord is risen today," *Adoremus Hymnal*, #415

Begin

Recreate the chalk talk at the right on the chalkboard. The children may want you to be more specific with the post-Resurrection appearances of Jesus.

Q. 105 *How can we know that our suffering and death will be turned into glory and everlasting life?*
Jesus' Resurrection proves Jesus' works and teachings, His power and divine authority. By Jesus' death, we are freed from sin and death. By Jesus' rising from the dead, the way to new life is opened for us (CCC 651, 654).

Q. 106 *Why did Jesus make Peter the first Pope?*
Jesus made Peter the first Pope so that Peter and the Apostles with him could rule and govern the Church according to Jesus' will and teachings (CCC 816)

Q. 107 *Why did Jesus send His Apostles to teach and baptize all people?*
Jesus sent the Apostles to teach and baptize all people so that all people could share in Jesus' life through the Church (CCC 1213, 1229, 1257).

Q. 108 *What was the Ascension?*
The Ascension was the moment when Jesus rose bodily into Heaven to sit at the Father's right hand. The Ascension happened forty days after the Resurrection (CCC 659, 663).

WE PRAY TO GOD AT MASS:

Welcome into Your Kingdom our departed brothers and sisters, and all who have left this world in Your friendship.

123

Develop

1. Finish reading the chapter with the children.

2. Using a children's Bible, read the following passages:
- Peter is told to "feed my sheep" (Jn 21:3–19)
- Apostles are told to go forth and baptize (Mt 28:16–20)
- Promise of the Holy Spirit and the Ascension (Acts 1:1–11)

The students may dramatize these biblical accounts

3. Discuss the importance of each biblical account:

A) Peter is told to "feed my sheep"
- Recount how Peter denied Jesus three times and proclaimed his love three times in order to be forgiven
- Peter is made the Pope of the Church. He is the leader and servant of all Catholics
- Peter has a special role among all the Apostles. They are all bishops, but Peter is the Pope, to whom they turn for guidance on matters of faith and morals. He is Jesus' representative on earth

B) Jesus commissions the Apostles
- Jesus tells the Apostles to baptize and teach all nations
- Our faith is Catholic, which means universal. We all have a duty to proclaim the Gospel to everyone
- Baptism is necessary for salvation. In Baptism we die with Christ and rise with Him to everlasting life
- It is not enough to baptize, we must also learn all that Jesus taught from Scripture and Tradition (that which is passed on through the teachings of the Church)

C) Jesus promises to send the Holy Spirit
- The Holy Spirit gives God's life to the Church. The Holy Spirit is God and the Third Person of the Blessed Trinity. The Holy Spirit helps us to remember all that Jesus taught

D) Jesus ascends to Heaven
- We see Jesus go to Heaven and we receive the promise of His return

Name:_____

The Holy Spirit

Color the picture below.

Jesus stayed with His Apostles for forty days after His Resurrection to teach them more about the faith and their mission on earth. He told Peter, the first Pope, to "feed my sheep." He taught all of them to go out to teach and baptize in the Name of the Father, and of the Son, and of the Holy Spirit. He promised He would send the Holy Spirit to help them. Jesus and God the Father sent the Holy Spirit on Pentecost.

Faith and Life Series • Grade 3 • Chapter 25 • Lesson 4   97

CHALK TALK: TIME LINE

Chalk Talk

appearances to disciples — Jesus makes Peter the first pope — The Ascension

Resurrection — Jesus teaches — Jesus' teaching to go out and baptize — Jesus gives promise of the Holy Spirit

Forty days before the Ascension

Reinforce

1. Have the students work on *Activity Book*, p. 97.

2. Have the students work on their Memorization Questions for this chapter and begin reviewing for the quiz.

Conclude

1. Lead the children in singing "Christ the Lord is risen today," *Adoremus Hymnal*, #415.

2. End class with the Prayer before the Crucifix.

Preview

In the next lesson, the students' knowledge of the material covered in this chapter will be reviewed and assessed.

NOTES

_____
_____
_____
_____
_____
_____
_____
_____
_____
_____

CHAPTER TWENTY FIVE
REVIEW AND ASSESSMENT

Aims

The students' knowledge and understanding of the material covered in this chapter will be reviewed and assessed.

Materials

- Quiz 25, Appendix, p. A-35
- Unit 6 Quiz, Appendix, pp. A-36 and A-37

Optional:
- "Christ the Lord is risen today," *Adoremus Hymnal*, #415

Review

1. Review the Resurrection accounts as well as the stories of Jesus' appearances, which the students have learned.

2. Review the significance of the Resurrection and our promise for eternal life, which we gain through Baptism.

3. Review the qualities of the risen body of the Lord: beautiful, spiritual, conforms to soul/will, not bound by time or space, will not suffer or die.

4. Review the four last things: death, judgment, Heaven, and hell.

5. Jesus stayed on earth for forty days after His Resurrection to prepare the Apostles for their mission.

6. Jesus made Peter the first Pope.

7. Jesus told the Apostles to go forth to baptize and teach all nations.

8. Jesus promised to send the Holy Spirit.

9. Jesus ascended into Heaven. At this time, the angel promised Jesus' return in glory.

Name: _____

Jesus Rises in Splendor   Quiz 25

"I am with you always, to the close of the age" (Matthew 28:20).

Word Bank

| Apostles | risen | sins | Holy Spirit |
| Peace | Resurrection | forty | Sunday |

Fill in the blanks with the correct words from the Word Bank.

1. Early on the *Sunday* morning after Jesus died, some women went to anoint His Sacred Body with spices and oils.

2. A beautiful angel told the women that Jesus was no longer dead, but alive. "He is *risen*!" the angel said, "Rejoice and tell the others."

3. The women ran to find the *Apostles* and tell them the news. Peter and John ran to the tomb and found only the burial cloths. Jesus had risen from the dead. He was alive.

4. Jesus first appeared to Mary Magdalene, the holy woman whose many *sins* He had forgiven. He said her name as she was weeping in the garden near the tomb.

5. Soon after, the disciples were all gathered together in an upper room. Even though the doors were locked, Jesus appeared and said "*Peace* be with you."

6. The Apostle Thomas was not present and would not believe. When Jesus appeared again, Thomas said "My Lord and my *God*."

7. On Good Friday, Jesus suffered and died on the Cross. On Easter Sunday He rose from the dead. Every Easter, we celebrate this miracle of the *Resurrection*.

8. After He rose from the dead, Jesus stayed among His disciples for *forty* days.

9. He told Peter, the first Pope, to "feed my sheep." He told all of them to go out to teach and baptize. He promised He would send the *Holy Spirit* to help them.

Faith and Life • Grade 3 • Appendix A   A - 35

Assess

1. Distribute the quizzes and read through them with the students to be sure they understand the questions.

2. Administer the quiz. As they hand in their work you may orally quiz them on the Memorization Questions for this chapter.

3. After all the quizzes have been handed in, you may wish to review the correct answers with the class.

Conclude

1. Lead the children in singing "Christ the Lord is risen today," *Adoremus Hymnal*, #415.

2. End class with a prayer.

CHAPTER TWENTY-SIX
THE COMING OF THE HOLY SPIRIT

Catechism of the Catholic Church References

Ascension: 659–67
Belief in the Holy Spirit: 687–88
Christ's Spirit in the Fullness of Time: 717–30, 745–46
Church Manifested by the Holy Spirit: 767–68
Gifts of the Holy Spirit: 768, 798–801, 1830–31, 1845
Holy Spirit: 683–86, 742
    In Baptism: 1266

Names, Titles, and Symbols of the Holy Spirit: 691–701
Mission of the Apostles: 858–60, 869
Pentecost: The Holy Spirit and the Church: 726, 731–41, 746–47, 767–68, 830, 1076
Pope and Bishops: Successors of Peter and the Apostles: 861–62, 880–87, 935–38

Scripture References

Pentecost, the Birthday of the Church: Acts 2

Background Reading: *The Fundamentals of Catholicism* by Fr. Kenneth Baker, S.J.

Volume 1:
"The Holy Spirit: Lord and Giver of Life," pp. 90–92
"Worship of the Holy Spirit," pp. 95–97

Volume 3:
"The Soul of the Church," pp. 128–31

Summary of Lesson Content

Lesson 1

Ten days after the Ascension of Jesus, the Holy Spirit descended upon the Apostles at Pentecost.

The Apostles were filled with grace to do the will of God in spreading the Good News.

Lesson 2

Peter preached the Good News and three thousand people were baptized.

Pentecost is the birthday of the Church.

Lesson 3

The Holy Spirit lives in us, too. He came to live in us at our Baptism.

We are temples of the Holy Spirit.

Optional: Confirmation is an outpouring of this same Holy Spirit.

Lesson 4

We receive the gifts of the Holy Spirit. These gifts are:
- Wisdom
- Understanding
- Council
- Knowledge
- Piety
- Fortitude
- Fear of the Lord

LESSON ONE: PENTECOST

Aims

The students will learn that the Holy Spirit descended upon the Apostles at Pentecost ten days after Jesus' Ascension into Heaven.

The Apostles were filled with the grace to do the will of God in spreading the Good News.

The students will learn about novenas.

Materials

- *Activity Book*, p. 98
- Novena prayer to the Holy Spirit
- Craft supplies

Optional:
- Pictures of Pentecost and symbols of the Holy Spirit
- "Come, Holy Ghost, Creator blest," *Adoremus Hymnal*, #443

Begin

Begin class by explaining why the Apostles and Mary were in the upper room. Forty days after the Resurrection of Jesus (Ascension Thursday), the Apostles returned to the upper room to wait for the Holy Spirit that Jesus had promised to send to them.

Ask the children these questions:
- Did the Apostles know what to expect?
- Why was Mary there with them?
- What were the Apostles like before Pentecost?

Develop

1. Read the first paragraph with the children.

2. The Apostles and Mary prayed for nine days and then, on the tenth day, the Holy Spirit came. A nine-day prayer asking for something is called a novena. There are many novenas in the Catholic Church. You may show some of them to the children. Give all of them a copy of the Novena to the Holy Spirit.

3. Have the students pray this novena nine times throughout the class (paralleling the nine days the Apostles prayed).

4. For what do the children think the Apostles were praying?
- *Courage?*
- *The ability to do the work Jesus wanted of them?*
- *Love?*

5. Have the students dramatize the story of Pentecost. Have one girl be Mary and some boys be the Apostles. You may assign "sound-effects" to some children, and give one the job of putting "tongues of fire" on the heads of all the Apostles and Mary. You may read the story in Acts 2 from a children's Bible.

6. Remind the children that the Holy Spirit is God and the Third Person of the Blessed Trinity. He brings God's life to the Church and to our souls. The Holy Spirit is the love between the Father and the Son.

7. The Holy Spirit came as tongues of fire at Pentecost. What other symbols are used for the Holy Spirit?
- *Dove*
- *Hand of God*
- *Eye of God*
- *Finger of God*
- *Wind*
- *Fire/light*

Discuss each of these symbols with the children, using pictures if possible.

---

26 The Coming of The Holy Spirit

"And the Spirit of the LORD shall rest upon him, the spirit of wisdom and understanding, the spirit of counsel and might, the spirit of knowledge and the fear of the LORD."

Isaiah 11:2

After Jesus rose up to Heaven on **Ascension** Thursday, the Apostles prayed and waited with Mary. They all stayed together in one home. Ten days later, a strong wind suddenly swept through the house. A bright flame of fire appeared over each one. These wonderful signs happened as the **Holy Spirit**, Who is God, the Third Person of the Holy Trinity, came into their hearts. The Holy Spirit filled them with courage and love.

The people outside heard the wind and gathered to listen. Peter and the other Apostles came out of the house in great excitement. They were full of joy and hope. The Holy Spirit created in them such a deep desire to carry on Jesus' work, that they began preaching at once. The Holy Spirit also gave them the power to speak in a way that all people could understand them. Men, women, and children of many countries and languages discovered the Good News that day for the first time.

Peter called out, "Men of Judea and all you who dwell in Jerusalem, hear these words: Jesus of Nazareth was a man sent among you by God. You know this by His miracles, signs, and wonders. God allowed Him to be crucified on a Cross. But now He has raised Him up again. We have seen Him. And now, from Heaven, He has poured out the Holy Spirit as His Father promised."

125

Name:_____

Pentecost

Color the picture below.

98   Faith and Life Series • Grade 3 • Chapter 26 • Lesson 1

HOLY SPIRIT PRAYER

Come Holy Spirit, fill the hearts of your faithful, and kindle in them the fire of Your Divine Love. Send forth Your Spirit and they shall be created, and You shall renew the face of the earth. Oh God, Who by the light of the Holy Spirit instructed the hearts of the faithful, grant that by the same Spirit we may be truly wise and ever rejoice in His consolation. We ask this through Christ Our Lord. *Amen.*

Reinforce

1. Have the children color *Activity Book*, p. 98.

2. Have the students make posters of the various symbols for the Holy Spirit. Each poster should also provide an explanation of the symbols.

3. Have the students present their finished posters to the class

Conclude

1. Teach the students to sing "Come, Holy Ghost, Creator blest," *Adoremus Hymnal*, #443.

2. Pray the Holy Spirit prayer. (See below left.)

Preview

In the next lesson, the students will learn about the Holy Spirit in the ministry of the Apostles.

NOTES

_____
_____
_____
_____
_____
_____
_____
_____
_____
_____

LESSON TWO:
LIFE OF THE CHURCH

Aims

The students will learn how the Holy Spirit gave graces and strength to the Apostles to help them fulfill their mission.

They will learn that Peter preached the Good News and that three thousand people were baptized in one day.

They will learn that Pentecost is the birthday of the Church.

Materials

- *Activity Book*, p. 99
- Birthday cake, candles, plates, and forks

Optional:
- "Come, Holy Ghost, Creator blest," *Adoremus Hymnal*, #443

Begin

Ask the children what would have been some of the obstacles for the Apostles to preach to the whole world and baptize all people:
- People might not want to be baptized
- The Apostles did not know what to say to them
- The Apostles did not speak their language
- The Apostles did not have any travel arrangements
- People were not ready to do Jesus' will

"What must we do?" the people asked. Peter answered, "Repent and be baptized, every one of you, in the name of Jesus Christ for the forgiveness of your sins, and you will receive the gift of the Holy Spirit. This promise is for you and your children, and for all those, everywhere, whom the Lord Our God calls to Himself." That **Pentecost** Sunday, three thousand people were baptized and the Church was born.

We do not hear a great wind or see tongues of fire, but the Holy Spirit is with us, too. He came to live in us on the day we were baptized. That is why we call ourselves temples of the Holy Spirit. We are His dwelling place.

> "Like mirrors we reflect the glory of the Lord. We grow brighter and brighter as we are changed into the image of Jesus. This is the work of the Holy Spirit."
>
> adapted from 2 Corinthians 3:18

Develop

1. Read paragraphs 2–4 with the children.

2. Using the student text, show how the Holy Spirit removed many of the obstacles for the Apostles:
- *Peter and the Apostles were excited to do Jesus' will and work*
- *They began preaching at once by the inspiration of the Holy Spirit*
- *They spoke in all the languages of the people there, which was a miracle. Imagine being able to speak German, Spanish, and French without studying these languages*
- *People were curious and wanted to hear the Gospel*
- *There were people from many countries because there was a great feast day for the Jews in Jerusalem*

3. What did Saint Peter preach?
- *Jesus was sent by God (as proven by miracles)*
- *Jesus was crucified and resurrected (he was a witness)*
- *Jesus went to Heaven and sent the Holy Spirit as promised*
You might explain this as a little Creed

4. What did Peter tell people that they must do?
- *Repent of their sins (confess and turn away from them)*
- *Be baptized in the name of Jesus Christ for the forgiveness of sins (Note: Baptism brought about the forgiveness of sins)*
- *Receive the Holy Spirit*
Remember that 3000 people were were baptized in one day

5. Why do we call Pentecost the birthday of the Church?
A birthday is a day we celebrate the new life of someone or the anniversary of the beginning of a new life. The Church was brought to life by the Holy Spirit who inspired the Apostles and the people to respond with open hearts. Even though the Church had been growing through Jesus' work—His teachings and plans—it came to life by the Holy Spirit at Pentecost. Celebrate Pentecost with a party.

Name:_____

1. When the Holy Spirit came into the hearts of the Apostles, what did people hear?
<u>They heard a strong wind.</u>
2. How did the Holy Spirit appear to the Apostles?
<u>The Holy Spirit appeared as tongues of fire.</u>
3. What did the Holy Spirit give the Apostles a desire to do?
<u>The Holy Spirit gave them a desire to carry on Jesus' work.</u>
4. How could all the people (even those from other nations) understand the Apostles?
<u>The Holy Spirit gave them the power to speak in a way that all people could understand.</u>
5. What day can we say is the birthday of the Church?
<u>Pentecost</u>

Faith and Life Series • Grade 3 • Chapter 26 • Lesson 2

Reinforce

1. Have the students work on *Activity Book*, p. 99.

2. Have the students make up speeches they would give if they were missionaries.

3. Have the students work on their Memorization Questions for this chapter.

Conclude

1. Lead the children in singing "Come, Holy Ghost, Creator blest," *Adoremus Hymnal*, #443.

2. Pray the novena prayer to the Holy Spirit.

Preview

In the next lesson, the students will learn about receiving the Holy Spirit.

THE HOLY SPIRIT IN THE LIFE OF MARY

"And Mary said to the angel, 'How can this be, since I have no husband?' And the angel said to her, 'The Holy Spirit will come upon you, and the power of the Most High will overshadow you . . .'" (Lk 1:34–35).

The Blessed Virgin Mary had an experience of the Holy Spirit that defies imagining. Filled with the Holy Spirit, she became the Mother of the Son of God.

Throughout her life on earth, Mary was guided by the Holy Spirit as a guide and companion.

NOTES
_____
_____
_____
_____
_____
_____
_____
_____
_____
_____

LESSON THREE: COME HOLY GHOST

Aims

The students will learn that the Holy Spirit lives in us, too. He first came to live in us at our Baptisms.

The students will learn about our great dignity as temples of the Holy Spirit.

Optional: The students may learn about the Sacrament of Confirmation as an outpouring of the Holy Spirit.

Materials

- *Activity Book*, p. 100
- Overhead projector, pencil, chart paper, tape, craft supplies
- Pictures (see the Begin section)

Optional:
- "Come, Holy Ghost, Creator blest," *Adoremus Hymnal*, #443

Begin

Show the students pictures of beautiful things and places such as rivers, mountains, Notre Dame des Paris, the Eiffel Tower, a cute puppy, or outer-space. Do not show them pictures of people. Explain to the children that although these things are beautiful, each and every one of the students is more beautiful and precious in the eyes of God because He lives in them. We are His temples.

Develop

1. Read paragraph 5 with the students.

2. Explain that we first receive the Holy Spirit at Baptism. When we receive God's life in us, the Holy Spirit comes to dwell in our souls. This is a great gift from God. We should take time to thank God for this gift and think about what an awesome grace this is!

3. Ask the children how they can keep the Holy Spirit living in their souls:
   - By receiving the Eucharist, praying, and doing good works

4. Ask the children how they lessen or remove the life of God in their souls:
   - They lessen the life of God in their souls by committing venial sin and remove the life of God by committing mortal sin

5. How can the life of the Holy Spirit be restored to our souls?
   - The Sacrament of Penance and perfect contrition for our sins

6. At Confirmation, you will receive an outpouring of the Holy Spirit and His gifts. He will make you, like the Apostles at Pentecost, capable of doing Jesus' work here on earth for the Church. He will help us live in a way that is pleasing to God. We will be called to witness to the truth of the Gospel, to worship God with all our hearts, and to trust in His love and mercy.

7. We are temples of the Holy Spirit, which calls us to great dignity. We must never act in a way that is displeasing to God. Having the Holy Spirit in us is a great grace, for He will lead us to God and Heaven. Have the students think of things they should and should not do.

"The fruit of the Spirit is love, joy, peace, patience, kindness, goodness, faithfulness."
— Galatians 5:22

Like the people baptized on Pentecost Sunday, we receive gifts from the Holy Spirit. The Holy Spirit teaches all truth and helps us to understand our lessons about our faith. He inspires us to love others, even when it is hard. He helps us to know and be sorry for our sins. He gives us the grace to be both strong and gentle like Jesus. He is with us always, wherever we go.

Words to Know:

Ascension   Holy Spirit   Pentecost

Q. 109 *What is Pentecost?*
Pentecost was the day when the Holy Spirit was poured out upon the hiding Apostles, bringing God's life to the Church. Pentecost happened ten days after the Ascension (CCC 731, 739).

Q. 110 *What is the role of the Holy Spirit in the Church?*
The Holy Spirit completes the mission of Jesus in the Church. The Holy Spirit prepares men to draw people to communion with God (CCC 737).

Name: _____

Pentecost

1. When did Jesus rise up to Heaven?
Jesus rose to Heaven on Ascension Thursday.
2. What did the Apostles do after the Ascension?
The Apostles prayed and waited with Mary.
3. How did the Holy Spirit come?
The Holy Spirit came as a strong wind and as tongues of fire.
4. What gifts did the Holy Spirit give to the Apostles?
The Holy Spirit gave them courage and love.
5. What did Peter preach?
Peter preached the good news that Jesus had been sent to them by God; that He had died on the Cross and rose again. He then sent them the Holy Spirit.
6. How many people were baptized?
3000
7. What do we call the day when the Holy Spirit came?
Pentecost
8. When does the Holy Spirit come to us?
Baptism
9. What gifts does the Holy Spirit give to each of us?
The Holy Spirit teaches us the truth, helps us to love others and be sorry for our sins, and gives us the grace to be strong and gentle like Jesus.

100 Faith and Life Series • Grade 3 • Chapter 26 • Lesson 3

Reinforce

1. Have the students work on *Activity Book*, p. 100

2. Have the students work on the Temples of the Holy Spirit activity described at the bottom left of this page.

3. Have the students work on the Memorization Questions for this chapter.

Conclude

1. Lead the children in singing "Come, Holy Ghost, Creator blest," *Adoremus Hymnal*, #443.

2. End class by praying to the Holy Spirit.

Preview

In the next lesson, the students will learn about the gifts of the Holy Spirit.

TEMPLES OF THE HOLY SPIRIT ACTIVITY

Have each of the students take a turn sitting on a stool in front of a sheet of chart paper.

Using the overhead projector to create a silhouette, trace the outline of each child's profile.

Have the students decorate the pictures of their profiles, showing how they are temples of the Holy Spirit.

You may wish to suggest some symbols for the Holy Spirit, such as fire or a dove.

(continued, see p. 259)

NOTES

LESSON FOUR: GOD'S GIFTS

Aims

The students will learn about the gifts of the Holy Spirit:
- Wisdom
- Understanding
- Council
- Knowledge
- Piety
- Fortitude
- Fear of the Lord

Materials

- *Activity Book*, p. 101
- Craft supplies

Optional:
- "Come, Holy Ghost, Creator blest," *Adoremus Hymnal*, #443

Begin

Read the rest of the chapter with the students. Ask the students to think of gifts that the Holy Spirit brings to our souls:
- Love
- Strength
- Awareness of the truth
- Sorrow for sin
- Understanding of our faith
- His presence with us

They may think of ones already mentioned in the chapter.

Q. 111 *When did you receive the Holy Spirit?*
I received the Holy Spirit when I was baptized (CCC 1257).

SONG OF PRAISE

Come, Holy Ghost, Creator blest,
   And in our hearts take up Your rest.
Come with Your grace and heavenly aid
   To fill the hearts which You have made.

Come, Holy Spirit, fill the hearts of Your faithful, and kindle in them the fire of Your love.

Develop

1. Explain that the Holy Spirit brings us many gifts. We should use them to grow closer to God. The greatest gifts that the Holy Spirit brings us are the virtues of faith, hope, and charity. These are called the theological virtues:
   - **Faith** helps us to believe all that God has revealed
   - **Hope** helps us to trust in God's revelations
   - **Charity** helps us to love God above all else and to love God in our neighbors because they are also temples of the Holy Spirit

2. Next, the Holy Spirit gives us special gifts called the gifts of the Holy Spirit. There are seven. As you go through them, have the students think of examples for each:
   - **Wisdom**: to see things as God sees them, to see the truth and know how to respond to it
   - **Understanding**: to be able to have a caring heart, to see God in others and to love them
   - **Council**: to be able to make good decisions, to know right from wrong, and to choose to do good
   - **Knowledge**: to know and understand our faith in order that we may live it well
   - **Piety**: to love God in our worship. This does not mean to "show off" at prayer, but rather to love God sincerely and to serve Him faithfully in humility
   - **Fortitude**: to do what is right even when it is hard to do so
   - **Fear of the Lord**: to know that God is almighty and that we are His dependent creatures. We should always be aware of His presence, obey His laws, and desire never to offend Him

Name: _____

Gifts of the Holy Spirit

1. WISDOM: the ability to see things as they really are.
2. UNDERSTANDING: means that your heart cares, listens, and encourages.
3. KNOWLEDGE: the ability to learn the faith and know the truth.
4. COUNSEL: the ability to make good decisions.
5. PIETY: means we have a deep love for God and His creation.
6. FORTITUDE: means we have the courage to do what is right.
7. FEAR OF THE LORD: means that we understand the greatness of God and that He is very near to us.

Name the gift of the Holy Spirit for each sentence.

1. I pray my Rosary every day. **Piety**
2. I forgive my friend for hurting my feelings. **Understanding**
3. I practice piano before going out to play. **Counsel**
4. I will not tell a lie because God hears everything. **Fear of the Lord**
5. I tell my friends not to make fun of someone. **Fortitude**
6. I pay attention at Mass. **Piety**
7. I studied hard for religion class and did well on a test. **Knowledge**
8. I would not steal because I know it is a sin. **Counsel**
9. I learned about God's laws and the sacraments. **Knowledge**
10. I feel bad about homeless people. **Understanding**
11. I see the greatness of God in everything around me. **Wisdom**

Faith and Life Series • Grade 3 • Chapter 26 • Lesson 4   101

Reinforce

1. Give the students time to complete their "Temple of the Holy Spirit" collages/pictures. Allow them to make presentations on their work.

2. Have the students work on *Activity Book*, 101.

3. Give them time to work on their Memorization Questions for this chapter and review for their quiz.

Conclude

1. Lead the children in singing "Come, Holy Ghost, Creator blest," *Adoremus Hymnal*, #443.

2. End class with a prayer to the Holy Spirit.

Preview

In the next lesson, the students' knowledge of the material covered in this chapter will be reviewed and assessed.

TEMPLES OF THE HOLY SPIRIT (continued)

Make a display of the Temples of the Holy Spirit pictures that the students worked on in the last class. Let the children make presentations on their pictures. Each child should explain why he chose to draw what he did to depict himself as a temple of the Holy Spirit.

Possible questions to the student might be:
- Why did you choose (X) to show the Holy Spirit?
- What do all these things say about you?
- As a temple of the Holy Spirit, what do you think makes you unique?
- What part of you is most pleasing to God?

NOTES

CHAPTER TWENTY SIX
REVIEW AND ASSESSMENT

Aims

The students' knowledge and understanding of the material covered in this chapter will be reviewed and assessed.

Materials

- Quiz 26, Appendix, p. A-38

Optional:
- "Come, Holy Ghost, Creator blest," *Adoremus Hymnal*, #443

Review

1. The students should know that the Apostles and Mary prayed for nine days after the Ascension of Jesus. On the tenth day, the Holy Spirit came. This day is called Pentecost.

2. When the Holy Spirit came, there was a loud wind and He descended like tongues of fire upon each of the Apostles and Mary. He brought many gifts so that they could do Jesus' work here on earth.

3. Peter preached the Good News and 3000 people were baptized that day. Pentecost is therefore called the birthday of the Church.

4. We receive the Holy Spirit at our Baptisms, and we are, therefore, temples of the Holy Spirit. We receive an outpouring of this same Spirit at Confirmation.

5. The Holy Spirit brings many gifts including the theological virtues of Faith, Hope, and Charity, and the gifts of the Holy Spirit: wisdom, understanding, council, knowledge, piety, fortitude, and fear of the Lord.

Name: _____

The Coming of The Holy Spirit — Quiz 26

"Do you not know that you are God's temple and that God's Spirit dwells in you?" (1 Corinthians 3:16).

Word Bank

| Ascension | temples | courage | miracles | Pentecost |
| flame | Heaven | baptized | Apostles | |

Fill in the blanks with the correct words from the Word Bank.

1. After Jesus rose up to Heaven on **Ascension** Thursday, the Apostles and Mary stayed together praying.

2. Ten days later, a strong wind suddenly swept through the house. A bright **flame** appeared over each one of the Apostles and Mary, the Mother of Jesus.

3. God the Holy Spirit, the Third Person of the Holy Trinity, came into their hearts and filled them with **courage** and love.

4. The **Apostles** began preaching at once. The Holy Spirit gave them the power to speak in a way that people of every language could understand.

5. Peter told the people, "Repent, and be **baptized**, every one of you in the name of Jesus Christ for the forgiveness of your sins, and you shall receive the gift of the Holy Spirit."

6. On that day of **Pentecost**, three thousand people were baptized. The people received the gifts of the Holy Spirit, as we received them when we were baptized.

7. The Holy Spirit came to live within us on the day we were baptized. We are **temples** of the Holy Spirit. He inspires us to love others, even when it seems difficult.

Assess

1. Distribute the quizzes and read through them with the students to be sure they understand the questions.

2. Administer the quiz. As they hand in their work you may orally quiz them on the Memorization Questions for this chapter.

3. After all the quizzes have been handed in you may wish to review the correct answers with the class.

Conclude

1. Lead the children in singing "Come, Holy Ghost, Creator blest," *Adoremus Hymnal*, #443.

2. End class with a prayer.

CHAPTER TWENTY-SEVEN
GOD'S FAMILY ON EARTH

Catechism of the Catholic Church References

Christ's Missionary Mandate: 849–56, 868
Christian Holiness: 2012–16, 2028–29
Church as the Body of Christ: 669, 787–96, 805–8
Church's Hierarchical Constitution: 871–96, 934–39, 1556–69
Church's Origin, Foundation, and Mission: 758–69, 778
Consecrated Life: 915–19, 931–33, 944–45
    Eremetical Life: 920–21
    Consecrated Virgins: 922–24
    Religious Life: 925–27
    Secular Institutes: 928–29

Societies of Apostolic Life: 930
Ecclesial Ministry: 874–79
Episcopal College and its Head, the Pope: 880–87
    Task of Teaching: 888–92
    Task of Sanctifying: 893
    Task of Governing: 894–96
Martyrdom: 2473–74, 2506
Meaning of "Catholic": 830–31
Mission of the Apostles: 858–60, 869
Vocation of the Laity: 782–86, 898–913, 928–39, 940–43

Scripture References

Missionary Mandate: Mt 28:18–20
Duties of a Bishop: 1 Tim 3:1–7

Tend the Flock of God: 1 Pet 5:1–4

Background Reading: *The Fundamentals of Catholicism* by Fr. Kenneth Baker, S.J.

Volume 3:
"A Hierarchical Church," pp. 101–4
"Bishops Are Successors of the Apostles," pp. 104–7

"What Is a Bishop?" pp. 119–22
"Church and World," pp. 158–60

Summary of Lesson Content

Lesson 1

Jesus founded the Church on earth, and entrusted her to the care and work of the Apostles.

Peter was given the role of leader in the Church.

Lesson 2

The Pope is the vicar of Christ.

All Popes can trace their lineage to Peter, the first Pope.

The Pope is the head of all bishops.

A bishop carries out the work of the Apostles: he teaches, guides, and preaches to a church in a geographical region called a diocese.

Lesson 3

Each bishop has many priests to help him. Priests bring us the grace of the sacraments.

Priests work in our parishes and neighborhoods.

There are missionary priests and religious brothers and sisters who also bring the good news to people.

God calls these people to serve His Church.

Lesson 4

The laity are the baptized in the Church. We help the priests to bring the Gospel out into the world.

Martyrs are people who witness through the laying down of their lives for the truth.

We are all destined for Heaven.

We are the Mystical Body of Christ.

LESSON ONE: THE POPE

Aims

The students will learn that Jesus founded the Church on earth and entrusted her to the care and work of the Apostles.

They will learn that Peter was the leader of the Church. His successor, the Pope, has the same role today.

Materials

- *Activity Book*, p. 102
- Catholic periodicals or diocesan newspapers
- Children's Bible

Optional:
- "The Church's one foundation," *Adoremus Hymnal*, #560

Begin

Hand out Catholic periodicals to the students. Point out a picture of the Pope and name him. Ask the children to find and read an article about the Pope and then report on it. After their reports, ask the children what the Pope does. Write descriptive words about the Pope and His ministry on the board.

---

27 God's Family on Earth

Now you are the body of Christ and individually members of it.
    1 Corinthians 12:27

Jesus founded the **Church** on earth, and He is her King. But before He ascended into Heaven, He asked His Apostles to spend the rest of their lives continuing His work. He gave them the power to teach and to guide the Church. He asked them to follow His footsteps in bringing truth, love, and grace into the world.

All of the Apostles embraced this mission, but Peter's mission was even greater. One day Jesus told him, "You are Peter and upon this rock I will build My Church. And the gates of Hell shall not prevail against it. I will entrust to you the keys of the Kingdom of Heaven. Whatever you declare bound on earth will be bound in Heaven."

With these words, Jesus invited Peter to take His place on earth. Peter accepted Christ's call. He became the first Pope, the head of the whole Church. Ever since that time, the Church has had an unbroken line of Popes to lead and guide her. We call the Pope the Vicar of Christ because he represents Jesus. Jesus Himself gave him that power. That is why Catholics everywhere respect and obey him.

The Pope is also the head of bishops all over the world. A bishop is like the Good Shepherd that Jesus spoke of in the Gospel. He watches over his flock, protecting it from danger. Today thousands of bishops all over the world carry on the work of the Apostles. They teach, preach, and guide. They deliver the message of Jesus. They explain the rules of the Church. They tell us how to avoid sin and lead good lives.

129

Develop

1. Read paragraphs 1–3 with the children.

2. Ask the children Who founded the Church. Tell them that Jesus founded the Church. Ask them Who gives life to the Church. Tell them that the Holy Spirit gives life to the Church. Who guides the Church in the absence of Jesus? The Pope. Who was the first Pope? Saint Peter. Who is the Pope now? Show his lineage to Saint Peter.

3. Read the story of the giving of keys to Saint Peter from the children's Bible in Mt 16:13–20. The students may dramatize this scene.

4. The keys are a sign of authority. Whoever has the keys can allow someone in or lock someone out. In the olden days, a master gave his keys to his top man or aide who would be responsible in his absence, like a vice president. The Pope is the Vicar of Christ.

5. What jobs does the Pope have? He must proclaim the truth in matters of faith and morals, which means he must uphold what we believe as Catholics. This is very important today, when not everything we must face is in the Bible. For example, human cloning is not in the Bible, but the Pope, who speaks on behalf of the Church, says that it is wrong.

The Pope must work with all the other bishops. Sometimes all the bishops meet with the Pope and together they teach the truth. These meetings are called ecumenical councils. There are also times when the Pope teaches the truth without all the other bishops. At these times he speaks ex cathedra (from the chair, i.e., with the authority, of Peter). He has done this twice to teach about Mary's Immaculate Conception and her Assumption into Heaven.

6. The Pope is infallible (protected from teaching error) when he teaches on matters of faith and morals.

Name:_____

The Pope

**Pope John Paul II,
The Successor of Saint Peter.**

Color the picture below.

102   Faith and Life Series • Grade 3 • Chapter 27 • Lesson 1

Reinforce

1. Have the students work on *Activity Book*, p. 102.

2. Have the students make their presentations on the Pope.

3. Teach the children to sing "The Church's one foundation," *Adoremus Hymnal*, #560.

Conclude

End class with a prayer for the Pope. Pray for the Holy Spirit to guide him and for good health.

Preview

In the next lesson the students will learn about bishops.

LIFE OF JOHN PAUL II

Pope John Paul II was born Karol Józef Wojtyla in a small town outside Cracow, Poland on May 18, 1920. Losing both of his parents and his elder brother by 1941, Karol was forced by the Nazis to work in a stone quarry. Nonetheless, it was during the disastrous days of World War II that he heard the call to the priesthood and studied secretly with the Archbishop of Cracow.

After the war he became a scholarly priest and was eventually made Archbishop of Cracow and later a Cardinal. As a Cardinal he took part in many of the important discussions of Vatican II, and was elected Pope in October of 1978.

NOTES

_____
_____
_____
_____
_____
_____
_____
_____
_____
_____
_____

LESSON TWO: BISHOPS

Aims

The students will learn that the Pope is the head of all bishops.

The students will learn the role of the bishops. A bishop continues the work of the Apostles: he teaches, guides, and preaches to a church in a geographical region called a diocese.

Materials

- *Activity Book*, p. 103
- A picture of the twelve Apostles
- Map of the world and of a diocese

Optional:
- "The Church's one foundation," *Adoremus Hymnal*, #560

Begin

Hold up a picture of the twelve Apostles. Point out Judas, the one who betrayed Jesus.

Next, point out Saint Peter, who was the first Pope. He acts as Jesus' representative on earth. All Popes can trace their lineage back to Saint Peter.

All the other Apostles were bishops. Even today the Pope is a bishop. He is the leader of the bishops. From the Apostles all bishops can trace their ordinations.

"I am the vine, you are the branches."

John 15:5

Each bishop has the help of many priests. Priests are very important to the Church because they bring us the grace of the sacraments. They share in the God-given power to forgive sins and offer Holy Mass. We are fortunate to have priests in our parishes, schools, and neighborhoods. Jesus comes into our lives through them.

Other priests bring the light of Christ to faraway parts of the earth. They are joined by **religious** sisters and brothers who want to give their whole lives to God by teaching and helping others. They are called **missionaries**. They make the Church rich in blessings by their sacrifices and love.

Bishops, priests, sisters, and brothers are called by God to serve the Church in a special way. God calls all of us to do special things in the Church, too. When we go to Mass every Sunday to pray and worship, we are answering God's call. When we learn about His Word and obey His Commandments, we are serving and loving Him. God wants parents and children and other people in the world to build up His Kingdom just as He calls priests and religious brothers and sisters. We are called the laity of the Church. We are baptized, believing members of God's family.

The laity help the bishops and priests in bringing the Word of God to all people. Sometimes in doing this work people are asked to offer their lives. We call these people **martyrs**. Faith in Christ means so much to them that they risk even death to proclaim it. Jesus said that when men persecute His followers for His name's sake, He will bless His followers with great reward in Heaven.

Develop

1. Read paragraph 4 with the children.

2. On a regional map, point out your diocese to the children. You may actually have a map of the diocese in your diocesan directory. Explain that a diocese is a geographical region for which a bishop is responsible.

3. A bishop is an apostle. He teaches, preaches to, and guides all the people in his diocese. He protects them from error. He is a good shepherd, like Jesus.

4. Each bishop has a cathedral church (like his home parish). At the cathedral, there is a special chair for the bishop. He usually will celebrate Mass at the cathedral. However, the bishop is responsible for all churches in his diocese.

5. Bishops must work with the Pope. Together they teach the truths of the Church. Sometimes all the bishops of the world meet with the Pope in an ecumenical council. During these councils they discuss things of importance for the whole Church. They must only teach what the Pope agrees with, though, because the Pope is the head of the Church.

6. The Pope is a bishop. He is bishop of the Diocese of Rome. Point to Rome on a map and show the children how far it is from your diocese.

7. We must all be obedient to our bishops and to the Pope. They are doing their best to help us to grow closer to Jesus and to serve His Church here on earth.

8. Using a local Catholic newspaper, have the students do research on their bishop. They should make presentations to the class. They should include a picture and tell how long he has been bishop and when he last visited your parish.

Name:_____

People in the Church

Write sentences using these words.

Church: **Answers will vary.**
_____

Catholic: _____
_____

Religious: _____
_____

Missionary: _____
_____

Martyr: _____
_____

Bishop: _____
_____

Pope: _____
_____

Saint: _____
_____

Disciples: _____
_____

Laity: _____
_____

Priest: _____
_____

Faith and Life Series • Grade 3 • Chapter 27 • Lesson 2

Reinforce

1. Have the students make presentations on their bishop.

2. Have the students work on *Activity Book*, p. 103. This will be helpful for the next lesson.

3. Have the students begin working on the Memorization Questions for this chapter.

Conclude

1. Lead the children in singing "The Church's one foundation," *Adoremus Hymnal*, #560.

2. End class with a prayer for your bishop. Pray for his intentions, his health, and for his many works in your diocese.

Preview

In the next lesson, the students will learn about priests and religious.

INFORMATION ABOUT THE BISHOP

Possible resources may include:
- Diocesan Newspaper
- Diocesan Directory
- Diocesan website (start at www.usccb.org)

Try calling his office. Ask a representative to fax you some biographical information and a photo.

You may also discuss the vestments of a bishop: mitre, crosier, ring, stole, dalmatic (what deacons wear), and chasuble (what priests wear).

NOTES

LESSON THREE: PRIESTS, RELIGIOUS, AND LAITY

Aims

The students will learn that each bishop has many priests to help him. Priests bring us the grace of the sacraments. Priests work in our parishes and neighborhoods.

The students will also learn that there are many missionary priests and religious brothers and sisters who are called by God to bring the good news of Jesus Christ to all people.

They will learn that members of the laity bring the Gospel to the world through their daily lives.

Materials

- *Activity Book*, p. 104
- Arrange for a priest, a religious, and a layman to visit, or bring pictures if visits cannot be arranged

Optional:
- "The Church's one foundation," *Adoremus Hymnal*, #560

Begin

Begin the class by reviewing *Activity Book*, p. 103 from the previous lesson. Play a review game to be sure they know the vocabulary words.

All of us are destined for Heaven. If we lead a good life on earth, God will take us to be with Him for ever. Members of God's family who have died and now live in Heaven are called saints. The saints were ordinary people, but they loved God with all their hearts and souls. This is the secret of how all of us, no matter what we do in the Church, can become saints.

Saint Paul told us that our Church is like a body with many parts. Whenever one small part is hurt, the whole body suffers. For example, we need our eyes to see, our lungs to breathe, and our feet to walk. If any one of these were taken away, our whole body would suffer the loss. So it is with our Church. Christ is the head and we make up all the other parts. Our good actions and prayers build up the health and strength of the whole Church. All of us are one united body under Christ.

This is why the Church is called **Catholic**. Catholic means "universal" or "for all." Christ founded the Church for everyone. Today because of good priests, missionaries, and lay people, the Church has spread to all nations. Even though we may never see these people in faraway lands, we are one with them because we share the same beliefs. We are all part of God's family on earth— the Catholic Church.

Words to Know:

Church   religious
missionary   martyr   Catholic

Develop

1. Read paragraphs 5–9 with the children.

2. Explain the various roles of different people in the Church:
   - *Priests*: priests help the bishops. Remember that the bishop is responsible for all the churches in his diocese. But he cannot be everywhere at once, so the priests act in his place to help him. Diocesan priests make vows of obedience to their bishop to be sure they do his work in the parish. Priests bring us the Sacraments of Baptism, Penance, Eucharist, Matrimony, and the Anointing of the Sick. Sometimes they bring us the Sacrament of Confirmation. They can never celebrate Holy Orders (only the Bishop can). The priests are assigned to a parish and work in a specific neighborhood. You can trace your parish boundaries on a map.
   - *Religious Brothers and Sisters*: these are people called by God to serve the Church. They are lay men and women who have consecrated their lives to God. They spend their lives helping others, praying, and being witnesses to the Gospel in anticipation of Heaven. They often take vows of poverty, chastity (they will not marry anyone), and obedience. They are members of various religious congregations, which tend to different needs in the Church.
   - *Laity*: all the other members of the Church. They live their lives either as single or married people. They bring the Gospel to the world through their work and their families.
   - *Martyrs*: those who are called to lay down their lives to witness to the truth of the Gospels.
   - *Saints*: those souls who are already in Heaven. They lived good lives on earth and are now enjoying their just reward.
   - *Holy Souls in Purgatory*: those who await Heaven while in a state of purification.

3. All of these people work together for the good of the Church. How will the students know their calling?

Name:_____

The Church

1. Who founded the Church?
Jesus Christ
2. Who was given the mission of continuing Christ's work?
The Apostles
3. Who had the greatest mission? What is the Pope's job?
Peter, the first Pope, had the greatest mission. The Pope's job is to take Jesus' place on earth to lead and guide the Church.
4. Who is the head of all the bishops in the world?
The Pope
5. What do bishops do?
The bishops watch over their flock, protecting it from danger. They preach, teach, and guide us. They deliver the message of Jesus. They explain the rules of the Church and help us to lead good lives.
6. What do priests do?
Priests bring us the grace of the sacraments.
7. What do missionaries do?
Missionaries bring the light of Christ to faraway parts of the earth.
8. What do brothers and sisters do?
Religious brothers and sisters give their whole lives to God by teaching and helping others.
9. What do members of the laity do?
The laity help the bishops and priests in bringing the word of God to all people.
10. Who are the saints?
The saints are ordinary people who loved God with all their hearts and souls and who now live in Heaven with God.

104   Faith and Life Series • Grade 3 • Chapter 27 • Lesson 3

Reinforce

1. Have the students work on *Activity Book*, p. 104.

2. If you have visitors, let them tell their vocation stories and have the students ask questions about their lives. Ask them what they do, how they felt called, etc.

3. Have the students work on their Memorization Questions for this chapter.

Conclude

1. Lead the children in singing "The Church's one foundation," *Adoremus Hymnal*, #560.

2. End class with a prayer asking God to know one's vocation.

Preview

In the next lesson, the students will learn about the Church as the Mystical Body of Christ.

CHALK TALK: ROLES IN THE CHURCH

NOTES

LESSON FOUR: THE MYSTICAL BODY OF CHRIST

Aims

The students will learn that the Church is the Mystical Body of Christ.

They will learn about the relationship between the Church Militant, the Church Suffering, and the Church Triumphant.

They may learn the marks of the Church.

Materials

- *Activity Book*, p. 105
- Children's Bible

Optional:
- "The Church's one foundation," *Adoremus Hymnal*, #560

Begin

Begin the class by reviewing all the different people that make up the Church. Have the students describe the Church hierarchy and the different roles. Also have them tell you about the Pope and their bishop. You may play a review game with the students. If they researched various religious congregations, they may make presentations on them, including a brief biography of their founder and their apostolic works.

Q. 112 *Who founded the Church?*
Jesus Christ founded the Church. Jesus gathered His faithful followers into one society, placed it under the direction of the Apostles with Saint Peter as its head, and gave it its Sacrifice, its sacraments, and the Holy Spirit, Who gives it life (CCC 763–65).

Q. 113 *Who are the pastors of the Church?*
The pastors of the Church are the Pope and the bishops united with him (CCC 816, 881).

Q. 114 *Who is the Pope?*
The Pope is the successor of Saint Peter as bishop of Rome. The Pope is the visible head of the entire Church (CCC 882).

"If you continue in my word, you are truly my disciples, and you shall know the truth, and the truth will make you free."
— John 8:31–32

Develop

1. Finish reading the chapter with the children.

2. Analyze the model of the Church as the Mystical Body of Christ. Read the following passage from a children's Bible: 1 Cor 12:1–31. Who is the head of the body? Christ. What are the parts of the body? Can they imagine a body with 10 left feet? What about with one with one hundred eyes but no mouth? Would not that be crazy? Everybody has a different role in the Mystical Body of Christ:
   - Apostles
   - Teachers
   - Healers
   - Administrators
   - Prophets
   - Workers of miracles
   - Helpers
   - Those who speak in tongues

3. How do the various people in the Church fulfill these roles? For example, bishops are the Apostles among us.

4. Is the Church made up of only those people we see here on earth? No. The people here on earth are called the Church Militant because we are fighting the good fight to get to Heaven. What about the people in Heaven? Are they part of the Church, too? Yes. They are the Church Triumphant because they are enjoying their just reward. What about the souls in Purgatory? They are the Church Suffering. They will go to Heaven, but must first be purified.

5. Explain the relationship between the people in Heaven, on earth, and in Purgatory.
   - On earth we can pray for one another and for the souls in Purgatory. We can also pray to the saints in Heaven.
   - The souls in Purgatory are suffering and cannot pray for themselves, so we must help them with our prayers and sacrifices.
   - The saints in Heaven can pray for us and intercede on our behalf before the throne of God. All souls are united in the Sacrifice of the Mass.

Name:_____

Mystical Body of Christ

1. What did Saint Paul say that the Church was like?
<ins>A body with many parts</ins>
2. Does each part affect the whole? How?
<ins>Whenever one small part is hurt, the whole body suffers. If any part is taken away, our whole body suffers the loss.</ins>
3. Who is the Head of the Body, the Church?
<ins>Jesus Christ</ins>
4. Who are all the parts of the Church?
<ins>The members of the Catholic Church</ins>

Draw a picture of the Mystical Body of Christ.

Faith and Life Series • Grade 3 • Chapter 27 • Lesson 4

Reinforce

1. Have the students work on *Activity Book*, p. 105.

2. Have the students draw pictures of the Mystical Body of Christ.

3. Have the students work on the Memorization Questions for this chapter and begin reviewing for the quiz.

Conclude

1. Lead the children in singing "The Church's one foundation," *Adoremus Hymnal*, #560.

2. End class by praying for the souls in Purgatory.

Preview

In the next lesson, the students' knowledge of the material covered in this chapter will be reviewed and assessed.

MARKS OF THE CHURCH

- One
- Holy
- Catholic
- Apostolic

RELIGIOUS ORDERS AND THEIR FOUNDERS

- Order of Preachers: Saint Dominic
- Order of Friars Minor: Saint Francis
- Poor Clares: Saint Clare
- Benedictines: Saint Benedict
- Cistercians: Saint Robert, Abbot of Molesme
- Society of Jesus: Saint Ignatius Loyola
- Society of Mary: William Joseph Chaminade
- Christian Brothers: Edmund Ignatius Rice

NOTES

CHAPTER TWENTY-SEVEN
REVIEW AND ASSESSMENT

Aims

The students' knowledge and understanding of the material covered in this chapter will be reviewed and assessed.

Materials

- Quiz 27, Appendix, p. A-39

Optional:
- "The Church's one foundation," *Adoremus Hymnal*, #560

Review

1. Review that Jesus founded the Church and made Saint Peter His representative on earth.

2. Review the role of the Pope. He is the leader of the bishops and the visible head of the Church on earth. Explain that he is infallible in matters of faith and morals (protected from teaching error). The students should know the name of the Pope.

3. Review the role of the bishop and the name of your bishop as well as the name of your diocese.

4. The students should know the role of the priests and the names of the priests at your parish.

5. The students should know what religious brothers and sisters are and what they do for the Church.

6. The students should know that the Church is comprised of the Church Militant, the Church Suffering, and the Church Triumphant.

7. The students should also understand the model of the Church as the Mystical Body of Christ.

Name:

God's Family on Earth   Quiz 27

"You did not choose me, but I chose you" (John 15:16).

Word Bank

sacraments	rock	martyrs	lives	Christ
Church	keys	spread	bishops	

Fill in the blanks with the correct words from the Word Bank.

1. Jesus founded the _Church_ on earth. Before He ascended into Heaven, He gave His Apostles the power to teach and guide her.

2. Jesus said to Peter, "You are Peter and upon this _rock_ I will build my Church. And the gates of hell shall not prevail against it."

3. Jesus said to Peter, "I will entrust to you the _keys_ of the Kingdom of Heaven. Whatever you declare bound on earth shall be bound in Heaven." Peter became the first Pope.

4. The Pope represents _Christ_ on earth. Jesus Himself gave the Pope that power. Catholics everywhere respect and obey Him.

5. The Pope is head of the thousands of _bishops_ all over the world. These are the teachers of the Church, who preach and guide all entrusted to their care.

6. Priests bring us the grace of the _sacraments_. They share in the God-given power to forgive sins and offer Holy Mass. Jesus comes into our lives through them.

7. Religious sisters and brothers give their whole _lives_ to God. Some are missionaries sacrificing to serve God and His people in far away lands.

8. Those who die for the Word of God are called _martyrs_.

9. The Church is called Catholic meaning "universal" or "for all." Because of good priests, missionaries, and lay people, the Church has _spread_ to all nations.

10. Write out the Scripture verse shown at the top of this page.

Faith and Life • Grade 3 • Appendix A

Assess

1. Distribute the quizzes, and read through them with the students to be sure they understand the questions.

2. Administer the quiz. As they hand in their work, you may orally quiz them on the Memorization Questions for this chapter.

3. After all the quizzes have been handed in you may wish to review the correct answers with the class.

Conclude

1. Lead the children in singing "The Church's one foundation," *Adoremus Hymnal*, #560.

2. End class with a prayer.

CHAPTER TWENTY-EIGHT
OUR LIFE IN THE CHURCH

Catechism of the Catholic Church References

Jesus as Our Teacher and Model of Holiness: 468–69, 516–21, 561
Sacramental Signs: 1145–62, 1189–92
Sacraments: 1113, 1131–34
Sacraments Instituted by Christ: 1114, 1123, 1129, 1210, 1988
Sacraments of Christ: 1114–16
Sacraments of the Church: 1117–21
Sacraments of Eternal Life: 1130
      Baptism: 1213–74, 1275–84
Confirmation: 1285–1314, 1315–21
Eucharist: 1322–1405, 1405–19
Penance and Reconciliation: 1422–98
Anointing of the Sick: 1499–1525, 1526–32
Holy Orders: 1536–89, 1590–1600
Marriage: 1601–58, 1659–66
Sacraments of Faith: 1122–26
Sacraments of Salvation: 1127–29
What Is Prayer?: 2559–65, 2590, 2644

Scripture References

Christ's Body, the Source of the Sacraments: Lk 5:17, 6:17–19, 8:46

Background Reading: *The Fundamentals of Catholicism* by Fr. Kenneth Baker, S.J.

Volume 1:
"Watch and Pray," pp. 144–46

Volume 3:
Essays on the Sacraments, pp. 163–355

Summary of Lesson Content

Lesson 1

Signs call our attention to a greater reality.

Sacraments are signs of grace. The matter and form used in each sacrament tells us what grace God is working in our souls.

Jesus instituted seven sacraments.

Lesson 2

The first sacrament is Baptism. The matter of Baptism is water. The form of Baptism is the pronouncement, "I baptize you in the Name of the Father and of the Son and of the Holy Spirit."

Baptism washes away all sin from the soul and infuses it with God's life of grace.

Lesson 3

The Sacrament of the Eucharist is the Body and Blood of Jesus, which nourishes our souls.

The Sacrament of Penance is the healing sacrament given for the forgiveness of sins.

In the Sacrament of Confirmation, we receive the outpouring of the Holy Spirit and His gifts, so we can do God's will in His Church.

Lesson 4

The Sacrament of Matrimony and Holy Orders help us to serve the Church.

The Sacrament of the Anointing of the Sick is a sacrament of healing, which prepares us for a happy death.

To keep the life of grace, we must obey the Commandments and pray.

LESSON ONE: SACRAMENTS

Aims

The students will learn that signs call our attention to a greater reality.

They will learn that the sacraments are signs of grace. The matter and form used in each sacrament tells us what grace God is working in our souls.

Jesus instituted seven sacraments.

Materials

- *Activity Book*, p. 106
- Water, oil (chrism if possible), bread and wine, a picture of a bride and groom, and a stole

Optional:
- "Sing praise to our Creator," *Adoremus Hymnal*, #500

Begin

Begin the class by explaining that signs point to something or tell us something. For example, yawn dramatically in front of the class, making a loud sound. Ask the children what this tells them. It tells them that you are sleepy. What about a road sign that says "stop"? The sign tells us to stop. What about a heart or a valentine? These signify love. Have the students think of some other signs and let everyone guess at their meanings.

---

28   Our Life in the Church

"My sheep hear my voice, and I know them, and they follow me; I give them eternal life, and they shall never perish, and no one shall snatch them out of my hand."

John 10:27–28

Signs help us every day of our life. Often they call our attention to important things we cannot see or hear. Smoke is a sign of fire. Red lights or sirens are signs of danger. A heart is a sign of love.

We cannot see love. It is invisible. But love is real. We can show it to others through our actions. For example, your mother may show you her love by kind words, a hug, or a smile. Hearing, feeling, or seeing these signs helps you to understand the love in your mother's heart. Without signs, her love would be hidden. With signs, you see and understand the wonderful gift that you are receiving.

In the Church, Jesus gave us signs of His grace in the seven sacraments. A **sacrament** is a sign. It uses things we can see and hear to tell us about something else that we cannot see or hear. Jesus and His grace are hidden from our eyes, but we know He is present in every sacrament. Jesus promised this when He instituted these sacraments during His public life on earth. He wanted to leave us visible signs of His grace being poured out to us.

The first sacrament we receive is Baptism. The signs of this sacrament are words and water. Most of us were baptized when we were little babies. Our parents and godparents took us to Church. They made our baptismal promises for us because we were too young to speak. Then the priest poured water over our heads. He

135

Develop

1. Read the first three paragraphs with the students.

2. Copy the Chalk Talk diagram at the right. Have the students name the seven sacraments as you draw them on the chalkboard. They may need some help remembering all seven.

3. Explain to the students that sacraments are signs. The matter and form used in each sacrament tells us what grace God is working in our souls:
   - *Baptism*: water, gestures, and the words of the priest. Ask the students what the water does. It washes and cleanses. With the words, "I baptize you . . . ," our souls are washed from sin and share in the death and Resurrection of Jesus. The life of grace is poured into the soul.
   - *Eucharist*: bread and wine and the words of consecration. Bread and wine are food and drink common to all cultures. They nourish our bodies and sustain us. When consecrated, the Eucharist nourishes our soul with the life of Christ.
   - *Penance*: in sorrow we tell our sins to a priest and he says the words of absolution. In Penance, Jesus forgives our sins.
   - *Holy Orders*: chrism (oil and balsam) and a stole. Oil is a sign of strength, nourishment, and beauty. Holy Orders ordains men to share in the ministry of Christ. A stole is a sign of his authority.
   - *Matrimony*: bride and groom make vows. Together they give themselves to each other for the rest of their lives.
   - *Confirmation*: chrism (same as above) and being sealed with the gift of the Holy Spirit. We receive the fullness of the Holy Spirit.
   - *Anointing of the Sick*: oil and prayers. The sick person is strengthened to suffer with Christ.

4. *Sacraments are different than the signs we talked about at the beginning of class because they cause what they signify.*

Name:_____

The Sacraments

Signs of God's grace poured out to us in the Church.

Use these pictures to reflect on the sacraments.

106   Faith and Life Series • Grade 3 • Chapter 28 • Lesson 1

Reinforce

1. Have the students color and label the images of the seven sacraments on *Activity Book*, p. 106.

2. Teach the students to sing "Sing praise to our Creator," *Adoremus Hymnal*, #500.

3. Have the students learn the Memorization Questions for this chapter as well as the chart at the end of this chapter.

Conclude

End class with a prayer asking God to give the students grace.

Preview

In the next lesson the students will learn more about Baptism, Eucharist, and Penance.

CHALK TALK: THE CHURCH

NOTES

_____
_____
_____
_____
_____
_____
_____
_____
_____
_____

LESSON TWO: SACRAMENTS WE HAVE ALREADY RECEIVED

Aims

The students will learn that the Sacrament of Baptism washes away all sin from the soul and infuses it with God's life of grace.

They will learn about Jesus's presence in the Eucharist and that the Sacrament of the Eucharist nourishes our souls.

They will learn that God forgives sins in the Sacrament of Penance.

Materials

- *Activity Book*, p. 107
- Water, doll, unconsecrated hosts, purple stole, rewards (e.g., candy or holy cards)
- Scripts for Baptism, Penance, and Eucharist (Appendix, pp. B-26–B-30)

Optional:
- "Sing praise to our Creator," *Adoremus Hymnal*, #500

Begin

Teach the children that grace is the life of God in us. It is a pure gift that keeps our souls alive and strong. We need grace to get to Heaven. Go over the Chalk Talk diagram from the previous lesson. Have the students note we are the only Church with all seven sacraments, which are channels of God's grace! Other Christian Churches have the Sacraments of Baptism and Matrimony. We pray, though, that all people will come to the Catholic Church where they can receive all the sacraments.

---

called us by name and said, "I baptize you in the Name of the Father and of the Son and of the Holy Spirit."

At that very moment, we become **Christians**: baptized followers of Christ. Our sin was washed away and our souls were filled with brilliant new life. This new life in our soul was God's own life, called grace. God shared grace with us on our Baptism day so that we could be His own precious children forever. He welcomed us with open arms into His family on earth. Because of our Baptism, He can one day welcome us with open arms into His Kingdom in Heaven.

As a result of our Baptism, we can spend the rest of our life keeping the life of grace alive in our soul. God understands us completely, so He knows that we need special help to do this. That is why He gave us the other sacraments: to keep God's grace. In this way, He can keep pouring His life and love into our hearts.

In the Sacrament of the Holy Eucharist, He gives us His own Son as food for our souls. Bread, wine, and the words of the priest are our signs that Jesus is present. Once the priest changes the bread and wine into Jesus' own Body and Blood, we can receive Him into our hearts. If we receive this sacrament often, the life of grace in our soul grows more and more strong.

In the Sacrament of Penance, God gives us the chance to win back grace that we have lost in sin. We know God is really present, because we have the sign of the priest's healing, forgiving words. When he says to us, "I absolve you from your sins in the Name of the Father and of the Son and of the Holy Spirit," Jesus Himself speaks through him, forgiving and blessing us.

When we receive the Sacrament of Confirmation, the Holy Spirit fills us with the grace to be even stronger members of the Church. This sacrament will help us to do whatever God asks us as members of His family.

Later in life, we may receive some of the other sacraments: Holy Orders, Matrimony (Marriage), and the Anointing of the Sick. The

136

Develop

1. Read paragraphs 4–8. These paragraphs talk about the sacraments the students have already received.

2. Have three stations set up in the classroom. You will need two other adult helpers for today's class, unless you wish to run these stations one after another.

Station 1: Baptism
Have the students each take turns playing parents and deacons or priests and baptize a doll using the proper baptismal formula and gestures (either pouring water or immersion). Then ask the students who participate in each "Baptism" what Baptism does for the soul. Sin is washed away and the life of grace is poured into the soul. Why is water used as a sign? It washes, gives life, nourishes, etc. What do the words mean? When the priest pours the water and says these words, we are baptized. What do the symbols of the candle and the white garment mean? The candle symbolizes our receiving of the light of Christ and the white garment symbolizes the purity of our souls.

Stations 2: Penance
Have the students give examples of mortal and venial sins. Have them tell you the steps to a good Penance (know your sins, be sorry for them, decide to not sin again, confess your sins to a priest in the Sacrament of Penance, do your penance).

Station 3: Eucharist
Have the students form a communion line. Ask them questions about the Eucharist, the matter, the form, the effects, Jesus' real presence, etc. If they get an answer correct they may practice receiving unconsecrated hosts and saying prayers of thanksgiving.

3. If the students complete all three stations successfully, they should receive a reward such as a holy card, medal, or candy.

Name:_____

Renewal of Baptismal Promises

Do you reject Satan? And all his works? And all his empty promises?
<u>Students respond with "I do."</u>
Do you reject sin so as to live in the freedom of God's children?

Do you reject the glamour of evil and refuse to be mastered by sin?

Do you reject satan, the father of sin and prince of darkness?

Do you believe in God, the Father Almighty, the Creator of Heaven and earth?

Do you believe in Jesus Christ, His only Son, Our Lord, Who was born of the Virgin Mary, was crucified, died, and was buried, rose from the dead and is now seated at the right hand of the Father?

Do you believe in the Holy Spirit, the Holy Catholic Church, the Communion of Saints, the forgiveness of sins, the resurrection of the body, and life everlasting.

God, the all-powerful Father of Our Lord Jesus Christ, has given us a new birth by water and the Holy Spirit, and forgiven our sins. May He also keep us faithful to Our Lord Jesus Christ forever and ever. Amen.

Name:_____

Faith and Life Series • Grade 3 • Chapter 28 • Lesson 2   107

SAMPLE QUESTIONS FOR STATION 3 ON EUCHARIST

- What is the Consecration?
- What does the priest say to change bread and wine into the Body, Blood, Soul, and Divinity of Jesus?
- In what part of the Mass does the Consecration occur?
- What happens to the Eucharist that remains after Mass?
- What is an adoration and benediction service?
- What are the chalice, paten, and ciborium?
- What is a monstrance and what is a tabernacle?
- Is the Mass a sacrifice, a meal, or both?
- Is the Mass the same Sacrifice as the one made on the Cross?

Reinforce

1. When the students have completed all three stations, they may help others or work on *Activity Book*, p. 107.

2. Have the students work on their Memorization Questions for this chapter.

Optional: you might arrange for your class to go to confession and you might have a class Mass during which the priest can explain the parts of the Mass.

Conclude

1. Lead the children in singing "Sing praise to our Creator," *Adoremus Hymnal*," #500

2. End class with a prayer thanking God for the Sacraments of Baptism, Penance, and Eucharist.

Preview

In the next lesson, the students will learn about the Sacraments of Confirmation, Matrimony, Holy Orders, and Anointing of the Sick.

NOTES
_____
_____
_____
_____
_____
_____
_____
_____
_____
_____

LESSON THREE: SACRAMENTS WE HAVEN'T YET RECEIVED

Aims

The students will learn that at the Sacrament of Confirmation, we receive an outpouring of the Holy Spirit and His gifts so we can do God's will in His Church.

They will learn that the Sacraments of Holy Orders and Matrimony help the Church to grow and live.

They will learn that the Sacrament of the Anointing of the Sick helps people to suffer with Jesus and die in peace.

Materials

- *Activity Book*, p. 108
- "Sing praise to our Creator," *Adoremus Hymnal*, #500

Optional:
- Arrange for a Confirmation class to visit

Begin

Review the Chalk Talk diagram from Lesson One. Ask the students which sacraments they have received and which ones they have not yet received. They are not old enough yet to receive some of them. Explain to the students that today we will learn about the sacraments we have not yet received. We should know about them and pray that one day we will receive them worthily.

Develop

1. Read paragraphs 9 and 10 with the students.

2. If possible, have the Confirmation class visit your class and explain the Sacrament of Confirmation. You may need to prompt the students with questions such as:
- What is the matter of Confirmation? Why?
- What is the form? What does it mean?
- Why are we confirmed?
- How do we share in the ministries of Christ as prophet, priest, and king? Why is this important to the Church?
- How is being confirmed like becoming an adult in the Church?
- What are the gifts and fruits of the Holy Spirit?

If they have already been confirmed ask:
- What was it like? How did you feel? Did you notice any difference?

3. Discuss vocations. God calls each of us to serve Him and His Church in a specific way of life. Most people are called to marriage, like your parents! They dedicate their lives to living the faith and helping the Church grow by having children and raising them Catholic. Some men are called to be priests, like Fr. _____. Priests celebrate the sacraments and give God's graces to the members of the Church through the sacraments. Some men and women are called to religious life. Discuss Holy Orders and Matrimony with the students. Tell them the matter, form, and effects of these sacraments. For Holy Orders, explain the varying degrees: deacon, priest, and bishop.

4. Discuss the Anointing of the Sick. Let the children know that they need only be sick in order to receive this sacrament and that it can be received more than once. The priest will anoint them with oil and pray that they will be strengthened to suffer in their illness with Jesus and, if it is God's will, to die in a state ready for Heaven.

---

important thing to remember is that God gave us the sacraments as a special invitation to share in His life. Receiving them strengthens our friendship with Him and unites us to Him. If we live up to the grace we receive in the sacraments, we really will begin to think, speak, and act like Christ. His own life will shine out of us.

When we are full of God's grace, it is easier to keep our promises to God and follow His Commandments. We love Him so much we want to go to Mass every Sunday, we want to practice our faith and witness it to others. We want to love God most of all, and love our neighbor as ourselves.

Prayer is one of the greatest ways we can show our love of our neighbor. God wants us to pray, not only for those in His family, the Church, but for others who do not have the gift of faith. Jesus told the Apostles that He came for everyone. He loves all people. He wants everyone in the world to belong to His family. Even if we cannot join the missionaries in distant lands, we can join them with our prayers. Prayer is powerful, and our prayers for people who do not yet know and love God can bring them closer to Him. Jesus said, "They will know you are My disciples by your love." To be His followers, we must love and pray for all the world.

Words to Know:

sacrament   Christian

> **Q. 115** *What are the sacraments?*
> The sacraments are signs of grace instituted by Jesus Christ to make us holy (CCC 1114, 1116, 1127).

Name:_____

Sacraments

1. What is a sacrament?
   A sacrament is a sign of grace instituted by Christ to make us holy.

2. What happens to us at Baptism?
   We become Christians. Our sin is washed away and our souls are filled with brilliant new life.

3. What are the signs of the Holy Eucharist? What happens when we receive this sacrament?
   Bread, wine, and the words of the priest are the signs. When we receive this sacrament the life of grace in our souls grows more and more strong.

4. What is the sign in the Sacrament of Penance? What happens when we receive this sacrament?
   The sign is the word is the priest, "I absolve you of your sins in the Name of the Father and of the Son and of the Holy Spirit." When we receive this sacrament, Jesus forgives our sins.

5. What happens when we receive the Sacrament of Confirmation?
   When we receive the Sacrament of Confirmation the Holy Spirit fills us with the grace to be even stronger members of the Church.

8. What happens when we receive the Sacraments of Matrimony and Holy Orders, and the Anointing of the Sick?
   Receiving these sacraments strengthens our friendship with God and unites us to Him.

108 Faith and Life Series • Grade 3 • Chapter 28 • Lesson 3

Reinforce

1. Have the students work on *Activity Book*, p. 108.

2. Have the students write thank you letters to the Confirmation class for coming to visit.

3. Have the students work on their Memorization Questions for this chapter.

Conclude

1. Lead the children in singing "Sing praise to our Creator," *Adoremus Hymnal*, #500.

2. Have the students pray to receive these sacraments worthily.

Preview

In the next lesson, the students will learn how the grace from the sacraments will help them to live the moral life, which should be supported by prayer.

THE SACRAMENT OF ANOINTING OF THE SICK

According to the *Catechism of the Catholic Church*, "The sacrament of Anointing of the Sick is given to those who are seriously ill by anointing them on the forehead and hands with duly blessed oil—pressed from olives or other plants—saying, only once: 'Through this holy anointing may the Lord in his love and mercy help you with the grace of the Holy Spirit. May the Lord who frees you from sin save you and raise you up'" (*CCC* 1513).

NOTES

LESSON FOUR: LIFE OF GRACE

Aims

To keep the life of grace that we receive in the sacraments we must obey the Commandments and pray.

Materials

- *Activity Book*, p. 109
- An assembly project such as a simple model

Optional:
- "Sing praise to our Creator," *Adoremus Hymnal*, #500

Q. 116 *How do the sacraments make us holy?*
The sacraments make us holy either by giving us the first sanctifying grace, which takes away sin, or by increasing that grace which we already possess (CCC 1123).

Q. 117 *What are the seven sacraments?*
The seven sacraments are: Baptism, Confirmation, Eucharist, Penance, Anointing of the Sick, Matrimony, and Holy Orders (CCC 1113).

". . . Put on love, which binds everything together in perfect harmony. And let the peace of Christ rule in your hearts, to which indeed you were called in the one body."

Colossians 3:14–15

Begin

Have the students work on the assembly project. They will need the proper tools, pieces for assembly, and the instructions. Assign tasks such as reading the instructions, keeping tools, etc. When they complete the project, ask them these questions:
- What role did they play?
- What did they need to do this project?
- Would the project have turned out well if they did not follow the instructions?
- Did they need help from each other?

Develop

1. Read the rest of the chapter from the student text.

2. Remind the students of the earlier Chalk Talk diagram which showed that the sacraments are the channels of grace given to the Church by Jesus Christ. We must believe the teachings of the Church in order to receive the sacraments. Then, when we receive the sacraments, we are given God's grace, which we need in order to live lives pleasing to God. In order to receive the sacrament worthily, we must avoid sin and keep the Commandments. When we are full of grace, it is easier to keep the Commandments. The sacraments help us overcome our temptations to sin (see effects of Penance and Eucharist). Finally, we need prayer. In prayer we speak with and listen to God. He gives us help along the way to keep the Commandments, to receive the sacraments worthily, and to help increase our faith. Prayer is very important, for we cannot do it all on our own. With these four pillars of our Catholic faith, we can live in a way that is pleasing to God as an offering or sacrifice of love to Him.

3. Review the moral life: the Ten Commandments, the beatitudes, the virtues and vices, and the works of mercy.

4. Discuss prayer. What is prayer? How do we pray? What are the forms of prayer? They are adoration and blessing, praise, petition and intercession, and thanksgiving. For whom can we pray? Where can we pray? Why should we pray in the presence of the Eucharist? What can prayer do? What are some prayers that we know? Must we pray memorized prayers or can we just talk with God? When is a good time to pray? What is the greatest prayer on earth? The greatest prayer on earth is the Mass.

Name:_____

Grace

1. What is grace?
Grace is the life of God in our souls.

2. How do we receive grace?
We receive grace from the sacraments, from prayer, and from doing good works.

3. Are there signs of grace in all seven sacraments?
Yes

4. Can we see grace?
No

5. Who gives us grace?
Answers will vary. (God, Jesus, etc.)

6. What weakens or removes grace from us?
Sin

7. What sacrament allows us to win back grace?
Penance

8. When we are full of grace, what is it easier to do?
It is easier to keep our promises to God and follow His Commandments.

Faith and Life Series • Grade 3 • Chapter 28 • Lesson 4

Reinforce

1. Have the students work on *Activity Book*, p. 109.

2. Have the students work on their Memorization Questions for this chapter and review for the chapter and unit quizzes.

Conclude

1. Lead the children in singing "Sing praise to our Creator," *Adoremus Hymnal*, #500.

2. End class with a prayer. Let the students choose the prayer or make up their own.

Preview

In the next lesson, the students' knowledge of the material covered in this chapter will be reviewed and assessed.

CREED, SACRAMENTS, COMMANDMENTS, PRAYER

Let the children pretend that they are workers in a factory. Use this parallel to explain:
- Creed: What we believe (our religion). This makes us who we are: God's family. The Creed is like a description of our job in the factory—to put things together.
- Sacraments: What we celebrate. The sacraments give us the life of grace. The sacraments are like the materials and tools we need in order to put things together.
- Commandments: What we live. We must live the Commandments to keep the life of grace in our souls. The Commandments are like the instruction manual that tells us how to put things together.
- Prayer: What we share with God. We ask God to give us strength that we may live our lives as pleasing offerings to God. Prayer is like helping one another.

NOTES

CHAPTER TWENTY-EIGHT
REVIEW AND ASSESSMENT

Aims

The students' knowledge and understanding of the material covered in this chapter will be reviewed and assessed.

Materials

- Quiz 28, Appendix, p. A-40

Optional:
- "Sing praise to our Creator," *Adoremus Hymnal*, #500

Review

1. The students should know the sacramental signs and that they bring about what they signify. Sacraments, by definition, are efficacious signs of God's grace.

2. The students should be able to explain each of the seven sacraments and what they effect in the soul.

3. The students should be able to describe in detail the Sacraments of Baptism, Penance, and Eucharist.

4. The students should have a basic understanding of the relationship of the 4 pillars of the Catholic faith: creed, sacraments, moral life, and prayer.

5. The students should be able to discuss the life of grace.

6. The students should be able to explain, at an age-appropriate level, the life of prayer.

Name: _____

Our Life in the Church — Quiz 28

Word Bank

| grace | Confirmation | name | life | powerful |
| love | Eucharist | sign | Baptism | |

Fill in the blanks with the correct words from the Word Bank.

1. Signs help us by calling our attention to important things we cannot see or hear. A mother's kiss is a sign of her <u>love</u>.

2. The sacraments are signs of <u>grace</u> instituted by Jesus Christ to make us holy. Jesus gave us signs of His grace in the seven sacraments.

3. A sacrament is a <u>sign</u> that fills us with grace. It uses things we can see and hear to tell us about something we cannot see or hear.

4. In the Sacrament of <u>Baptism</u>, our parents and godparents made our baptismal promises for us.

5. At our Baptism, the priest or deacon poured water over our head, called us by <u>name</u>, and said, "I baptize you in the Name of the Father and of the Son and of the Holy Spirit."

6. At the very moment of Baptism, Original Sin is washed away and our souls are filled with God's own <u>life</u>, called grace.

7. We can spend the rest of our lives keeping grace in our souls by receiving the Sacrament of the <u>Eucharist</u> and the Sacrament of Penance often.

8. The seven sacraments are Baptism, <u>Confirmation</u>, Eucharist, Penance, Anointing of the Sick, Holy Orders, and Matrimony (Marriage). Receiving the sacraments gives us grace and unites us to God.

9. Prayer is <u>powerful</u>. Prayers for people who do not yet know and love God can bring them closer to Him.

A - 40 — Faith and Life • Grade 3 • Appendix A

Assess

1. Distribute the quizzes and read through them with the students to be sure they understand the questions.

2. Administer the quiz. As they hand in their work you may orally quiz them on the Memorization Questions for this chapter.

3. After all the quizzes have been handed in you may wish to review the correct answers with the class.

4. Repeat steps 1–3 for the unit quiz.

Conclude

1. Lead the children in singing "Sing praise to our Creator," *Adoremus Hymnal*, #500.

2. End class with a prayer.

CHAPTER TWENTY-NINE
MARY, OUR MOTHER AND QUEEN

Catechism of the Catholic Church References

Devotion to the Blessed Virgin: 971
Full of Grace: 485, 490, 509, 723
Immaculate Conception: 490–93, 508
Intercessor: 490, 723, 969, 975
Mary as Our Mother: 963–70, 973–75
Mary in the Church: 963–72
Mary's Consent: 494, 511
Mary's Divine Motherhood: 495, 509
Mary's Predestination: 488–89

Mediator of Grace: 970
Meditation on the Rosary: 2705–8, 2723
Mother of the Church: 963
Obedience of Mary's Faith: 148–49
Payer in Union with Mary: 2673–79, 2682
Prayer of Mary: 2617–19, 2622
Queen of Heaven: 966, 974
Virginity of Mary: 496–507
Virtues: 144, 494, 511, 2030

Scripture References

Mary's Fiat: Lk 1:38
Wedding at Cana: Jn 2:1–11

"Behold your Mother": Jn 19:26–27

Background Reading: *The Fundamentals of Catholicism* by Fr. Kenneth Baker, S.J.

Volume 2:
"Mariology," pp. 315–85

Summary of Lesson Content

Lesson 1

Jesus gave Mary to all men to be their Mother.

By Mary's "Yes" to God, she helped to bring salvation to all people, becoming Mother to the Son of God.

Lesson 2

God prepared Mary for her role in salvation history by her Immaculate Conception (she was conceived without Original Sin).

Lesson 3

Mary lived her whole life without sin.

Mary holds the highest place in Heaven, after her Son.

Mary helps to bring us closer to Jesus—sometimes through visions and messages.

Lesson 4

We can ask Mary to pray for us as an intercessor.

Mary interceded for the married couple at the wedding at Cana.

Mary is Queen of Heaven

LESSON ONE: MOTHER MARY

Aims

The students will learn that Jesus gave Mary to all men to be our Mother.

The students will understand that by Mary's "Yes" to God, she helped bring salvation to all people. She became the Mother of the Son of God.

Materials

- *Activity Book*, p. 110
- Children's Bible
- Posterboard, markers, and craft supplies
- Litany of Loreto
- Statue, candle, and flowers in a vase

Optional:
- "Hail, holy Queen enthroned above," *Adoremus Hymnal*, #530

Begin

Ask the children the following questions: Who is your favorite lady? Why? What do you like about her? How is Mary the perfect woman? We know that all good qualities in women are only shadows of what Mary is like.

Develop

1. Read the first two paragraphs with the students.

2. Explain that God loves us very much. He is our Father and He sent His only Son to suffer and die for us. He also sent His Holy Spirit to dwell in us. He knew that we needed the love of a Mother. His mother was so perfect that He wanted to share her with us. When Jesus gave Mary to John, the beloved disciple, at the foot of His Cross, He gave Mary to all his disciples—and to all of us—to be our Mother.

3. Mary is also the Mother of all people in the order of grace. Just as Eve was the mother of all the living because she and Adam were our first parents, so Mary was Mother of all the living in grace since she was the first to have grace. Because she gave us Her Son, we can all have the grace that He won for us on the Cross.

4. Ask the students to recount stories they know about Mary.

Using a children's Bible read the the accounts of the Annunciation, Visitation, Nativity, Presentation in the Temple, and Finding of the Child Jesus in Lk 1:26—2:52.

5. Ask the students to name good things that Mary did (from the reading) and some of her good works. Ask the students how they can follow her example.

6. Using the Litany of the Blessed Virgin Mary (see right), expand upon the virtues and qualities of Mary that are pleasing to God. Help the students to understand how happy we should be to have Mary as our Mother. She can teach us how to be pleasing to God and also pray for us.

7. Have the students set up a Marian altar and pray the litany. They may make posters of Mary using their favorite title for her.

LITANY OF LORETO

Lord, have mercy on us.
Christ, have mercy on us.
Lord, have mercy on us.
Christ, hear us.
Christ, graciously hear us.
God the Father of heaven,
have mercy on us.
God the Son, Redeemer of the world,
have mercy on us.
God the Holy Spirit,
have mercy on us.
Holy Trinity, One God,
have mercy on us.

Holy Mary, *pray for us.**
Holy Mother of God,
Holy Virgin of virgins,
Mother of Christ,
Mother of divine grace,
Mother most pure,
Mother most chaste,
Mother inviolate,
Mother undefiled,
Mother most amiable,
Mother most admirable,
Mother of good counsel,
Mother of the Church,
Mother of our Creator,
Mother of our Savior,
Virgin most prudent,
Virgin most venerable,
Virgin most renowned,
Virgin most powerful,
Virgin most merciful,
Virgin most faithful,
Mirror of justice,
Seat of wisdom,
Cause of our joy,
Spiritual vessel,
Vessel of honor,
Singular vessel of devotion,
Mystical rose,
Tower of David,
Tower of ivory,
House of gold,
Ark of the covenant,
Gate of Heaven,
Morning star,
Health of the sick,
Refuge of sinners,
Comforter of the afflicted,
Help of Christians,
Queen of Angels,
Queen of Patriarchs,
Queen of Prophets,
Queen of Apostles,
Queen of Martyrs,
Queen of Confessors,
Queen of Virgins,
Queen of all Saints,
Queen conceived without original sin,
Queen assumed into heaven,
Queen of the most holy Rosary,
Queen of peace,

Lamb of God, who take away the sins of the world,
spare us, O Lord.

Lamb of God, who take away the sins of the world,
graciously hear us, O Lord.

Lamb of God, who take away the sins of the world,
have mercy on us.

Pray for us, O holy Mother of God.
That we may be made worthy of the promises of Christ.

Let us pray: Grant, we beseech Thee, O Lord God, unto us Thy servants, that we may rejoice in continual health of mind and body; and, by the glorious intercession of blessed Mary ever Virgin, may be delivered from present sadness, and enter into the joy of Thine eternal gladness. Through Christ our Lord. *Amen.*

* Pray for us is repeated after each invocation.

Reinforce

1. Have the students work on *Activity Book*, p. 110 (not shown).

2. Have the students make posters of Mary using the titles given to her in the Litany of the Blessed Virgin Mary.

3. Teach the students to sing "Hail, holy Queen enthroned above," *Adoremus Hymnal*, #530.

Conclude

End class by praying the litany and singing "Hail, holy Queen enthroned above," *Adoremus Hymnal*, #530, before your classroom Marian altar.

Preview

In the next lesson, the students will make rosaries and learn about Mary's Immaculate Conception.

LITANY OF LORETO

Composed in the Middle Ages, the Litany of Loreto was officially recognized and accepted by Pope Sixtus V in 1587. At this time all other litanies to the Blessed Virgin Mary were suppressed.

The Litany of Loreto likely survived because of the dedication of the Holy House of Loreto, whose members kept the prayer alive through the centuries.

Invoking numerous titles for Our Lady, the Litany of Loreto calls upon Mary as our Mother, friend, source of joy, and protectress.

LESSON TWO: IMMACULATE MARY

Aims

The students will learn that God prepared Mary for her role in salvation history by her Immaculate Conception, which means that she was conceived without Original Sin.

They will make rosaries. Packages of mission rosaries may be purchased from the Lewis Rosary Company.

Materials

- Make a rosary beforehand so you are clear on the instructions
- *Activity Book*, p. 111
- Supplies for making rosaries

Optional:
- "Hail, holy Queen enthroned above," *Adoremus Hymnal*, #530
- Miraculous medals
- "Bernadette, Princess of Lourdes," video; CCC of America, available through Ignatius Press

Begin

Begin class by reading paragraph 3 with the children. Help them to understand the difference between the Immaculate Conception (Mary being conceived without Original Sin) and the Virginal Conception (Jesus conceived by the power of the Holy Spirit). Review the words of Gabriel, "Hail Mary, full of grace," in the story of the Annunciation.

---

29   Mary, Our Mother And Queen

> When Jesus saw his mother, and the disciple whom he loved standing near, he said to his mother, "Woman, behold, your son!" Then he said to the disciple, "Behold, your mother!" And from that hour the disciple took her to his own home.
> — John 19:26–27

Jesus asked Mary, His own Mother, to be our Mother too, the day she and Saint John stood at the foot of His Cross. "Mother," He said, "behold your son. Son, behold your Mother." With that, Mary inherited many, many children—the whole Church!

Mary actually became the Mother of the Church long before that, as a young woman who bravely said "Yes" to God's plan. She was free to say "No." But she wanted to do whatever God asked. Because of her trust, obedience, and love, Jesus came into the world as a little Child Who would grow into Our Savior. Mary helped God keep His promise to His people. Her choice brought salvation and light to the world.

God prepared Mary in a very special way for her role in our salvation. He allowed her to be the one person in the world, besides Jesus, who was conceived without Original Sin. In other words, Mary never needed to be baptized like all of us. We were born with the effects of our first parents' sin. But Mary was born with no trace of sin. That is why she is called the **Immaculate Conception**. She came into the world already filled with God's life. That is why the angel Gabriel approached her with the words, "Hail Mary, **full of grace**."

Develop

1. Set up tables with 4–6 children at each. On each table, place the materials for making rosaries: cords with Crucifixes attached to them, a box of beads, spaces, and middle/center (Hail Holy Queen) pieces. Because children are still developing their hand-eye coordination, they may need help (particularly the boys). The girls may excel at this project and should be encouraged to be helpful to others.

2. Lead the children in making their rosaries. You will need to walk around the room, checking the number of beads for each decade, etc.

3. Say the prayers of the rosary as you are assembling them. Pray the Joyful Mysteries as you would have reviewed these mysteries in the previous lesson. Ask the students questions about each mystery before you begin that decade.

4. The students usually need help with the Hail Holy Queen piece and with cutting the cord.

5. Ask the students to clean up. Often they want to make a second rosary for a sibling. Depending on your supplies, they may do so.

6. You may watch a video on Lourdes, such as "Bernadette Princess of Lourdes," by CCC Video. This video refers to Mary as the Immaculate Conception. The children will also see a role model close to their own age. You may discuss Saint Bernadette with the children.

7. If possible, have a priest come in and bless the rosaries. If you have Miraculous Medals, you may give them to the children to attach to their rosaries. Have them pray: "O Mary, conceived without Original Sin, pray for us who have recourse to Thee."

Name: _____

Immaculate Heart of Mary

Jesus, I am thine, and all that I have is thine through the Immaculate Heart of Mary.

Color the picture below.

Faith and Life Series • Grade 3 • Chapter 29 • Lesson 2   111

15 MYSTERIES OF THE ROSARY

Joyful Mysteries
1. Annunciation
2. Visitation
3. Nativity
4. Presentation
5. Finding of Jesus in the Temple

Sorrowful Mysteries
1. Agony in the Garden
2. Scourging at the Pillar
3. Crowning with Thorns
4. Carrying of Cross
5. Crucifixion

Glorious Mysteries
1. Resurrection
2. Ascension
3. Pentecost
4. Assumption
5. Coronation of Mary

Reinforce

1. Have the students make rosaries and have them blessed.

2. Have the students work on *Activity Book*, p. 111.

3. Have the students begin work on their Memorization Questions for this chapter.

Conclude

Lead the children in singing "Hail, holy Queen enthroned above," *Adoremus Hymnal*, #530.

Preview

In the next lesson the students will learn about Mary as Queen of Heaven and Earth and how she intercedes on our behalf.

Rosary Kit Source

Rosary kits may be purchased from:
The Lewis Rosary Company,
2600 Fifth Avenue, Troy, NY 12180
Telephone: 800-342-2400
Email: lewis@readyfund.com
Web Site: www.rosaryparts.com

NOTES

_____
_____
_____
_____
_____
_____
_____
_____
_____

LESSON THREE: PRAY FOR US SINNERS...

Aims

The students will learn that Mary holds the highest place in Heaven after her Son.

They will understand that Mary helps to bring us closer to Jesus—sometimes through visions and messages.

They will understand that Mary intercedes on their behalf so they should turn to her for prayers.

Materials

- *Activity Book*, p. 112
- Appendix, p. B-31
- Children's Bible

Optional:
- "Hail, holy Queen enthroned above," *Adoremus Hymnal*, #530

Begin

Begin today's class by reading the story of the Wedding at Cana from the children's Bible in John 2:1–11. Ask the children what role Mary had in this story. Explain that to ask on the behalf of another is to intercede. Did Jesus answer her prayer? Why? What did Mary tell the servants to do? Was this good advice?

Mary brought Jesus into our world, and she lived her whole life without sin. That is why she holds the highest place in Heaven after her Son. Just as she brought Jesus to us, so she brings us to Jesus. Sometimes Mary appears on earth with a message from Him. Usually the message is to stop sinning, to love God, and to pray. She tells us these things as a loving Mother, inspiring us gently to be good.

We are wise to ask Mary to pray for us, because Jesus always listens to His Mother. His first miracle at the wedding feast in Cana happened at her request. She told Him, "Son, they have no wine." Jesus had not planned to work a miracle that day, but Mary's request won over His heart. He changed six jars of water into delicious wine for the guests of the bride and groom. Just like the couple in Cana, we can go to Mary for help. We can ask her to tell Jesus what we need. Then we can patiently wait for His generous love to answer.

We please God when we try to imitate the virtues of Mary. Mary's greatest desire was to do His will, and she did it in each hour of her life. In Nazareth, she did His will by keeping a happy, comfortable home for Jesus and Joseph. At the foot of the Cross, she did His will in quiet, helpless suffering. After the feast of Pentecost, she did His will by helping the Apostles build the early Church.

Now Mary is the Queen of Heaven, but she still does whatever God wills. His will is that she remain a loving Mother in our lives, leading us to Jesus and our heavenly home.

Words to Know:

Immaculate Conception   full of grace

Develop

1. Read paragraphs 4 and 5 with the children.

2. Ask the children if they know of an example when Mary came down from Heaven with a message from Jesus. They should know the story of Lourdes from the previous lesson (they may know of other apparitions as well). Ask them questions about the story of Lourdes:
   - When did Mary appear?
   - To whom did Mary appear?
   - What did Mary tell Bernadette?
   - Did Mary sound mean in telling us what to do? Why would she tell us what to do?
   - How would Mary know what is pleasing to her Son?
   - Should we listen to Mary? Should we follow her example?

3. Explain that Mary will pray for us and with us if we ask her to. Ask the children what Marian prayers they know.

Remind them that in the Hail Mary we are asking Mary to pray for us. Surely her prayers must be very powerful before the throne of God. Just as Jesus answered Mary's petition at Cana, He will surely answer the prayer which she will offer to Him on our behalf.

4. Teach the children about Our Lady of Guadalupe and Juan Diego (pertinent facts at right). He was made a saint in July 2002 by Pope John Paul II.

5. Have the students work on their Our Lady of Guadalupe stained glass window crafts. Put a large image of Our Lady of Guadalupe on display for reference. Use the image on p. B-31 in the Appendix from which to make transparencies. Have the students color them with markers and hang them in the window. They will look like stained glass!

Name:_____

Mary

1. Who gave us Mary to be our Mother? When did He do this, and how?

Jesus did it while he was on the Cross by saying, "Mother, behold your son. Son, behold your Mother."

2. What did Mary do to allow Jesus to come into the world?

Mary said "Yes" to God's plan.

3. How did God prepare Mary to be the Mother of Jesus and of the Church?

God allowed Mary to be the one person in the world besides Jesus who was conceived without Original Sin.

4. Did Mary ever sin? What is the title we give to Mary because of this?

Mary never sinned. She was born without Original Sin and this is why we call her the Immaculate Conception.

5. Does Mary ever appear on earth? Why?

Sometimes Mary appears on earth with a message from Jesus.

6. Why should we ask Mary to pray for us?

We should always ask Mary to pray for us because Jesus always listens to His Mother.

7. What was Mary's greatest desire? How can we follow her example?

Mary's greatest desire was to do God's will. We can follow her example by trying to do God's will too.

112 Faith and Life Series • Grade 3 • Chapter 29 • Lesson 3

Reinforce

1. Have the students work on their Our Lady of Guadalupe stained glass craft.

2. Have the students work on *Activity Book*, p. 112.

3. Have the students work on their Memorization Questions for this chapter.

Conclude

Lead the children in singing "Hail, holy Queen enthroned above," *Adoremus Hymnal*, #530, and pray a decade of the rosary before your classroom Marian altar.

Preview

In the next lesson the students will learn about Mary's Assumption and Coronation. You may have a Crowning of Mary ceremony.

JUAN DIEGO AND OUR LADY OF GUADALUPE

Juan Diego was a poor Mexican-Indian who lived about 14 miles north of Mexico City. He would walk those 14 miles every Sunday in order to be on time for Mass. One Sunday morning, as he was walking, he saw an image of the Blessed Virgin Mary. She addressed him in his native language and said, "Juanito, Juan Dieguito, the most humble of my sons, my son the least, my little dear." After his encounter with Mary, the image of the Virgin was emblazoned upon his native cloak, or tilma. Juan Diego told his story, gave away all of his possessions, and lived in the church for the rest of his life, sharing the account of his vision. He was canonized in 2002.

NOTES

LESSON FOUR: HAIL HOLY QUEEN

Aims

The children will learn that Mary was taken up to Heaven, body and soul.

They will know that because of her virtue and obedience to God, Mary was crowned Queen of Heaven and earth.

Your class may have a Crowning of Mary Ceremony.

Materials

- *Activity Book*, p. 113
- Crown for Mary (if your statues did not come with one, you may make one from flowers or construction paper)
- Images of the Assumption and Coronation

Optional:
- "Hail, holy Queen enthroned above," *Adoremus Hymnal*, #530

Begin

Discuss the daily life of Mary in Nazareth. She kept house for Joseph and Jesus. She prepared their meals, made clothes, did handiwork, spent time in prayer, and was obedient to the will of God. Ask the children what sorts of things they think Mary did. Tell them that she did these things joyfully and obediently.

Our Lady has appeared to her children on earth many times. Each time, she brings a special message to build our hope and faith. In the winter of 1531, Mary appeared in Mexico to a humble man named Juan Diego. In this apparition, we call the Mother of God "Our Lady of Guadalupe." Mary's words to Juan Diego are meant for each one of us:

> "Hear me, my dear little child. Let nothing discourage you or make you sad. Do not be afraid of illness, worry, or pain. Am I not here, your Mother? Have I not put you on my lap and sheltered you in my arms? Are you not tucked in the folds of my mantle? Is there anything else you need?"

These words show us that Mary cares for us with the heart of a loving Mother. If we honor and obey her, she will never leave us in this life. She will help us be happy on earth and find our way home to Heaven.

Q. 118 *What was the Immaculate Conception?*
The Immaculate Conception was a unique gift from God to prepare Mary to be the Mother of Jesus. Mary was "full of grace" and free from Original Sin from the first moment of her existence (CCC 490–91).

Develop

1. Read paragraphs 6 and 7 from the textbook.

2. Ask the children about the different virtues of Mary. List them in a chart; cite some examples of how to keep these virtues, as well as examples of how not to keep them. Have the students name as many different virtues as possible. You may refer to the Litany of the Blessed Virgin Mary used in Lesson One for help.

3. Review the Immaculate Conception and remind them that she was conceived without Original Sin. Also tell the children that death and corruption of the body are consequences of Original Sin. Because Mary was sinless—she never had Original Sin—God gave her a special grace. When her time on earth was finished, God took Mary to Heaven body and soul. This mystery is called the "Assumption of Mary." You may show the children a picture of the Assumption.

4. Mary holds the highest place in Heaven after God. God elevated Mary to such a high level because of her life of virtue and as a reward for her faithfulness and love of God. God crowned Mary Queen of Heaven and Earth. This mystery is called the "Coronation." Have the children ever seen the coronation of Queen Elizabeth II or other royalty? It is a great ceremony and a great honor. Jesus is the King of Heaven and Earth, and Mary is His Queen. In the Old Testament, the mother of the king was made queen (see 1 Kings 2:19). You may read Revelations 12:1 so they can visualize the great beauty and royalty of Mary.

5. Explain that just as God crowned Mary, we too should honor her as our Queen. Have a Crowning of Mary ceremony. They may have a procession with the Mary statue, pray the rosary, bring her fresh flowers, crown Mary as Queen, pray the Litany of the Blessed Virgin Mary, and sing "Hail, holy Queen enthroned above," *Adoremus Hymnal, #530.*

Name:_____

Mary, Our Mother

Can you unscramble these words to learn about Mary?

1. Mary was free from sin, and we call this the Immaculate Conception. When it was time for Mary to leave this world, she was taken up to Heaven with her body and soul. This is called the:

   SUMSAPTNOI = **Assumption**

2. There is a prayer, the Hail Mary, that asks Mary to pray for us. If we combine this prayer with the Our Father and the Glory Be and meditate on some mysteries, we have:

   EHT SORRAY = **The Rosary**

3. This is the title of the Glorious Mystery that teaches that Mary was crowned Queen of Heaven and Earth:

   NORCOTONIA = **Coronation**

4. This is the name of the Joyful Mystery that tells us about the Archangel Gabriel's visit to Mary at which time he asks her to be the Mother of Jesus:

   INNNNAAITUCO = **Annunciation**

5. Mary was so blessed! She was with the Apostles when they received the Holy Spirit. What was the name given to that glorious day?

   TEPNCSEOT = **Pentecost**

Faith and Life Series • Grade 3 • Chapter 29 • Lesson 4   113

CHART OF VIRTUES

Virtues	Keeping	Not Keeping
Humility	Thank God for His works	Brag about our works
Faith	Believe in what God tells us	Deny Church teachings
Purity	Guard our words and thoughts	Watch bad movies, speak badly of another

Reinforce

1. Have the students work on page *Activity Book*, p. 113.

2. Give each student a job in the Crowning of Mary ceremony.

3. Have the students write their prayers as a letter to Mary.

4. Have the students work on their Memorization Questions for this chapter and review for the quiz.

Conclude

End class with the Crowning of Mary ceremony and sing "Hail, holy Queen enthroned above," *Adoremus Hymnal*, #530.

Preview

In the next lesson the students' knowledge of the material covered this week will be reviewed and assessed.

NOTES
_____
_____
_____
_____
_____
_____
_____
_____
_____

CHAPTER TWENTY NINE
REVIEW AND ASSESSMENT

Aims

The student's knowledge and understanding of the material covered this week will be reviewed and assessed.

Materials

- Quiz 29, Appendix, p. A-41

Optional:
- "Hail, holy Queen enthroned above," *Adoremus Hymnal*, #530

Review

1. Briefly review the following biblical stories:
   - Annunciation
   - Visitation
   - Nativity
   - Presentation in the Temple
   - Finding of the Child Jesus in the Temple

2. Review the following mysteries:
   - Immaculate Conception
   - Virginal Conception
   - Mother of God
   - Assumption
   - Coronation

3. Review the Marian apparitions you studied in this chapter.

4. Review Mary's virtues and how the children can follow her example.

5. Review the titles of Mary found in the Litany of the Blessed Virgin Mary and discuss what they mean.

Name: _____

Mary, Our Mother And Queen Quiz 29

"Blessed are you among women and blessed is the fruit of your womb" (Luke 1:42).

Word Bank

home	will	Immaculate Conception
grace	pray	
Mother	Guadalupe	

Fill in the blanks with the correct words from the Word Bank.

1. When Jesus said "Behold your Mother," he was speaking to the Apostle John and to the whole Church. Mary is our Heavenly **Mother**. She is the Mother of the Church.

2. Mary was born with no trace of sin. From the moment of her conception she was free from Original Sin. That is why she is called the **Immaculate Conception**.

3. Mary came into the world already filled with God's life. This is why the angel Gabriel said to her, "Hail Mary, full of **grace**.

4. We are wise to ask Mary to **pray** for us, because Jesus always listens to His Mother.

5. Mary's greatest desire was to do God's **will**.

6. Now Mary is the Queen of Heaven, but she still does whatever God wills. His will is that she remain a loving Mother in our lives, leading us to Jesus and our heavenly **home**.

7. In 1531, Mary appeared in Mexico to Juan Diego. She asked him to go to the bishop and ask for a church to be built. We call her "Our Lady of **Guadalupe**."

8. Write out the Scripture verse shown at the top of this page.

_____

Faith and Life • Grade 3 • Appendix A   A - 41

Assess

1. Distribute the quizzes and read through them with the students to be sure they understand the questions.

2. Administer the quiz. As they hand in their work, you may orally quiz them on the Memorization Questions for this chapter.

3. After all the quizzes have been handed in you may wish to review the correct answers with the class.

Conclude

End class by singing, "Hail, holy Queen enthroned above," *Adoremus Hymnal*, #530.

CHAPTER THIRTY
THE COMMUNION OF SAINTS

Catechism of the Catholic Church References

Christian Beatitude: 1720–24, 1728–29
Christian Holiness: 2012–16, 2028–29
Communion of Saints: 946–59, 960–62
Heaven: 1023–29, 1053
Individual Judgment: 1021–22, 1051

Last Judgment: 1038–41, 1059
Prayer for the Dead: 1032, 1055
Purgatory: 1030–32, 1054
Resurrection of the Body: 988–91
To Die in Christ Jesus: 1005–14, 1018–20, 1052

Scripture References

Heaven Described: 1 Cor 2:9; Rev 22:9; 1 Jn 3:2
Life Eternal: Jn 3:16

Purgatory: 2 Macc 12:46
Resurrection of the Body: Jn 6:39–40

Background Reading: *The Fundamentals of Catholicism* by Fr. Kenneth Baker, S.J.

Volume 2:
"The Ascension of Jesus," pp. 308–311

Volume 3:
"Eschatology," pp. 361–88

Summary of Lesson Content

Lesson 1

Death is not the end of life, but its real beginning

Jesus won eternal life by His death on the Cross and Resurrection from the dead.

People who live with God in Heaven are called saints.

Lesson 2

Saints must love God with all their hearts and live according to His Laws.

God called even great sinners to be great saints.

Lesson 3

Many people die in the friendship of God, but are not ready for Heaven. These souls go to Purgatory and are purified so they may go to Heaven.

We can help the souls in Purgatory by praying for them and by offering Masses and sacrifices for them.

The saints in Heaven, the souls in Purgatory, and all people on earth make up the Communion of Saints.

Lesson 4

At then end of the world, God will judge all people.

LESSON ONE: ETERNAL LIFE

Aims

The students will learn that death is not the end of life, but its real beginning

They will learn that Jesus won eternal life for us by His death on the Cross and His Resurrection from the dead.

They will learn that the people who live with God in Heaven are called saints.

Materials

- *Activity Book*, p. 114
- Rite of funerals

Optional:
- "For all the saints," *Adoremus Hymnal*, #590

Begin

Ask the children if they know anyone in Heaven. They will likely start with Mary and the saints. Do they know anyone from their family or any of their friends who are in Heaven? Maybe their grandparents, great aunts, or uncles are in Heaven. How did they get there? You may review the four last things, which were covered in a previous lesson. Tell them that our life's purpose is to know, love, and serve God in this world so that we can be happy with Him in the next.

Develop

1. Read paragraph 1 with the children.

2. Tell the students that we hope in eternal life because of the example Jesus gave us by His own death and Resurrection.

3. Explain that death is very normal but often we feel sad when someone dies. Why? We miss that person. Explain that when a person dies, his body and soul are separated and the soul goes on to eternal life. Our soul is a spiritual being, so it cannot die (only physical things die). Our body, however, stops living.

4. Explain that we must respect our bodies because they are temples of the Holy Spirit. How must we treat our bodies in life? We nourish them and give them exercise. We must take special care of them and not harm them.

5. So, too, in death we must honor the body especially since we believe in the resurrection of the body at the end of this world! At the end of time when Jesus comes for the final judgment, our bodies will share in the eternal life of our souls and share in their rewards! We know this because both Jesus and Mary are in Heaven with their bodies!

6. Explain that as Catholics, when a person dies, we celebrate their passing into eternal life with a funeral. You may explain a funeral rite to the children. Let them know that at some time they may need to go to a funeral. There is no need to be afraid, especially when they see the body, for we are honoring that person and preparing him for eternal glory. Review proper etiquette for funerals. For example, you may remind the children that at funerals, people are sad, so they may say things like: "I'm sorry for your loss. Mr./Ms. _____ was a good person." They should be on their best behavior and they should pray for the deceased.

Name:_____

Heaven

1. To what is death the doorway?
Heaven

2. How was Heaven opened after the sin of Adam and Eve?
By Jesus' death on the Cross

3. What is Heaven?
Heaven is the state of perfect happiness with God forever.

4. Who is in Heaven besides the Blessed Trinity and Mary?
The saints and angels are in Heaven.

5. Is Heaven our true home? How do we know this?
Yes. Answers will vary.

6. Does everyone go to Heaven? What must we do?
No. Answers will vary.

7. What can we do to prepare ourselves for Heaven?
Answers will vary.

8. How can we help others to go to Heaven?
Answers will vary.

114 *Faith and Life Series • Grade 3 • Chapter 30 • Lesson 1*

Reinforce

1. Have the students work on *Activity Book*, p. 114.

2. Have the students begin working on their Memorization Questions for this chapter.

3. Teach the children to sing "For all the saints," *Adoremus Hymnal*, #590.

Conclude

1. Lead the children in singing "For all the saints," *Adoremus Hymnal*, #590.

2. You may teach the children to pray for a happy death. If you do not have such a prayer, pray for the children's deceased family members with a Hail Mary and then conclude with, "Saint Joseph, patron of a happy death, pray for us."

Preview

In the next lesson, the students will learn about the saints in Heaven and how they accepted God's great mercy. They, too, can trust in God's mercy.

RITE OF FUNERALS

The idea of a Christian funeral is to provide a source of communion with the person who has died, as well as a celebration of eternal life, through the Church.

According to the *Catechism of the Catholic Church*, "The Christian funeral is a liturgical celebration of the Church. The ministry of the Church in this instance aims at expressing efficacious communion with *the deceased*, at the participation in that communion of *the community* gathered for the funeral, and at the proclamation of eternal life to the community" (*CCC* #1684).

NOTES

LESSON TWO: DIVINE MERCY

Aims

The students will learn that Saints must love God with all their hearts and live according to His laws.

They will see that God called even great sinners to be great saints. He calls them because of His Divine Mercy.

Materials

- *Activity Book*, p. 115
- Rosaries that the children made in a previous lesson
- Image of Divine Mercy and Divine Mercy Chaplet prayer cards
- Saints kit or stories of saints as examples

Optional:
- "For all the saints," *Adoremus Hymnal*, #590

Begin

Remind the children that our life's purpose is to know, love, and serve God in this world so that we can be happy with Him in the next. We should also help other people do the same.

Our goal is to get to Heaven, for it is there that we will be happy forever! If we love others—and we should love all our neighbors—we should want them to get to Heaven too! Today we can learn from the lives of some saints.

Develop

1. Read paragraph 2 with the children.

2. Using stories of the saints or a saints kit, help the children to research their name–saints and learn how they knew, loved, and served God while on earth. Have them make presentations to one another on their name–saints. (This could be assigned as homework from the previous lesson and they could use the internet–www.catholicsaints.com or www.CatecheticalResources.com. They could dress up as their saint for class.)

3. Tell the story of Saint Faustina Kowalska. She was a religious sister who lived in Poland in the early 20th century. Jesus appeared to her and spoke with her about the need for the conversion of sinners and that His Mercy be spread throughout the world. Jesus had Saint Faustina commission an image (show this image), so that we could develop a devotion to the image of Divine Mercy. When we honor Jesus and His mercy, He will give His Mercy to poor sinners. They can be given the grace of conversion and the grace of Heaven at the end of their lives on earth. If you have prayer cards of the Divine Mercy with the chaplet on the back, hand them out to the children.

4. Teach the children to pray the chaplet of Divine Mercy (see right). It usually takes about fifteen minutes. They may use the rosaries which they have made for this prayer.

5. Explain that it is important to pray for the living and the dead so that we will all know and experience Jesus' Mercy. Teach them to pray "Jesus, I trust in You!" Remind them that it is a spiritual work of mercy to pray for souls!

6. Using the examples of some of the saints that were discussed in this class, show how God's mercy touched each of their souls.

---

30 The Communion of Saints

> "What no eye has seen, nor ear heard, nor the heart of man conceived, what God has prepared for those who love him. . . ."
>
> 1 Corinthians 2:9

Jesus taught us that death is not the end of life, but its real beginning. Death is the doorway to Heaven. Jesus made this possible by His Sacrifice on the Cross. His gift of Himself to the Father was so pleasing that it destroyed death, earning us the gift of eternal life. People who live with God in Heaven after they die are called saints. God welcomes the saints into glorious and everlasting happiness.

While Jesus' death on the Cross opened the gates of Heaven, we must do our part to live there one day. The saints earned their heavenly reward. They loved God and kept His laws. They found many ways to know, love, and serve Him during their lives. They were human, so sometimes they sinned or made mistakes. But they came to God, told Him they were sorry, and started all over again. Some of the greatest saints in Heaven, like Mary Magdalen, Saint Paul, and Saint Augustine, were sinners for a long, long time. But each one finally turned to God and gave Him his whole heart. This love turned them from great sinners into great saints.

Many people who love God and die in His friendship are not fully ready for Heaven. First they go to **Purgatory** to be cleansed of their venial sins. Souls in Purgatory suffer because they miss God, but the suffering is mixed with joy because they know they will see Him soon. We can help the souls in Purgatory reach Heaven faster by offering our Masses, prayers, and sacrifices for them.

Name:_____

Communion of Saints

A spiritual bond of love exists among all the branches in the True Vine wherever they may be: in Heaven, in Purgatory, or on earth. Christ is the vine and we are the branches. In the space below, draw branches and write the names of those you know who are united in Christ, wherever they may be. Now think of Mass, at the end of the Eucharistic Prayer, where the priest raises up the Body and Blood of Christ. Imagine that your prayer is joined to all those in heaven and earth when the priest says: "Through Him, with Him, in Him, in the unity of the Holy Spirit, all glory and honor is yours, almighty Father, forever and ever.

Faith and Life Series • Grade 3 • Chapter 30 • Lesson 2   115

SAINT FAUSTINA KOWALSKA

Saint Faustina Kowalska was a poor girl who received little education, worked as a domestic servant, and became a nun in the Congregation of the Sisters of Our Lady of Mercy in Warsaw when she was still very young. A quiet sister with a deep prayer life, Saint Faustina began to have visions of the Blessed Virgin and received the stigmata. She recorded her experiences in more than 700 pages of phonetically spelled, unpunctuated diary entries. While a bad translation of her diary was labeled heretical, Pope John Paul II called for a better translation, and Faustina was recognized as a saint.

Reinforce

1. Have the students work on *Activity Book*, p. 115.

2. Have the students visit Jesus in the Blessed Sacrament and pray for their loved ones.

3. Have the students work on their Memorization Questions for this chapter.

Conclude

1. Lead the children in singing "For all the saints," *Adoremus Hymnal*, #590.

2. Pray for the living and the dead, asking that God's Divine Mercy will bring them to eternal happiness in Heaven. End class by praying "Jesus, I trust in You!"

Preview

In the next lesson, the students will learn about the Communion of Saints.

CHAPLET OF DIVINE MERCY
(Said on regular rosary beads)

Our Father,
Hail Mary,
Glory Be,
Apostles' Creed

Large Beads:
Eternal Father,
I offer You the Body, Blood,
Soul and Divinity,
of Your Dearly Beloved Son,
Our Lord, Jesus Christ,
in atonement for our sins,
and those of the whole world.

Small Beads of each decade:
For the sake of His sorrowful Passion,
have mercy on us and on the whole world.

Conclude with saying, three times:
Holy God,
Holy Mighty One,
Holy Immortal One,
Have mercy on us,
and on the whole world.

LESSON THREE: COMMUNION OF SAINTS

Aims

The children will learn about the Communion of Saints. Remind them about the Church Militant, the Church Suffering, and the Church Triumphant.

The students will learn how prayer helps all members of the Church through the Communion of Saints.

Materials

- *Activity Book*, p. 116
- Drawing paper, pencil crayons/craft supplies

Optional:
- "For all the saints," *Adoremus Hymnal*, #590

Begin

Begin the class by praying the chaplet of Divine Mercy. You may sing it if you wish.

You may ask the students to share how they have experienced God's Mercy in their lives—maybe through the Sacrament of Penance or an experience of God's love and forgiveness. They may talk about how their name–saints received God's Mercy.

WE PRAY TO GOD AT MASS:

There we hope to share in Your glory when every tear will be wiped away. On that day we shall see You, Our God, as You are. We shall become like You and praise You for ever through Christ Our Lord, from Whom all good things come.

The saints in Heaven, the souls in Purgatory, and the members of the Church on earth make up the whole family of God's people. We call our one great family the **Communion of Saints**. This Communion of Saints can love and help each other across the barriers of time. Even though the saints are in Heaven, and we are on earth, we can call on them for prayers and help. Even though the souls in Purgatory seem so far away, our prayers make us close to them.

One day this world we live in will come to an end. God will gather all of the people who have ever lived and judge each one. That day will be the **Last Judgment**. On that day our good actions will be like treasures. God will see them and He will offer us back a crown of glory. Jesus will say, "Come, you who have My Father's blessing. Inherit the Kingdom prepared for you from the beginning of the world!"

We can look forward to this day of rejoicing by preparing our hearts now, today, on earth. We must always keep our eyes and hearts on Heaven because that is our true home. We will get there if we keep knowing, loving, and serving God, our King and final destiny.

Develop

1. Read paragraphs 3 and 4 with the children.

2. Review:
   - Earth—our time to know, love, and serve God
   - Hell—an eternal state for those who choose not to love and serve God (note: we choose hell by our mortal sins and our rejection of God's love and mercy)
   - Purgatory—a temporary state for souls who die in God's friendship but have either venial sins or have not done penance for the sins they committed on earth. This is a state of being made pure so we can joyfully spend eternity with God in Heaven
   - Heaven—an eternal state for those who die in the friendship with God and are completely purified from sin

3. Use the Chalk Talk diagram at the right to talk about the Communion of Saints. Let the children see how we help one another get to Heaven. Explain that the souls in Heaven help us with their prayers. We simply need to ask them for help. Also, our guardian angels will help us along the way. The souls in Heaven and the souls on earth must pray for the souls in Purgatory that they might get to Heaven faster. The souls on earth can pray for one another as well as for the souls in Purgatory. The souls in Heaven do not need our prayers, but they pray with us and for us to help us get to Heaven, where we will be with them forever.

4. Explain that the entire Communion of Saints benefits from the Mass—at Mass we pray for the souls in Purgatory and they are relieved of their sufferings. The angels and saints are around the altar and we benefit from the Mass and Holy Communion (a foretaste of Heaven!).

Name:_____

Communion of Saints

1. What is the Communion of the Saints?
The Communion of Saints is our one great family made up of the saints in Heaven, the souls in Purgatory, and the members of the Church on earth.

2. The Church is God's family. There are three places where His family may be. What are these three places?
Heaven, Purgatory, and the Church on earth

3. What is Purgatory?
Purgatory is a state in which a soul is made clean from all venial sin and receives punishment due to sins not forgiven before the soul can go to Heaven.

4. What is the Church on earth? What must we do?
The Church on earth is made up of all the followers of Jesus who believe the same faith, receive the sacraments, and obey the Pope.

Faith and Life Series • Grade 3 • Chapter 30 • Lesson 3

Reinforce

1. Have a class Mass and offer it for the souls in Purgatory.

2. Have the students work on *Activity Book*, p. 116.

3. Have the students work on their Memorization Questions for this chapter.

Conclude

1. Lead the children in singing "For all the saints," *Adoremus Hymnal*, #590.

2. End class by praying for the souls in Purgatory and thanking the angels and saints for their help.

Preview

In the next lesson the students will learn about being called to Heaven.

CHALK TALK: COMMUNION OF SAINTS

NOTES

LESSON FOUR: INHERIT THE KINGDOM

Aims

The students will learn that at the end of our lives and at the end of the world, God will judge all people.

They will learn about some of the rewards in Heaven.

Materials

- Appendix, p. B-32
- Craft supplies (note: "jewel" beads may be purchased at craft store)

Optional:
- "For all the saints," *Adoremus Hymnal*, #590

Begin

Read paragraphs 5 and 6 from the student text.

Help the children to contemplate the glories of Heaven using sentences starters (allowing them to finish the sentences), such as:
- Heaven is more beautiful than...
- Heaven is greater than...
- What I most look forward to in Heaven is...
- The saint I want to meet first is...
- In Heaven, I want to...

Words to Know:

Purgatory   Communion of Saints   Last Judgment

Q. 119 *What does "Communion of Saints" mean?*
The *Communion of Saints* means all the faithful who form one single body in Jesus Christ: the victorious souls in Heaven, the suffering souls in Purgatory, and the militant souls on earth (CCC 947, 954).

"Our hearts are made for You, O Lord, and will not rest until they rest in You."

Saint Augustine

Develop

1. Explain that every saint in Heaven is crowned with glory for the way he lived his life and served God. For example, we remember Saint Francis for his great love of the poor. We remember Saint Faustina for teaching us about God's Mercy. We remember Saint Clare for her love of the Eucharist, etc. (you may use any of the saints the children know). We know that Mary was crowned Queen of Heaven and Earth.

2. Explain that these saintly qualities or virtues are what all of us must possess if we hope to join the saints in Heaven. Give some examples of virtues.

3. Explain that these virtues are like jewels in our own crowns of glory.

4. Furthermore, we know that there are other great crowns of glory in Heaven: crowns for virgins (those consecrated to God), crowns for martyrs (those who give their lives witnessing to the truths of God), and crowns for teachers (those who teach others about the truths of God by word and deed).

5. Have the students think about their virtues and the ones they most want to possess. Tell them that they all have some virtues and the ability to grow in all virtues with the help of the Holy Spirit. Let them know that you see some virtues in each of the students. If they have a hard time recognizing a virtue in themselves, help them recognize their virtues and affirm this for them.

6. Ask the students to make crowns using the template in their activity books, or they can make their own. They may use a white crown for virgins, a red crown for martyrs, and a gold crown for teachers. Have them label each jewel with a virtue, using as many as they wish. Let them show their work to the class and explain the crown they want in Heaven.

B - 32
Faith and Life • Grade 3 • Appendix B

Reinforce

1. Have the students present their crowns of glory to the class and tell how they want to get to Heaven. Have them explain the virtues they wish to achieve and why they chose the color of crown they did (red, white, or gold).

2. You have a party to celebrate the end of the year.

3. Have the children review for their quiz.

Conclude

Lead the children in singing "For all the saints," *Adoremus Hymnal*, #590.

Preview

In the next lesson the students' knowledge of the material covered this week will be reviewed and assessed.

CROWN REFERENCES IN HOLY SCRIPTURE

- Phil 4:1
- 1 Th 2:19
- 2 Timothy 4:8
- James 1:12
- 1 Peter 5:4
- Revelations 2:10
- Revelations 3:11

NOTES

CHAPTER THIRTY
REVIEW AND ASSESSMENT

Aims

The student's knowledge and understanding of the material covered this week will be reviewed and assessed.

Materials

- Quiz 30, Appendix, p. A-42
- Unit 7 Quiz, Appendix, pp. A-43 and A-44

Optional:
- "For all the saints," *Adoremus Hymnal*, #590

Review

1. The students should understand that death leads to eternal life. It is the separation of the body and soul. They should be familiar with proper funeral etiquette.

2. The students should know about the four last things: death, judgment, Heaven, and hell.

3. The students should know who is included in the Communion of Saints and how they can help one another to get to Heaven by prayers.

4. The students should know about various saints including their name-saints.

5. The students should understand the need for Divine Mercy.

Name: _____

The Communion of Saints — Quiz 30

"As you did it to one of the least of my brethren, you did it to me" (Matthew 25:40).

Word Bank

| venial | suffer | prayers | Heaven | Last Judgment |
| Cross | Saints | life | serve | |

Fill in the blanks with the correct words from the Word Bank.

1. Jesus taught us that death is not the end of **life** but rather the beginning of eternal happiness that will never end.

2. The Sacrifice on the **Cross** was Jesus' gift of Himself to the Father. It was so pleasing that it destroyed death, earning us the gift of eternal life.

3. Saints are people who live with God in Heaven after they die. On earth the saints loved God and kept His laws. They found many ways to know, love, and **serve** Him.

4. People who love God and die in His friendship but are not fully ready for Heaven go to Purgatory to be cleansed of their **venial** sins.

5. Souls in Purgatory **suffer** because they miss God, but they know they will see Him.

6. We can help the souls in Purgatory reach Heaven faster by offering our Masses, **prayers**, and sacrifices for them.

7. The members of the Church here on earth with those in Heaven and in Purgatory make up one great family called the Communion of **Saints**.

8. At the end of the world, God will judge each one of us. This day is called the **Last Judgment**. God will see all our good actions and give us a crown of glory.

9. We must always keep our eyes and hearts on **Heaven**, because it is our true home.

A - 42   Faith and Life • Grade 3 • Appendix A

Assess

1. Distribute the quizzes and read through them with the students to be sure they understand the questions.

2. Administer the quiz. As they hand in their work, you may orally quiz them on the Memorization Questions for this chapter. After all the quizzes have been handed in you may wish to review the correct answers with the class.

Conclude

1. Lead the children in singing "For all the saints," *Adoremus Hymnal*, #590.

2. End class with a prayer asking God to keep the children safe over the summer so that they may return next year. Send home all of their books and the work they did throughout the year.

Faith and Life series: Our Life With Jesus Appendices

APPENDIX A: QUIZZES AND UNIT TESTS

Unit 1	A-1
Unit 2	A-7
Unit 3	A-13
Unit 4	A-19
Unit 5	A-25
Unit 6	A-31
Unit 7	A-38

APPENDIX B: STORIES, GAMES, CRAFTS, AND SKITS

Play: Creation and the Fall	B-1
Parable Plays	B-7
An Exploration of Angels in Art	B-11
Play: Creation and the Fall	B-12
Creation and the Fall - Act Two: Temptation and the Fall	B-13
Bible Lands Map	B-14
The Ten Commandments Song	B-15
The Church's Calendar	B-16
Jewish Holidays	B-18
The Twelve Apostles	B-21
Jesus' Apostles / Who Am I? (Game)	B-22
Devotion to the Sacred Heart of Jesus	B-23
Baptism Script	B-26
Penance Script	B-28
Eucharist Script	B-29
Our Lady of Guadalupe	B-31
Crown of Glory	B-32

Name: _____

God Loves Us Quiz 1

Word Bank

never	love	star	see	end	talking
lived	all wise	voice	fault	everything	three

Fill in the blanks with the correct words from the Word Bank.

1. God has _____ forever. Billions of years ago God was alive. Billions of years from now He will be just as powerful and alive.

2. God is eternal, which means He had no beginning and He will _____ die.

3. God is all perfect, which means that all good is found in God. He is without any _____ .

4. God is almighty, all holy, and _____ .

5. His power and beauty are infinite, which means without _____ .

6. There is only one God, but in God there are _____ Persons: God the Father, God the Son, and God the Holy Spirit.

7. God was thinking of you, loving you from all eternity. Long before He put one _____ in the sky, He knew you.

8. He knew your name. He knew your face. He knew the color of your eyes and the sound of your _____ . You are precious to Him.

9. God knows _____ about us, even our thoughts.

10. God gave each of us a soul that will never die. He gave us souls so that we could _____ Him.

11. God is pure spirit. We cannot _____ or hear Him but we know He is always with us.

12. Prayer is _____ with God. We need to do it everyday because it keeps us close to Him.

Faith and Life • Grade 3 • Appendix A

Name: _____

God Created the World   Quiz 2

"I have loved you with an everlasting love" (Jeremiah 31:3).

Word Bank

love	created	Heaven	darkness
earth	God	good	Sin
image	everlasting	Lord	life

Fill in the blanks with the correct word from the Word Bank.

1. In the beginning, there was _____, and then God created light.

2. God was happy, but He wanted to share His _____ with us.

3. God _____ the world, which means He made it out of nothing.

4. God created Heaven and _____ .

5. God made a man and a woman in His own _____ and likeness.

6. We believe that God is the _____ , or Master of all things.

7. Everything that God created is _____ .

8. We will be completely happy forever in _____ for we will see God.

9. God promised that He will take us to Heaven if we _____ and serve Him.

10. _____ is any wrong we do on purpose, which turns us away from God.

11. Our Bible verse for today is: "I have loved you with an _____ love."

12. Who loves us with an everlasting love? _____ .

Faith and Life • Grade 3 • Appendix A

Name: _____

Learning About God

Quiz 3

"All Scripture is inspired by God and profitable for teaching." (2 Timothy 3:16).

Word Bank

Shepherd	Jesus	Second	Savior
Bible	New Testament	Church	
Prophets	Parables	Pope	

Fill in the blanks with the correct words from the Word Bank.

1. _____ were men who prepared the people for the coming of the Savior.

2. Jesus is God the Son, the _____ Person of the Trinity.

3. The _____ is a holy book God gave us to tell us of his love for us.

4. The Bible is divided into two parts: the Old Testament and the _____.

5. The Old Testament tells of creation and God's people waiting for the _____.

6. The New Testament tells about _____, our Savior, and the things He said and did.

7. _____ are stories that Jesus used to teach about the Kingdom of God.

8. Jesus, our Teacher, once called Himself the Good _____.

9. Jesus gave us another shepherd to take his place on this earth called the _____.

10. The Pope teaches and guides the _____ for Christ.

11. Write out the Scripture verse shown at the top of this page.

Faith and Life • Grade 3 • Appendix A

Name: _____

The Promise of a Savior   Quiz 4

"Therefore the child to be born will be called holy, the Son of God" (Luke 1:35).

Word Bank

Cross	chose	obey	children
Original	bodies	Adam	
promise	created	Savior	

Fill in the blanks with the correct words from the Word Bank.

1. We cannot see the angels because they are pure spirits. They have no _____.

2. God _____ the angels and gave them free will.

3. The good angels _____ God but the bad angels refused God.

4. Adam and Eve promised to _____ God when He told them not to eat the fruit of the one tree in their beautiful garden.

5. Eve broke her _____ to God by listening to the devil.

6. Eve helped _____ break his promise to God. This first sin was called Original Sin.

7. Because Adam was the father of all people on earth, the effects of his sin are passed on to each one of us. We are all born with _____ Sin on our soul.

8. God promised a _____ who would make up for Adam's sin and reopen the gates of Heaven.

9. Jesus is the Savior. He died on the _____ to make up for our sins.

10. Baptism is the sacrament that takes away Original Sin. We receive grace, which is God's life in us, and we become _____ of God when we are baptized.

11. Write out the Scripture verse shown at the top of this page.

Name: _____

Unit 1 Test   Chapters 1 – 4

Word Bank

Parables	see	everything	life
New Testament	die	Trinity	sin
Bible	three	grace	talking
Original	Baptism	Jesus	

Fill in the blanks with the correct words from the Word Bank.

1. God is eternal, which means He had no beginning and He will never _____ .

2. There is only one God, but in God there are _____ Persons: God the Father, God the Son, and God the Holy Spirit.

3. God knows _____ about us, even our thoughts.

4. God is pure spirit. We can't _____ or hear Him, but we know He is always with us.

5. Prayer is _____ with God. We need to do it everyday because it keeps us close to Him.

6. Jesus is God the Son, the Second Person of the Holy _____ .

7. _____ Sin was the first sin committed, when Adam and Eve disobeyed God.

8. The _____ is a holy book God gave us to tell us of His love for us.

9. The Bible is divided into two parts: the Old Testament and the _____ .

10. The New Testament tells about _____ , our Savior, and the things He said and did.

11. _____ are stories that Jesus used to teach about the Kingdom of God.

Faith and Life • Grade 3 • Appendix A

Unit 1 Test (continued)

12. The sacrament that takes away Original Sin, gives us God's grace, and makes us His children is called the Sacrament of _____.

13. Any wrong we do on purpose which turns us away from God is called _____.

14. Grace is God's _____ within our soul.

15. We receive _____ from the sacraments, prayer, and doing good works.

Write out the following Scripture verses.

"I will not forget you. Behold, I have graven you on the palms of my hands" (Isaiah 49:15-16).

"I have loved you with an everlasting love" (Jeremiah 31:3).

"All Scripture is inspired by God and profitable for teaching . . ." (2 Timothy 3:16).

"Therefore the child to be born will be called holy, the Son of God" (Luke 1:35).

Name:

Abraham: The Father Of God's People Quiz 5

"Wait for the Lord, and he will help you" (Proverbs 20:22).

Word Bank

| Savior | faith | everyone | born | forgot |
| gods | promise | angel | country | Abraham |

Fill in the blanks with the correct words from the Word Bank.

1. The people waited a long time for the promised _____.

2. Some of the people got tired of waiting and began to worship their own _____.

3. These people _____ God, but God did not forget them.

4. He remembered his _____ to send a Savior.

5. _____ was one of the men God chose to prepare the people for the coming of the Savior.

6. Abraham had a great gift from God called _____.

7. God asked Abraham to take his family to a faraway _____ called Canaan.

8. God asked Abraham to offer his son Isaac in sacrifice, but as Abraham was about to strike his son an _____ stopped him.

9. God told Abraham that, out of his family, the Savior of the world would be _____.

10. God asks you to obey your parents right away and to be kind to _____, even to people who have hurt you.

11. Write out the Scripture verse shown at the top of this page.

Name: _____

The Prophet Moses   Quiz 6

"Trust in the Lord for ever, for the Lord God is an everlasting rock"
(Isaiah 26:1-4).

Word Bank

bush	slaves	covenant	Egypt
manna	Passover	Death	
meal	plagues	Commandments	

Fill in the blanks with the correct word from the Word Bank.

1. The Pharaoh in Egypt made God's chosen people his _____ because he was jealous of their loyalty to the one, true God.

2. God spoke to Moses from a burning _____ and told him to tell the Pharaoh to "Let my people go."

3. Pharaoh refused. God sent many disasters or _____ to the land. There were hailstorms, illnesses, frogs, and bugs.

4. Pharaoh continued to say "No," so the Angel of _____ was sent to destroy the firstborn child of every Egyptian family.

5. God commanded that each Israelite family share a special _____ after killing a lamb and sprinkling the lamb's blood on the doorpost.

6. The homes of God's chosen people were passed over by the angel. This was called the _____ .

7. Pharaoh let the Israelites go. Moses led the people out of _____ .

8. God protected His people on their long journey to Canaan. On their journey they received bread from Heaven, called _____ , and fresh water from a rock.

9. Moses received the Ten _____ from God on a mountain-top.

10. God lived up to His promise, or _____ . "You will be My people and I will be your God."

Name: _____

God's Laws of Love Quiz 7

"The Lord is my shepherd, I shall not want" (Psalm 23:1).

Word Bank

anoint	Saul	talking	shepherd	conquered
Goliath	Psalms	David	help	near

Fill in the blanks with the correct words from the Word Bank.

1. The Israelites wanted a king. God told Samuel to _____ the new king by pouring oil over his head. This was a sign of God's gift of power.

2. The first king of Israel was _____ . He was weak and disobedient to God.

3. God chose another king named _____ to rule over His people after Saul died.

4. David was only a young _____ , but he turned out to be a great and wonderful king.

5. David trusted God enough to fight the giant named _____ .

6. David _____ Jerusalem and made it the city of his people.

7. David taught his people the importance of prayer, or _____ with God.

8. David taught his people that, when all hope seems lost, God is _____ us.

9. God's strength and _____ are more powerful than anything in the world.

10. David wrote the _____, which are songs for God that we sing or recite after the first reading at Mass.

11. Write out the Scripture verse shown at the top of this page.

Faith and Life • Grade 3 • Appendix A

Name: _____

King David Quiz 8

"If you love me, you will keep my commandments" (John 14:15).

Word Bank

honor	seven	neighbor	lie	manna
heart	three	joys	Mount Sinai	holy

Fill in the blanks with the correct words from the Word Bank.

1. On the journey to the Promised Land, God fed the Israelites with _____ .

2. On top of _____ , God gave Moses the tablets of the Ten Commandments.

3. The first _____ Commandments tell us how to worship and respect God.

4. The last _____ Commandments tell us how to be kind and fair to each other.

5. Jesus said, "You shall love the Lord your God with your whole _____ , with your whole soul, and with your whole mind. This is the greatest and the first commandment."

6. "And the second is like it, you shall love your _____ as yourself."

7. If we follow His Commandments, God promises to share with us the _____ of Heaven which last forever.

8. God wants me to follow the Ten Commandments always, which means:
    a. To _____ my mother and father.

    b. To keep _____ the Lord's Day by going to church, praying, and not doing unnecessary work.

    c. To tell the truth and not to _____ .

9. Write out the Scripture verse shown at the top of this page.

A - 10   Faith and Life • Grade 3 • Appendix A

Name: _____

Unit 2 Test — Chapters 5 – 8

Word Bank

Abraham	Trust	Faith
Commandments	Mount Sinai	King
Moses	Anoint	Canaan
Covenant	David	Pharaoh

Fill in the blanks with the correct words from the Word Bank.

1. _____ the father of God's chosen people.

2. _____ a gift from God by which we believe in Him and everything He teaches us.

3. _____ to depend on or hope in.

4. _____ ruler in ancient Egypt.

5. _____ a leader of the Israelites to whom God gave the Ten Commandments.

6. _____ name of the Promised Land that God gave to the Israelites.

7. _____ a promise, or agreement, between two persons or groups. God made a covenant with the Israelites, His chosen people.

8. _____ the mountain on which God made a covenant with the Israelites and gave them the Ten Commandments.

9. _____ God's Laws.

10. _____ a man who rules a kingdom.

11. _____ to put oil on someone as a sign that God is giving him power to rule.

12. _____ the boy who killed Goliath and grew up to be a king of Israel.

Faith and Life • Grade 3 • Appendix A

Unit 2 Test (continued)

Write out the following Scripture verses.

"Wait for the Lord, and he will help you" (Proverbs 20:22).

"Trust in the Lord for ever, for the Lord God is an everlasting rock" (Isaiah 26:1-4).

"The Lord is my shepherd, I shall not want" (Psalm 23:1).

"If you love me, you will keep my commandments" (John 14:15).

Name: _____

Loving God Most of All Quiz 9

"Every day I will bless thee and praise thy name for ever" (Psalm 145:2).

Word Bank

anything	gods	tabernacle	name	superstitious
love	Lord	holy	loving	

Fill in the blanks with the correct words from the Word Bank.

1. The First Commandment is "I am the Lord your God; you shall not have other _____ before Me."

2. The First Commandment tells us to adore and worship God. We pray to Him, believe in Him, hope in Him, and _____ Him.

3. The First Commandment tells us not to put anyone or _____ before God.

4. God does not want us to be _____, believing that created things have powers that only God possesses.

5. The Second Commandment is "You shall not take the name of the _____ your God in vain. We must never curse God's Holy Name.

6. The Second Commandment tells us to use the name of God to speak to Him or about Him in a reverent or _____ way.

7. Sentences such as "O God" or "O my God," when one is angry, frightened, or surprised, use God's _____ in the wrong way.

8. In the Our Father we say "Our Father, Who art in Heaven, hallowed by Thy Name." Hallowed means _____ .

9. We are to show respect in holy places. In church while waiting for Mass to begin we can look at the _____ or Jesus on the crucifix and we can pray.

10. Write out the Scripture verse shown at the top of this page.

Faith and Life • Grade 3 • Appendix A

Name: _____

The Lord's Day — Quiz 10

"This is the day, which the Lord has made; let us rejoice and be glad in it" (Psalm 118:24).

Word Bank

holy	happiness	Days	Christmas
serious	Mass	offer	Son

Fill in the blanks with the correct words from the Word Bank.

1. The Third Commandment is "Remember to keep _____ the Lord's Day."

2. The greatest gift that we can offer to God on His day is to participate in the _____ faithfully.

3. At every Mass, we are able to _____ ourselves to God and join ourselves with Christ's gift of Himself to God the Father.

4. In the Mass, the Father gives us His own _____ as "the Bread of Life" in Holy Communion.

5. The Church teaches that there is a _____ obligation for us to participate in the Mass on Saturday evening or Sunday each week unless we are unable to because of sickness, lack of transportation, or other reasons.

6. Sunday is a special day for family and a time for spreading _____ to others.

7. Holy _____ of Obligation are special holy days, besides Sunday, which God wants us to keep those days holy by participating in the Mass.

8. The Holy Day of Obligation we celebrate on December 25 is _____.

9. Write out the Scripture verse shown at the top of this page.

A - 14 *Faith and Life • Grade 3 • Appendix A*

Name: _____

Obedience and Love   Quiz 11

"Children, obey your parents in everything, for this pleases the Lord"
(Colossians 3:20).

Word Bank

others	helped	sacred	difficult	respect
God	kind	obey	happiness	

Fill in the blanks with the correct words from the Word Bank.

1. The Fourth Commandment is "Honor your father and your mother." Honor means to love, respect, and _____ .

2. We bring _____ to our home when we live up to God's Fourth Commandment.

3. Some days it is _____ to obey our parents because we would rather play outside or go somewhere with our friends.

4. We must _____ and obey our parents and teachers and not talk back to them.

5. Jesus wants us to act the way the Good Samaritan did when he _____ the man who had been attacked by robbers.

6. God will reward us if we show a readiness to make sacrifices for _____ and show good will by always wanting to do what is right.

7. The Fifth Commandment is "You shall not kill." The life of every person, no matter how poor, old, weak, or small, belongs to _____ and is precious.

8. The life of every baby inside of his mother is _____ and we must respect it.

9. We must be _____ . We must not argue, fight, hurt others, say mean things to others, or refuse to make up with someone after a fight.

10. Write out the Scripture verse shown at the top of this page.

Faith and Life • Grade 3 • Appendix A

Name: _____

Purity and Truth Quiz 12

"Blessed are the pure in heart, for they shall see God" (Matthew 5:8).

Word Bank

| satisfied | Law | false | truth |
| want | respect | day | Commandment |

Fill in the blanks with the correct words from the Word Bank.

1. The Sixth commandment is "You shall not commit adultery." The Ninth Commandment is "You shall not covet your neighbor's wife." Covet means to _____ what is not yours.

2. In the Sixth and Ninth Commandments, God told us to _____ our bodies and the bodies of other people.

3. Your body is holy because on the _____ of your Baptism, the Holy Spirit came to live inside of it.

4. The Seventh _____ is "You shall not steal." The Tenth Commandment is "You shall not covet your neighbor's goods."

5. The Seventh and Tenth Commandments tell us not to want what others have. We should be _____ with the things we have and share them.

6. If someone takes money or other property that belongs to someone else, he is breaking God's _____ and must make up for it in order to receive forgiveness.

7. The Eighth Commandment is "You shall not bear _____ witness against your neighbor." This commandment tells us not to tell a lie about our neighbor.

8. Sometimes we are afraid to tell the _____, or we want to blame someone else for something we did. God asks us to be honest.

9. Write out the Scripture verse shown at the top of this page.

A - 16 Faith and Life • Grade 3 • Appendix A

Name: _____

Unit 3 Test   Chapters 9 – 12

Word Bank

belong	lie	God	Seventh	wrong
kind	life	Name	talking	day
holy	love	respect	Tenth	

Fill in the blanks with the correct words from the Word Bank.

1. The First Commandment tells us to adore and worship God. We pray to Him, believe in Him, hope in Him, and _____ Him.

2. The Second Commandment teaches us always to honor God's Holy _____. We must never curse God's Holy Name or use His Name in an unholy way.

3. Sentences such as "O God" or "O my God," when one is angry, frightened, or surprised, use God's Holy Name in the _____ way.

4. The Third Commandment tells us to keep _____ the Lord's Day, especially by participating in the Mass every Sunday or Saturday evening.

5. The Fourth Commandment, "Honor your father and your mother," tells us to love, respect, and obey our parents and teachers, without _____ back to them.

6. The Fifth Commandment is "You shall not kill." The life of every person, no matter how poor, old, weak, or small, belongs to _____.

7. Every baby inside of his mother is alive. We respect all _____.

8. In obeying the Fifth Commandment, we must be _____ to others, rather than argue, fight, or say mean and hurtful things to them.

9. The Sixth Commandment is "You shall not commit adultery." We must _____ the Sacrament of Marriage by being pure in thoughts, words, and actions.

Faith and Life • Grade 3 • Appendix A   A - 17

Unit 3 Test (continued)

10. The Ninth Commandment is "You shall not covet your neighbor's wife." The word covet means to want something that does not _____ to you.

11. Your body is holy because, on the _____ of your Baptism, God the Holy Spirit came to live within you. We must respect our bodies and the bodies of others.

12. The _____ Commandment, "You shall not steal," means that we are not to take what belongs to someone else. We are to return what we have stolen.

13. The _____ Commandment is "You shall not covet your neighbor's goods."

14. The Eighth Commandment tells us not to _____ about our neighbor.

List the correct number of the Commandment followed:

15. _____ Honoring God's Holy Name and not using His name in a bad way.
16. _____ Always being honest and telling the truth.
17. _____ Staying away from fighting, hitting, or hurting another person.
18. _____ Adoring and loving God. Always putting God first in one's life.
19. _____ Wanting to receive Holy Communion every Sunday or Saturday evening.
20. _____ Never lying about someone or ruining his good name.
21. _____ Being pure in thoughts, words, and actions.
22. _____ Honoring our parents by doing what they ask and not talking back to them.
23. _____ Being satisfied with what one has, rather than wanting other people's things.
24. _____ Wearing clothes and speaking words according to God's holy will.
25. _____ Respecting life within the mother. Respecting the elderly and disabled.
26. _____ Trusting in God instead of thinking that objects have powers.
27. _____ Staying away from movies and television programs that show things against God's Commandments.
28. _____ Saying a prayer if we hear God's name used wrongly.
29. _____ Return or pay for anything one has ever taken from another person.
30. _____ Looking forward to participating in Mass every Sunday.

Name:

God's Tender Mercy   Quiz 13

"Blessed are the merciful, for they shall obtain mercy" (Matthew 5:7).

Word Bank

sheep	Christ	sins	priests	forgiven
venial	Easter	go	grace	

Fill in the blanks with the correct words from the Word Bank.

1. God's love follows us wherever we _____ .

2. Jesus told us that He is the Good Shepherd and we are His _____ .

3. Only God can forgive sins. On that first _____ Sunday night, Jesus gave His Apostles the power to forgive sins in His Name.

4. Jesus breathed on the Apostles and said, "Peace be with you. Receive the Holy Spirit; if you forgive men's sins, they are _____."

5. The Apostles were the early _____ of the Church. Our priests today have the same power to forgive sins through the Sacrament of Penance.

6. The Sacrament of Penance frees our souls of any mortal sins that remove God's life of _____ from our souls.

7. The Sacrament of Penance or Reconciliation frees us of less serious, _____ sins that weaken our love toward God and our neighbor.

8. When we go to a priest in the Sacrament of Penance, we can be sure that _____ Himself is present and He washes away all our sins.

9. God will never turn us away when we are truly sorry for our _____ .

10. Write out the Scripture verse shown at the top of this page.

Faith and Life • Grade 3 • Appendix A

Name: _____

Meeting Jesus in Confession — Quiz 14

"If you forgive the sins of any, they are forgiven" (John 20:23).

Word Bank

forgiving	receive	sorry	Jesus
penance	sins	absolution	offend

Fill in the blanks with the correct words from the Word Bank.

1. If we hurt someone, we tell that person that we are _____.

2. In the Sacrament of Penance we tell _____ that we are sorry.

3. We prepare to _____ the sacrament by making an examination of conscience. We think about what we have done wrong and about how many times we have done it.

4. Next, we think about how our sins _____ Jesus and how we are sorry for them. We make up our mind not to commit the same sins again. We say the Act of Contrition.

5. We go into the confessional or reconciliation room and tell our _____ to the priest. After we are finished, the priest talks to us about what we have told him.

6. The priest then gives us a _____ which can be prayers or things to do to make up for the wrong we have done to God and others. Then we say the Act of Contrition.

7. We receive _____, the forgiveness of our sins, when the priest says, "I absolve you from your sins in the Name of the Father and of the Son and of the Holy Spirit."

8. Every time we hear the words of absolution, we know that Jesus Himself is _____ us through the priest.

9. Write out the Scripture verse shown at the top of this page.

Name: _____

The Christ Child Is Born Quiz 15

"Glory to God in the highest, and on earth peace among men with whom he is pleased!" (Luke 2:14).

Word Bank

| gifts | Jesus | Savior | Bethlehem |
| word | news | Mary | Joseph |

Fill in the blanks with the correct words from the Word Bank.

1. Angel Gabriel said to Mary: "Hail, full of grace, the Lord is with you! Blessed are you among women! You will bear a son and call His name _____."

2. Mary told the angel, "Behold the handmaid of the Lord, let it be done to me according to your _____."

3. God prepared _____ to be the mother of the Savior. From the first moment of her life, she was full of grace, without Original Sin. This is called Mary's Immaculate Conception.

4. God chose a good man named _____ to be the foster father of Jesus.

5. Jesus was born in poverty in a stable at _____.

6. An angel appeared to shepherds and said "Behold I bring you good _____ of great joy."

7. "Today in the town of David, has been born to you _____, Who is Christ the Lord. You will find him lying in a manger."

8. The shepherds ran to adore Him. Later three wise men brought him precious gifts. We can bring the Christ child our hearts as our _____ for Him.

9. Write out the Scripture verse shown at the top of this page.

Faith and Life • Grade 3 • Appendix A

Name: _____

Jesus Grows In Age and Wisdom Quiz 16

"Thou art my beloved Son; with thee I am well pleased" (Luke 3:22).

Word Bank

baptized	Jewish	thirty	prophets	Nazareth
carpenter	Joseph	dove	blesses	

Fill in the blanks with the correct words from the Word Bank.

1. As a boy growing up in _____, Jesus led an ordinary life. He ate, slept, laughed, played, worked, and studied.

2. Since Jesus was _____ , He learned all the Jewish customs and traditions of His time.

3. Joseph, a skilled _____ , probably taught Jesus how to make fine things from wood.

4. No one knew He was God's own Son except Mary and _____ .

5. We call the first _____ years of Jesus' time on earth "His hidden life."

6. God _____ us for acting as Jesus did when He was growing up.

7. John the Baptist was the last of the _____ to prepare the way for Jesus.

8. Jesus was _____ by John the Baptist in the River Jordan.

9. At His Baptism, the Holy Spirit came down upon Jesus in the form of a _____ . The voice of His Father called from Heaven: "This is my Beloved Son; with whom I am well pleased."

10. Write out the Scripture verse shown at the top of this page.

Name: _____

Unit 4 Test   Chapters 13 – 16

Match the letter of the correct answer with the word or phrase on the left.

___ 1. grace

___ 2. Act of Contrition

___ 3. Nazareth

___ 4. Apostles

___ 5. Angel Gabriel

___ 6. Immaculate Conception

___ 7. dove

___ 8. parables

___ 9. Bethlehem

___ 10. River Jordan

___ 11. John the Baptist

___ 12. Our Savior

A. The town where Jesus was born

B. The holy man who baptized Jesus

C. God's life in us

D. A prayer telling God we are sorry for our sins

E. God's messenger to Mary

F. Mary was created free from Original Sin

G. Christ the Lord

H. Place where Jesus was baptized

I. A symbol of the Holy Spirit

J. Jesus' chosen disciples

K. The town in which Jesus grew up

L. Stories Jesus told to explain the Kingdom of God

Faith and Life • Grade 3 • Appendix A

Name: _____

Unit 4 Test (continued)

Word Bank

offended	sins	resolve
detest	grace	
penance	all good	

Fill in the blanks with the correct words from the Word Bank.

Act of Contrition

O my God, I am heartily sorry for having _____ You.

I _____ all my _____ because of Your just punishments, but

most of all because they offend You, my God, Who are _____ and

deserving of all my love. I firmly _____ , with the help of Your

_____ , to confess my sins, to do _____ , and to amend

my life. *Amen.*

A - 24   Faith and Life • Grade 3 • Appendix A

Name: _____

Signs and Wonders   Quiz 17

"I am with you always, to the close of the age" (Matthew 28:20).

Word Bank

Lazarus	man	miracles	cured	parables
fish	wine	faith	Galilee	seed

Fill in the blanks with the correct words from the Word Bank.

1. When Jesus was about thirty years old, He began teaching in a place called _____.

2. Jesus performed many _____ to prove that He was the Savior and the Son of God.

3. When a bride and groom ran out of wine at their wedding feast in Cana, Jesus changed the water in six stone jars into good _____.

4. Jesus fed a crowd of over five thousand with five loaves of bread and two _____.

5. At the word of Jesus, the blind saw, the lame walked, and the sick were cured. All of this gave people great _____ in Jesus.

6. Jesus _____ a Roman soldier's servant from a distance because of the soldier's belief in Jesus.

7. Jesus raised _____ from the dead.

8. Jesus used ordinary stories, called _____ , to teach about God and Heaven.

9. He compared the tiny mustard _____ with His own Kingdom, which had small beginnings but would cover the whole world.

10. Jesus Christ is true God and true _____ .

11. Write out the Scripture verse shown at the top of this page.

Name: _____

The Last Supper, Our First Mass Quiz 18

"Love one another as I have loved you" (John 15:12).

Word Bank

Mass	wash	bread	Passover
wine	changed	Jesus	Sacrament

Fill in the blanks with the correct words from the Word Bank.

1. On Holy Thursday, the night before He died, Jesus and His Apostles gathered to celebrate the feast of the _____, a holy dinner in memory of the time God saved the Israelites from slavery in Egypt.

2. That night Jesus knelt down to _____ the feet of His Apostles, telling them that He had given them an example that they should follow.

3. During the meal, Jesus took _____, blessed and broke it, and gave it to His Apostles saying "This is My Body which will be given up for you."

4. Then He took a cup of _____. He gave thanks and gave it to them saying, "This is the cup of My Blood, the Blood of the new and everlasting covenant. It will be shed for you and for all, so that sins may be forgiven."

5. At the moment Jesus spoke the words, the bread and wine were _____ into His Body and Blood. It looked and tasted like bread and wine, but it was now Jesus.

6. Jesus told the Apostles, "Do this in remembrance of Me." With these words, _____ gave the Apostles the power to do the same.

7. At every Holy _____ the priest says the same words over bread and wine, and they become the Body and Blood of Jesus.

8. We call this the _____ of the Holy Eucharist. When we receive this sacrament, Jesus comes into our hearts alive and full of love.

9. Write out the Scripture verse shown at the top of this page.

Name: _____

Jesus Gives His Life for Us — Quiz 19

"Could you not watch with me one hour?" (Matthew 26:40).

Word Bank

forgive	unpopular	Heaven	Calvary	sacrifice
Passion	head	Cross	John	pray

Fill in the blanks with the correct words from the Word Bank.

1. After the supper, Jesus went to the Garden of Olives to _____ . In His Agony in the Garden, He asked His Apostles, "Could you not watch with me one hour."

2. Pilate knew Jesus was innocent, but he was afraid of being _____ .

3. The soldiers beat Jesus with whips and pushed a crown of sharp thorns on his _____ .

4. They made Him carry a heavy _____ . He fell three times.

5. When Jesus reached the top of Mount _____ , the soldiers nailed His hands and feet to the wood of the Cross, raised the Cross upright, and left Him to die in pain.

6. Jesus asked His Father to _____ the cruel soldiers.

7. He gave His Mother to be the Mother of His Apostle _____ and of all people.

8. Jesus wanted to redeem us and to buy our freedom, so we could go to _____ .

9. A _____ is something that is offered to God. Jesus offered Himself as a sacrifice to God so we could receive God's life within us and become His children.

10. The _____ and death of Jesus saved the world.

11. Write out the Scripture verse shown at the top of this page.

Faith and Life • Grade 3 • Appendix A

Name: _____

Offering Gifts of Love   Quiz 20

"I am the living bread which came down from heaven" (John 6:51).

Word Bank

Son	destroyed	Temple	Blood
Christ	offered	Apostles	Sacrifice

Fill in the blanks with the correct words from the Word Bank.

1. All through the ages, God's children have _____ sacrifices to Him as a sign of their worship and love.

2. Whenever a person offered up something in sacrifice, he burned or _____ it. This showed that he was giving it completely back to God.

3. Jewish families went to worship God at the _____ in Jerusalem. They offered up lambs, doves, and food.

4. When Jesus shed His _____ on the Cross, He gave God the perfect gift: the Sacrifice of Himself on the Cross.

5. Jesus made it possible for the perfect gift of His Body and Blood to be offered continually. At the Last Supper, Jesus gave His _____ the power to change bread and wine into His Body and Blood.

6. Today all over the world the Sacrifice of the Mass continues in the same way. Every time we go to Holy Mass, we offer _____ Himself to the Father.

7. Mass is the very same _____ as the one that took place on Calvary.

8. Jesus, the _____ of God, is being offered continually to save our world. With the priest we offer Jesus to the Father—the best gift we can give.

9. Write out the Scripture verse shown at the top of this page.

Name: _____

Unit 5 Test　　　　　　　　　　　　　　　Chapter 17 – 20

Match the events on the left with the sentences on the right. Place the letter of the correct answer next to the sentence.

A. Last Supper

B. Agony in the Garden

C. Good Friday

D. Easter Sunday Morning

E. Easter Sunday Evening

1. Jesus washed the feet of His Apostles. ____

2. "Could you not watch with me one hour?" ____

3. "This is My Body which will be given up for you." ____

4. "Receive the Holy Spirit. If you forgive the sins of any, they are forgiven." ____

5. "He has risen." ____

6. "Woman, behold your Son!" ____

7. "This is the cup of my Blood." ____

8. "Do this in remembrance of Me." ____

9. The solders beat Him with whips and pushed a crown of sharp thorns on His head. ____

10. "Father, forgive them." ____

Faith and Life • Grade 3 • Appendix A

Unit 5 Test (continued)

Write the letter of the phrase from the right column that matches the items on the left.

_____ 1. Calvary

_____ 2. Sacrifice

_____ 3. Mass

_____ 4. Covenant

_____ 5. Holy Thursday

_____ 6. Redeem

_____ 7. Remembrance

_____ 8. Temple

A. The Sacrifice of Jesus on the Cross, offered by the priest.

B. The building in Jerusalem where the Jews worshipped God.

C. The day the Holy Eucharist was given at the Passover Meal.

D. The hilltop where Jesus died.

E. A word that means in memory of something.

F. To free someone by buying his freedom.

G. Something that is offered to God. At every Mass, the _____ of Christ on the Cross is offered.

H. An agreement; a promise. God had a _____ with His Chosen people.

Name: _____

The Holy Mass   Quiz 21

"I am the living bread, which came down from heaven" (John 6:51).

Word Bank

Father	God	priest	Calvary	News
belief	adore	Cross	Gospel	Mass

Fill in the blanks with the correct words from the Word Bank.

1. At every Mass a miracle happens. Through the _____, God changes the bread and wine into Christ's own Body and Blood.

2. The priest lifts up the Sacred Host and the Cup of Salvation and offers them to the _____.

3. Christ, the Lamb of God, is sacrificed on the altar at Mass just as He was on _____. It is in a different way, but it is the very same Sacrifice.

4. We are obliged to go to Mass every Sunday and on Holy Days of Obligation to offer Jesus to the Father with the priest. We are to worship and _____ Him.

5. At the beginning of Mass, we make the Sign of the _____. We call to mind our sins and ask God's forgiveness.

6. We listen to the readings from the Old and New Testament. We stand for the _____ reading because we are hearing Jesus' own words.

7. The Gospel means Good _____. The Good News of Christ's miracles, parables, and teachings are meant for us today, as it was meant for those who lived two thousand years ago.

8. After the homily, we stand and say the Creed. The word Creed means _____. We say out loud that we believe in God, the Father, Son, and Holy Spirit.

9. Jesus comes into our hearts and lives at Mass. He teaches us through the readings. He offers Himself for us to _____ our Father.

10. Jesus unites Himself to us in Holy Communion. The Holy _____ is the greatest prayer.

Faith and Life • Grade 3 • Appendix A

Name: _____

Offering Jesus to the Father Quiz 22

Match the letter of the correct response on the right to the statement on the left.

WHAT THE PRIEST SAYS	WHAT WE SAY
1. Blessed are you, Lord, God of all creation. Through your goodness we have this bread to offer, which earth has given and human hands have made. It will become for us the bread of life. _____	A. It is right to give Him thanks and praise.
2. Pray, brethren, that our sacrifice may be acceptable to God, the Almighty Father. _____	B. Christ has died, Christ is risen, Christ will come again.
3. The Lord be with you. _____	C. Amen.
4. Lift up your hearts. _____	D. And also with you.
5. Let us give thanks to the Lord our God. _____	E. Blessed be God forever.
6. Let us proclaim the mystery of faith. _____	F. May the Lord accept the sacrifice at your hands for the praise and glory of his Name, for our good, and the good of all His Church.
7. Through Him, with Him, in Him, in the unity of the Holy Spirit, all glory and honor is yours almighty Father, forever and ever. _____	G. We lift them up to the Lord.

Name: _____

The Bread of Life — Quiz 23

"I am the bread of life; he who comes to me shall not hunger" (John 6:35).

Word Bank

closer	God	supper	worthy	friendship
Lamb	unbreakable	family	Bread	

Fill in the blanks with the correct words from the Word Bank.

1. In the Old Testament, the people would offer up a lamb. It was killed and the family would eat the lamb as a sacred meal and as a sign of their covenant and friendship with _____ .

2. They wanted to be _____ to Him by eating something offered as a sacrifice to Him.

3. Under the New Covenant, we lift up the _____ of God. Then we share in this Sacrifice by receiving God's own Son in Holy Communion.

4. The priest holds Jesus before us and says, "This is the Lamb of God who takes away the sins of the world. Happy are those who are called to His _____ ."

5. We look at Jesus and answer, "Lord, I am not _____ to receive You, but only say the word and I shall be healed."

6. To share fully in the New Covenant or full _____ with God, we must share in Jesus' Sacrifice and the meal of the Sacrifice.

7. The Eucharist, the _____ of Life, keeps the life of grace alive in our hearts.

8. Sharing this sacred banquet unites us in friendship with the Father. Our faith in the one, true God makes us a _____ .

9. The New Covenant is the perfect and _____ friendship with God. Jesus won the New Covenant for us.

10. Write out the Scripture verse shown at the top of this page.

Name: _____

Jesus Comes to Us in the Holy Eucharist   Quiz 24

"He who believes in me shall never thirst" (John 6:35).

Word Bank

bread	Life	5,000	Mass	God
close	listens	kind	grace	thanks

Fill in the blanks with the correct words from the Word Bank.

1. Jesus changed five loaves of bread and two fish into food for over _____ people.

2. He promised them a more wonderful bread when He said, "I am the _____ of life; he who comes to me shall not hunger, and he who believes in me shall never thirst" (John 6:35).

3. The Holy Eucharist is the Bread of _____ that Jesus promised.

4. We are so fortunate because we can receive the Holy Eucharist at every _____ .

5. For a worthy reception of Holy Communion, three things are necessary: to be in the grace of _____ , to realize and consider whom we are about to receive, and to observe the Eucharistic fast (CCC1385–88).

6. After we receive Jesus, we kneel down to make a thanksgiving. We give _____ to Jesus for being with us.

7. We silently pray to Him and He _____ . If we are having trouble being kind or good, Jesus understands. He will help us.

8. Every time Jesus comes to us in Holy Communion, He fills our souls with His own life. God's life within us is called _____ . Our venial sins are taken away.

9. When we receive the Holy Eucharist our charity (our love for God and our neighbor) increases. We receive the strength to be generous, forgiving, and _____ .

10. The best way to stay _____ to Jesus is to go to Mass and receive Holy Communion, even every day if possible.

11. Write out the Scripture verse shown at the top of this page.

Name: _____

Jesus Rises in Splendor   Quiz 25

"I am with you always, to the close of the age" (Matthew 28:20).

Word Bank

Apostles	risen	sins	Holy Spirit
Peace	Resurrection	forty	Sunday

Fill in the blanks with the correct words from the Word Bank.

1. Early on the _____ morning after Jesus died, some women went to anoint His Sacred Body with spices and oils.

2. A beautiful angel told the women that Jesus was no longer dead, but alive. "He is _____ !" the angel said, "Rejoice and tell the others."

3. The women ran to find the _____ and tell them the news. Peter and John ran to the tomb and found only the burial cloths. Jesus had risen from the dead. He was alive.

4. Jesus first appeared to Mary Magdalene, the holy woman whose many _____ He had forgiven. He said her name as she was weeping in the garden near the tomb.

5. Soon after, the disciples were all gathered together in an upper room. Even though the doors were locked, Jesus appeared and said " _____ be with you."

6. The Apostle Thomas was not present and would not believe. When Jesus appeared again, Thomas said "My Lord and my _____ ."

7. On Good Friday, Jesus suffered and died on the Cross. On Easter Sunday He rose from the dead. Every Easter, we celebrate this miracle of the _____ .

8. After He rose from the dead, Jesus stayed among His disciples for _____ days.

9. He told Peter, the first Pope, to "feed my sheep." He told all of them to go out to teach and baptize. He promised He would send the _____ to help them.

Name: _____

Unit 6 Test   Chapters 21 – 25

Word Bank

Offertory	Creed	Disciple	Divinity
Eucharist	Thanksgiving	Covenant	Gospel
Consecration	Appearance	Worship	Easter
Good Friday	Worthy	Host	Resurrection

Fill in the blanks with the correct words from the Word Bank.

1. _____ Love, honor, and adoration, which we give to God.

2. _____ Good News. The story of the Life, Death, and Resurrection of Jesus.

3. _____ A prayer telling what we believe.

4. _____ The part of the Mass in which bread and wine are offered as a gift.

5. _____ The part of the Mass in which the priest changes the bread and wine into the Body and Blood of Jesus.

6. _____ The round wafer of bread used at Mass.

7. _____ The Sacrament of the Body and Blood of Jesus. He comes to us in the appearance of bread and wine.

8. _____ The nature of God.

9. _____ The way something looks or appears to be.

A - 36   Faith and Life • Grade 3 • Appendix A

Unit 6 Test (continued)

10. _____ Deserving.

11. _____ A promise or an agreement. God made one with the Israelites.

12. _____ Giving thanks.

13. _____ A follower of Jesus.

14. _____ The day Jesus suffered and died for us.

15. _____ The day Jesus rose from the dead.

16. _____ The event of Jesus' rising from the dead.

Name: _____

The Coming of The Holy Spirit — Quiz 26

"Do you not know that you are God's temple and that God's Spirit dwells in you?" (1 Corinthians 3:16).

Word Bank

Ascension	temples	courage	miracles	Pentecost
flame	Heaven	baptized	Apostles	

Fill in the blanks with the correct words from the Word Bank.

1. After Jesus rose up to Heaven on _____ Thursday, the Apostles and Mary stayed together praying.

2. Ten days later, a strong wind suddenly swept through the house. A bright _____ appeared over each one of the Apostles and Mary, the Mother of Jesus.

3. God the Holy Spirit, the Third Person of the Holy Trinity, came into their hearts and filled them with _____ and love.

4. The _____ began preaching at once. The Holy Spirit gave them the power to speak in a way that people of every language could understand.

5. Peter told the people, "Repent, and be _____, every one of you in the name of Jesus Christ for the forgiveness of your sins, and you shall receive the gift of the Holy Spirit."

6. On that day of _____, three thousand people were baptized. The people received the gifts of the Holy Spirit, as we received them when we were baptized.

7. The Holy Spirit came to live within us on the day we were baptized. We are _____ of the Holy Spirit. He inspires us to love others, even when it seems difficult.

Name: _____

God's Family on Earth   Quiz 27

"You did not choose me, but I chose you" (John 15:16).

Word Bank

| sacraments | rock | martyrs | lives | Christ |
| Church | keys | spread | bishops | |

Fill in the blanks with the correct words from the Word Bank.

1. Jesus founded the _____ on earth. Before He ascended into Heaven, He gave His Apostles the power to teach and guide her.

2. Jesus said to Peter, "You are Peter and upon this _____ I will build my church. And the gates of hell shall not prevail against it."

3. Jesus said to Peter, "I will entrust to you the _____ of the Kingdom of Heaven. Whatever you declare bound on earth shall be bound in Heaven." Peter became the first Pope.

4. The Pope represents _____ on earth. Jesus Himself gave the Pope that power. Catholics everywhere respect and obey Him.

5. The Pope is head of the thousands of _____ all over the world. These are the teachers of the Church, who preach and guide all entrusted to their care.

6. Priests bring us the grace of the _____ . They share in the God-given power to forgive sins and offer Holy Mass. Jesus comes into our lives through them.

7. Religious sisters and brothers give their whole _____ to God. Some are missionaries sacrificing to serve God and His people in far away lands.

8. Those who die for the Word of God are called _____ .

9. The Church is called Catholic, meaning "universal" or "for all." Because of good priests, missionaries, and lay people, the Church has _____ to all nations.

10. Write out the Scripture verse shown at the top of this page.

Name: _____

Our Life in the Church Quiz 28

Word Bank

grace	Confirmation	name	life	powerful
love	Eucharist	sign	Baptism	

Fill in the blanks with the correct words from the Word Bank.

1. Signs help us by calling our attention to important things we cannot see or hear. A mother's kiss is a sign of her _____ .

2. The sacraments are signs of _____ instituted by Jesus Christ to make us holy. Jesus gave us signs of His grace in the seven sacraments.

3. A sacrament is a _____ that fills us with grace. It uses things we can see and hear to tell us about something we cannot see or hear.

4. In the Sacrament of _____ , our parents and godparents made our baptismal promises for us.

5. At our Baptism, the priest or deacon poured water over our head, called us by _____ , and said, "I baptize you in the Name of the Father and of the Son and of the Holy Spirit."

6. At the very moment of Baptism, Original Sin is washed away and our souls are filled with God's own _____ , called grace.

7. We can spend the rest of our lives keeping grace in our souls by receiving the Sacrament of the _____ and the Sacrament of Penance often.

8. The seven sacraments are Baptism, _____ , Eucharist, Penance, Anointing of the Sick, Holy Orders, and Matrimony (Marriage). Receiving the sacraments gives us grace and unites us to God.

9. Prayer is _____ . Prayers for people who do not yet know and love God can bring them closer to Him.

Name: _____

Mary, Our Mother and Queen — Quiz 29

"Blessed are you among women and blessed is the fruit of your womb" (Luke 1:42).

Word Bank

home	will	Immaculate Conception
grace	pray	
Mother	Guadalupe	

Fill in the blanks with the correct words from the Word Bank.

1. When Jesus said "Behold your Mother," he was speaking to the Apostle John and to the whole Church. Mary is our Heavenly _____. She is the Mother of the Church.

2. Mary was born with no trace of sin. From the moment of her conception, she was free from Original Sin. That is why she is called the
_____.

3. Mary came into the world already filled with God's life. This is why the angel Gabriel said to her, "Hail Mary, full of _____."

4. We are wise to ask Mary to _____ for us, because Jesus always listens to His Mother.

5. Mary's greatest desire was to do God's _____.

6. Now Mary is the Queen of Heaven, but she still does whatever God wills. His will is that she remain a loving Mother in our lives, leading us to Jesus and our heavenly _____.

7. In 1531, Mary appeared in Mexico to Juan Diego. She asked him to go to the bishop and ask for a church to be built. We call her "Our Lady of _____."

8. Write out the Scripture verse shown at the top of this page.

Faith and Life • Grade 3 • Appendix A

A - 41

Name: _____

The Communion of Saints Quiz 30

"As you did it to one of the least of my brethren, you did it to me" (Matthew 25:40).

Word Bank

venial	suffer	prayers	Heaven	Last Judgment
Cross	Saints	life	serve	

Fill in the blanks with the correct words from the Word Bank.

1. Jesus taught us that death is not the end of _____ but rather the beginning of eternal happiness that will never end.

2. The Sacrifice on the _____ was Jesus' gift of Himself to the Father. It was so pleasing that it destroyed death, earning us the gift of eternal life.

3. Saints are people who live with God in Heaven after they die. On earth the saints loved God and kept His Laws. They found many ways to know, love, and _____ Him.

4. People who love God and die in His friendship but are not fully ready for Heaven go to Purgatory to be cleansed of their _____ sins.

5. Souls in Purgatory _____ because they miss God, but they know they will see Him.

6. We can help the souls in Purgatory reach Heaven faster by offering our Masses, _____, and sacrifices for them.

7. The members of the Church here on earth with those in Heaven and in Purgatory make up one great family called the Communion of _____.

8. At the end of the world God will judge each one of us. This day is called the _____. God will see all our good actions and give us a crown of glory.

9. We must always keep our eyes and hearts on _____ because it is our true home.

Name: _____

Unit 7 Test — Chapters 26 – 30

Write the letter of the phrase from the right column that matches the item on the left.

_____ 1. Grace	A. God's life within us.
_____ 2. Holy Spirit	B. God, the Third Person of the Holy Trinity.
_____ 3. Pentecost	C. The day that the Holy Spirit appeared as tongues of fire above Mary and the Apostles.
_____ 4. Ascension	D. Our Heavenly Mother
_____ 5. Sacraments	E. Jesus rising to Heaven in front of His Apostles.
_____ 6. Martyrs	F. Mary's life began with no trace of sin.
_____ 7. Immaculate Conception	G. Represents Christ on earth. Head of the Catholic Church.
_____ 8. Mary	H. Persons who gave their lives for God.
_____ 9. Pope	I. Signs of grace given by Jesus to make us holy. The first sign of grace is Baptism.
_____ 10. Purgatory	J. The Sacrament of the Body and Blood of Jesus Christ.
_____ 11. Communion of Saints	K. The place where a soul goes to be made clean of venial sins.
_____ 12. Last Judgment	L. The sacrament in which all our sins are forgiven.
_____ 13. Holy Eucharist	M. All members of the Church: on earth, in Purgatory, and in Heaven.
_____ 14. Penance	N. The event at the end of the world when God will judge us.
_____ 15. Heaven	O. Our true home.

Faith and Life • Grade 3 • Appendix A

Unit 7 Test (continued)

Word Bank

| all good | penance | grace | resolve |
| sins | offended | detest | |

Use the words in the Word Bank to fill in the missing parts of the Act of Contrition.

Act of Contrition

O my God, I am heartily sorry for having _____ You.

I _____ all my _____ because of Your just punishments, but

most of all because they offend You, my God, Who are _____ and

deserving of all my love. I firmly _____ , with the help of

Your _____ , to confess my sins, to do _____ ,

and to amend my life. *Amen.*

Play: Creation and the Fall

Materials:

Costumes

pink or flesh-colored tights and T-shirts for Adam and Eve; black or red cape, tights, and T-shirt for devil.

Props

two kitchen brooms for tree trunks

poster board: two yellow for sun and stars; six brown for dry land and tree trunks; three blue for water; four green for trees, leaves, and grass; three white for clouds and miscellaneous planets; scraps for fish and birds.

artificial fruit to hang on a tree, glue sticks, scissors, yarn (a few yards any color, for birds, fish, and strings of leaves), tape, stuffed animals, potted plants.

Characters:

Narrator
God
Adam
Eve
Devil
Two Clouds
Three students for Water
Four students for Land
Two Trees
One Sun
One Moon
Stars and Planets

Direct Aim: to learn the story of creation and the Fall as recorded in the first chapters of Genesis

Making props:

Patterns for several shapes are printed on pages B-3–B-6.

Draw the following shapes on poster board and cut them out:

1 large yellow sun

1 medium white moon

2 large white clouds (see pattern)

3 large blue waves of water (see pattern)

4 brown pieces of land

2 large green tops of trees

2 brown tree trunks (piece them together so each is about 40 inches high and 4 inches wide)

several clumps of green grass

green plants

green seaweed

stars and planets

colored birds (see pattern)

colored fishes (see pattern)

Using tape, attach a length of yarn to the top edge of each bird and fish. Then attach the opposite end of the yarn to the back of the clouds or the water. Use only enough yarn to allow the birds and fish to hang in the center of a cloud or the water when flipped from back to front.

Using the same method, attach yarn to some green plants and to the land, and attach yarn to the seaweed and to the water.

Attach the tree tops to the straw end of a broom and attach the trunk to the handle. Leave the trunk loosely attached so a student can place both hands about mid-length on the handle. Attach a few pieces of fruit to each tree. Be sure the "forbidden fruit" is easy to remove.

Glue or tape the grass clumps to the brown land.

Tape or staple green "leaves" to yarn to form "clothes" for Adam and Eve. Leave long ends of yarn on each side to tie around the child's waist.

Faith and Life • Grade 3 • Appendix B

CREATION AND THE FALL

ACT ONE: CREATION

(Begin in silence with the lights out. The two speakers stand on either side of the stage, preferably with microphones.)

Narrator: In the beginning, God created the heavens and the earth. On the first day of creation, God said:

God: Let there be light!

(Turn on the lights.)

Narrator: And there was light. (*pause*) Then God looked at what He had made and saw that it was good! On the second day of creation, God said:

God: Let there be a dome in the sky, with clouds above and water below!

(Two Clouds stand on either side of the stage. Three students who are Water stand in the center, with water overlapping.)

Narrator: And so it happened. (*pause*) Then God looked at what He had made and saw that it was good! (*pause*) On the third day of creation, God said:

God: Let the waters separate into their own places so the dry land can appear!

(Four students who are Land take places between the Waters.)

Narrator: And so it happened. (*pause*) Then God said:

God: Let there be green plants to grow on the land and in the sea!

(Students flip plants from behind the pieces of Land and seaweed from behind the Water. Two Trees come and stand in front of Land and Water.)

Narrator: And so it happened. (*pause*) Then God looked at what He had made and saw that it was good! (*pause*) On the fourth day of creation God said:

God: Let there be a sun to rule the day and a moon to rule the night, and many stars and planets!

(Sun, Moon, Stars, and Planets scatter themselves randomly behind Land and Water.)

Narrator: And so it happened. (*pause*) Then God looked at what He had made and saw that it was good! (*pause*) On the fifth day of creation God said:

God: Let there be birds to fly in the air and fish to swim in the sea!

(The Waters flip fishes and Clouds flip birds down.)

Narrator: And so it happened. (*pause*) Then God gave the birds and the fish a command:

God: Be fruitful and multiply!

Narrator: Then God looked at what He had made and saw that it was good! (*pause*) On the sixth day of creation God said:

God: Let there be all kinds of animals to live upon the earth!

(Students place stuffed animals about the stage.)

Narrator: And so it happened. Then God gave the animals a command:

God: Be fruitful and multiply!

Narrator: Then God looked at what He had made and saw that it was good! (*pause*) Then God said:

God: Let us make man in our own image and likeness! *(Adam and Eve come center stage.)*

Narrator: And so it happened. (*pause*) God made a man and a woman. He made them like Himself, to think and to love. God gave them to each other so they could form the first family. And because they could think and love, God gave the man and the woman charge over all the animals and all the other things that He had made. Then God gave the man and the woman a command:

God: Be fruitful and multiply! Fill the earth!

Narrator: Then God looked at everything He had made and saw that it was very good! (*pause*) On the seventh day, God rested from all His work of creation. He blessed the seventh day and made it holy so people could rest on that day and remember to thank Him for all the gifts of creation He has given them!

(All creatures take a bow, then all but the two Trees exit, leaving the stuffed animals behind.)

Cloud Pattern

Faith and Life • Grade 3 • Appendix B

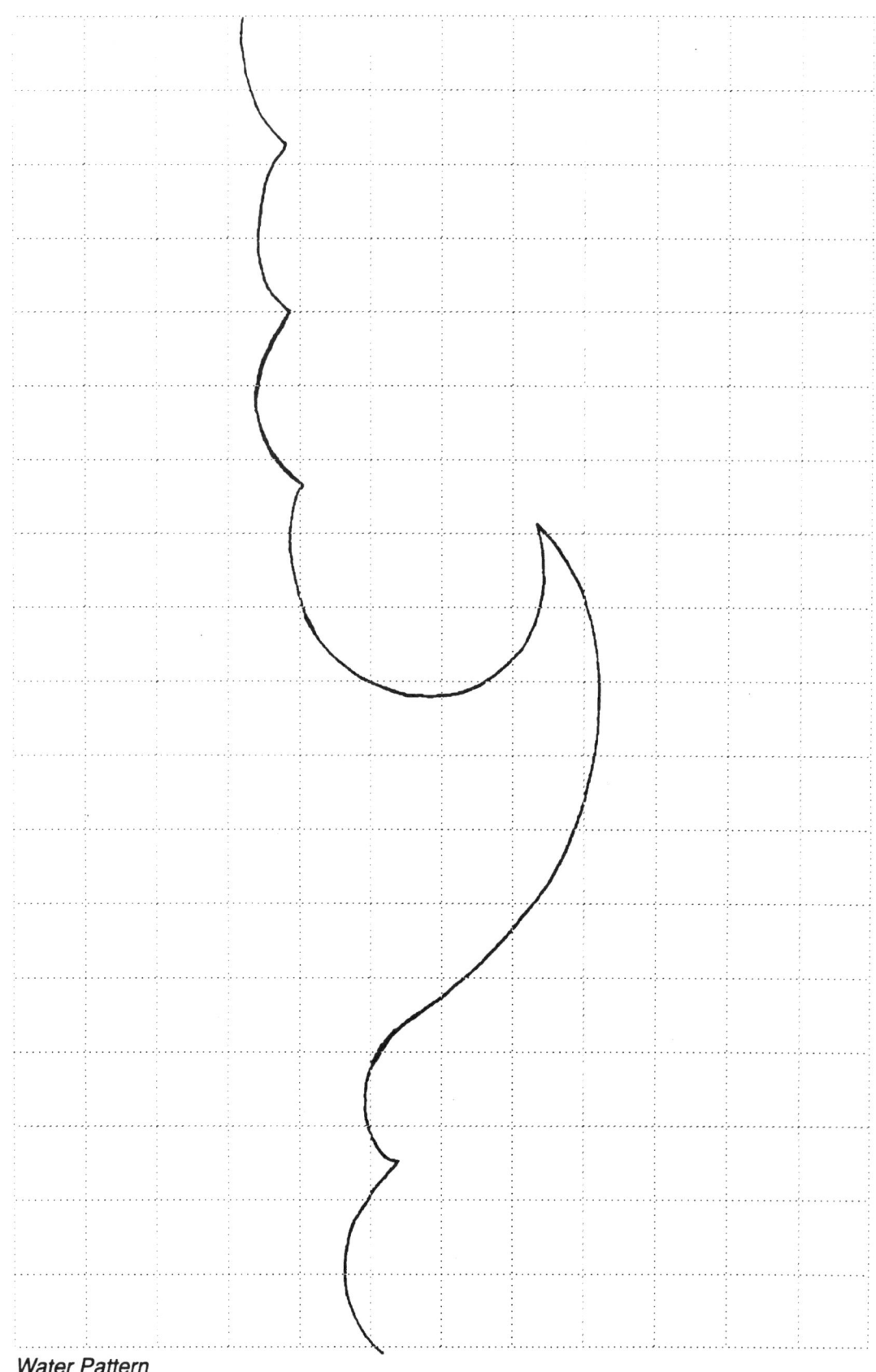

Water Pattern

Fish Pattern

Bird Pattern

Parable Plays

Materials: copies of the scripts (pages B-8–B-10), simple props (these can be mimed or made by the students), costumes (optional).

Direct Aim: to learn more about God's Kingdom as revealed to us in the parables of Jesus

What to Do and Say

Make as many copies of each script as you will need to involve as many students as possible in the acting. If you have students who do not wish to take a speaking part, give them a non-speaking role or ask them to make props or backdrops or to gather costume pieces. Try to get everyone involved in some way. Assign parts and give the students a few minutes to look over the script. It helps to do several read-throughs before planning the movements. The students can usually hear the words and understand the meanings better when they are not moving around. Say:

> Jesus often spoke to His followers in parables. Parables are stories that make us think about our behavior. Even though they are made-up stories, they teach us about some of the important messages Jesus wants us to learn. They teach us about forgiveness and mercy, about being alert and persistent, about the value God places on each and every person, and many other truths. As we grow, we will hear these stories again and again, but they will never get old. We will always be able to hear Jesus speaking through them.

The Wise and Foolish Bridesmaids
based on Matthew 25:1–13

Characters
Narrator
Bridegroom
Bridesmaids 1–5 (carrying lamps and flasks)
Bridesmaids 6–10 (carrying only lamps)

The Rich Man and Lazarus
based on Luke 16:19–31

Characters
Narrator
Rich Man
Lazarus, a poor man
Father Abraham
Two Angels

Props
chair and table with "food"
chair for Father Abraham
a self-standing backdrop painted with flames.

The Good Samaritan
based on Luke 10:25–37

Characters
Narrator
Victim
Priest
Levite
Samaritan
Innkeeper

Props
saddlebags
money bag
reasonable facsimile of a donkey.

THE WISE AND FOOLISH BRIDESMAIDS

A Parable Play

Narrator: Jesus once told this parable to his followers: You can compare the Kingdom of Heaven to this situation—Ten bridesmaids took their lamps and went out to meet the bridegroom.

(*The bridesmaids enter and look anxiously about in all directions.*)

Bridesmaid 1: Does anyone see him yet?

Bridesmaid 6: Not yet. I wonder what's taking him so long?

Bridesmaid 7: I thought he'd be here by now.

Bridesmaid 8: I'm so sleepy. It's way past my bedtime.

Bridesmaid 9: If he doesn't get here soon, my lamp is going to burn out! I'm nearly out of oil.

Bridesmaid 10: Me too.

Bridesmaid 2: (*yawning*) I can't stay awake another minute.

(*She sits down and soon all the bridesmaids sit or lie down and go to sleep.*)

Narrator: Of the ten bridesmaids, only five had been wise enough to bring along extra oil for their lamps. The bridegroom was very late, and all of the girls fell asleep waiting. But about midnight, a cry awoke them announcing, "The bridegroom is here! Light his way to the wedding banquet!"

Bridesmaid 3: At last, he's here. I'm so excited!

Bridesmaid 4: (*Pouring oil from the flask into her lamp.*) Quickly, let's fill our lamps and hold them high so he can see the way!

Bridesmaid 5: Good thing we brought along a refill.

(*Bridesmaids One through Five finish filling their lamps.*)

Bridesmaid 6: Hey, my lamp is sputtering. It's nearly out of oil.

Bridesmaid 7: Mine's completely dry. (*To Bridesmaid 1*) Here, give me some of your oil.

Bridesmaid 1: I'm sorry, but if I did that, my own lamp would burn out, and I'd be no help to the Bridegroom.

Bridesmaid 2: Go wake the oil merchant. Perhaps he'll sell you what you need.

(*The five foolish bridesmaids rush off with their empty lamps.*)

Narrator: Shortly after the foolish bridesmaids left to buy more oil, the bridegroom arrived.

Bridegroom: At last, the hour has come for my wedding feast. Light my way into the hall where I will meet my bride.

Narrator: The five wise bridesmaids held their lamps high as they went into the feast together. Then the doors were shut.

(*Bridesmaids Four and Five mime closing two great doors.*)

The splendid feast began. When the foolish bridesmaids returned . . .

Bridesmaid 7: Where is everybody?

Bridesmaid 8: They must have gone in already.

(*They knock at the doors.*)

Bridesmaid 9: Open up. We're supposed to be bridesmaids too.

Bridegroom: (*Through the heavy doors*) I'm sorry, but my bridesmaids are with me already. I don't recognize you.

Narrator: Jesus ended the parable with a warning: Stay awake, because you do not know the day or the hour when the Son of Man will return.

THE GOOD SAMARITAN

A Parable Play

As the play opens, the Victim is lying unconscious at the side of the road.

Narrator: Jesus once told this parable to some teachers who wanted to know whom He meant by "neighbor" when He said, "Love your neighbor as you love yourself." A certain man had been traveling on a dangerous road to Jericho, when he was assaulted by robbers, beaten up, and left for dead at the side of the road.

Victim: (*coming to*) Ohhhhhhhhh! Ahhhhhhhhhhhh! (*in great pain*)

Narrator: A priest happened to be traveling the same road that morning, and when he saw the fellow lying by the roadside, he said to himself:

Priest: Oh dear. What have we here? How distasteful. I'd better not get involved. This fellow looks as if he's about to die, and if I touch him, I'll be considered unclean. Then I won't be able to perform the sacrifices as usual at the Temple.

Narrator: With these and other excuses, he decided to continue on his way. He crossed to the other side of the road and walked on. A little while later, a Levite, who also worked at the Temple, came by. He heard the groans and said to himself:

Levite: Oh, how dreadful. What a sorry sight! I wish I weren't in such a hurry to get to the Temple. I really can't stop right now. Poor fellow!

Narrator: The Levite too passed the victim by. Finally, a Samaritan came along the road, leading his donkey. He saw the victim lying by the side of the road and knew that he was a Jewish man. Samaritans and Jews avoided any contact with one another, and it had been this way for many generations of hatred and mutual distrust. The Samaritan was on a business trip and could have passed the victim by, but he had pity on him and decided to stop and help.

Samaritan: Oh my goodness, there's a man over there who looks badly hurt. Poor Jewish fellow—someone has beat him up terribly. (*He kneels down beside the victim.*) Here, it's OK. I'm here to help. Let me give you some wine to deaden the pain. (*He gets some supplies out of his saddlebags.*) I'll bandage the wounds the best I can, but we're going to need to get you to a doctor. Can you stand up enough to get on my donkey? We'll go slowly.

Narrator: The Samaritan put the victim on his donkey and led him to a nearby town. He checked into an inn and got further help for him. When he had to leave the next day to continue his trip, he told the innkeeper:

Samaritan: Please take care of this gentleman until he is completely recovered.

Innkeeper: But sir, I cannot afford to take in charity cases.

Samaritan: I'm not asking you to. Here in this bag you'll find payment for the time we've already spent and an amount to cover a room and food for the hurt man until he recovers completely. If you should need more money, I'll settle our accounts on my return trip.

Innkeeper: You, a Samaritan, will do all this for a Jewish man?

Narrator: Then Jesus asked his listeners to identify which of the three—Priest, Levite or Samaritan—proved himself to be a neighbor to the victim. The teachers answered, "the one who took pity on him." Jesus replied, "Go then and do the same."

THE GOOD SAMARITAN

A Parable Play

As the play opens, the Victim is lying unconscious at the side of the road.

Narrator: Jesus once told this parable to some teachers who wanted to know whom He meant by "neighbor" when He said, "Love your neighbor as you love yourself." A certain man had been traveling on a dangerous road to Jericho, when he was assaulted by robbers, beaten up, and left for dead at the side of the road.

Victim: (*coming to*) Ohhhhhhhh! Ahhhhhhhhhhhh! (*in great pain*)

Narrator: A priest happened to be traveling the same road that morning, and when he saw the fellow lying by the roadside, he said to himself:

Priest: Oh dear. What have we here? How distasteful. I'd better not get involved. This fellow looks as if he's about to die, and if I touch him, I'll be considered unclean. Then I won't be able to perform the sacrifices as usual at the Temple.

Narrator: With these and other excuses, he decided to continue on his way. He crossed to the other side of the road and walked on. A little while later, a Levite, who also worked at the Temple, came by. He heard the groans and said to himself:

Levite: Oh, how dreadful. What a sorry sight! I wish I weren't in such a hurry to get to the Temple. I really can't stop right now. Poor fellow!

Narrator: The Levite too passed the victim by. Finally, a Samaritan came along the road, leading his donkey. He saw the victim lying by the side of the road and knew that he was a Jewish man. Samaritans and Jews avoided any contact with one another, and it had been this way for many generations of hatred and mutual distrust. The Samaritan was on a business trip and could have passed the victim by, but he had pity on him and decided to stop and help.

Samaritan: Oh my goodness, there's a man over there who looks badly hurt. Poor Jewish fellow—someone has beat him up terribly. (*He kneels down beside the victim.*) Here, it's OK. I'm here to help. Let me give you some wine to deaden the pain. (*He gets some supplies out of his saddlebags.*) I'll bandage the wounds the best I can, but we're going to need to get you to a doctor. Can you stand up enough to get on my donkey? We'll go slowly.

Narrator: The Samaritan put the victim on his donkey and led him to a nearby town. He checked into an inn and got further help for him. When he had to leave the next day to continue his trip, he told the innkeeper:

Samaritan: Please take care of this gentleman until he is completely recovered.

Innkeeper: But sir, I cannot afford to take in charity cases.

Samaritan: I'm not asking you to. Here in this bag you'll find payment for the time we've already spent and an amount to cover a room and food for the hurt man until he recovers completely. If you should need more money, I'll settle our accounts on my return trip.

Innkeeper: You, a Samaritan, will do all this for a Jewish man?

Narrator: Then Jesus asked his listeners to identify which of the three—Priest, Levite or Samaritan—proved himself to be a neighbor to the victim. The teachers answered, "the one who took pity on him." Jesus replied, "Go then and do the same."

An Exploration of Angels in Art

Materials: art prints of religious paintings, sculptures, or frescoes depicting angels; paint and brushes, pastels, colored chalk, clay, and other available art supplies; paper of various sizes and textures.

Direct Aims

- to learn about the nature of angels
- to express the idea of angel in an original artwork

What to Do and Say

Christian art is full of examples of artists' ideas of angels. The following art activity can start a discussion about the nature of the angels, their gifts and attributes, the services to which they have been called, and their role in human history. Bring in several prints of paintings, drawings, or sculptures that depict angels. Angels can be among the main characters (the angel Gabriel announcing to Mary that she was to be the Mother of God, or they can be background characters, filling up the sky or carrying someone to heaven. If you do not have pictures such as these, use the pictures of angels from the student text.

> Today we will be looking at the way artists from different historical periods have portrayed angels. Because we know so little about angels, artists have used their imaginations freely when depicting angels. I invite you to move freely about the classroom and note some of the details of the angels in the art prints I have posted throughout the room.

Have the students examine several depictions of angels closely. Circulate about the classroom as they are looking at the pictures and keep them focused on the subject of angels. Point out features they might not readily notice. Suggest that they look for similarities and differences among the pictures. After a suitable amount of viewing time, ask them to return to their seats for a discussion. Ask:

> What did you notice about angels in these examples of sacred art? What were some of the common features that you noticed?

Solicit replies. The students will probably mention such features as wings, brightness, haloes, and motion. As they mention items, expand on their remarks. For example, say:

> Wings are a common feature in angelic portrayals. Why is this so? Angels are usually shown to look like humans. Why might this be so? What are some of the activities the angels are doing? Do they look happy? sad? serene? busy? What colors are used to portray angels? Are they wearing clothing? Do angels need clothes? When might they need clothes or need to look like humans? What does a halo signify? Do the angels in any of these pictures seem to be singing? Playing musical instruments? Praising God? What else do you notice about them?

Continue the discussion for as long as it is fruitful. Then say:

> You will now have the opportunity to portray an angel. First, close your eyes for a few minutes and think of a Bible story about an angel or several angels. Or think about your own guardian angel and how you would show your angel in art. I have different kinds of art supplies, so that you can choose the kind of picture or sculpture you would like to do. The one requirement for this project is that you include an angel or angels in your work.

Help the students select the materials they need to do their own portrayals of angels. Display their finished work in the classroom or in a school art show.

Play: Creation and the Fall

Materials:

Costumes

pink or flesh-colored tights and T-shirts for Adam and Eve; black or red cape, tights, and T-shirt for devil.

Props

two kitchen brooms for tree trunks

poster board: two yellow for sun and stars; six brown for dry land and tree trunks; three blue for water; four green for trees, leaves, and grass; three white for clouds and miscellaneous planets; scraps for fish and birds.

artificial fruit to hang on a tree, glue sticks, scissors, yarn (a few yards any color, for birds, fish, and strings of leaves), tape, stuffed animals, potted plants.

Characters:

Narrator
God
Adam
Eve
Devil
Two Clouds
Three students for Water
Four students for Land
Two Trees
One Sun
One Moon
Stars and Planets

Direct Aim: to learn the story of creation and the Fall as recorded in the first chapters of Genesis

Making props:

Patterns for several shapes are printed on pages B-3–B-6.

Draw the following shapes on poster board and cut them out:

1 large yellow sun

1 medium white moon

2 large white clouds (see pattern)

3 large blue waves of water (see pattern)

4 brown pieces of land

2 large green tops of trees

2 brown tree trunks (piece them together so each is about 40 inches high and 4 inches wide)

several clumps of green grass

green plants

green seaweed

stars and planets

colored birds (see pattern)

colored fishes (see pattern)

Using tape, attach a length of yarn to the top edge of each bird and fish. Then attach the opposite end of the yarn to the back of the clouds or the water. Use only enough yarn to allow the birds and fish to hang in the center of a cloud or the water when flipped from back to front.

Using the same method, attach yarn to some green plants and to the land, and attach yarn to the seaweed and to the water.

Attach the tree tops to the straw end of a broom and attach the trunk to the handle. Leave the trunk loosely attached so a student can place both hands about mid-length on the handle. Attach a few pieces of fruit to each tree. Be sure the "forbidden fruit" is easy to remove.

Glue or tape the grass clumps to the brown land.

Tape or staple green "leaves" to yarn to form "clothes" for Adam and Eve. Leave long ends of yarn on each side to tie around the child's waist.

CREATION AND THE FALL

ACT TWO: TEMPTATION AND THE FALL

(Two Trees are center stage; strings of leaves are on the ground; stuffed animals and pots of flowers are randomly placed. As Narrator speaks, Eve slowly walks on stage carrying a bouquet of flowers. She stops at each pot to pick a flower, then sits down beneath the tree of the knowledge of good and evil to arrange her flowers.)

Narrator: When God made the world, He made everything good! The trees were good, the flowers were good, the land was good, the water was good, the animals were good, and Adam and Eve were good! *(pause)* But the devil and his bad angels were in hell, and when the devil heard that God had made a beautiful world for Adam and Eve, he hurried right over to cause trouble!

(The devil sneaks on stage, hides behind one tree, then the other. He reaches up and picks a fruit from the tree under which Eve is sitting, jumps out in front of her, and offers the fruit to her. Eve, startled, shakes her head vigorously and covers her mouth.)

Narrator: The devil knew God had commanded Adam and Eve not to eat the fruit from a certain tree. But he pretended that he didn't know. He wanted to trick Eve.

(The devil offers the fruit again. Again Eve refuses, but this time not so strongly.)

Narrator: Then the devil lied to Eve and told her that the fruit would make her wise—like God.

(The devil breathes on the fruit, polishes it on his sleeve, and offers it with his other hand.)

Narrator: This time the fruit looked good to Eve. She decided she would rather be wise than obedient, so she took the fruit and ate it.

(Eve takes a bite of the fruit. The devil laughs wickedly, rubs his hands together in glee, and slinks away. Adam enters and goes to sit by Eve. She motions in the direction of the serpent, shows Adam the fruit, and urges him to eat. He does. Then both suddenly notice their nakedness and cover themselves with the strings of leaves lying nearby.)

Narrator: It didn't take long for Adam and Eve to understand what a terrible sin they had committed when they chose to obey the devil instead of God. Now they were afraid of God, and they were ashamed of their nakedness. Nothing seemed right anymore.

(Looking miserable, Adam and Eve stand up and walk off the stage, weeping.)

Narrator: But God's love for Adam and Eve did not change because of their disobedience. He still loved them very much and wanted to show them how to love Him again. So He promised to send a savior into the world to win back the hearts of all people. But mankind would have to wait for thousands of years until the promise of a savior would be fulfilled.

(The three Waters come forward and turn their props so the reverse side shows. Written on the back is: TO BE CONTINUED . . . All bow.)

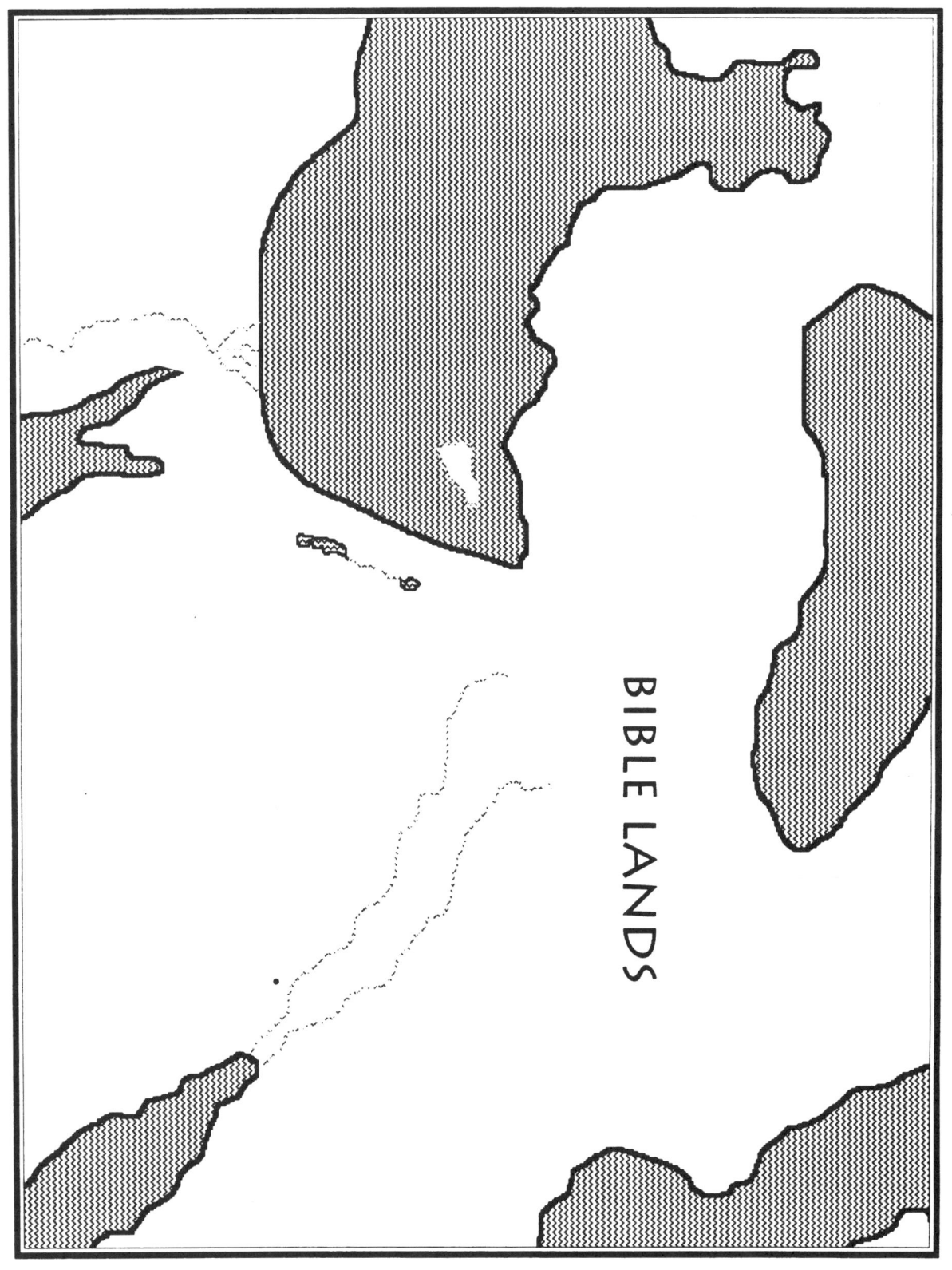

Ten Commandments Song

Learn this song with your teacher to help you remember the Ten Commandments that God gave us.

Use the tune of "Farmer in the Dell".

Have no gods but Me. (*2x*)
This is the First Commandment:
Have no gods but Me.

Don't use God's name in vain. (*2x*)
This is the Second Commandment:
Don't use God's name in vain.

Keep holy the Sabbath day. (*2x*)
This is the Third Commandment:
Keep holy the Sabbath day.

Honor your mom and dad. (*2x*)
This is the Fourth Commandment:
Honor your mom and dad.

You shall not kill. (*2x*)
This is the Fifth Commandment:
You shall not kill.

Do not commit adultery. (*2x*)
This is the Sixth Commandment:
Do not commit adultery.

You shall not steal. (*2x*)
This is the Seventh Commandment:
You shall not steal.

You shall not lie. (*2x*)
This is the Eighth Commandment:
You shall not lie.

Don't covet your neighbor's wife. (*2x*)
This is the Ninth Commandment:
Don't covet your neighbor's wife.

Don't covet your neighbor's goods. (*2x*)
This is the Tenth Commandment:
Don't covet your neighbor's goods.

God gave us laws of love. (*2x*)
They are the Ten Commandments.
God gave us laws of love.

The Church's Calendar

Read the following to know how to color in the circular calendar on the next page. (You will need these colors: purple, green, red, and possibly a golden yellow.)

When the priest celebrates Mass, you have probably noticed that the color of his vestments changes according to the liturgical season. This liturgical calendar is basically divided into the fifty-two Sundays of the Church year.

There are two very great feasts: 1) the feast of Easter, most important for the Christian because in it we celebrate the death and Resurrection of Jesus; and 2) the feast of Christmas, December 25, which falls on a Sunday every few years, and which has three Sundays of feast after it. The priest wears white, the color of light, during these feasts; but you can use gold, too, to color in the cross and star.

Purple is a symbol of waiting and a preparing for a feast. The greater the preparation, the greater the feast! Color the four Sundays of Advent and the six Sundays of Lent in purple.

From Easter to Pentecost is "the Great Sunday": seven Sundays of feast. The priest wears white all during this Easter Season.

The eighth Sunday is Pentecost, the feast of the Holy Spirit. (Remember the meaning of the number eight!) Color Pentecost red.

The other Sundays the priest wears green. They are called Sundays in Ordinary Time.

After you have colored in your liturgical calendar, you can use it to help you and your family keep track of the liturgical seasons of the year.

The Church's Calendar

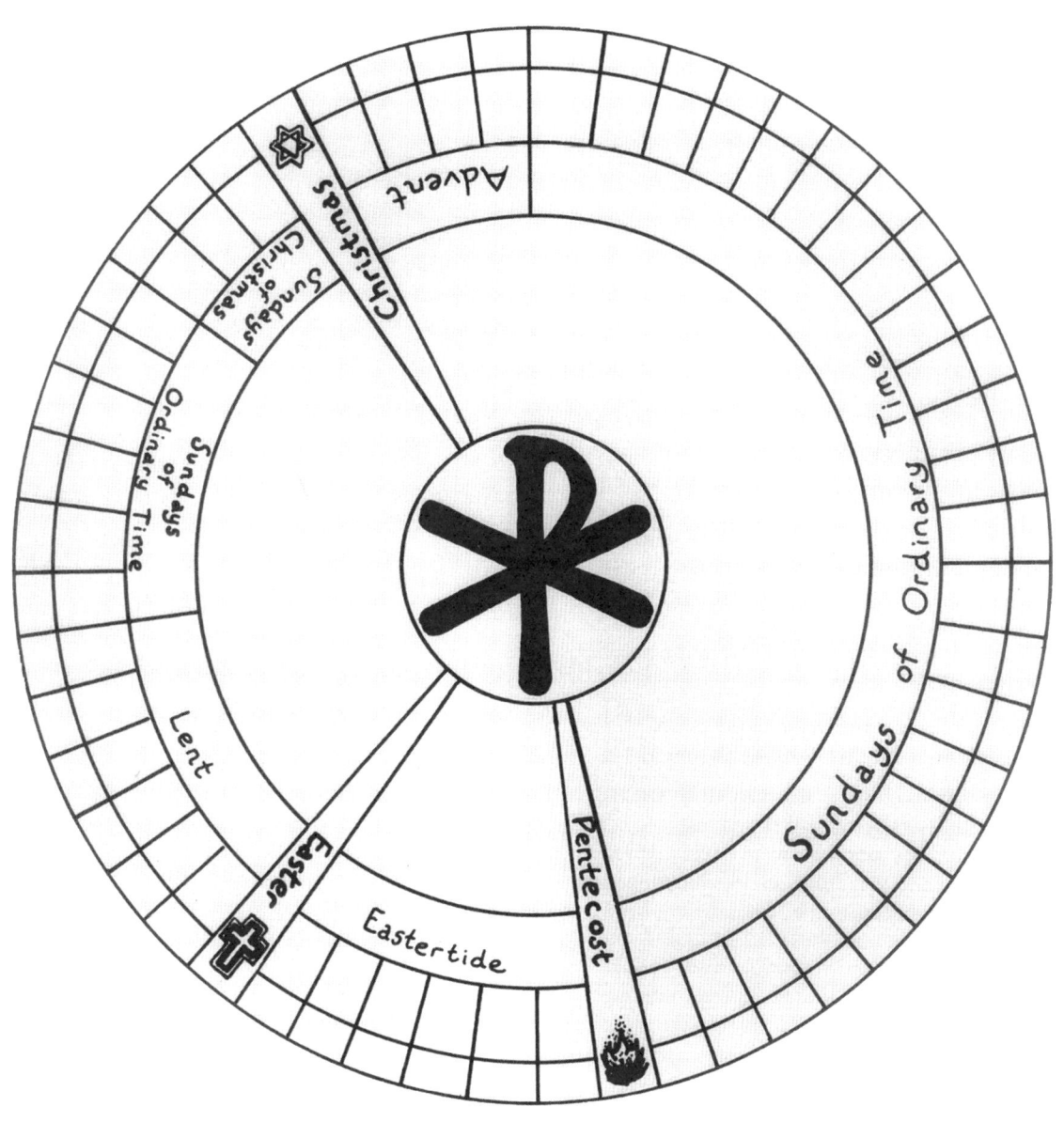

Faith and Life • Grade 3 • Appendix B

Jewish Holidays

Materials: chalkboard, photocopies of holiday symbols (page B-20) on card stock, scissors, markers or crayons, hole punch, yarn or colored string, key-ring holders or curtain rings, Bible.

Direct Aims

- to help students learn about the holidays Jesus and His family celebrated
- to learn the Jewish feasts that find their fulfillment in Jesus and His mission

Preparation: Read Leviticus, chapter 23. Prepare a sample of the holiday symbols wall-hanging.

What to Do and Say

Introduce the theme for this activity.

> When we think about Jesus growing up in a small Jewish village nearly two thousand years ago, we might wonder what His everyday life was like. What games did He play with His friends? What chores did He do for Mary and Joseph? What foods did He like best? I wonder what holidays He celebrated with His family and friends. The holidays we celebrate not only give us a chance to get together with people we like but also help us learn about important events from the past. Let's list some of our favorite holidays on the board, along with the events from the past the holidays celebrate.

Solicit replies and write them on the board. Show the students your sample hanging. Say:

> Today we're going to learn about five religious holidays Jesus and His family celebrated because they were devout Jews. Each of the five symbols on this hanging represents one of those five feasts. Many Jews today still celebrate these feasts, and if you pay close attention, you might discover that we celebrate some of them as well, although in different ways.

As you give the following presentation, write the name and a brief description of each feast on the board and point out the corresponding symbol on the hanging. In brackets are the Christian feasts in which the Jewish holidays find their fulfillment or in which there are similarities to Jewish celebrations. Say:

1. One feast we know Jesus celebrated was **Passover**. This feast is celebrated by the Jews each spring to recall the deliverance of their ancestors from slavery in Egypt. They retell the story of Moses, who asked the Egyptian Pharaoh to let the Jewish people go free. The Pharaoh refused again and again, and each time God sent a plague. The last plague brought death to the firstborn in every Egyptian household, which finally convinced Pharaoh to let the Jewish slaves go free. The firstborn of the Jews were saved from the slaughter, because God commanded each Jewish family to kill a lamb and sprinkle its blood on their doorposts so the Angel of Death would pass over their house. Because of the blood of the lamb, the Jews were spared. Since then, Jewish families have continued to celebrate that event. We know that Jesus ate a Passover meal with His apostles on the night before He died. The Last Supper was a Passover meal. The lamb on the hanging represents the feast of Passover (Lev 23:4–5). [Holy Thursday]

2. The feast of **First Fruits** occurs at the beginning of the spring grain harvest. In Temple times it was celebrated by taking the first of the barley and wheat harvest to the Temple to offer them to God. This took place two days after the feast of Passover, or on the "third day". Crossed stalks of wheat represent the feast of First Fruits (Lev 23:9–14). [Easter: St. Paul refers to the risen Christ as "first fruits" (1 Cor 15:20, 23). We unite the fruits of our labor with the offering of Jesus at every Mass.]

3. The feast of **Weeks** is the great celebration at the end of the spring grain harvest. It is held fifty days (a "week" of Sabbaths) after the feast of First Fruits. It recalls the giving of the Law (that is, the Torah, which includes the Ten Commandments) to Moses on Mt. Sinai. It is celebrated by decorating the home and synagogue with flowers and ripe fruits. Loaves of leavened bread are waved in the air in joyful thanks. The loaf of bread represents the feast of Weeks (Lev 23:15–22). [Pentecost: God had promised the Jews that there would be a day when He would write His laws on their hearts. This was fulfilled with the coming of the Holy Spirit.]

4. In the fall, the feast of **Trumpets** marks the beginning of the Jewish year. On that day, a ram's horn is blown, calling the Jews to synagogue for prayer. The ram's horn reminds them of their ancestor Abraham, who showed great faith in God by being willing to sacrifice his son, Isaac. God instead accepted the sacrifice of a ram in Isaac's place. The celebration ends ten days later with the holiest day of the year—the Day of Atonement. On that day, New Year's vows or promises are made solemnly to God, and people seek forgiveness from those they have hurt. During the Temple age, the High Priest entered the Holy of Holies in the Temple to ask pardon for the people's sins. It is a time of fasting and prayer for all. A ram's horn represents the feast of Trumpets (Lev 23:23–25). [Our Advent and Lent are seasons of prayer, fasting, and penance.]

5. The feast of **Tabernacles** or **Booths** is the fall harvest festival. It lasts for eight days and begins just five days after the Day of Atonement. The mood changes from a solemn focus on one's own actions to great joy and thanksgiving for the blessings of God. The people build booths or tents out in their fields and eat outside for the eight days. Some even sleep in these makeshift shelters. They remember the years their ancestors spent wandering in the desert on their way to the Promised Land. They hang their tents with fruits, vegetables, and other products of the harvest. On the eighth day, they pray for good rains and renewal of the fields before the planting of next year's crops. A tent represents the feast of Tabernacles (Lev 23:33–43). [Our octaves of Christmas and Easter are seasons of joy marked by feasting and celebration.]

Color and cut out the symbols. Punch holes where indicated. Cut five-inch lengths of yarn or string to tie between the symbols. Attach the top length of string to the ring. Keep the symbols in proper chronological order so the connection can be made between Jewish and Christian feasts.

Source: *What Everyone Should Know about Jewish Holidays, Festivals and Fast Days* (Channing L. Bete Co.: 1986). Address: South Deerfield, MA 01373.

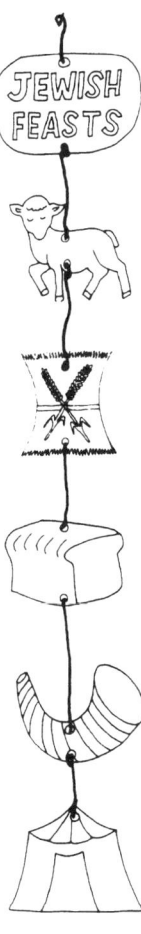

Faith and Life • Grade 3 • Appendix B

Clue	Apostle
I followed Jesus after John the Baptist pointed Him out.	PHILIP
I was Jesus' first follower. I met Him at the Sea of Galilee.	ANDREW
Jesus nicknamed me "Rock". I ruled the Church from Rome.	PETER
My friend Philip brought me to Jesus.	BARTHOLOMEW
My brother Peter was also an apostle.	ANDREW
I first followed Jesus because I hoped He would help us to overthrow the Romans.	SIMON
I was the apostle in charge of the group's money.	JUDAS
I am the patron saint of impossible causes.	THADDEUS (JUDE)
I doubted that Jesus had risen because I had not seen Him with my own eyes.	THOMAS
I betrayed Jesus for thirty pieces of silver.	JUDAS
I was bishop of Jerusalem. I was martyred by being thrown off a high tower.	JAMES THE LESS
James and Jude were my brothers. I preached the gospel in Arabia, where I was martyred.	SIMON
I was a tax collector.	MATTHEW
I was the youngest apostle.	JOHN
My brother John was also an apostle. I went as far as Spain to preach the gospel.	JAMES THE GREATER
At the Last Supper, I asked Jesus to tell us where He was going.	THOMAS
My brother Jude and I were cousins of Jesus.	JAMES THE LESS
My brothers James and Simon and I were cousins of Jesus.	THADDEUS (JUDE)
At the Last Supper, I asked Jesus to "show us the Father".	PHILIP
Because I had the same name as another apostle, I was nicknamed "the Greater".	JAMES THE GREATER
Because I was afraid, I denied that I even knew Jesus—three times!	PETER
Besides John, I was the other apostle who wrote a Gospel account of Jesus' life.	MATTHEW
I am often referred to as the "beloved disciple".	JOHN
I preached the gospel in Arabia, India, and Armenia. I suffered a martyr's death.	BARTHOLOMEW

Faith and Life • Grade 3 • Appendix B

Jesus' Apostles / Who Am I? Game

Materials: copies of student worksheet (page B-21) on heavy paper, scissors.

Direct Aim: To familiarize the students with the Twelve Apostles as men who answered a call to follow Christ and who willingly shared in His death by giving up their own lives for the Faith

What to Do and Say

Look at the picture of the Last Supper from the student text. The Last Supper is a frequently depicted event from the life of Christ. Each artist's version of the Last Supper tries to show us the personalities of the men we call the Twelve Apostles. Have you ever thought about the fact that these men (except for Judas) became the first priests and bishops of the Catholic Church? We owe a great deal to the apostles, who spread the Good News about Jesus to many parts of the world. There are several facts about the apostles that every Catholic should know.

Pass out the student worksheets. Familiarize the students with the information in several different ways. Some suggestions follow:

1. Read through the clues and discuss them as a class.

2. Make booklets. Draw a picture of an apostle on each page and write the clues as a caption.

3. Cut the clues apart, leaving names off. Have students put them into twelve matching pairs, two for each apostle.

4. Have students locate on a map any place names mentioned in the clues. Pin the names of the apostles at the locations that are significant for each.

5. Match up the apostles who were brothers. (Seven apostles came from only three families!)

6. Fold the apostles' names to the back, or cut them off the clue cards. Have the students take turns drawing a clue and trying to match it with the correct apostle.

7. Collect a holy card of each apostle. Glue the clues, minus the names, to card stock. Use as a matching game.

Devotion to the Sacred Heart of Jesus

Materials: copies of student worksheet (page B-23); scissors; coloring pencils; an image of the Sacred Heart of Jesus; red, brown, and yellow felt or construction paper.

Direct Aims

- to learn of the love Jesus has for us as manifested by His Sacred Heart
- to introduce devotion to the Sacred Heart to the students and their families

Preparation: Enlarge and cut out one set of components of the Sacred Heart symbol (see page B-25) from construction paper or felt.

What to Do and Say

In the chapter titled "Jesus Gives His Life for Us", we read of the great pain and suffering Jesus felt when He was humiliated, tortured, and crucified. All this He endured because He loves us so much He wanted to make up for our sins (*reparation*).

Many years after the Crucifixion, between 1673 and 1675, Jesus appeared several times to a holy woman named Margaret Mary. In the visions, Jesus was wearing a red and white robe and showing a heart on His chest. Jesus told Margaret Mary how much He loves us all, how deeply He desires us to love Him, how much He continues to suffer when people do not love Him in return, and how He desires that each of us make reparation for our sins and those of others.

Hold up your felt or paper heart. Ask:

What does this symbol mean to us? [love] On which holiday do we see hearts used? [St. Valentine's Day]. Yes, on Valentine's Day we celebrate the love and friendship we share with our families and friends. For a long time the human heart was thought to be the center of a person's life, the origin of feelings, thoughts, and emotions. When we say to someone, "I give you my heart", we mean "I give you myself." That is what Jesus meant when he appeared to Margaret Mary with a heart on His chest.

Place the heart on the board and hold up the flame. Ask:

What is this? [fire, flame] What is fire like? What happens to a fire if no one puts it out? [it spreads, it grows larger] One time when Jesus appeared to Margaret Mary, He told her, "My Divine Heart is so inflamed with love for everyone that it is not able to contain the flames of its burning love. This love wants to draw all people to holiness and salvation." Jesus asked this saint to tell others of His love and to share with them the desires of His Sacred Heart.

Classroom Activities

Place the flame above the heart on the board. Hold up the thorns and say:

> These thorns look pretty sharp, don't they? They would hurt badly if they were pressed into your skin! Where have we seen thorns before? [Jesus' crown of thorns] Yes, when Jesus was crucified, He wore a crown of thorns on His head. But when He appeared to St. Margaret Mary, He wore thorns across His heart. The thorns remind us that love often means suffering. Because Jesus loves us, He was willing to suffer for us. If we truly love someone, we too will be willing to suffer for that person.

Place the thorns across the heart and hold up the cross. Say:

> When we say "He's carrying a cross" or "He has a great cross to bear", we mean that the person has a great burden or difficulty in his life. From the moment He became man, Jesus had to carry many crosses, or difficulties. Let's name some of the burdens Jesus bore because of His love for us. [poverty, hunger, thirst, pain, humiliation, rejection, scourging, death] The symbol of the cross reminds us that we too must be willing to suffer and die for our love of Jesus. This dying is letting go of our sinful, selfish ways, "dying to ourselves". What are some ways you yourselves can do this?

Allow time for discussion. Place the cross behind the heart and flame. Hold up the wound and say:

> The wound in Jesus' heart is caused by mortal sin. Jesus told St. Margaret Mary, "If only men would make some return for My love . . . but the sole return they give is to reject me and treat me with coldness." He told her that we can console Him in His suffering by receiving Holy Communion as often as possible, by displaying His Sacred Heart image in our homes (show the students an example of the image), by praying for our own souls and the souls of others, and by trying to live and love as He did. The wound stays open to allow us to come into Jesus' heart. Sometimes our mother or father might say to us, "You have a special place in my heart", and this means they love us. Jesus also tells each of us that we have a special place in His heart, and there we can be comforted and strengthened. Pretty big heart, isn't it!

Place wound on lower left edge of the heart. You may wish to make a bulletin board display using your completed Sacred Heart symbol. Pass out student worksheets for students to color.

Additional Activity: Copy the parts of the Sacred Heart symbol onto brown, red, and yellow paper as required, and let each student assemble his own.

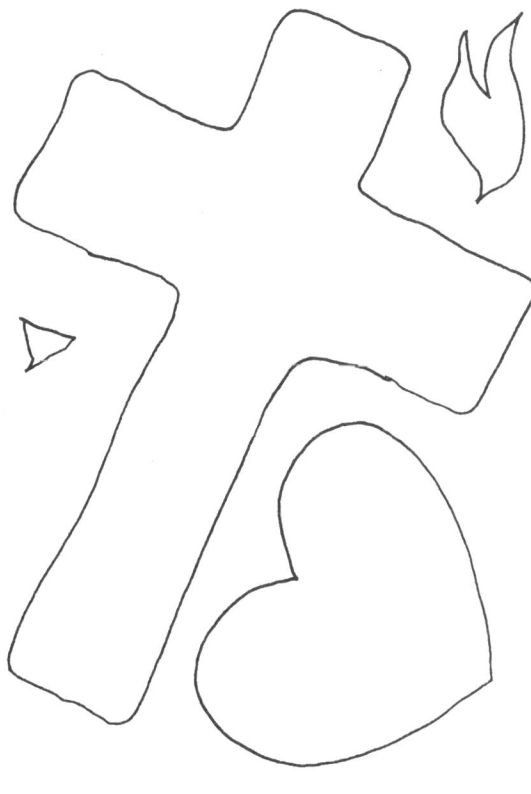

Enlarge the components of the Sacred Heart symbol and transfer to felt or construction paper (brown for cross, red for heart, yellow for thorns). Assemble as shown below.

Baptism Script

Gather the children around and begin with the Sign of the Cross.
Welcome the children to the Baptism of the doll or stuffed animal, and have two children act as parents, and two as godparents.

Ask the parents: What name have you given your child? Parents: N.
Ask the parents: What do you ask of God's Church for N.? Parents: Baptism.

Explain to the children that in asking for N. to be baptized, the parents are also responsible for raising N. in the Catholic faith. It is their duty to help their children keep the Commandments of loving God and neighbor.

Ask the parents: Do you clearly understand what you are undertaking? Parents: We do.
Ask the Godparents: Godparents, are you ready to help these parents in their duty as Christian mothers and fathers? Godparents: We are.

Liturgy of the Word: Read the Baptism of Jesus: Lk 3:2b-23.

Intercessions: R/ Lord Hear our Prayer.
We pray for N. who will be baptized here today. R/
We pray for N.'s parents, help them to raise N. according to the faith. R/
We pray for N.'s godparents, may they support N.'s parents in the rearing of N. R/
We pray for all God's family, united in one Baptism for the forgiveness of sins.
We pray that you renew the grace of our Baptism that we may be more faithful to you. R/

Anointing before Baptism (Oil of Catechumens—on the chest):
We anoint you with the oil of salvation in the name of Christ our Savior; may he strengthen you with his power who lives and reigns for ever and ever. All: *Amen.*

Explain to the children that the priest would then bless the water for Baptism. (Bless + this water in which N. will be baptized) Ask the students what water is symbolic of.
We drink it for life, we can die in it by drowning, it is fun, it is cool and refreshing, it washes, etc.
Make these parallels to the spiritual life: we die and rise to new life with Christ through Baptism, we are washed free from sin, and we are filled with the life of grace, which nourishes our souls.

Renewal of Baptismal Promises (all present may do this)
Do you reject sin so as to live in the freedom of God's children? (I do.)
Do you reject the glamour of evil, and refuse to be mastered by sin? (I do.)
Do you reject Satan, father of sin and prince of darkness? (I do.)
Do you believe in God, the Father almighty, creator of heaven and earth? (I do)
Do you believe in Jesus Christ, His only Son, Our Lord, who was born of the Virgin Mary, was crucified, died, and was buried, rose from the dead, and is seated at the right hand of the Father? (I do).
Do you believe in the Holy Spirit, the holy catholic Church, the communion of saints, the forgiveness of sins, the resurrection of the body and life everlasting? (I do.)
This is our faith. This is the faith of the Church. We are proud to profess it, in Christ Jesus our Lord. (*Amen.*)

Baptism Script Continued

Ask parents and godparents: Is it your will that N. should be baptized in the faith of the Church, which we have all professed with you? Parents and Godparents: It is.

(Pouring water over N.'s head 3 times): N. I baptize you in the Name of the Father, and of the Son, and of the Holy Spirit. All: *Amen.*

Explain to the students that now N. will be anointed on the crown of the head with Chrism to share in the threefold ministry of Christ as Prophet, Priest, and King.

Next, N. will be clothed in a white garment as a reminder of how pure N. is, and that just as we must work hard to keep white clothes clean, so too we must work to keep our soul free from sin. We put on clothes as we are now clothed in Christ:
N. you have become a new creation, and have clothed yourself in Christ. See in this white garment the outward sign of your Christian dignity. With your family and friends to help you by word and example, bring that dignity unstained into the everlasting life of heaven.
All: *Amen.*

Next N. will receive a lighted candle, which represents receiving the light of Christ. Light the candle and give it to the godparents: Receive the light of Christ.
Say: Parent and godparents, this light is entrusted to you to be kept burning brightly. This child of yours has been enlightened by Christ. He is to walk always as a child of the light. May he keep the flame of faith alive in his heart. When the Lord comes may he go out to meet him with all the saints in the heavenly kingdom.
All: *Amen.*

Ephphetha (optional) (bless ears & mouth of N): The Lord Jesus made the deaf hear and the dumb speak. May he soon touch your ears to receive his word, and your mouth to proclaim his faith, to the praise and glory of God the Father.
All: *Amen.*

Explain that now the newly baptized has been reborn as a child of God, and so together with them, we pray the Lord's Prayer: Our Father...

Final blessing:
May almighty God the Father and the Son and the Holy Sprit + bless you.
All: *Amen.*
Go in Peace:
All: Thanks be to God.

You may sing a song (example: For all the Saints).

Penance Script

The celebration ideally follows these steps:

1. The priest may say a prayer to help you remember God's forgiving love. He may also read some words from the Bible. Say "Amen" after his prayer for you.

2. Make the Sign of the Cross with the priest after he welcomes you and say, "Bless me father, for I have sinned." Tell him how long it has been since your last confession.

3. Confess your sins. Follow the Ten Commandments or say your mortal sins first, if you have any. You may want to choose one or two areas of your life where you are failing to love as Jesus asks, and where you most strongly feel the need to change.

4. Accept the prayer, work of charity, or other action the priest gives you as your penance.

5. Express your sorrow either in you own words or by saying an Act of Contrition that you have memorized:

    O God, I am heartily sorry for offending thee. I detest my sins because of your just punishment, but most of all because they have offended thee, My God, whom I should love above all things. I firmly intend, with they help of they grace to sin no more and to avoid the near occasions of sin. Amen.

6. The priest will give you absolution.

    God, the Father of mercies, through the death and Resurrection of his Son has reconciled the world to himself and sent the Holy Spirit among us for the forgiveness of sins; through the ministry of the Church, may God give you pardon and peace, and I absolve you from your sins in the Name of the Father, and of the Son, and of the Holy Spirit.

    Respond: Amen.

7. The priest says, "Give thanks to the Lord, for he is good."

    Respond: For his mercy endures forever.

8. You may conclude by saying "Thank you" or by saying "Thanks be to God."

9. After confession, spend a few moments in prayerful reflection.

Eucharist Script

When we enter the Church, we bless ourselves with Holy Water to remind us of our baptism. We then genuflect to the tabernacle. If the tabernacle is not in the Church, we bow (from the waist) to the altar.

Entrance Song: Choose one you have learned as a class.
Greeting: In the +Name of the Father and of the Son and of the Holy Spirit. R/ Amen.

The Lord be with you. R/ And also with you.

My brothers and sisters, to prepare ourselves to celebrate the sacred mysteries let us call to mind our sins. (You may ask what are the sacred mysteries? What kinds of sins can we recall? Would we have any mortal sins on our soul at this time?)

Pray the Confiteor: I confess...
Lord have Mercy. R/ Lord have Mercy.
Christ have Mercy. R/ Christ have Mercy.
Lord have Mercy. R/ Lord have Mercy.

Pray the Gloria: Glory to God in the Highest...

Explain that the priest will lead us in the opening prayer, and then we sit for the Liturgy of the Word. (You may have a Liturgy of the Word or just review what occurs during the Liturgy of the Word; tell the students God speaks to us through His word and is present in His word.) The Liturgy of the Word consists in the following: First Reading, Psalm, Second Reading, Alleluia, Gospel, and Homily.

Together pray the Creed/Profession of Faith: We believe in one God....
You may pray for the students' intentions. R/ Lord hear our prayer.

Liturgy of the Eucharist. You may set the altar and explain all that is used: corporal, chalice, paten, purificator, pall, finger basin, water and wine cruets, candles, and hosts in ciborium.

The Priest will then bless God and the gifts offered, and then call down the Holy Spirit so that the bread and wine will become the Body, Blood, Soul, and Divinity of Jesus Christ. We also offer ourselves to God in this Holy Sacrifice:

The Lord be with you. R/ And also with you.
Lift up your hearts. R/ We lift them up to the Lord.
Let us give thanks to the Lord our God. R/ It is right to give Him thanks and praise.

The priest continues then we all pray the Sanctus: Holy, Holy, Holy Lord...

The priest then prays the prayer called the Canon. I highly discourage the leader (unless it is a priest) to dramatize this. What words does He say to change the Bread into the Body, Blood, Soul and Divinity of Jesus Christ? Take this, all of you, and it eat: this is my body, which will be given up for you. What words does He say to change the Wine into the Body, Blood, Soul and Divinity of Jesus Christ? Take this, all of you, and drink from it: this is the cup of my blood, the blood of the new and everlasting covenant. It will be shed for you and for all so that sins may be forgiven. Do this in memory of me.

Eucharist Script Continued

We can then pray the memorial acclamation:
Christ has died…
Dying you destroyed our death…
When we eat this bread….
Lord, by your cross and resurrection…

The priest then prays: Through Him, with Him, in Him, in the unity of the Holy Spirit, all glory and honor is Yours almighty Father, forever and ever. R/ Amen.

Together we pray the Our Father….

Have the students give each other the Sign of Peace.

Together pray the Agnus Dei: Lamb of God…

When the priest says: This is the Lamb of God who takes away the sins of the world, Happy are those who are called to His supper. What should we respond? R/ Lord, I am not worthy to receive you, but only say the word, and I shall be healed.

The priest then receives Holy Communion, and gives communion to those worthily prepared to receive our Lord.

Have the students walk through a Communion procession. If you give them hosts, say: "This is a Host." If you are using crackers, say "This is a cracker." DO NOT SAY: "THE BODY OF CHRIST"—because what you are giving them is not the Body of Christ. The students need to understand that when a priest says it, it is true and this is why we say "Amen," because we profess our faith that indeed it is the Body of Christ that we receive in Holy Communion.

For the Eucharist, the matter is bread and wine, the form is "This is My Body; This is the Cup of My Blood," and the minister is the priest. In the Host is the Body, Blood, Soul and Divinity, just as in the Chalice. If the Host is broken, Jesus is entirely present in all the parts of the Host. Jesus remains present after consecration, and this is why we reserve Him in the tabernacle and can go there to pray.

Together sing a Communion Song.

The priest then prays a closing prayer. At the end, he will say: The Lord be with you. R/ And also with you. May almighty God bless you, the Father, and the Son, and the Holy Spirit +. R/ Amen.
The Mass is ended, go in peace. R/ Thanks be to God.

Together sing a closing hymn.